NURSERY
MANAGEMENT
Administration
and Culture

NURSERY MANAGEMENT
Administration and Culture

Harold Davidson

Department of Horticulture
Michigan State University
East Lansing, Michigan

Roy Mecklenburg

Chicago Botanic Garden
Chicago Horticultural Society
Glencoe, Illinois

Prentice-Hall, Inc., Englewood Cliffs, New Jersey 07632

Library of Congress Cataloging in Publication Data

Davidson, Harold, (date)
  Nursery management.

  Includes bibliographies and index.
  1. Nurseries (Horticulture)—Management.
  2. Nurseries (Horticulture)—United States.
  I. Mecklenburg, Roy, joint author. II. Title.
  SB88.5.D38   635'.068   80-19440
  ISBN 0-13-627455-2

Printed in the United States of America

10 9 8 7 6 5 4 3 2

Editorial/production supervision
  and interior design by Leslie I. Nadell
Cover design by Suzanne Behnke
Manufacturing buyer: John Hall

Prentice-Hall International, Inc., *London*
Prentice-Hall of Australia Pty. Limited, *Sydney*
Prentice-Hall of Canada, Ltd., *Toronto*
Prentice-Hall of India Private Limited, *New Delhi*
Prentice-Hall of Japan, Inc., *Tokyo*
Prentice-Hall of Southeast Asia Pte. Ltd., *Singapore*
Whitehall Books Limited, *Wellington, New Zealand*

Dedicated to

H. JOHN CAREW

Friend, Colleague, Horticulturalist
Former professor and chairman
Department of Horticulture
Michigan State University

Contents

Preface

This book is intended as an introductory text for students and others interested either in starting or managing a nursery. The stimulus for writing the book came from both students and professional nurserymen requesting guidance in various areas of nursery management. The text is divided into two primary areas: 1) administration and 2) culture. Within these areas the principles of business management and plant science as they pertain to nursery management have been interpreted by the authors as they viewed the state of the art in the late 1970s. All topics are not covered in detail, but hopefully they are presented so that the information will be useful to the reader. Where appropriate, additional readings have been suggested for those readers who may wish to pursue a subject in greater depth. The topics of plant propagation and pest control were purposely omitted since they are thoroughly covered in other publications (see Appendix A). Garden center management and retailing of nursery products were decidedly beyond the scope of the text.

The chapters on the history of the nursery industry and current status of the industry are included to acquaint the reader with: 1) the development of the nursery business in the United States and how it has changed through the years due to various economic, social, technical, and political pressures; 2) the major centers of nursery production in the United States; and 3) the many types of organizations within the industry and the purposes for which they exist.

Since the nursery industry is very diversified, no single text can cover in detail all of the various aspects of the business. The information set forth in this text is intended to provide both general and specific information on topics related to nursery management which can be used in exercising sound management decisions. Young people would be well-advised to seek a period of "intelligent employment" within the industry prior to starting a nursery business. The production and marketing of quality plants are fascinating businesses, but both require considerable knowledge and skill if they are to be done productively and profitably.

Botanical names within the text conform to *Hortus Third*, which is an excellent dictionary of botanical nomenclature for nurserymen and others interested in the proper nomenclature for plants. The appendices contain various tables and nomographs that a nursery manager may find useful. Also included is a list of publications related to nursery management.

The authors solicit suggestions from both teachers and professional nurserymen as to how future editions can be improved in both content and manner of presentation.

Acknowledgements

The authors wish to acknowledge the many authors of the technical articles on which much of this text is based. Without published results of their research, the science information relative to nursery production would be limited. Their names, along with the journals of publication, are listed in the references following the appropriate chapters. We also wish to express our appreciation to the many nurserymen who have been our teachers and who have provided information that has proven useful in writing this text. Individuals and/or companies who provided illustrations and photographs are mentioned in the appropriate legends. Special thanks go to the following individuals for supplying specifically-requested information or for offering critical reviews of various chapters: Richard Brickman, Richard H. Brolick, Martin J. Bukovac, Donald H. Dewey, Arthur G.

Farley, David C. Farley, Harold E. Hicks, Harold Hunziker, Ernest H. Kidder, John J.B. Light III, George W. Maentz, Alfred A. Manbeck, Paul E. Rieke, Richard A. Schroeder, Hugh Steavenson, Herman R. Struck, William R. Studebaker, and John G. Zelenka.

Finally, we acknowledge the patience and assistance of our wives, Martha and Ellie, in proofreading and critiquing the manuscripts and the patience and deftness of Karen Krzanowski, Sharon Roback, and Betty Uphaus, for typing and retyping them; and we thank Leslie Nadell and the staff at Prentice-Hall for their constructive, critical reviews.

Harold Davidson
East Lansing, Michigan

Roy Mecklenburg
Glencoe, Illinois

Chapter 1

Brief History of the Nursery Industry

The American nursery industry undoubtedly began in Massachusetts Bay Colony, where the settlers grew young fruit trees as part of the general farm operation. As early as 1648, for example, according to a note in his journal, John Endicott traded 500 apple trees for 250 acres of land. Earlier, in a letter to Governor Winthrop in 1644, he stated:

> I humblie and heartilie thanck you for your last lettre of newes and for the trees you sent mee. . . . I haue not sent you any trees because I heard not from you, but I haue trees for you if you please to accept them whensoeuer you shall send. I thinck it is to late to sett or remoue. I could wish you to remoue in the latter end of the years your trees, and I pray you send mee what you want and I will supply what I can.

Since that time the industry has progressed steadily, although sometimes with difficulty. The short survey that follows comments

1

on some of the historically important nurseries and nurserymen as well as modern ones (largely by regions) and discusses the major factors in the development of the industry. The chapter is summarized with a chronology of events from 1737 to 1977. For more details, the reader should consult the references and suggested readings at the end of the chapter.

EARLY EASTERN NURSERIES

The first major commercial nursery established in the United States was the Prince Nursery, also known for many years as the Linnaean Botanic Garden, at Flushing, New York. In 1737 William Prince started by cultivating a few trees to landscape his property. His success led him to commercial production, and shortly thereafter he published a catalog listing several hundred varieties. From it were stocked nearly all of the grafted apple, cherry, and pear orchards of New York, New Jersey, Massachusetts, and Connecticut. His nursery became so outstanding for its diversity of species, particularly fruit, that in 1777, following the battle of Long Island, General Howe made it a British protectorate.

Prince Nursery continued for over a century and introduced many outstanding foreign plants to the New World. By 1827 it contained over 100 species of plants from Australia alone, including *Eucalyptus* and *Banksias*. The nursery also experimented with plant breeding and introduced a number of new selections. As a result, its catalogs during the first half of the nineteenth century were considered the best in the trade. But Prince Nursery did more than grow trees: they also trained nurserymen, including Patrick Barry, one of the founders of the famous Mount Hope Nursery.

Another early nursery was Thomas Young's on Long Island. In 1768 Young was cited by the New York Society for the Promotion of Arts for having the largest number of apple trees (over 27,000) in rows. Other well-known Long Island nurseries started prior to 1900 were James Bloodgood's (1790), Andre Parmenter's (1825), Parsons's (1838), and Hicks's (1853). Mr. Parmenter, the first practitioner of the art of landscape gardening in America, frequently visited other parts of the country to lay out gardens and pleasure grounds for gentlemen of that century. By the early 1800s nurseries flourished in New York City. Michael Flay, for example, an immigrant from England, operated nurseries at the corner of Broadway and 12th Street and in Harlem. He was noted for the introduction of several very fine camellia varieties.

With the opening of the Erie Canal in 1825 and the development of a large orchard industry in western New York, a large nursery center developed near Geneva. According to Hedrick, David Thomas was the pioneer nurseryman of western New York; by 1830 he had the most extensive collection of fruit trees west of the Hudson River. One of the first nurseries in this area was founded by Reynolds and Bateman in 1830; it consisted of 6 acres about 1 mile from the center of Rochester. In 1839 they sold it to George Ellwanger and Patrick Barry, who established the Mount Hope Nursery. It was destined to become the leading nursery of the country during the latter part of the nineteenth century.

Patrick Barry was born in Ireland, emigrated to the United States when he was 20 years old, and obtained a job at the Prince Nursery in Flushing. After a period of "intelligent employment," he took part of his wages in nursery stock, moved to Rochester, and established a partnership with Ellwanger. Following a visit to the nursery in 1893, George Nicholson, curator of the Royal Gardens at Kew, England, noted that the cultivation of fruit trees had reached "enormous proportions," with 400 of the 600 acres devoted to the production of fruit trees. The Mount Hope Nursery was the primary source of liners, cuttings, and scion wood for the development of many of the nurseries in the Midwest. Another famous nursery near Rochester was Asa Rowe's, the oldest and most extensive in that area in 1841 and the source of stock and scions for many of the nurseries that developed in the Michigan territory.

The first nursery in Dansville, New York, was started in 1855 by O. B. Maxwell. After he and his brother Joshua inspected the site they were convinced that the soil and climate were well adapted to growing nursery stock. They were correct: by the early 1890s, Dansville—with 1200 acres of nursery products—was on a par with the great nurseries of Geneva and Rochester. George A. Sweet, the largest grower, had 125 acres in nursery stock; he was followed by J. B. Morly and T. Kennedy & Sons, with 75 acres each.

By 1850 western New York had become the nursery center of the nation, and the number of large nurseries increased rapidly. By about 1865, besides the previously mentioned nurseries, there was the W. & T. Smith Company; T. C. Maxwell and Brothers of Geneva; A. M. Purdy of Palmyra, known the country over as a specialist in small fruit; the Maloney Brothers Nursery; and Jackson and Perkins of Newark.

Jackson and Perkins began in 1864 as market gardeners, specializing in small fruits. About 1879 they began growing a few roses and hardy ornamentals. By 1894 they were producing about 175,000 roses yearly, and by 1900 they were known not only for their roses but for their outstanding collection of clematis, peonies, and other hardy ornamental plants.

One of the finest nurseries in New England in the late 1700s and mid-1800s was John and William Kenrick's of Newton, Massachusetts. John began his horticultural work by planting peach pits. Although he was acquainted with the art of grafting, he was not acquainted with "inoculation" (budding) as a method of vegetative propagation. When he learned the art about 1794, he began a commercial fruit production nursery that became the leading business of its kind in New England. About 1797 he added ornamental trees, including the Lombardy poplar, the most salable ornamental tree in New England at that time. After John died, William continued the nursery until his own death in 1870. William also experimented in silk culture, growing thousands of mulberry trees for his silkworms.

Another outstanding New England orchardist-nurseryman was Robert Manning of Salem, Massachusetts. In 1823 he began collecting, propagating, and offering for sale fruit varieties that were hardy in New England. Through his contacts with leading horticulturists, he obtained the best varieties available from Europe. By the time of his death in 1842, he had a collection of some 2000 fruit varieties, the largest ever assembled by an American up to that time. At one of the annual exhibitions of the Massachusetts Horticultural Society, he exhibited over 160 kinds of pears.

C. M. Hovey's 36-acre nursery in Cambridge also grew a remarkable number of varieties; besides 100 varieties of forest and ornamental trees, he sold 600 varieties of pears, 200 of apples, 100 of plums, 100 of cherries, 75 of peaches, and 50 each of grapes and gooseberries, as well as varieties of currents, apricots, raspberries, and strawberries. Hovey was also the editor of *The Magazine of Horticulture* and author of *The Fruit Trees of America,* a beautifully illustrated book on native and exotic fruits. Other early nurseries of New England were Ephraim Goodale's of Arlington, Massachusetts, and Benjamin and Charles Vaughan's in Hallowell, Maine.

One of the first nurseries in New Jersey was begun about 1794 by William Coxe in partnership with Daniel Smith. Coxe was an outstanding pomologist and wrote the first book on pomology (fruit production) published (1817) in this country. He collected all the best varieties of fruits available in the United States and from many parts of Europe and was one of the first to successfully graft the better varieties of grape onto the more vigorous stocks.

Philadelphia also had an extensive nursery area. Thomas Meehan & Sons was started in 1854 on 6 acres of land, and by 1908 there were 265 acres in production as well as good retail and landscape departments. Thomas Meehan popularized the planting of American trees so extensively that Nicholson refers to him as "the Nestor among American tree lovers and planters." By 1893 Meehan's nursery contained the largest collection of native American trees and shrubs to be found in any nursery in the world.

In 1897 the Conard and Jones Company of Pennsylvania pioneered the sale of seeds and plants by mail order. A few years later it became the Conard-Pyle Company, the producers of the famous "Star Roses." In 1920 Robert Pyle, who specialized in roses, introduced *Rosa hugonis* ("The Golden Rose of China") at the unheard of price of $5 per plant. Conard-Pyle is still the largest grower of roses in the eastern United States.

Bernard McMahon was another leading Pennsylvania horticulturist, with extensive plantings, nurseries, and greenhouses. McMahon received, propagated, and disseminated many of the plants collected by Lewis and Clarke on their expedition to the Northwest. The fine broadleaved evergreen *Mahonia* now bears his name. Hoopes Brothers and Thomas, established in 1853 at West Chester, was also large, with 600 acres in production, and was widely known for its fine stock. Josiah Hoopes's *Book of Evergreens,* published in 1868, was a valuable contribution to the literature on conifers.

EARLY MIDWESTERN NURSERIES

The famous nursery production area of Lake County, Ohio, had its initial impetus in 1853, when Jesse Storrs, a farmer-nurseryman from Cortland, New York, located on 80 acres of farm land near the village of Painsville. In 1858 Storrs offered a partnership to J. J. Harrison, a skilled propagator, because in his opinion there was not room for two nurseries in the county. By 1970, however, the county contained more than 200 nurseries, with a combined acreage of over 5000 acres. The excellent climate of Lake Erie, the wide variety of soils, and the strategic geographic location within a developing nation all contributed to Lake County's success as a major nursery center.

Storrs and Harrison soon became the largest nursery in the country—about 1400 acres. Most of the land was worked with mules, but these were gradually replaced with Percheron draft horses. The firm grew not only woody plants but also large quantities of tropical plants, greenhouse crops, and vegetable seeds. Facilities included modern greenhouses as well as storage and packing houses, one large enough to accommodate several railroad cars.

Another famous nursery of Lake County was owned and operated by Henry Kohankie. Kohankie had been foreman of the ornamental department of Storrs and Harrison Company for 15 years before starting his own nursery in 1900. The nursery developed a nationwide reputation for its wide selection of high-quality ornamental plants, and for a long time its catalog was considered the "Bible" of ornamental plants by many landscape architects.

Bloomington, Illinois, also became an important nursery center, since five important railroads intersected there and the soil and climate were well suited to all types of plants. The Bloomington Nursery, later the Phoenix Nursery Company, started in 1852 by Franklin K. Phoenix, grew a general line of nursery stock, and at one time was the largest in the country. Its packing houses, cold-storage cellars, and other buildings covered more than 20 acres.

The foundation of the famous nursery industry of Missouri was laid following the War of 1812, when young James (Judge) Stark moved from his home in Bourbon County, Kentucky, to the wilderness on the west banks of the Mississippi River. He came on horseback carrying fruit tree scions in old-fashioned saddlebags. In 1816 he started a small nursery, destined to become Stark Bros. Nurseries and Orchard Company. The judge was a great believer in advertising and used it unsparingly to promote the sale of his stock.

The horse also brought the nursery industry to Shenandoah, Iowa, in 1869. D. S. Lake, an employee of a nursery at Prairie City, Illinois, traveled the Midwest on horseback selling osage orange, hedge plants, and forest tree seedlings. In 1869 he and his wife moved to the Iowa frontier and started a fruit tree nursery on a few acres of land. One hundred years later it covered some 3000 acres, with about one-third in nursery stock. Because of the fine climate and soil, Shenandoah soon became one of the major centers of the country. Its nurseries pioneered in the development of mechanized equipment for field operations, storage, packing, and shipping.

Many of the fine nurseries of Ohio, Michigan, Illinois, Missouri, Iowa, and other midwestern states that were established in the mid-1800s had direct or indirect contact with the nursery centers of New York. One of the first nurseries established in Michigan was that of Z. K. and E. D. Lay near Ypsilanti in 1833. From Asa Rowe's nursery near Rochester, New York, they brought 25,000 cultivated trees, mostly of one season's growth. One year later Timothy W. Dunham of Orleans County, New York, came to Michigan to establish a nursery and brought with him "a chest of drawers or shallow boxes filled with apple tree root grafts, about 3000 in number." Like the

Lays, Dunham obtained most of his scions and plant material from Asa Rowe.

EARLY WESTERN NURSERIES

The development of the nursery industry in Oregon began with a load of nursery stock that was transported by prairie schooner from Salem, Iowa, to Milwaukee, Oregon, in 1847. In the spring of that year Henderson Lewelling (Luelling), a nurseryman, planted about 700 small trees and shrubs in stout wagon boxes filled with a compost of soil and charcoal. In April he hitched his nursery wagon to three yoke of cattle and began the long trip to Oregon. The hazardous journey across the plains and over the Rocky Mountains took about 9 months, but the following year he joined William Meek and together they established the first orchard-nursery of grafted trees in the Northwest. Their trees, along with others obtained from the nurseries of Ellwanger and Barry and A. J. Downing, shipped via the Isthmus of Panama, formed the nucleus of the nursery-orchard industry of the Northwest. Roots from seedling apples, sprouts from wild cherry, and roots of the wild plum supplied the first understocks for grafting, and good nurseries developed rapidly. About 1850, for instance, George Settlemeir began a nursery at Oregon City, later moved it to Mt. Angel, and soon had the largest variety of fruit and ornamental trees in the Oregon territory. The nursery business expanded chiefly because of the demand for quality apples, which sold for $12–15 per bushel.

Spanish missionaries, who undoubtedly began the California nursery industry before 1700, introduced most of the deciduous and evergreen fruiting plants. Unfortunately, according to Williamson, as a result of many unscrupulous, ignorant adventurers plunging into the production of fruit trees, the early California nurserymen were looked upon as little better than highwaymen. But once the ecological requirements of the newly introduced fruits were learned, the industry became stabilized.

The first commercial nursery of record in California was started by A. P. Smith of Sacramento in the early 1850s on land purchased from Captain John Sutter. By 1857 Smith had some 1200 roses of 200 varieties as well as many other plants. Like the nursery industry of the other states, the early California nurseries produced mainly fruit trees and grape vines to supply the heavy demands for these species.

EARLY INDUSTRY OBSERVATIONS

Most of the nurserymen of the late 1700s and early 1800s were orchardists-nurserymen; that is, they produced fruit trees for their orchards and sold the excess. In later years nurserymen produced trees for sale and either planted or burned the excess. Initially, the primary method of propagation of fruit tree varieties was by grafting onto wild stocks; later, understocks obtained from France were used. Most of their trees were sold direct and delivered by oxcart, often over primitive roads or no roads at all. The large nurseries contained hundreds of acres—some over 1000—and catered to the wholesale trade and nursery agents.

The 1870s to the 1890s was the era of the itinerant nursery agents, many of whom were unscrupulous in their claims and careless about deliveries. Nevertheless, the results were not all evil. Traveling by horse and wagon, they sold nursery stock from farm to farm. They were responsible for the extensive plantings of elms and silver maples throughout the eastern and midwestern cities and for the familiar plantings of Norway spruce in the dooryards of most New York and midwestern farms.

Of course, not all nurserymen and agents were scalawags; most packed their goods carefully and labeled them accurately. Many nurserymen were held in high esteem, as the report of the orchard committee of the Michigan Pomological Society of 1873 testifies. When the committee evaluated the Ilgenfritz Nursery of Monroe in 1877, they stated that it had a "fine arrangement of packing houses and extensive cellars in which to heel-in stock. All the land upon which it is grown is thoroughly prepared and under-drained before planting is begun."

LEGISLATION AND THE AUTOMOBILE
AFFECT DEVELOPMENT

For the nursery industry 1912 was a significant year: the first national plant quarantine act was passed and parcel post went into effect. The Plant Quarantine Act prohibited the importation of certain plants into the country; and Plant Quarantine No. 37, effective in 1919, created a favorable economic situation for American nurserymen by severely restricting plant imports. In fact, American nurseries soon found it necessary to import skilled plant propagators from Europe.

Passage of the parcel post bill paved the way for various changes.

First, it led to the rapid development of the mail-order business. Most of the major firms became established in the primary production areas, including: western New York; Lake County, Ohio; and Shenandoah, Iowa. This facet of the business, which relied heavily on the U.S. mail and on catalog, magazine, and newspaper advertising, prospered immediately. It is still a huge business, but when the "horseless carriage" arrived and as better roads were built and more people could afford automobiles, nurserymen also found it advantageous to develop retail outlets. Retail sales, in turn, led some of the more enterprising nurserymen to sell various types of soil amendments, garden tools and equipment, pesticides, garden ornaments, and outdoor furniture. This was the genesis of the modern garden center industry, which in 1972 accounted for more than $829 million in sales. California had the largest number of garden supply stores and recorded the greatest sales volume ($117 million); Pennsylvania, New York, Michigan, Texas, and Ohio each had sales in excess of $45 million.

EARLY GARDEN CENTERS

Garden centers started by way of seed houses, sometimes accidentally. Sometime around 1784, David Landreth established the seed house of David Landreth and Sons in Philadelphia. This was probably the first establishment of its kind in the United States. Another famous seed house was that of the Thorburns, for many years a center for horticultural interest in New York City. In 1801 its founder, Grant Thorburn, sold a rose geranium that he had placed in a pot on his grocery store counter to draw attention to the flowerpots he sold. From that insignificant beginning the establishment grew to a complete emporium of everything required in the practice of horticulture. A similar circumstance was responsible 150 years later for the formation of Frank's Nurseries of Detroit, currently the largest garden center chain store business in the country.

CENSUS DATA ON NURSERIES

The first special census of nurseries, conducted in 1890, revealed that 4500 nurseries occupied about 173,000 acres of land and employed more than 45,000 men, 2000 women, and 14,000 animals. Two-thirds of the nurseries were small (2–25 acres) and produced a variety of materials for local demand. Another group produced

Table 1-1 Major nursery production states, 1890 versus 1974^a

1890	Value of nurseries	1974	Value of sales
New York	10.6	California	127.8
California	4.2	Florida	42.8
Illinois	3.6	Ohio	25.6
Ohio	3.2	Illinois	21.6
Pennsylvania	3.1	Pennsylvania	19.9
Missouri	2.6	Oregon	19.7
New Jersey	1.7	New Jersey	18.9
Massachusetts	1.4	New York	17.9
Nebraska	1.4	Michigan	15.8
Iowa	1.4	Tennessee	15.0
Kansas	1.3	Texas	14.3
U.S. total	42.0		506.5

^aCensus data for 1890 are in value of nurseries, whereas the 1974 data are in value of sales. All values are in millions of dollars.

SOURCE: U.S. Census of Agriculture, 1890 and 1974.

either a general line of nursery stock or specialized in a few items, such as small fruit, and relied on newspaper advertising and catalogs for their orders. They delivered by mail, freight, or express. A third group, the large producers, catered to the wholesale trade by issuing trade catalogs to other nurserymen, to extensive planters, and to nursery agents. Some of these nurseries were 1000 acres or more, shipped in railroad-car lots, and in the busy season, by the trainload. A fourth group produced a general assortment of stock and sold through salesmen who canvassed from house to house and farm to farm selling millions of plants. Total nursery production in 1890 was estimated to be approximately 3.4 billion plants, primarily fruit trees and small fruit plants. Major production was centered in New York, California, Illinois, Ohio, and Pennsylvania (Table 1-1).

In 1974 these five states were still among the leaders in the production of nursery products, but their ranking had changed. California had become the leading state, with wholesale sales close to $130 million—almost seven times that of New York, the leader in 1890. The nursery center of the country was comprised of three southern California counties (Kern, Los Angeles, and Orange), with a combined production of $72 million. Ornamental plants have led all other categories of nursery products in total sales in the United States since 1950 (Table 1-2).

Table 1-2 Wholesale value of nursery products, by year

Nursery product	1950	1960	1970
	(millions of dollars)		
Ornamental plants	57	125	233
Deciduous fruit and nuts	6	11	26
Lining-out stock	3	6	13
Citrus and subtropical fruit	2	7	6
Small fruit plants	3	4	6

SOURCE: U.S. Census of Agriculture, 1969.

A CHANGING INDUSTRY

During the 1950s and 1960s, the total number of nurseries declined almost 50% in the 10 leading nursery states. Although the total acreage in nursery stock in seven of these states increased, Florida, New York, and Texas showed a decrease.

In addition to a change from fruit tree production to ornamental plant production, the nursery industry of the United States has experienced major changes in its methods of production and transportation. Machines, of course, have gradually replaced animals and reduced the need for hand labor. The introduction of hydraulic power made possible the development of mechanical planters, tree diggers, lifting and loading equipment, and high-speed packaging and potting machines.

Changes in digging and root pruning illustrate the dramatic effect of machines and hydraulic power. Earlier all plants were dug by hand, and little, if any, root pruning was done. Even with the development of the "U-blade," root pruning and digging of bare-root plants needed 6–14 teams of horses (Fig. 1-1). The operation also required 6–18 people to drive the teams and operate the equipment. Beginning in the early 1900s, however, the steam engine gradually replaced horses. A large, 16-horsepower steam engine (Fig. 1-2) supplied the power for a double-barreled winch which pulled the cables attached to the U-blade. Currently, the power to root prune or dig bare-root trees is supplied by a 100-horsepower twin-engine high-clearance tractor operated by one worker (Fig. 1-3). A hydraulic tree spade, also operated by one person, can dig and lift, in a matter of minutes, a 20- to 40-ft tree with a soil ball 5 ft in diameter.

The development of selective chemical weed control agents, improved pesticides, and slow- or controlled-release fertilizers also

Figure 1-1 Root pruning shade trees in the nursery with the aid of horsepower in the 1800s. (Courtesy Isaac Hicks & Son, Westbury Nurseries.)

changed cultural practices significantly. But the most pronounced change in the industry was the large-scale production of container-grown plants. Although the system of growing plants in containers was known for centuries, it was not adapted to large-scale production of small plants until after World War II. California pioneered in its development, but it soon spread to the other parts of the nation. The system allows nurserymen to grow, ship, and market their plants in the same container. It lends itself to a high degree of automation and eliminates the need to dig the crop just prior to sale.

The development of national highway systems in the mid-1950s and 1960s brought about another major change in the shipping of nursery stock. Rapid truck delivery permitted pick up at the site of production and delivery to the point of sale or of planting in the landscape. This eliminated the double and triple handling of plants shipped by railroad. Truck delivery has also contributed to greater

Figure 1-2 Digging bare-root trees in a nursery with the aid of a U-blade, double-barreled winch, and 16 HP steam engine. (Source: 1847 Catalog, Monroe Nursery.)

specialization. Nurserymen now tend to produce only plants that grow well in their area. They may specialize in shade trees, evergreens, shrubs or ground covers, or even in a limited selection of shade trees or evergreens. Nurserymen who formerly produced a wide assortment of species may concentrate on only a few species and buy the balance of their catalog needs from other sources. The relatively low cost of truck transportation and the savings from reduced handling have been responsible for this. On the other hand, a significant increase in trucking rates could change this situation.

Figure 1-3 Digging bare-root trees in a nursery with the aid of a U-blade and high clearance tractor. (Courtesy Bailey Nursery.)

SUMMARY

Some of the more significant events and developments in the brief history of the nursery industry of the United States are summarized in the following chronology.

Chronology of Nursery Industry of the United States

1737	Establishment of the first commercial nursery (Prince Nursery of Flushing, N.Y.) in the United States.
1847	The "Nursery Wagon" transported container-growing plants from Iowa to Oregon.
1869	Gypsy moth brought into the United States from Europe. This voracious pest was confined primarily to the New England states.
1870	San Jose scale accidentally introduced into this country

from China on ornamental plants (via San Jose, California). This serious pest was widely distributed throughout the country in the late 1800s by interstate shipment of infested nursery stock.

1870   The first large tree-moving equipment developed by the Hicks Nursery on Long Island.

1873-74   A severe freeze throughout the Midwest caused the loss of thousands of plants and the failure of many nurseries.

1875   American Association of Nurserymen founded (incorporated 1921).

1881   California law passed to prevent distribution of the grape gall louse.

1890-91   A blizzard killed millions of trees in nurseries and orchards throughout the country, causing serious financial loss to many nurserymen.

1891   *The Nursery Book* by Liberty Hyde Bailey was published.

1893   Publication of the *National Nurseryman*, a trade journal for the nursery industry.

1896   Maryland legislature passed the first law providing that all nursery stock being shipped into that state must be accompanied by a certificate, issued by an authorized official, stating that the stock was duly inspected and found to be free from indications of the presence of dangerously injurious insects and plant diseases (San Jose scale, peach yellows, rosette). Many other states soon followed this example and passed similar laws.

1896-98   A serious overproduction of nursery stock lowered prices; many nursery firms were forced out of business.

1898   Introduction of the white pine blister rust into New England. This disease was probably introduced on plants imported from Europe.

1898-99   A serious drought in the California area caused the loss of many plants, forcing a number of nurseries out of business.

1904   Discovery of chestnut blight on the grounds of the New York Zoological Park. This disease, which caused the demise of the American chestnut, was apparently introduced on plant material imported from China.

1912   Passage of the Plant Quarantine Act of 1912, the first federal plant quarantine designed to provide the necessary federal legislation to protect against the entry of dangerous insects and diseases on plants or plant products imported from foreign countries.

1912   Passage of the Parcel Post Act, which spawned the development of many mail-order nurseries.

1916   The Japanese beetle found in New Jersey was probably introduced by the importation of plants from Japan.

1919   Plant Quarantine No. 37 enacted into law.

1920   Photoperiodism recognized as an important factor in the control of growth and flowering of certain plants.

1929   The Dutch elm disease discovered in Cleveland, Ohio. This disease and its vector were most likely introduced into the United States on elm logs imported from Europe.

1930   Passage of the Plant Patent Law.

1934   Auxins, such as indoleacetic acid, recognized as having considerable practical value in stimulating the rooting of cuttings.

1936   DDT recognized as an insecticide of major importance in the control of insects.

1944   2,4–D first used as a selective herbicide in the removal of broadleaved weeds from lawns and for the control of selected weeds in nurseries.

1946   Development of garden center industry following World War II revolutionized the marketing of nursery stock.

1949   Container production of nursery stock developed on a large scale.

1949   Introduction of the first patented ornamental tree, "Moraine" honey locust (Plant Patent 836).

1956   Passage of Interstate and National Defense Highway Act, which led to rapid truck transport of nursery products.

1956   Introduction of hydraulic tree diggers revolutionized digging plants in nurseries.

1959   Development of selective chemical weed control for nursery crops.

1959   Drip or "spaghetti" irrigation methods developed for container production of nursery stock.

1960   Fertilizer injections introduced into the nursery industry.

1965   Federal Highway Beautification Act was enacted.

1967   Polyethylene film used to modify environment about nursery plants.

1975	Trickle irrigation introduced to field production of nursery stock.
1975	Photoperiod and light intensity used to control juvenile growth of woody plants.
1977	Nursery Marketing Council was established.

REFERENCES

ANONYMOUS. 1908. A group of pioneer nurserymen and pomologists. Natl. Nurseryman 16(6):200–203.

_____. 1908. The nurseries of Pennsylvania. Natl. Nurseryman 16(6):187.

_____. 1908. The Storrs and Harrison Company. Natl. Nurseryman 16(11):361–364.

_____. 1967. Census of Agriculture. U.S. Bureau of Census. Government Printing Office, Washington, D.C.

_____. 1968. Scope of the nursery industry. Horticultural Research Institute, Inc., 230 Southern Building, Washington, D.C. 20005.

BAILEY, L. H. 1895. A century of American horticulture. Florist Exchange 7 (17):387–394.

BARRY, W. C. 1894. The nursery industry of the East. Natl. Nurseryman 2(6): 70.

COATES, L. 1908. The nursery business in California. Natl. Nurseryman 16:337.

DURUZ, W. P. 1941. Notes on the early history of horticulture in Oregon with special reference to fruit tree nurseries. Agric. Hist. 15(2):84–97.

GREENING, C. E. 1902. Evaluation of the nursery business. Michigan State Horticultural Society. P. 91.

HALE, J. H. 1891. Nurseries. Bulletin of the 11th census. Michigan State Horticultural Society. Pp. 470–474.

LEWIS, C. E. 1953. Hicks nurseries celebrate centennial. Am. Nurseryman 98 (2):20.

MANNING, R. 1880. Sketch of the history of horticulture in the U.S. up to the year 1829. History of the Massachusetts Horticultural Society 1829–1878.

POTTER, C. H. 1965. Lewelling's legacy—the Oregon nursery trade. Am. Nurseryman 122(2):9.

THOMAS, J. J. 1873. Horticulture for the people. Michigan Pomological Society. Pp. 489–491.

THOMPSON, B. F. 1843. The history of Long Island. Vol. 2, pp. 83–87, 239.

WILLIAMSON, R. 1893. Nursery business on the Pacific Coast. Natl. Nurseryman 1(8):95.

WOOD, J. 1900. Pioneer nurserymen. Natl. Nurseryman 8(3):27.

SUGGESTED READING

DAVIDSON, H., and D. A. SNELL. 1971. Growth and development of the garden center industry in the U.S. HortScience 6(1):12–15.

DOUGLAS, G., et al. 1947. The history of the Southern Nurserymen's Association. Southern Nurserymen's Association, Nashville, Tenn.

HEDRICK, U. P. 1950. A history of horticulture in America. Oxford University Press, Inc., New York.

Chapter 2

The Nursery Industry

The nursery industry of the United States has grown from its embryonic beginning on Long Island in 1737 to a multimillion-dollar, nationwide complex of businesses today. It is composed of many interrelated parts, including nurseries that produce plants, landscape firms that use plants and related materials to develop attractive and functional landscapes, garden centers that sell plant materials and garden-related items, plus maintenance firms that specialize in maintaining plants and landscaped areas.

NURSERY CLASSIFICATION

A plant nursery is a place where hardy trees, shrubs, ground covers, vines, and herbaceous plants are propagated and grown. Nurseries in the United States are very diversified and may be classified and de-

Table 2–1 Classification of nurseries

I. *Ownership*	IV. *Product*
1. Private industry	1. General, diversified, catalog; offering many types of hardy plants
a. Proprietorship	2. Specialty, limited catalog; specialty in one major class, but may offer some species from several subclasses
b. Partnership	
c. Corporation	
2. Government agencies	
a. County	a. Fruit
b. City	(1) General
c. State	(2) Tree fruits, including nuts
d. Federal	(3) Small fruits
3. Educational institutions	b. Ornamental
a. Arboretia	(1) General
b. Botanical gardens	(2) Shade and flowering trees
c. Universities	(3) Evergreens
II. *Function*	(a) Narrowleaved
1. Production	(b) Broadleaved
a. Wholesale	(4) Shrubs
b. Retail	(5) Roses
c. Nonprofit	(6) Ground covers and vines
2. Mail-order	(7) Herbaceous perennials
3. Landscape	(8) Indoor plants (house plants)
4. Wholesale plant materials distribution	c. Forest and conservation
5. Quarantine	(1) Reforestation
6. Research	(2) Wildlife habitat
III. *Production system*	(3) Erosion control
1. Field production	d. Propagation and liner materials
a. Bare-root	(1) Budded plants
b. Soil-balled	(2) Grafted plants
2. Container production	(3) Rooted cuttings
	(4) Seedlings
	(5) Rootstocks

scribed according to four major criteria: (1) ownership, (2) function, (3) production system, and (4) type of plant material produced (Table 2–1).

Ownership

Nurseries are owned and operated either by private industry or by various governmental agencies and educational institutions. Within the private sector they may be either a proprietorship, a partnership, or a corporation. The advantages and disadvantages of these legal forms are discussed in Chapter 3. Government agencies operate nurseries to supply part or all of their plant material needs, to furnish planting stock for various reforestation and conservation programs, and for quarantine purposes. Educational institutions operate nurseries to support their many and diverse programs in research, teaching, extension, and to landscape their campuses.

Function

Production nurseries propagate and produce plants for a variety of purposes, including fruit production, environmental quality improvement programs, conservation projects, and research and educational programs. Production nurseries may be either profit- or nonprofit-oriented. Those that are profit-oriented are in the private sector of the industry; the nonprofit production nurseries are operated by various governmental agencies and educational institutions. Those that are profit-oriented can be subclassified as either retail or wholesale production.

Retail production nurseries are generally small in size, commonly 50 acres or less, and sell their production directly to the ultimate user, in most cases homeowners.

Wholesale production nurseries are primarily large establishments that sell their plants in wholesale units to industry-related buyers (e.g., landscape contractors, garden centers). Wholesale production nurseries may specialize in a particular type of plant material and locate in areas where climate and soil are most favorable for production. In 1975 there were over 5000 wholesale nurseries in the United States, with combined sales in excess of $900 million.

Mail-order nurseries deliver the products that they merchandise via the U.S. mail, the United Parcel Service, or by bus. Their contact with customers is primarily through catalogs and literature sent directly to the customer or advertisements placed with one or more of the mass communication media. Most of the material is herbaceous perennials, small fruit, or small trees and shrubs. Potted material is grown and shipped in a lightweight medium to reduce shipping costs.

Landscape nurseries design and construct attractive and functional landscapes utilizing the resources available within the organization. Modern landscape firms are staffed with designers that produce the landscape plans, growers that produce the plant material, and construction specialists who carry out the plans. Landscape nurseries produce woody ornamental plants that are larger than those available from most wholesale production nurseries. However, they seldom produce all their plant material needs and usually supplement their production by purchasing smaller, readily available material from other nurseries. Some landscape nurseries subcontract parts of a landscape project to other firms. For example, it is common to sub-contract lawn work to a lawn specialist, and large pools, patios, and sundecks to a building contractor. In some states a builder's license is required to do this type of construction, especially if the construction is attached to a building.

A *plant material distribution center* (PMDC) is a nursery whose primary function is to locate, purchase, and assemble in a convenient location landscape plants which, in turn, are resold to landscape nurserymen or contractors. The PMDC takes title to the plant material and either holds it in a sales yard or grows it in a nursery to enhance quality prior to sale. The center may also stock for resale various items associated with planting (e.g., peat moss, tree wrap, mulch, etc.).

Quarantine nurseries are, as the name implies, nurseries where plants are held during a period of quarantine. They are operated by federal or state agencies charged with the responsibility of administering federal and state laws related to importation of plants.

Production System

On the basis of production systems, nurseries may be classified as either field production or container production. Field production nurseries (Fig. 2-1) may be subclassified by the method used in digging and processing their plants; they may be either bare-root or soil-balled. Plants that are dug bare-root have the soil removed from their roots as they are harvested, whereas soil-balled plants are dug with a soil ball about their roots, which is then contained in some manner. The most common method used to contain soil-balled plants is to secure the soil ball with burlap, known in the industry as balled and burlapped (B&B). Other methods include boxing, potting, and basketing. Boxing is used for large plants, dug with large soil balls, shaped as an inverted, truncated pyramid, which is then contained with specially designed wood forms. Potting is used on small plants which are dug and lifted out of the ground with a soil ball and placed into pots. Basketing is a technique that has developed to containerize soil balls of plants that are dug with various types of tree diggers (Fig. 2-2).

Growing plants in containers has been practiced for centuries, but container production of plants in the nursery is a relatively modern practice (Fig. 2-3). Since the early 1950s it has evolved into a highly scientific and successful method of nursery production. It is an excellent example of nurserymen and scientists working to-

Figure 2-1 Field production of evergreens. (Source: Kluck Nursery.)

gether in solving problems and developing a highly effective and efficient system of growing and marketing plants in containers (Table 2-2).

In the early development of container production of plants, nurserymen used tin cans, tar-paper pots, or standard clay pots as the container. The growing medium was whatever field soil was readily available. Fertilizer and irrigation system practices were adapted from field culture. Since container production, as a large commercial venture, began in the warmer parts of the country, there was no problem with overwintering of plants. But as the practice was adopted by nurserymen in the colder parts of the country, overwintering of plants in containers became a problem that had to be solved if the practice was to be successful for northern nurseries.

Since the 1950s major changes have been effected in the container production of plants. The containers are no longer the rusted food cans of the early years, but are designed and manufactured especially for the nursery industry. Metal containers are crimped so that they nest for shipping and storage, and dipped in a rustproof paint so that they last for 2 or more years and make an attractive

Figure 2-2 Digging B&B trees in a nursery with the aid of a hydraulic digging machine. Note the wire basket lined with burlap. (Source: Farley Bros. Nursery.)

market container. Plastic containers may be obtained that serve various needs, including thin wall for inexpensive short-term crops and thick wall for long-term crops and for stacking during transport.

Various types and sizes of woodfiber containers are also available. They are best used either for potting field-grown plants that will be shipped and then marketed within a few weeks or for plants that will be produced and marketed the same growing season by retail production nurseries. Fiber pots are structurally weak and should not be stacked when shipping the potted plants. Also, when they become wet they deteriorate. This can be either an advantage or disadvantage, depending upon the situation. In retail production it may be an advantage in that the exposed roots, which grow through the walls of the container, can be used as an indication of a good vigorous root system. These plants must be carefully handled and planted without too much delay following purchase by retail customers. However, in wholesale production rapid deterioration of containers is undesirable, since it necessitates repotting, which is an added cost of production. Other types of containers used in nursery

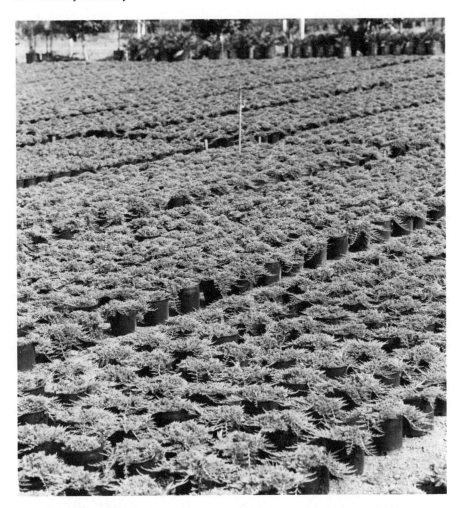

Figure 2-3 Container-grown evergreens in a production nursery. (Courtesy Monrovia Nursery Co.)

production include tar-paper pots, wood or wire baskets, thin-walled polyethylene bags, and polyethylene-lined baskets, pots, or boxes.

The growing medium is blended to specifications. By using various ingredients, nurserymen can obtain a medium that meets their particular production and market requirements. Soil fertility regimes are carefully planned and monitored to optimize growth and quality. Various types of slow-release and soluble fertilizers have been developed to aid in maintaining fertility levels at optimum. Irrigation practices are specifically designed for the effective and efficient use of water and water-soluble fertilizers. And container-grown plants

Table 2-2 Advantages and challenges of producing and marketing plants in containers

---

Production Advantages

---

1. More uniform plants. This is a result of providing optimum conditions for growth of the plants (e.g., medium, nutrition, water, light, spacing).
2. Provides a method of producing plants that are difficult to transplant.
3. Greater numbers of plants produced per unit area. Avoids need of land in rotation (cover crops) and reduces loss of plants due to cultivator injury.
4. Permits use of areas normally not usable for field production.
5. Avoids the digging operation.
6. Improves cash flow. Invested capital has a faster turnover rate.
7. Greater potential for mechanization of materials handling [e.g., potting (Fig. 2-4), pickup, and delivery to and from production site].

Production Challenges

---

1. Total dependence upon artificial irrigation (offset by greater control of moisture levels).
2. Root development is limited by the size and shape of the container.
3. Need for repotting of plants if they are not used on schedule (potential for container-bound roots).
4. Need for winter protection in colder climates.
5. Greater need to supplement and monitor levels of chemical supplements.
6. Need to leach medium periodically (to avoid excess soluble salts).
7. Need for good water drainage. On some sites it is necessary to develop wastewater disposal systems.
8. Relatively high cost production system (offset with improved cash flow).

Marketing Advantages

---

1. Reduces transportation costs, due to lightweight medium.
2. Extends marketing season (both wholesale and retail).
3. Extends planting season.
4. Convenient prepackaged cash-and-carry item.
5. Relatively easy to maintain (water and fertilize) in sales area; no need to mulch or heel-in.
6. Better display of plants.
7. Less handling damage. Workers tend to carry plants in pots by the container rather than by their tops.

Marketing Challenges

---

1. Medium has a tendency to dry out faster, requiring greater attention to watering.
2. Plants in unsightly containers are unattractive to customers.
3. Difficult to remove plants from some types of containers, such as cylindrical metal containers.
4. Container-bound roots, if present, limit growth and life expectancy of plants in landscape sites.

Figure 2-4 Potting machine aids in planting container-grown nursery stock. (Courtesy Cottage Gardens Nursery.)

can be overwintered in northern climates with a high probability of success if certain practices are followed relative to avoiding desiccation of the foliage, cold-temperature injury of the roots, and girdling damage by rodents.

Product

Nurseries can also be classified and described on the basis of the types of plant material that they produce. Historically, the early nurseries of the nation produced fruit plants for the developing nation. Gradually, they included plants for landscaping, and as the need developed they produced seedlings of forest tree species for the forest industries and plants with special characteristics for conservation purposes and erosion control. When a nursery produces species from two or more of the foregoing categories, it is best classified as a general nursery, producing a diversified catalog of hardy plants. With the development of the railroads and especially with the advent of rapid truck transportation, large wholesale nurseries began to specialize in one or a limited number of species. Some wholesale production nurseries grow only one type of plant material, such as: shade trees, evergreens, shrubs, roses, or herbaceous perennials. Some specialize in one or two genera (e.g., rhododendrons or taxus and hemlock). Other nurseries specialize in the production of seedlings for reforestation, conservation, and Christmas tree plantations. There are also nurseries that specialize in propagating materials for other nurseries. Their production may include dwarf rootstocks, grafted plants, rooted cuttings, seedlings, or shade tree whips. These firms are mostly located in the major nursery production areas or on sites that provide a major climatic advantage.

ALLIED AREAS

Within the industry there are a number of businesses that are closely allied to nursery production. They do not produce but buy, sell, and distribute plant material or provide a closely related service.

Landscape contractors perform the major construction operations associated with the development of large landscapes. Typical projects include shopping malls, industry-headquarters sites, industrial parks, golf courses, amusement parks, and so on. Landscape contractors purchase almost all of their plant material from nurseries that specialize in the production of large landscape plants. Arrangements for purchase and delivery of plants are often made through a nursery broker.

Nursery brokers are independent sales agents whose primary function is to arrange purchase-sales agreements between members of the nursery industry. They help to locate plants for the buyers and sell the products of the producers. Brokers may also arrange shipping and transportation schedules. They do not take title to the plant material but are paid a commission on sales booked with each nursery that they represent.

The *horticultural broker or distributor* is the primary supplier of the hard goods for the nursery industry. They purchase and stock for resale all types of tools, equipment, and supplies for the horticultural industries. Good horticultural brokers specialize in service to their customers by having the needed materials and supplying them when and where they are needed in the proper quantities.

The *modern garden center* is the outgrowth of the small retail nursery sales lot or fruit stand of the pre-World War II years. It is not only a retail center for plants, but it is the place where people come to purchase all their gardening supplies. Garden centers vary considerably in size, quality, and services offered. The larger, chain-operated garden centers are primarily self-service. Many operate on a low margin of profit based on a fast turnover and do a large volume of business, whereas the smaller, generally family operated garden centers provide many special services, operate on a higher percentage markup, but do a lower volume of business. However, there are many variations between the two groups.

Sometimes the price of plants in a large garden center may be higher than those in smaller garden centers. And some fairly large garden centers offer special services to their customers. The marketing system varies with the philosophy of management and the level of competition in the market area. Most garden centers have found it necessary and profitable to broaden their product mix. Large investments in buildings, high rents for prime locations, and other high overhead costs make it necessary for garden center managers to be alert to various means of assuring sales during all months of the year, rather than being satisfied with only two peak sales periods, spring and fall, as was the situation in past years. Handicrafts, home decorations, garden furniture, pet supplies, and Christmas decorations are examples of items used to improve the cash flow at garden centers when plant sales are slow.

Landscape maintenance firms, as the name implies, specialize in maintaining the landscape plantings for individuals and businesses. Tree maintenance, as performed by the arborist, is a very specialized branch of the landscape maintenance business. The arborist is responsible for all types of specialized activities associated with large trees, including moving, pruning, and repairing damaged trees; bracing, spraying, and fertilizing of living trees; plus the removal of dead or dying trees. Specialized training is needed to perform the functions of the arborist.

Although most home lawns and landscapes are maintained by homeowners or by hiring a neighbor boy, some are maintained by professional maintenance firms; in some parts of the country there are franchised lawn maintenance firms. Industrial and institutional landscape maintenance has become a relatively large business since the mid-1950s. There are also firms that rent and maintain plants for use in interior landscapes, including offices, malls, and public buildings.

Within the industry can be found many combinations of the foregoing groups or classifications. Some nurseries, for example, may produce plants by both field and container culture. Also, some businesses may be made up of two or more divisions. Many mail-order nurseries commonly operate garden centers. Some large nursery businesses operate a wholesale production nursery specializing in ornamental plants, a garden center, a landscape construction department, and a landscape maintenance department. In another situation the business may start as a small retail nursery and gradually develop over a period of years into a large wholesale production nursery with one or more allied businesses. At first it may be a proprietorship, which then becomes a partnership and finally a corporation. As a corporation it may be involved in producing evergreen seedlings for Christmas tree plantations and reforestation; ornamental evergreens and shade trees for landscape purposes—the latter produced by both field and container culture; and operate a garden center.

TRADE ORGANIZATIONS*

Trade organizations that serve the nursery industry are primarily oriented about the functional aspect of the business and to some degree about the type of plant material produced. But most of the trade organizations are organized on a geographic basis.

The *American Association of Nurserymen* (AAN) was first organized in 1875 as the National Association of Nurserymen, Florists, and Seedsmen. By 1883 the seedsmen and florists had organized their own trade association. Thus, the name was changed in 1884 to the American Association of Nurserymen and was incorporated as a nonprofit corporation in 1921. The AAN is active in many types of programs, including education, promotion, and legislation that enhance the efficient and economic progress of the nursery industry. They publish a nursery trade and supply directory, special AAN summaries on topics of current interest, and a quarterly magazine, *ALI*, with in-depth articles of concern to nurserymen.

The annual meeting of the AAN held in July is a forum for the discussion of industry problems and the dissemination of information. At the first meeting four topics were discussed: costs and inequities of freight rates, grades for nursery stock, statistics on the annual production, and condition of crops and postal rates. These topics have held high priority in many meetings since and will undoubtedly have high priority at future meetings.

The AAN staff in Washington, D.C., provide the management and administrative staff for each of the next six trade organizations. They are the umbrella under which these organizations are united for economy of force and unity of purpose. The AAN also offers an opportunity to its members to subscribe to a group accident insurance program and to the Dodson Savings Classification Plan for workmen's compensation insurance.

*See Appendix B for addresses.

The *Horticultural Research Institute* (HRI) was organized in 1962 by a group of progressive nurserymen as a nonprofit, tax-exempt organization to plan and support research for the nursery industry. Members of HRI are informed of all research results through the newsletter "Horizons." HRI also publishes special research reports on many topics of interest to the nursery industry. Examples of subjects addressed are antitrust, credit, estate planning, labor, wage-hour, tax accounting, truth in lending, and a technical glossary of horticulture and landscape terminology. Tax-deductible contributions can be made to HRI for the support of research programs.

The *National Landscape Association* (NLA) was founded in 1939 as the National Landscape Nurserymen's Association to promote better landscaping and to provide a means for the exchange of ideas and knowledge related to the profession. The association supports the publication of literature relative to landscape beautification and sponsors management clinics. In 1967 NLA came under the umbrella of the AAN for administration and promotion. Membership in NLA is open to nursery firms that do landscape work and are members of the American Association of Nurserymen.

The *Wholesale Nursery Growers of America, Inc.* (WNGA) was organized in 1964 with the major purpose of providing a forum for the exchange of ideas and information relative to the production of nursery products. The WNGA has developed a useful crop reporting system and has stimulated interest in and aided HRI in the conduct of a business analysis of the nursery industry. They are active in seeking scientific answers to problems of production and postharvest physiology of nursery crops. A quarterly newsletter contains information on technological advancements in growing and production, general business news pertaining to wholesale nurserymen, trend reports, and the latest developments in mechanization and transportation. Their meetings coincide with the annual summer meeting of the AAN and the midwinter meeting in Chicago. Membership is open to nurserymen engaged in the production of nursery stock at the wholesale level.

The *American Association of Nurserymen's Group Insurance Trust* is one of the oldest and most successful group insurance programs in existence. It is designed to provide life insurance and hospitalization with major medical insurance for the owners and full-time employees of AAN member firms. Members may select between two excellent life and health insurance plans, both featuring $100,000 major medical, double-life insurance option, and supplemental benefits to Medicare. It is composed of over 300 nursery firms and is managed by nurserymen trustees.

Garden Centers of America is the trade association for the garden center industry. It is management-oriented to give the nation's garden center operators the management information they need to operate a more profitable business. Garden Centers of America was organized in 1972 and functions under the AAN umbrella.

The *Nursery Marketing Council* (NMC) was established in 1977 to provide the nursery industry, through the AAN, with a market research and analysis capability to produce advertising and public relations that ultimately will increase the use of plant materials and related products. Its activities benefit the entire nursery industry and are supported by voluntary contributions.

SPECIALIZED ASSOCIATIONS

The *International Plant Propagator's Society* (IPPS) was organized in 1951 to secure recognition for the plant propagator as a craftsman and to provide a forum for the dissemination of knowledge in this field. The society is divided into the eastern, western, and southern regions in North America, each division sponsoring an annual meeting. In addition, there is a region of Great Britain and Ireland, an Australian region, and a New Zealand chapter. The combined proceedings are published by the society, which also publishes *The Plant Propagator,* a quarterly magazine available to members only.

Mail-Order Association of Nurserymen, Inc. was founded in 1934 to promote the general interests of mail-order nurserymen by providing a forum for discussion of matters pertaining to the business. The association meets twice a year, in the summer with the AAN and in the winter at the Mid-America Trade Show.

All-American Rose Selections (AARS) was organized in 1938 in an attempt to bring some order out of the confusion that existed in the yearly introduction of roses. Prior to its inception, literally hundreds of inferior varieties of roses were introduced each year. Through its program of variety trials in selected test gardens, AARS has succeeded in establishing in the minds of home gardeners a high degree of confidence in its seal of quality. In 1976 All-American award winners comprised over 40% of all roses sold in the United States annually. This is a real tribute to All-American roses, since the award winners comprise less than 1% of the more than 8000 known named varieties of roses. The rose industry of the United States sells in excess of 40 million plants annually. AARS is a nonprofit organization whose sole function is to test new rose selections and to give recognition to those of merit in the form of an All-American award.

Landscape Materials Information Service (LMIS), incorporated in January 1954 as a self-supporting, nonprofit association, was organized to act as a clearinghouse for the collection, evaluation, and dissemination of information pertinent to the interests of arborists, horticulturists, landscape contractors, nurserymen, various public agencies, and suppliers of landscape materials.

Members receive an updated plant materials availability list twice a year, a biweekly bulletin announcing contracted and planned landscape projects, and advice on the procurement of scarce plant material or other landscape supplies. Membership is centered primarily in the northeastern states.

The *Associated Landscape Contractors of America* (ALCA) was incorporated in 1961 as a nonprofit corporation (business league) to provide cohesion and coordination among industry members and to enhance the image of landscape contracting as a profession. The association publishes the monthly "ALCA Action Letter."

The *International Society of Arboriculture* was organized as the International Shade Tree Conference in 1924 (name was changed in 1975) to promote and improve the planting and preservation of trees and to assist in the beautification of the countryside. Its publications include *The Journal of Arboriculture,* the monthly *Arborists News,* and special publications and films issued on an irregular basis.

The *National Arborists Association,* founded in 1938, is an organization of commercial people engaged in arboriculture. It is interested in the business aspects of tree services and good public relations programs.

The *Nurserymen's Protective Association* provides credit information on other nurserymen (wholesale, construction, and retail) to its members.

National Association of Plant Patent Owners is a private trade organization whose members own one or more plant patents. The objective of the association is to keep its members informed on the rules and regulations of the Patent Office pertaining to filing for and the granting of plant patents. Its constant legislative arm is a vital force in protecting the plant patent system.

The *Garden Center Symposium* (GCS), organized in 1964, is a midwestern garden center trade association composed of small independent merchants who operate garden centers. The purpose of the symposium is to provide a means for the exchange of management information on garden center operations and a vehicle for gathering and disseminating data of value to garden center managers. The symposium compiles and maintains up-to-date lists of plants and supplies.

STATE, REGIONAL, AND LOCAL ORGANIZATIONS

In addition to the many national associations, most states have nurserymen's associations which embrace growers, contractors, landscape maintenance personnel, and garden center operators. The state associations promote and support legislation that affects the nursery industries within each state. They also conduct, in cooperation with state university extension services, educational meetings and demonstrations. Some of the larger state associations employ an executive secretary and publish a trade paper and buyer's guide.

In a few places, nurserymen within a geographic area have formed associations, either formal or informal, for the purpose of conducting seminars, sponsoring garden shows and trade shows, and supporting field demonstrations. These groups may be within the metropolitan area of a city (e.g., the Metropolitan Detroit Landscape Association), an area of the state (e.g., Long Island Nurserymen's Association), or they may involve a number of states (e.g., Southern Nurserymen's Association, a consortium of state nurserymen's associations in the South for the purpose of conducting a joint summer meeting at Atlanta, Georgia).

CENTERS OF PRODUCTION

The centers of nursery production in the United States have changed with the development of the nation and have tended to follow the westward migration. For many years Geneva, New York, was the primary center of production. But this gradually shifted to Lake County, Ohio, which became known as the nursery capital of the country in the late 1800s and in the early twentieth century. However, other areas were gradually developing: central Illinois; Shenandoah, Iowa; and Tyler, Texas. By the mid-twentieth century, the primary center of nursery production in the United States was in southern California. The leading areas of production, as indicated by the 1974 Census of Agriculture, are California, Florida, Ohio, Illinois, Pennsylvania, Oregon, New Jersey, New York, Tennessee, Texas, and Iowa, with a few centers located in other states (Table 1-1).

California

If two words could characterize the nursery industry of a state, "container production" would do it for California. Growing plants in containers has become a science with California nurserymen. Soil has been replaced with mixtures of sand, peat moss, soil, and redwood sawdust. Plant nutrients are supplied by constant injection feed. Moisture control is obtained by "spaghetti" or overhead irrigation. Hand labor has been substantially replaced by machines. California nurserymen propagate, grow, and ship container-grown stock 12 months of the year. Most of the ornamental evergreens produced in southern and central California nurseries are shipped to eastern and midwestern markets. In 1969 California nurseries sold over 19 million ornamental plants in containers, almost one-half of the total U.S. production.

In addition to container-grown ornamentals, California is also the leading rose-producing area of the nation. Most of the rose growers are located in southern California, south of the Tehachopi Mountains, but because of urban pressure, are gradually moving to the Bakersfield area.

California nurserymen produce large quantities of grapes and citrus and other fruit trees for the large fruit industry of the state. They grow palms, cycads, and various other subtropical plants in either container or field soils for use in interior and exterior landscapes. Production is increasing in bedding plants, ground covers, succulents, and cacti.

Florida

The nursery industry of Florida is centered in three distinct areas as a result of Florida's peninsular topography and its associated climatic zones. The lower-east-coast nurseries, located in Dade, Broward, and Palm Beach counties, produce most of the tropical and subtropical material used in northern conservatories or in Florida's beautiful tropical landscapes. The central region produces the hardier subtropical material, citrus, and foliage plants used for indoor landscaping. Apopka, located in the center of the state, is known as "The Foliage Capital of the Nation." In the northern region, particularly in Baker County, camellias and azaleas are produced as well as many of the hardier ornamental plants associated with the gracious landscapes of the South. Although the state plant board lists some 4000 certified nurseries, most of the state's $42 million wholesale nursery crop was produced by less than 20% of the nurseries and most of the plants were container-grown.

Ohio

The nursery center of the nation, prior to 1960, was considered by many to be Lake County, Ohio. In 1854 Jesse Storrs purchased a small farm in Lake County and soon founded the nursery firm of Storrs and Harrison, which became one of the largest nurseries of the late 1800s. By 1960 some 200 nurseries were producing a wide variety of nursery stock in a narrow belt 6 to 10 miles in width and about 20 miles long along the southern shore of Lake Erie. Because of the moderating influence of Lake Erie, plus a deep, rich, slightly acid soil, nurserymen grow ericaceous plants, narrowleaved evergreens, shrubs, shade trees, roses, perennials, bulbous plants, and some fruit trees and small fruit plants.

Industrialization and urbanization of this area have caused some nurseries to move to locations in other parts of the state. Southwestern and central Ohio, which are less industrialized, but have good agricultural lands and a mild climate, may become the new center for nursery production in Ohio. Many nurseries are relocating in the Ohio River valley; an interesting trend, since the first nurseries of Ohio established in 1790 were located in the Ohio River area.

Illinois

Most of the major nurseries of Illinois are located in five counties (Cook, Lake, DuPage, Kane, and Iroquois) close to Chicago. They have the advantages of a relatively mild climate and rich loam prairie soil which favor B&B production, plus central geographical locations within the nation and many large, rapidly growing urban centers within a radius of 300 miles.

Illinois nurseries, like most others that had their beginning with the opening of the West, were at first oriented toward the production of fruit plants. However, by the mid-1950s, production of ornamental plants dominated. Illinois nurseries are famous for the production of narrowleaved evergreens, shade and flowering trees, and specimen plants for the landscape industry. The winter meeting of the Illinois State Nurserymen's Association (ISNA), held in Chicago in mid-January, gradually developed into the Mid-America Trade Show and is now jointly sponsored by ISNA, the Illinois Landscape Contractors Association, and the Wisconsin Landscape Federation.

Pennsylvania

The history of the Pennsylvania nursery industry dates back to the times of David Landreth (1784) and Bernard McMahon (about 1800), when these men were engaged in the seed and nursery business in Philadelphia. The nurseries with the largest production are located in the counties of Indiana, Erie, Butler, and Allegheny, which are situated west of the Allegheny Mountains, where there is a good distribution of rainfall, or they are located in the southeastern counties, Chester, Montgomery, Bucks, and Lancaster, close to major market areas.

The state is known for the production of ornamental plants, including conifers, broadleaved evergreens, shade and flowering trees, and roses. The rose production is centered in the southeastern area near West Chester. The production of broadleaved evergreens has increased considerably over the past few years because of the increased demand for such plants. Pennsylvania nurseries are favored by a mild climate and well-drained acidic soils. A number of the Pennsylvania nurseries are known for their quality production of seedlings and liners.

Oregon-Washington

The Oregon–Washington area is one of the major producers of nursery stock, bulbs, flower, and turf seed crops. The coastal area, west of the Cascade Mountains, particularly the Willamette Valley, has a maritime climate favorable to the production of shade tree whips, broadleaved evergreens, and conifers. The inland area, east of the Cascade Mountains, has a less favorable climate, characterized by hot, dry summers and cold winters, and is thus limited to plants that are winter-hardy in that area. Many fruit tree nurseries are located on the eastern slopes of the Cascade Mountains.

Oregon and parts of Washington are also famous for their bulb production. Some 100 million bulbs are shipped from Oregon and Washington each year. Narcissus, tulip, and iris production is centered primarily in Washington, but lily and gladiolus production predominates in Oregon. Oregon is also a major producer of cut holly, which is sold for Christmas decorations. One of the large holly farms near Portland ships over 100 tons of berried holly branches each year to various parts of the United States.

New Jersey

The Garden State has been a major nursery area since colonial times. Major production centers are located in Middlesex and Monmouth counties, in close proximity to two major population centers, New York and Philadelphia, both important market areas for ornamental plants. In addition to a major market area, New Jersey also has a mild, maritime climate and some of the finest agricultural land in the nation, which make it a site that is ideal for the production of nursery stock. However, high land values and zoning laws unfavorable to agriculture, brought on by increased urbanization and industrialization, are limiting growth of nursery production in the central part of the state. Nursery production is almost totally directed to ornamental plants, including everything from ground covers up to 6-in.-caliper shade trees.

New York

Although New York state is best known for its skyscraper cities and giant industries, it is also a major nursery production state. In the 1890 Census of Agriculture, New York ranked first in the nation in the value of all nurseries. Wholesale production nurseries are concentrated primarily in the central and western counties, including Wayne, Ontario, Livingston, Erie, Monroe, and Chautauqua and in Suffolk County on eastern Long Island.

New York produces a wide selection of nursery crops, but ornamentals account for nearly 90% of the total wholesale value. Fruit trees and grape vines, although a small part of the state's total production, represent a major contribution to the nation's fruit-plant production.

Tennessee

The central portion of Tennessee in the vicinity of McMinnville and Winchester, known as the Highland Rim area of Tennessee, produces a substantial amount of nursery stock, including coniferous and broadleaved evergreens, ornamental trees and shrubs, nut trees, standard and dwarf fruit trees, ground covers, and vines. Tennessee is particularly well known for the production of flowering dogwoods (*Cornus florida*). The area is favored with a long growing season, productive soils, and a good distribution of rainfall. Some 400 certified growers operate close to 15,000 acres in nursery production in this center of horticulture.

Texas

Texas is a substantial producer of nursery stock. In 1964 the wholesale dollar volume of nursery products was in excess of 8.6 million, with over 87% of the production centered in ornamental plants; roses accounted for approximately 44% of the total value. By 1969 total sales were $9.4 million, with 77% in ornamental plants; roses accounted for only 23% of the total value. Texas also produces broadleaved evergreens, citrus, nuts, and a wide variety of deciduous ornamentals, which are marketed primarily in the southern and southeastern states. Rose production is centered in the vicinity of Tyler, which was known as the "Rose Capital of the Nation" in the mid-1960s. In 1962 Texas produced over 19 million rose bushes. The rose-growing area surrounding Tyler, in Smith County, has a very favorable combination of climate and soil conducive to the growth of roses. The area has about 314 growing days each year, with sufficient cool weather in the fall to mature plants. It has a good distribution of rainfall, and fertile, well-drained sandy loam soil that is slightly acidic.

Iowa

Shenandoah and adjacent Hamburg in southwestern Iowa are the center of a major nursery production area, producing fruit trees and ornamentals of all types. Large quantities of packaged and potted nursery stock are sold to garden centers, and bare-root material is sold to wholesale nurseries in other parts of the country. Shenandoah and Hamburg are major mail-order centers. Being centrally located in the nation, with good soils and a mild climate, accounts in part for the growth and development of Shenandoah as a nursery center.

New England Area

The New England states, particularly Rhode Island, Connecticut, and Massachusetts, are known for quality production of evergreens, especially *Taxus,* which seems to be ideally adapted to the climatic conditions along New England's southern coast. A 1959 survey of the Rhode Island nursery industry revealed that 78% of the nurseries were 3 acres or less in size, whereas 10.6% of the nurseries controlled 85% of the acreage under production. The small and large nurseries both concentrated in the production of relatively few species, the small nurseries because of space limitations and the large nurseries to gain production efficiency. The medium-sized nurseries grew a variety of plants, primarily for local retailing and landscape construction.

Michigan

Located in the heart of the Great Lakes area, Michigan has for over 100 years been a major producer of nursery stock. Most of the early production was directed toward supplying the rapidly expanding fruit industry. Even today, Michigan produces large quantities of fruit plants; however, more than 75% of its production is classified as ornamental plants. Michigan is a leader in the production of evergreen seedlings for reforestation and Christmas tree planting. The major production areas are located in the lower half of the southern peninsula, with the major nurseries located in the western, southwestern, and southeastern counties.

Oklahoma

Since the late 1950s a substantial nursery production area has developed in northeastern Oklahoma in the vicinity of Tahlequah. One large nursery specializes in container production of plants, whereas the others produce by field culture.

Southern States

The nursery industry of the southern states has expanded rapidly since 1969, growing from $75 million wholesale sales value to a value estimated at $148 million in 1974. Broadleaved evergreens accounted for 40% of the total production of ornamentals in the southern nurseries, deciduous shrubs 34%, narrowleaved evergreens 18%, and ornamental trees 8%. Mobile, Alabama, is a major production area for azaleas.

SUMMARY

The nursery industry of the United States is a very dynamic, rapidly growing, changing industry. It is made up of nurseries that are very diversified in function and species produced. In the early development of the industry, most production centered about bare-root fruit trees, whereas currently the emphasis is on ornamental plants that are produced by various methods, including both field- and container-production. Many are sold as large B&B specimen plants, which are used to produce immediate effects in the landscape. Centers of production moved with the development of the nation. At first the major nursery centers were located in the East (New York, New Jersey, Pennsylvania), with a gradual shift to the Midwest (Ohio, Illinois, and Iowa), and finally to the West, with the major center located in southern California. The past 30 years have seen many production changes, which will be discussed in subsequent chapters.

REFERENCES

BOYER, C. A. 1952. Nurseries big business in Michigan. Am. Nurseryman 96 (2):9.

CHADWICK, L. C. 1960. Nursery industry thrives in Ohio. Am. Nurseryman 92 (1):19.

DAVIDSON, H., C. E. LEWIS, and R. A. MECKLENBURG. 1966. The Michigan nursery industry project 80. Mich. Coop. Ext. Serv. Rep. 43.

GARTNER, J., J. E. BREWER, and H. F. FLINT. 1959. The Rhode Island nursery industry. R.I. Agric. Exp. Sta. Misc. Publ. 50 rev.

GORTZIG, C. F. 1969. State of the trade in the empire state. Am. Nurseryman 130(2):18.

HUDSON, A. C., and H. B. SORENSON. 1957. The Texas nursery industry. Tex. Agric. Exp. Sta. MP222.

JARVESOO, E. 1964. Nursery trade flourishes in Bay State. Am. Nurseryman 120(2):12.

LYLE, E. W. 1963. Roses, glamour crop of the Texas trade. Am. Nurseryman 118(2):9.

MEAHL, R. P. 1961. The Pennsylvania nursery industry. Agric. Ind. Adjustment Conf. Rep. Pa. State Univ.

PAULS, D. E., and A. H. HARRINGTON. 1960. The nursery industry of Washington. Wash. Agric. Exp. Sta. Circ. 372.

POTTER, F. 1953. Nurseries play a major role in agriculture of New York state. Am. Nurseryman 98(2):9.

RESEARCH SUMMARY. 1977. Scope III of the nursery industry. American Association of Nurserymen, 230 Southern Building, Washington, D.C. 20005.

SMITH, C. N. 1969. A fact book on the Florida wholesale woody ornamental nursery industry. Dept. Agric. Econ. Univ. Fla. Mimeo Rep. EC69–11.

SORENSON, H. B. 1963. The nursery industry of Texas. Am. Nurseryman 118(2):8.

TECH. COMMITTEE SM–33. 1969. Marketing woody ornamentals. South. Coop. Serv. Bull. 143.

SUGGESTED READING

WHITE, R. P. 1975. A century of service. American Association of Nurserymen, 230 Southern Building, Washington, D.C. 20005.

Chapter 3

Management Applied to Nurseries

There are many definitions of management, but the one that states it best is: *Management* is the bringing together of **men, money**, and **materials,** in a framework of time, for an economic or sociologic purpose. Simply stated, management brings together the three primary factors of production that managers use, places them together in a framework of time, and gives them a reason or purpose for being.

How do managers manage? What are their primary responsibilities? Naturally, a manager is a person and as such is subject to all the past, present, and future forces that have molded, are molding, and will mold the person into the individual that he or she is now and will be in the future. As a result, no two managers are exactly alike, and no two managers can be expected to manage exactly alike. Each will be different as a result of his or her individual personality and past experiences. But each manager by definition will have a purpose, the factors of production, and time. How a manager uses the factors of production and time determines how successful he or she will be in accomplishing his or her purpose.

A manager's primary responsibilities are basically six in number. He or she must:

1. Determine goals
2. Plan
3. Organize and staff
4. Direct, control, and coordinate
5. Motivate
6. Evaluate and reward

These six responsibilities apply to all levels of management, from foreman to president. How they are applied depends upon the purpose or objective of the organization and the level of management. They are fully applicable in the management of nurseries.

DETERMINING GOALS

The purpose or goal is known by various names within a nursery. In the production department it is the production goal; in marketing it is the sales objective; in propagation it is the percent rooting or "take" in grafting; and to the average laborer it is the job. But to the owner or the stockholder, it is profit. In each situation, the purpose should be clearly understood. We will look at individual objectives in some detail under organization and staffing, but the overall objective of the nursery business should be clearly established and stated in such a manner that it gives direction to all units of the organization.

To arrive at the overall objective, management must give consideration to four integral questions: (1) what products or services are needed, (2) by whom, (3) at what price and quantity, and (4) does the organization have the interest and the ability to provide the products or services? For example, assume that a person or firm is thinking of producing shade trees. They may have heard that there is a shortage of shade trees, and they have some idle land from which they would like to derive an income. Assume that the land will produce the trees and that water is available. Now a series of questions must be asked to define the objective. What is the nature of the target market? Is it homeowners in a local area, garden centers in a limited geographic area, landscape contractors in a limited area or large geographic area, or other nurseries in a local or national market area? Or is the target market some combination of these?

If the market comprises homeowners or garden centers, the demand may be for small trees that can be transported in the family car. If it is landscape contractors, the demand will be primarily for large trees processed with a ball of earth. If it is other nurseries or a combination of markets, the demand may be for a combination of sizes. What species and cultivars does the market demand, and what price will the market support? Consideration must also be given to similar products and services currently available or to be available in the market area.

Following the market study, it is necessary to formulate and state the company objective in such a manner that it will give direction to the production and marketing effort needed to accomplish the objective. For example: objective A: to produce $1\frac{1}{2}$- to 2-in.-caliper shade trees hardy in climatic zones 4 and 5 for the garden center market (Fig. 6–5). This objective limits size, geographic area, and type of market. It does not limit cultivar selection; objective B: to produce large ($3\frac{1}{2}$- to 4-in. DBH) specimen trees for landscape projects. This objective sets the course for a long-time investment in trees of large diameter requiring powerful equipment for handling. It limits customers primarily to landscape contractors.

Either objective sets the direction for the production and marketing effort. In objective A, the production effort will be toward producing small shade trees as quickly and economically as possible. This will result in rotations of relatively short duration, relatively close spacing of trees in the nursery blocks, and a need to use practices and equipment that will meet the objective. The intended market is identified, and the merchandising program can be directed to reach the garden center market. The cash turnover is rapid, owing to the short rotations, which is an advantage when interest rates are high. In objective B, the production effort will be directed to producing large specimen trees which will require wide spacing and long rotations, and the need to develop techniques that will effectively produce high-quality trees for immediate effect in the landscape. It will require powerful equipment to move the large, heavy material. The marketing effort will be concentrated on contacting sources that have a need for large, well-developed trees, primarily landscape contractors, city park departments, golf courses, and so on. However, the cash turnover is delayed by a number of years, which is a disadvantage when interest rates are high.

Provision must also be made for modifying long-range objectives.

Management must constantly evaluate the market and be responsive to trends. But all actions taken should be in keeping with the primary goal and the professional image of the nursery.

PLANNING

Planning is for the future, but it is based on past history. It is done to accomplish an objective, with the best expenditure of resources (personnel, money, materials), in the time period specified or implied. It should be a logical process of selecting the best course of action from a number of alternatives. Unfortunately, this is easier said than done. In some organizations decisions are made by default or without sound background information. When this happens too often, objectives are seldom attained and the organization fails.

When planning, a good manager consults with advisers. He or she will try to clearly define the problem to be solved or state the objective to be attained. The manager then encourages input from the staff. Depending upon the situation, it may require the gathering and evaluating of information by staff members, followed by the development of several possible courses of action. Upon an analysis of the situation and with the best possible information available, the manager must make a decision; this is one of management's responsibilities. The manager should not avoid it by trying to get a subordinate to make it; if the manager does this, especially if it is done too often, he or she will soon become ineffective. The decision should be clear and understood by the units involved in implementing the decision.

ORGANIZATION

The organization of a nursery business needs to be considered under three categories: (1) organization of the physical facilities, (2) the functional organization, and (3) the legal organization.

Organization of the physical facilities has to do with the physical relationship of production and administrative units one to the other and to the layout of propagation units and production fields for maximum efficiency. This information is discussed in Chapter 5.

Organization for function relates to developing the organization to maximize efficient use of people and their support systems: machines, facilities, supplies, and so on, to accomplish the various functions. It is the staffing and delegation of authority to accomplish an objective. In a group of workers, it is common that one will be more assertive than the others, and he or she becomes the leader. At that point the leader-follower organization is formed.

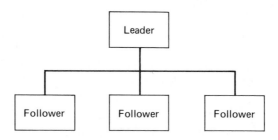

The leader-foreman is generally the most skilled in the particular physical skill that is being performed. He or she is expected to lead (manage) the others, and if a good working relationship exists with the followers, the job will get done. If not, there are problems and the leader will probably be replaced. This form of organization is limited by the span of control of the leader. Can he or she effectively control 3, 10, or 100 people?

The Bible (*Exodus,* 18:17-22) tells of Jethro's advice to Moses in 1450 B.C. when he was trying singlehandedly to lead the Israelites out of Egypt.

> What you are doing is not good. You and the people will wear yourselves out, you are not able to perform it alone. Listen to my counsel: You shall represent the people before God, and bring their cases to God; and you shall teach them the statutes and the decisions. . . . Choose able men from all the people, such as fear God, men who are trustworthy and who hate a bribe; and place such men over the people as rulers of thousands, of hundreds, of fifties and of tens. And let them judge the people at all times; every great matter they shall bring to you, but any small matter they shall decide themselves; so it will be easier for you, and they will bear the burden with you.

This passage from the Bible is the earliest known record of the principles of management and organization. By accepting the advice of his father-in-law, Moses created a simple, workable, line organization that accomplished the mission.

The *line organization* has been used for centuries in the functional development of organizations. It is the most common structural form found in most small- to medium-sized nurseries. When tailored to fit the needs of the nursery manager, it can be quite

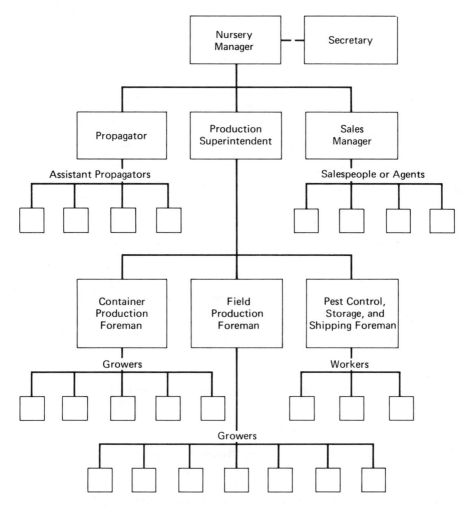

Figure 3-1 Example of line organization for a medium-sized nursery.

functional. The structure of an average, medium-sized production nursery can be represented as in Fig. 3-1. This structure illustrates the chain of responsibility for three basic functional areas: propagation, production, and sales.

Since propagation is a specialized area, it is headed by a skilled propagator who has the responsibility (goal, mission) of propagating the materials needed for field production and the implied responsi-

Figure 3-2 Example of line and staff organization for a large-sized nursery.

bility of keeping posted on new methods of propagation related to the type of plants being produced by the nursery.

The nursery superintendent has the largest division and is charged with the responsibility of meeting the production goals. This division is organized into three subsections and staffed accordingly. The sales division is responsible for marketing of the products produced.

As an organization grows in size, its functional units increase. But the ultimate size of each unit is determined by the span of control of the individual leader (foreman or superintendent) in charge. At some point the business may become too large for the manager to control effectively without assistance; he or she then gradually obtains a staff, and the business is reorganized.

The *line and staff organization* (Fig. 3-2) is designed to accomplish this objective. The various staff people aid the manager in developing plans and coordinating the activities of the various functional units. In some situations it is desirable to add various service units that provide a service function (e.g., mechanical maintenance) to the overall organization.

The two most common staff positions are the comptroller, in charge of financial matters, and the personnel manager, in charge of labor relations. These two staff assistants aid the manager in the area of money and interior personnel management. If a customer relations director is added, his or her responsibilities should relate to exterior people relationships as opposed to interior. The position would have to do with public and government relations.

The research and development director is responsible for developing new products that the nursery might produce; testing new products that the firm might use; and developing, in cooperation with one or more of the functional units, new methods of operation. The mechanic heads the service unit and is responsible for keeping all mechanical equipment operational. It is important that the chain of command be clearly established in a line and staff organization. Basically, staff members have no command control over the functional units. They are advisory to the manager, who alone directs and controls the functional units.

Sometimes the organization becomes too large for one person to maintain effective control over the functional units, at which time the manager delegates to the staff certain specific aspects of overall authority. When this is done, the business becomes an *executive organization* in which the manager is known as president and is assisted by a group of executive vice-presidents who have authority over functional units in their specific areas of responsibility.

In organizing and staffing a nursery, it is important to keep in mind the overall goal of the organization and the span of control of individual department heads, and to develop logical groupings of functional and staff units. Also, a nursery organization must be flexible and capable of meeting the constantly changing demands for labor as influenced by season, weather conditions, and the changing demands of the marketplace.

The organizing and staffing of a large production nursery is a challenging task. The demand for labor fluctuates with the season of the year and by operations within and between divisions. For many field production nurseries, there is a maximum need for labor in the spring and fall, with a minimum need in the winter months. In early spring the demand is greatest in the areas of digging and shipping, followed in midspring by planting (Fig. 3-3) and June budding. Then during the summer the primary need is for cultivation and pest control, in August for fall budding operations, followed in the fall months by digging and storage operations.

Figure 3-3 Planting small flowering trees with the aid of a planting machine. (Courtesy Mechanical Transplanter Co.)

Nursery managers need to develop good labor management techniques, since labor often accounts for 50% or more of the cost of production. Also, federal, state, and union regulations place specific restraints upon employers relative to conditions of employment and pay schedules.

The *legal form of organization* is another consideration in organizing the nursery business. The three commonly used legal forms of organization are the proprietorship, the partnership, and the corporation. Each form has advantages and disadvantages which should be evaluated prior to legally constituting the business, and periodically during the life of the organization.

The *proprietorship* is the easiest to form. Anyone who can acquire the land and wants to start a nursery can do so, as long as he or she complies with state and local laws related to zoning and taxation. In the proprietorship, responsibility is centered in one individual; there is no sharing of the profits. But the business is limited by the capabilities and limitations of the owner, and the business usually terminates upon the owner's death. This is a serious weakness of the proprietorship form of business. Many excellent small nurseries have failed to continue following the death of the owner, because no provision was made for continuation of the business.

The *partnership* is an agreement between two or more parties. It is easy to form, but at times it may be difficult to divest an undesirable partner or to market a share of a partnership. Partnerships in which the abilities of each partner complement one another are generally more successful than those in which they duplicate each other. In the nursery industry one partner may be an excellent production worker and the other a salesperson. Or one partner may be excellent in landscape design and construction, whereas the other is an excellent garden center manager. Problems sometimes develop when both partners are both growers and neither is good at administration or sales.

The major weakness in the partnership form of business relates to resolving problems that arise between partners or between the spouses of partners. It can be a very precarious legal form of business and should be constituted with considerable forethought. It is well to have the articles of agreement developed by a lawyer, following careful consideration by all parties. It is possible to develop limited partnerships and open-end-agreement contracts. The limited partnership allows some partners to limit their liability while at least one partner remains fully liable for the debts of the business. Open-end partnership agreements allow for taking in new partners and for the death, retirement, or resignation of partners.

The *corporation* is another legal form of business, designed to provide for the continuity of a business and to limit the liability of a stockholder. Many nurseries that start as proprietorships convert to a corporate form as they grow and develop in size. The corporation is limited by a charter that must be obtained from the state in which the business is incorporated. Also, the business must be managed by a board of directors, hold an annual meeting of stockholders, and file an annual report, generally with the secretary of state in the state of incorporation.

There are many ways that the corporation can be constituted, including public and private. In the public corporation, the stock is for sale to the general public, whereas in the private corporation (commonly referred to as subchapter S) the stock is kept within a closed, private group (commonly within a family). Many commercial nurseries are private (subchapter S) corporations. In general, the private form of corporation meets the needs of most nursery businesses. But when there is serious disagreement within the group and a stockholder wishes to divest himself or herself of one portion of the business, it may be difficult to obtain fair market value for the stock, since there may be a charter limitation on whom it can be sold to.

In organizing a nursery business, it may be desirable to have multiple forms of legal structure to gain the advantages of each. For example, it may be more desirable for a proprietor to own the land and structures, and lease these to the nursery. The production nursery may be a private corporation engaged in agricultural production, which in turn sells its product to another corporation, a sales-oriented organization, which markets it in interstate commerce. The two corporations remain smaller than one large corporation that owns all land and capital assets; this may provide a tax advantage. It limits restrictions placed upon businesses that engage in interstate commerce to only that corporation that is so engaged. It also reduces the size of capitalization, which may permit young people to buy into the nursery at considerably less equity than if the nursery owned all the land and capital assets. It also permits the landowner to sell or will his or her lands without consent of the corporation. This may present a problem to the production nurseries renting land, but by long-term lease arrangements it can generally be managed in an equitable manner. In any case, when developing a corporation or a combination of business forms, it is advisable to obtain the services of a lawyer who is familiar with the various legal and financial requirements, advantages, and limitations.

CONTROL AND COORDINATION

Control and coordination involves those activities that are needed to keep an organization headed on the course that it was assigned or that it chose to follow. Control relates to activities within a unit, whereas coordination relates to activities between units. In a small operational unit, control is direct and is accomplished primarily by voice; there is little need for written directives or written communication, but as an organization grows and the levels or echelons of management increase and the functional units are spread over a greater geographic area, control becomes indirect and must be accomplished by written directives or written communications, and direct control becomes minimal. One effective indirect means of obtaining control is to develop and publish a policy manual for standard procedures and policies. It is best developed in cooperation with key employees and staff advisers. Some items that might be covered in the manual are tabulated in Table 3-1.

Another control mechanism is to set attainable goals for each

Table 3-1   Suggested topics to be covered in policy manual for a
nursery

Administrative	*Personnel*
Mail handling	Affirmative action policy
Private use of facilities	Clothing and dress
Workers in administration area	Grievances
Equipment	Hours of work
Borrowing	Lost and found
Use	Lunchroom
Care and servicing	Parking
Purchasing	Promotion
Returning to storage	Safety
Finance	Sick leave
Insurance	Tardiness and absenteeism
Loans to employees	Termination
Medical benefits	Vacations
Overtime pay	Work rules
Pay periods and paydays	*Plants*
Paid holidays	Handling and care
Retirement programs	Sale to employees
Wage review	*Supplies*
	Obtaining within the nursery
	Purchases for the nursery
	Returning to storage

functional unit. Depending upon the type of unit, the goals may be
daily, weekly, monthly, seasonal, or yearly. For a digging crew, daily
goals are in order, whereas for a propagator it may be x thousands of
cuttings per month, season, or year; for the production and sales
managers, the goal may be x number of plants/species/season; and
for the general manager, the goal is dollars of profit.

Since there are objectives to be obtained, there must be some
form of reporting. Records and reports are another means that managers use to gain control over their operational units. Records and
reports should contain accurate, up-to-date information if they are
to be valuable to the manager. Collecting and processing data that are
not going to be used in making management decisions is a worthless
practice that should be discouraged. But collecting data that, when
processed, will be used for evaluation purposes and as a basis for
future planning and management decisions is an implied responsibility of all levels of management.

Two excellent tools that can be used by management as a guide
to labor productivity are, the reasonable-expectancy table (Tables

3-2a and 3-2b) for individual performance and the staffing table (Table 3-3) for crew performance. Both are developed from labor productivity records maintained by the production foremen. The data, from records kept on the various functions performed within the nursery, can be processed into meaningful information that can be used in planning labor needs, estimating future cost of production and cash flow requirements for the business, and evaluating production. Table 3-3 is an example of how raw data can be converted into a more meaningful unit: average labor-hours per 1000 trees.

Digging and planting of large trees vary considerably by the size of the ball and with the type of equipment used. Therefore, average

Table 3-2a Reasonable-expectancy tables: Digging evergreens

		Plants per labor-hour[a]		
Plant size		Spreading (e.g., yews, mugho pine)	Compact upright (e.g., yews)	Large type (e.g., spruce, pine)
12–15 in.	FP[b]	12.0		
12–15 in.	B&B	8.5		
15–18 in.	B&B	7.5	8.5	
18–24 in.	B&B	6.0	7.8	6.9
2–2½ ft	B&B		6.9	4.5
2½–3 ft	B&B		6.0	
3–4 ft	B&B			3.0
4–5 ft	B&B			2.0

[a]Based on data from 6- to 10-worker digging crews. Includes carrying out and loading on pallets.
[b]Fiber pot.

Table 3-2b Reasonable-expectancy table: Digging B&B trees by hand

Caliper	Trees per labor-hour[a]
1–1¼ in.	24
1½–2 in.	14
2½–3½ in.	9
4 in.	3.5

[a]Based on data from 8-worker crew. Includes burlapping, topping, and tying tops.

labor-hours to dig and plant shade trees have been converted to graphs (Figs. 3-4 and 3-5) which can be used to estimate labor-hour requirements when digging and planting large trees.

Record taking and reporting must be made as simple as possible. Various types of forms are available or can be designed to obtain data on individual work performance, use of equipment and supplies,

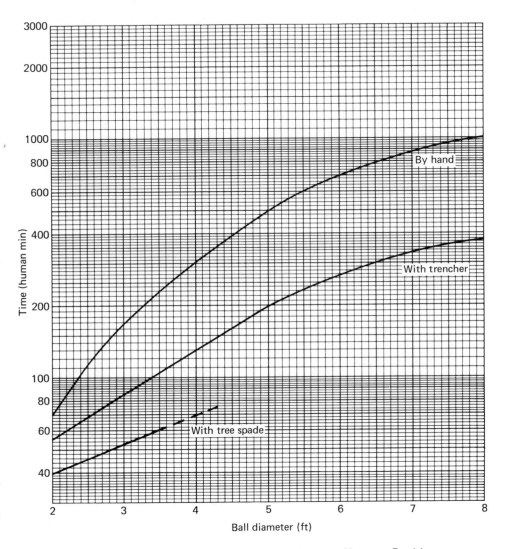

Figure 3-4 Average time for digging B&B trees. (Source: Davidson and Speakman, 1969.)

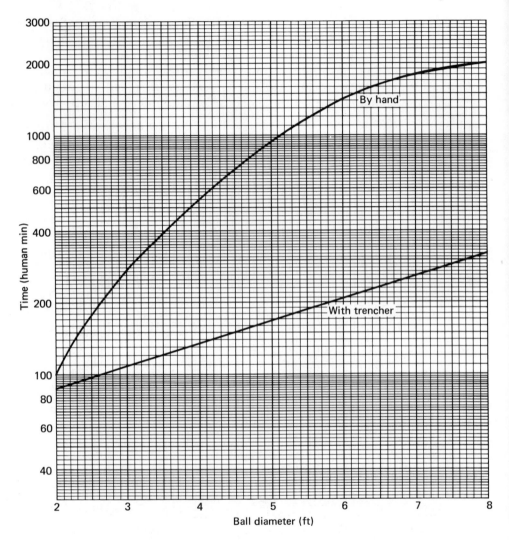

Figure 3-5 Average time for planting B&B trees. (Source: Davidson and Speakman, 1969.)

expenditure of funds, and so on. The uniform chart of accounts for use in financial management developed by the Horticultural Research Institute can be a useful management tool in this area. There are charts for nursery production, landscape, and retail operations.

Each operational unit manager should establish contact with other operational units to coordinate activities, especially when the

Table 3-3 Nursery staffing tables[a]

Planting in the nursery	Average labor-hours/1000
Shade tree whips, 1½-in. caliper	
With tractor-drawn planting machine (V-shaped plow to open trench, plus closing disks and packing wheels), 8-worker crew	
Planted on 8-ft centers in rows $\bar{x} = 4000/10$-hr day	20.0
Shade tree whips, 1–1¼-in. caliper	
Hole marking and digging 10×10 ft (cleared land, experienced crew, good weather)	64.0
$\bar{x} = 2100$ holes/134 labor-hours	
Preplant pruning (remove from storage rack, prune roots and top, return to rack)	62.5
$\bar{x} = 16$ trees/labor-hour	
Planting by hand into predug holes; fill and water	185.2
$\bar{x} = 5.4$ trees/labor-hour	
Evergreen transplants	
With tractor-drawn mechanical transplanter, Model 2000, two-row, 10-worker crew,	
9–10-in., spreading, BR	
Long rows $\bar{x} = 10,000/10$-hr day	10.0
Short rows (<1000 ft) $\bar{x} = 8000/10$-hr day	12.5

(continued)

Table 3-3 continued

Pruning or trimming		Average labor-hours/1000
Shade trees		
From the ground		
1–1¼-in.	$\bar{x}$ = 5850 trees/148 labor-hours	25.3
¾–1½-in.	$\bar{x}$ = 300/10-hr day	34.0
With pole trimmers		
1½–2½-in.	$\bar{x}$ = 300/10-hr day	34.0
With step ladders		
1½–2½-in.	$\bar{x}$ = 200/10-hr day	50.0
Evergreens cone-shaped 2–4-ft (i.e., Capitata Yews)		
With long-bladed knife	$\bar{x}$ = 10,000/10-hr day	1.0
With power-pack hedge shears	$\bar{x}$ = 4500/10-hr day	2.2
With long-bladed hedge shears	$\bar{x}$ = 2000/10-hr day	5.0
Evergreens spreading 18–24-in. (i.e., Pfitzer juniper)		
With power-pack hedge shears (winter only for junipers)	$\bar{x}$ = 7000/10-hr day	1.5
With long-bladed hedge shears	$\bar{x}$ = 4000/10-hr day	2.5

Digging		Average labor-hours/1000
Evergreens		
By hand B&B		
15- or 18-in. spreading, 10-in. ball	$\bar{x}$ = 10 workers: 450/10-hr day	220
4-ft upright 12–14-in. ball	$\bar{x}$ = 10 workers: 200/10-hr day	500
5–6-ft upright, 18-in. ball	$\bar{x}$ = 8 workers: 130/10-hr day	615
With Jiffy balling machine		
15–18-in. plants, digging and potting	$\bar{x}$ = 8 workers: 900/10-hr day	88.8
15–18-in. plants, digging and B&B	$\bar{x}$ = 12 workers: 800/10-hr day	100
Shade trees		
By hand (varies with size of ball, see Figs. 3–4 and 3–5)		
With tree-spade digging machine (includes tying branches, digging, packaging into burlapped wire baskets, secured, trunks wrapped) 10-hr day, from barn to digging area, minimum moving from field to field and back to barn at end of day		
66-in. Vermeer, truck-mounted	$\bar{x}$ = 10-worker crew: 25/10-hr day (2.8 labor-hr/tree)	2800
44-in. Vermeer, on tractor	$\bar{x}$ = 7-worker crew: 80/10-hr day (53 min/tree)	875
30-in. Vermeer, on tractor	$\bar{x}$ = 7-worker crew: 150/10-hr day (28 min/tree)	467
28-in. Caretree, on Bob Cat (skid tractor)	$\bar{x}$ = 10-worker crew: 230/10-hr day (26 min/tree)	435

[a] Average labor productivity for selected nursery operations. Data obtained from a number of nurseries. Each nursery manager should develop manning tables for the particular set of conditions, methods of operation, machines, and work force.

59

manager is highly dependent upon coordinated or sequential activities.

EMPLOYEE MOTIVATION, EVALUATION, AND REWARDS

Motivating, evaluating, and rewarding employees are important management functions. They sometimes do not receive the attention from nursery managers that they deserve. The three functions are closely interrelated. For example, a spontaneous statement such as "Well done," "A good job," or "Excellent" made by a manager as an evaluation of employee performance is one of the most appreciated rewards and one of the best positive motivators that is available to management. But all too often, its impact and value are overlooked. The proper and timely granting of employee rewards can have a major impact upon the success or failure of the business. Every employee is entitled to have his or her performance evaluated: to receive praise and advancement for work well done, rebuke for failure, and punishment for unacceptable behavior or performance.

A good nursery manager is cognizant of the fact that the most important factor of production relates to the employees. The manager must never forget that employees are people, and that they have needs and aspirations, skills, and ideas. It is how the manager perceives employees and satisfies these needs and skills that determines to a large degree the productivity of the employees and, ultimately, the success of the business.

Each person has a basic need for food, clothing, and shelter. And most people have a need to be with others. Human beings are social; they like to be with others of their own kind and enjoy the company of members of the opposite sex. People work to satisfy these physiological and sociological needs. However, people also have dreams and aspirations that go beyond these basic needs. They are called the ego or psychological needs: the need to be recognized as an individual and not just a statistic, the need to express and carry out ideas, and the need for praise and recognition.

When an employee is hired, he or she should be informed what is expected—duties and responsibilities. The person should also be told the procedure for evaluation and reward. Communicating the job responsibilities varies with the position. For temporary, seasonal employees the communication may be verbal and rather specific. For top management the communication may be in writing, but general in nature. However, for middle management a detailed job description, in writing, may be in order, because it is necessary to clearly define the scope of the position and the limits of responsibility.

An application form should be used for most positions. The form serves a number of functions: to obtain (1) personal data on the applicant (name, address, date of birth, medical history, etc.), (2) pertinent information on the applicant relative to the position; (3) a history of previous employment, and (4) if applicable, a statement of the applicant's expectations. The form thus serves as the first step in the evaluation process. The form also screens out those applicants who do not wish to complete formal, written documents for one reason or another. A follow-up interview provides the nursery manager with a second opportunity to evaluate the potential employee. At this time the manager should also explain the unique characteristics and philosophy of the nursery and try to determine if the applicant has the desired qualifications for the position.

Once an employee has been hired, he or she should undergo training appropriate to the position and his or her skills and background. All too often managers fail to train new employees properly. The initial period, after a person joins a nursery, is extremely important both to the person and to the nursery. New employees must learn what is expected of them and how far they can proceed on their own. Also, the employer must learn how to best motivate the new employee and how much responsibility can be delegated to the employee as he or she matures and develops as a productive part of the labor–management team.

Young people, especially those who have made a substantial investment in their education, by devoting two or more years of their lives to obtaining a college education, will need to obtain training in the work ethic. Unfortunately, people from urban areas have little opportunity to learn and practice the physical skills associated with the nursery industry. Academic institutions are not equipped to provide these, which are best learned on the job. They will need to serve a period of apprenticeship, learning the art and skills associated with the nursery industry. However, nursery managers have an obligation to these young employees, to the nursery industry, and to themselves to provide this period of internship. By doing so, they will be making an investment in a human resource that will pay substantial dividends in the future.

It has been said that a good supervisor is someone who can get people to do what he or she wants done, the way he or she wants it done, when he or she wants it done by people who want to do it. How is this accomplished? By incentives. Incentives will vary with individuals, groups, and situations. Some of the most common in-centives are commendation, pay, time off, titles, and various fringe benefits. But one of the best incentives is participation. When people are asked for their advice relative to achieving an objective, they feel a part of the organization. They feel personally involved and have a sense of importance. Employees, especially in middle-management positions, must feel that they are essential to the organization meeting its objective. A manager who solicits advice must be pre-pared to utilize that advice and provide appropriate recognition (reward) when it is deserved.

For the applicant the evaluation process commences at first contact with the employer. The applicant should be sure the contact is appropriate for the position. A letter should be neatly typed and supported by a vita sheet or completed application form. At the interview the applicant should be clean and dressed appropriately for the position. The applicant should remember that he or she is apply-ing for a position and should represent himself or herself as well as possible.

At an appropriate time each person and each unit of the nursery should be evaluated and rewarded. Each manager must arrive at his or her own method or methods that will contribute to the overall success of the nursery operation.

After working for some predetermined time period, the new employee should be made aware of his or her standing. The evalua-tion should not be made too quickly on insufficient evidence, but slowly and deliberately. The employee should be commended for his or her accomplishments and counseled in areas that could be improved upon. Also, when appropriate, an increase in salary should be given, since incentive pay is an important means of rewarding good performance.

Most new employees begin as *hourly workers* whose primary function is the performance of physical skills. Although they work with materials, the skills employed require little technical knowledge. They may include such jobs as digging holes to plant trees, digging and lifting plants, packing, or making cuttings. Hourly workers can be evaluated on the basis of quantity and to some degree the quality of production. In most nurseries, standards of quality are set by management. In some establishments the quality standards are high and must not be sacrificed for quantity, whereas in other establish-ments, by design, the standards of quality are somewhat lower, in the interest of obtaining quantity of production. Nevertheless, the objec-tive set for the worker is generally some type of daily goal, and the compensation is wages paid at an hourly rate. In establishments where quality of performance is appreciated, superior performance should be provided with additional rewards, such as a rate of pay greater than the average or a bonus paid at the end of a season or at some other predetermined time period. However, in addition to these standard methods of earned or contractual rewards for labor, management should also be cognizant of other methods of reward appropriate to the age level, social background, and the desires and expectations of the workers. Young people hoeing weeds in the nursery will often work better and faster if they know they will be rewarded with time off with pay. Most people will do a better job if they know that their work is appreciated and will be rewarded accordingly. An hourly worker usually moves up to "skilled worker" when he or she has acquired a degree of technical knowledge and skill.

Skilled workers also work with materials, but the jobs are more demanding of technical knowledge and ability. Examples are budding and grafting; application of fertilizers and pesticides; and operating equipment, such as tree diggers. Skilled workers are evaluated both on the quantity and quality of their performance. Their earned rewards may include in addition to a higher wage rate such fringe benefits as days off with pay, paid vacation, and health insurance. Various supplementary rewards may be expense-paid trips to professional meetings or an opportunity to obtain additional training at company expense.

Foremen are the first level of management. They are charged with the responsibility of getting a job done; this is most commonly accomplished by managing people and materials. Therefore, one of the foreman's responsibilities is to motivate, evaluate, and reward the workers. However, foremen are evaluated by their superiors on how well they get the job done. Since the foreman's job is a management position, he or she should also be charged with the responsibility of maintaining records on the use of the resources (workers and materials) over which he or she has responsibility. A simple but meaningful system is one that accounts for both the workers and machine-hours that go into each job, plus a record of the materials that were expended. In a nursery the job may either be plant-production-oriented or it may be nonproductive, such as maintenance of roads, digging a pond, and so on. Nevertheless, it is important to management to obtain data on productivity to evaluate the crews' performances. The data can also be used to develop staffing tables (Tables 3-2a and 3-2b) for use in estimating cost of production and cash-flow analysis.

The foreman's earned rewards are similar to those of the skilled laborer: higher salary, various fringe benefits, and so on. In addition, there should be certain supplementary rewards for jobs that are well done, particularly under adverse situations: weather, time, shortage of personnel. These supplementary rewards might be a cash bonus or a gift appropriate to the person and the situation. Care must be exercised in giving a bonus on a regular basis; it can easily become an expected, earned reward. Foremen should seldom, if ever, be evaluated on a monetary productivity basis, although this is done in some nurseries or landscape construction firms. A couple of examples will illustrate the point.

In a landscape construction firm, a job is bid at a monetary value, and the foreman who is assigned to the job is sometimes evaluated on how much money was made on the job. If the job is profitable, he or she may share in a bonus, whereas if the job lost money, he or she may be reprimanded or even be discharged. But foremen in most firms, either landscape or nursery, have control over only two factors of production, workers and materials; they should be evaluated only on their ability to use these two factors effectively. If they bid the job or have a degree of financial control, it is reasonable to evaluate them on profitability of the job.

A foreman in charge of a digging crew in a nursery is provided with a mechanical tree digger, a crew of workers, and the needed materials, such as burlap, wire baskets, pinning nails, twine, and so on. His or her job is to harvest a certain number of trees per day (week or season). Implied within the objective is that the trees be firmly balled and that no damage be done to the trees being dug or to the trees that remain in the block to grow on to larger sizes. If this objective is attained (assuming it was attainable), he or she is rewarded with a good monthly salary. However, if his or her unit performs better than average, the trees are well balled, there is no damage to any of the trees, and the customers of the nursery are pleased with the quality of the product, the foreman should be given an appropriate supplementary reward, generally a bonus. He or she should be praised and thanked for doing a superior job. The foreman, in turn, should praise the workers and share a portion of the bonus with them.

In making the evaluation of the crews' performances, various means are utilized. visual observation of the crews on the job, comments from customers on the quality of the product, and digging records of the number of trees dug and the labor-hours utilized to accomplish the job. From the digging records, the nursery superintendent or the nursery manager will obtain the data needed to arrive at average times to dig and process trees of various size classes and to estimate costs to harvest plants of various sizes. Since management has the data on wage rates and costs of supplies, equipment, and so on, they are in a position to make the necessary calculations to evaluate the economic productivity of the system and to make the appropriate rewards or effect changes in the system.

Similar types of evaluations can be made for all the divisions of the nursery if the goals or objectives are clearly defined. In propagation the goal is output of young plants, seedlings, cuttings, grafts, and so on. In the nursery it is the production of saleable plants to meet a market objective. In each case the foreman and his or her unit are evaluated and rewarded on the basis of productivity and quality.

The goal of top management is to produce a profit for the organization. Therefore, management is evaluated on the basis of profitability and is rewarded accordingly. This topic is discussed in Chapter 7.

SUMMARY

Although the management process can be divided into and discussed as six component parts—(1) setting goals, (2) planning, (3) organizing and staffing, (4) directing and controlling, (5) motivating, and (6) evaluating and rewarding—it is a unified process with each part dependent upon all others. Successful managers constantly evaluate and seek ways to improve the use of their resources. Managers must keep abreast of changing demands in the marketplace and changing methods of production in order to make sound management decisions relative to the long-range goals of the organization. Changes in goals or in methods of production will of necessity affect the organizational structure, which in turn will modify methods of control, coordination, motivation, and so on. And once the new structure is developed to meet the newly developed objectives, the process starts over again. Management is a never-ending process. It is a logical process that good managers understand and practice in a successful manner. Poor managers either fail to understand the process or fail to practice one or more of the parts that make up good management.

For additional information on management, the reader should consult one or more books on the topic; a few are listed as Suggested Reading. Another source of good management information is the Small Business Management Series, published by the Small Business Administration and sold by the Superintendent of Documents, Washington, D.C. 20402.

SUGGESTED READING

CARROLL, S. J., JR., and H. L. TOSI, JR. 1973. Management by objectives. Macmillan Publishing Co., Inc., New York.

DALE, E. 1973. Management: theory and practice. McGraw-Hill Book Company, New York.

DRUCKER, P. F. 1977. An introductory view of management. Harper's College Press, New York.

STRONG, E. P. 1965. The management of business. Harper & Row, Publishers, New York.

Chapter 4

Selection of
a Nursery Site

The selection of a site for a nursery should be done with considerable care and thought, since location will have a major effect on the overall success of the organization. Soil, water, and environment are factors of paramount importance in the selection of a site for a production nursery, whereas for a garden center the important considerations are population density, social customs, and traffic patterns. However, each factor should be considered and evaluated for the effect it will have on the overall success of the business. The factors are grouped into three convenient categories for discussion: ecological, economic, and sociological.

ECOLOGICAL FACTORS

Climate

For the production of nursery stock, either field-grown or container-grown, a mild climate with a long growing season and an even distribution of rainfall is most desirable. Areas with extremes in temperature, especially rapid fluctuating temperatures, or those that are subject to wind, hail, or ice storms should be avoided. Sites should be selected that afford protection from drying winds and alternate freezing and thawing. Within a large geographic area, there are sites to be found that have a favorable microclimate for the growth of plants. Sites close to a large body of water are often temperature-moderated by the lake effect up to 2 or more miles from the shore line.

Topography

The land for efficient operation should be relatively level; steep slopes should be avoided, but rolling land can be terraced. Sites that are subject to flooding or are known to be frost pockets should be avoided. Areas with large outcroppings of rock and large stones are less desirable as sites for a field production nursery than those that are free of such obstructions, which impede many operations associated with modern nursery practices.

Soil

The media for container-grown plants is generally artificially blended (Chapter 9). Therefore, the native soil is not an important site factor for a container production nursery. But it is an important consideration relative to drainage and trafficability. Container production nurseries need a dependable source of supply for sand, peat moss, water, fertilizer, containers, and so on, and these materials should be available at reasonable prices.

The selection of soil type for a field production nursery will vary with the type of nursery stock to be produced. Seedlings and bare-root plants can be produced best when grown on sandy or sandy loam soil because (1) it does not crust over following rains or irrigation, allowing better seedling emergence; (2) it exhibits less tendency to heave, minimizing injury due to lifting of the plants out of the ground when the ground thaws in the spring; (3) it can be worked earlier in the spring and sooner after rains; (4) it requires less power for cultural operations; and (5) plants can be removed from it with less damage to the roots. Plants that are marketed with a soil ball about their roots are best produced in either a silty loam or a clay loam soil.

Soils for the production of quality nursery stock must have good structure and porosity. These characteristics have a strong influence upon air–water relationships, nutrient availability, the activity of microorganisms, and ultimately upon plant growth and development. Soils with a granular or crumb structure make excellent soils for field production nurseries. These soils have good drainage characteristics while retaining adequate moisture for plant growth. They contain a balanced supply of clay minerals and soil colloids, which function as adsorption sites for plant nutrients. And they permit digging operations even in wet seasons.

The optimum soil reaction (pH) for the production of most woody plants is between 5.0 and 7.2. Therefore, it is desirable that the proposed nursery site have a pH within or close to this range. Soils with a pH greater than 7.2 should be avoided because it is difficult and costly to lower their pH. Acid soils can be corrected fairly easily with lime.

Although it is desirable that the soil have an optimum level of fertility, it is not an absolute requirement, since the intensity and balance of most elements can be modified fairly readily with commercial fertilizers. However, soils that test high in calcium and magnesium should be avoided as sites for the production of woody species, since high levels of these two bases will induce trace element deficiencies. Soils for field production nurseries should contain 2–5% organic matter and must be free of pests, including noxious weeds, nematodes, insects, disease organisms, and herbicide residue, which might restrict the growth or impair the quality of nursery crops.

A valuable guide in selecting a site for a field production nursery is the past agronomic history of the site. A soil that is currently producing or recently produced a productive agricultural crop is to be desired over one that has a past history of low productivity. In addition, the native vegetation of the area can be a clue to the productive potential of the site. Assistance in evaluating potential nursery sites may be obtained from the U.S. Soil Conservation Service, county agricultural agents, the state department of agriculture, and soil, insect, disease, and horticulture specialists located at the state university.

Water

An ideal nursery site, with respect to water, would be one where there is good rainfall distribution throughout the planting and growing season, with a minimum of rain (or snow) during the digging and shipping season. Since this is almost impossible to find, it is best to locate a site where there is access to a dependable supply of quality water. The delivery capability will vary from a few hundred gallons per minute to many thousands of gallons per minute, depending on the size and type of nursery to be established (see Chapter 10).

Water can be obtained either from a municipal water system or from streams, rivers, ponds, lakes, or wells. It should be free of alkalies, excessive salts, or industrial wastes that might be detrimental to plant growth. Irrigation water for use on seedlings and young transplants should have less than 200 parts per million (ppm) of dissolved solids. Whereas, the water used on larger field-grown or container-grown plants may have from two to three times this amount. A Solu-bridge can be used to estimate this value. A reading of 330 micromhos per centimeter at 25°C is equivalent to 200 ppm of dissolved solids. Irrigation water that contains calcium in excess of 500 ppm is likely to raise the pH of the soil, which in time could have an adverse effect upon the growth of the plants.

In some areas of the country, sodium and boron can cause problems in the propagation and production of young plants. The sodium absorption ratio of the irrigation water should be less than 10 and the boron content less than one-half part per million (ppm). In addition to a supply of water for the nursery stock, a source of safe drinking water must be available for employees. Prior to making the final selection of the site for a nursery, consult with the state geologist or with the state department of natural resources relative to state laws pertaining to water rights.

Air

Air pollution is a problem to be considered in selecting a site for a nursery. Air that is polluted with sulfur dioxide (SO_2), fluorides [e.g., hydrogen fluoride (HF)] photochemical smog, and ozone (O_3) should be avoided. These phototoxic pollutants are produced primarily by industry, motor transportation, and by the generation of electricity. Therefore, it is undesirable to locate either downwind from an industrial site that could be a potential source of pollution or in a confined geological area where photochemical smog concentrates due to poor air circulation.

ECONOMIC FACTORS

Cost of Land

The initial cost of the land will often determine if a nursery establishment can be started on a given site. Generally, it is thought that a production nursery engaged in extensive production cannot afford to produce plants on high-priced land. On the other hand, nurseries engaged in intensive production, landscape nurseries, or garden centers can afford higher-priced land provided that other factors do not limit productivity or sales. In addition to land costs, the annual taxes and property assessments will affect the net return on the investment and may in some cases preclude the operation of a nursery on the site. Many fine nurseries have or are closing out operations on certain sites as a result of increased taxes caused by higher land values, brought about by urbanization.

One solution to high land costs is for an individual to own the land and lease it to the nursery on a long-term lease. This allows an individual to capitalize on appreciation of land values but permits a nursery to program production. In some states tax advantages can be obtained if the land is committed by contract to long-term (at least 10 years) agriculture. Information on these contracts can be obtained from the Cooperative Extension Service in the various states or from real estate agents who specialize in farm properties.

Labor

Since nurseries rely on considerable hand labor to perform much of the work associated with production and landscape construction, a supply of manual labor must be available. Field production nurseries, because of the seasonal nature of their operations, experience periods of peak demand for labor followed by periods where there is little need for labor. This seasonal need for unskilled labor is met in part by the employment of migrant laborers. However, with the passage of labor laws, many nurseries are finding it difficult to obtain seasonal labor. Some have solved this problem by employing high school students, off-duty firemen, retirees, homemakers, and so on, on a part-time basis, whereas others are contracting for the employment of laborers from the various territories of the United States. Still other nurserymen are either contracting out some of the production operation (e.g., digging and packaging) or they are mechanizing many of the traditional hand operations associated with the nursery industry. In addition to manual laborers, nurseries also need individuals capable of performing various skilled operations (e.g., propagators, pesticide applicators) and others who have abilities as foremen or managers.

Facilities

Power is needed by most nurseries; some need only one form while others may require many forms. Electric power is needed for lighting and the operation of equipment, including irrigation pumps, refrigerators, potting machines, computers, typewriters, and so on. Three-phase electric power is desirable to operate certain types of machines (e.g., soil mixing, potting, packaging, and computers). If the three-phase lines are not close to the site, it can be costly to have the power brought to the site. This cost might be avoided by careful selection of the site or by using alternative sources of power, such as diesel-powered generators.

Oil, gas, or coal is necessary for the operation of the heating plant. Since the energy crisis of the mid-1970s, it is necessary to check on the availability of a dependable, noninterrupted supply of heating fuel at a cost that the business can afford. Gasoline is needed in large quantities to power trucks, tractors, cars, and other equipment used in the nursery. This should be contracted for delivery to the nursery so that the business can take advantage of bulk rates and submit the associated charges for a federal tax credit, which is permitted for off-the-road use.

Good transportation facilities are necessary for most nurseries. A high percentage of the nursery stock shipped in the United States is transported by motor truck. However, substantial amounts are also transported by railroad, particularly from the Northwest, and some is transported by airplane. Since motor freight is the primary means of transport, nurseries should locate so that trucks carrying heavy loads may have access without restriction. This is particularly important for nurseries located in the northern parts of the country, where weight limitations are often imposed on county roads during the spring-thaw period.

A garden center located on a road or highway that affords easy access is much more desirable than one located on a superhighway or on a second-class or unpaved road, where access is difficult. In some situations a site located on the right-hand side of the road for people going home from work in large urban areas may be more desirable than one located on the left side.

Competition

Competition should always be evaluated before starting a new business. This is particularly true when the establishment will serve a limited clientele or market in a limited geographic area. The number of similar establishments and the progressiveness of each should be carefully considered. An elementary question that should be answered prior to starting a new business is: "What can I produce (product or service) that is superior to my competition, is needed by others, and can be sold for a profit?" However, competition is not a problem in selecting a site for a production nursery that will have a large market area (e.g., many states or the nation). In fact, the presence of other nurseries in the area may be an asset. Nurserymen often cooperate with each other on the use of specialized equipment, human resources, and in shipping arrangements.

SOCIOLOGICAL FACTORS

Many sociological factors have influenced and will continue to influence the development of the nursery industry just as they influence many other segments of the economy. Increased population, wealth, and leisure time all point to a greater demand for nursery products. But these factors vary considerably between communities, and it behooves enterprising nurserymen to know these trends. The mode of life and the ethnic background of the people may also influence the acceptance of the products and services to be offered or the manner by which they can be merchandised.

City or township clerks should be contacted relative to zoning restrictions, building codes, permits, and business licenses prior to buying land to develop a nursery or prior to improving the present facilities. Local zoning laws may prohibit or restrict the development of a nursery, landscape construction firm, or a garden center on a given site.

The availability and quality of the schools, churches, hospitals, civic associations, and cultural centers are also important considerations for all segments of the nursery industry. Communities that support these facilities are prone to support good landscapes and are therefore good sites for garden centers and landscape nurseries. The availability of these facilities will indirectly affect a wholesale nursery's ability to attract and keep good personnel.

SUMMARY

Establishing a successful nursery, landscape operation, or garden center is not a simple matter. It requires a large investment in land and facilities, familiarity with the laws and restrictions on all levels and units of government, and the assembling of a cohesive, productive group of people to accomplish the goals of the organization. Therefore, prior to selecting the site, all factors should be considered and evaluated. Advice from specialists in the area of real estate, soil science, horticulture, entomology, pathology, water resources, and associated areas should be solicited and evaluated. Considerable assistance may be obtained from county agricultural agents, soil conservation service, and extension specialists located at land grant universities. And it is highly desirable to have worked in the industry for a number of years prior to starting a nursery business. There is no substitute for experience.

REFERENCES

DAVIDSON, H. and T. SPEAKMAN. 1969. Time study for planting trees. Weeds, Trees, and Turf. Vol. 8, No. 8, p. 18.

DAVIS, D. D. 1973. Air pollution damages trees. USDA Forest Service.

ENGSTROM, H. E. 1941. Nursery practice for trees and shrubs suitable for planting on the prairie plains. USDA Misc. Publ. 434.

PETERSON, G. W., and R. S. SMITH, JR. 1975. Forest nursery division in the U.S. USDA Agricultural Handbook 470.

RICHARDS, L. A. 1954. Diagnosis and improvement of saline and alkali soils. USDA Agricultural Handbook 60.

STOECKELER, J. H., and G. W. JONES. 1957. Forest nursery practice in the Lake States. USDA Agricultural Handbook 110.

____, and P. E. SLABAUGH. 1965. Conifer nursery practice in the prairie plains. USDA Agricultural Handbook 279.

Chapter 5

Organization
and Development
of the Nursery

The organization and development of a nursery site should be done with considerable care and forethought to maximize efficiency of production and to minimize loss of time. Some thought should also be given to future expansion and ways of attaining long-range goals. A detailed planometric map (Fig. 5–1) of the site, locating all existing facilities, natural or man-made, should be developed. Then with the aid of overlays, plans can be made to develop the site, including the location of production areas, irrigation facilities, shipping–receiving–storage areas, administrative headquarters, residences, circulation and parking, windbreaks, and beautification. A separate overlay should be made diagramming the location of all underground utilities, including depths, location of valves, and so on.

GENERAL CONSIDERATIONS

The actual size and location of the individual units within the nursery will vary with the size and type of the operation, topography, soil type, cultural practices, equipment and extent of mechanization, availability of labor, and various economic factors.

75

Figure 5–1 Planometric map of a production nursery illustrating physical layout, control, and expansion potential. Dash lines indicate areas for expansion.

The *best sites* in a field production nursery should be allocated to the production areas, since soil is one of the major production assets. When possible, irrigation facilities should be centrally located within the production area to minimize the length of main lines and laterals.

Shipping–receiving–storage facilities are best located at a site that will be easily accessible from a major highway. The area should include adequate parking and turnaround area, elevated docks, adequate assembly areas, and restroom facilities for employees and truck drivers.

The *administrative headquarters* should be located to provide centralized control over production, shipping, and sales. In planning the building, consideration should be given to the interrelationship and coordination required by the various departments that will be housed in the headquarters. Adequate parking and convenient access to the sales area need to be provided for customers. If residences are to be constructed on the property, they should be located away from the commercial areas but conveniently connected to them.

Circulation and parking are important considerations in the development of nurseries and garden centers. Access and parking for customers should be made as easy and as convenient as possible. Preferably, these facilities should be blacktopped. Roads to the shipping–receiving–storage areas should also be readily accessible, about 30 feet in width, with no sharp-angle turns. In parts of the country where snow is a problem, it is advisable to locate the facility close to a major roadway to minimize snowplowing. Also, space at the sides of roads and parking areas must be available for piling of snow. Roads within the production area can be of crushed stone or gravel. They should be between 20 and 30 ft in width, but the gravel area can be confined to a 12- to 15-ft strip in the center. Roadways within the production area often serve as turnaround areas for field-operation equipment.

Windbreaks, if used, are planted on the windward side of seed beds and young transplant areas to reduce the dehydrating, eroding, and abusive effects of strong winds. Unfortunately, as the plants in the windbreak grow, so do their roots, which soon compete with the nursery crops for the available water and nutrients. Windbreaks that support vegetation 6 ft or more in height can materially reduce the yield of crops immediately adjacent to and up to several feet from the windbreak. The distance is roughly proportional to the height of the windbreak. Also, plants in the windbreak can harbor insects, diseases, and mammals that could be injurious to the nursery crops. If windbreaks are planted, avoid species that are known to be an alternate or primary host to a disease or insect that is a pest of nursery crops. Two good uses of evergreen plantings in a nursery are for protecting outdoor propagation areas with sheared hedges and the screening of storage room walls from the heating rays of the sun. These plantings can also serve as a source for seed or cuttings if the appropriate species or cultivar is planted. In areas where a permanent natural windbreak is undesirable, it could be advantageous to construct a windbreak out of snow fencing or to interplant with an annual crop such as corn between every two or three seed or liner beds.

In developing the overall plan for the nursery, consideration must also be given to constructing storage areas for equipment, tools, fertilizer, pesticides, and other materials. Container production nurseries will need storage areas for the basic ingredients of their growing media (sand, peat, bark, and so on); a holding area for containers; and special storage tanks for fertilizer concentrate.

Employee facilities, such as parking areas, locker rooms, lunchrooms, restroom facilities, and foremen's offices, should be carefully planned and properly constructed and maintained. Clean, neat facilities for employees are important in maintaining morale, which will have a direct effect upon production efficiency.

Public areas of the nursery should be planned and landscaped. Mature, well-maintained specimen plants can be developed into attractive synoptic plantings, which will aid in selling smaller nursery plants.

SPECIFIC CONSIDERATIONS

Production areas of nurseries include propagation greenhouses, seed beds, cold frames, liner beds, and the blocks or container yards. In most nurseries, production is centered on one farm, but in large nurseries production is often distributed over a number of farms. When a nursery offers a diverse product mix, it is desirable to organize the production effort either by method of production (field vs. container) or by plant type (herbaceous vs. woody; evergreen vs. deciduous; trees vs. shrubs vs. ground covers; etc.). When a number of farms are utilized, it is good management to concentrate compatible plant types onto one farm to gain production efficiency.

Seed bed areas are best situated on level, well-drained sandy loam or silty loam sites with a moderate level of nutrition and the pH appropriate to the crop (Chapter 8). The beds should be oriented in an east-west direction if lath or snow fence is to be employed for shade, so that the lath strips will be oriented in a north-south direction. This orientation produces a moving sun–shade pattern during bright sunny days, which will prevent sunscalding of the seedlings or newly rooted cuttings beneath, which could occur if the lath strips were oriented in an east-west direction.

The width of the seed beds is generally determined by the width of equipment used in working the area. The wheels of all heavy equipment should be confined to pathways between the beds. Some commonly used widths are 36, 42, and 48 in. Prior to planting, it is highly desirable to obtain a soil analysis to determine levels of nutrients and presence or absence of nematodes. In many situations, it is also desirable to fumigate or sterilize the soil prior to planting to assure freedom from diseases, weeds, and other pests.

Liner beds are areas of the nursery where young plants are grown under intensive culture for a period of 1–2 years prior to planting, either in the field or in containers. The liner beds may be open fields exposed to the elements, or they may be protected by shade houses (Fig. 5-2). Shade houses are utilized to temper the climate to produce better-quality plants for transplanting.

Figure 5-2 Young evergreens planted in liner beds, protected by a shade house. (Courtesy Zelenka Nurseries.)

Figure 5-3 Liner beds 52 in. on centers.

Plantings in the liner area are either in beds or in long, narrowly spaced rows. The spacing between the rows is determined primarily by the equipment utilized to plant, care for, and dig the plants. Spacings of 3, 4, 5, and 6 in. between rows are common. The actual spacing in the rows is determined by species, growth rate, and desired size of the transplants. Where beds are utilized, the width is adjusted to accommodate the equipment, but a 3½ or 4-ft bed with 10-in. pathways is common (Fig. 5-3). A 100-ft liner bed, 42 in. wide, planted to eight 5-in. rows with plants 4 in. in the row would support a population of 2520 plants. If the offset system of planting is utilized, that is, four rows are mechanically planted at a time followed by four additional rows interplanted between the others, the width of the pathway may have to be increased by one row width to accommodate the offset of the equipment.

Prior to planting of liner areas, the land must be properly prepared, including plowing, disking, leveling, sterilizing, or preplant weed control and subsoiling if necessary. The soil should be prepared to a depth of at least 6 in., although deeper preparation is needed for tap-rooted species. Moisture is critical to producing optimum growth

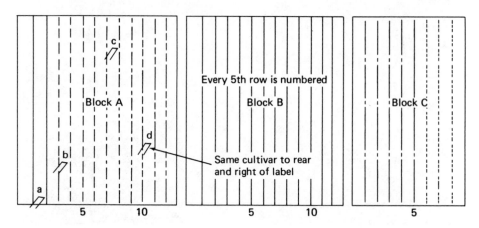

Figure 5-4 Designation of blocks and rows in a field production nursery.

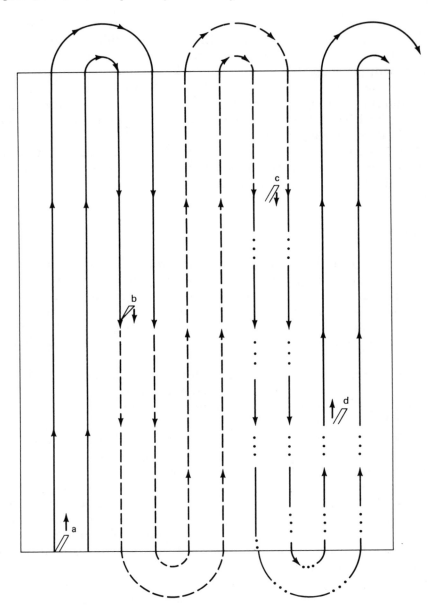

Figure 5-5 Labeling of nursery rows, conforming to the direction in which the rows were planted.

in this intensive production area. Therefore, a readily available source of quality water is an essential factor in the proper management of the area.

Field production areas of large nurseries may consist of one or more farms designated by name. Each farm is subdivided into blocks and rows. For ease of management, some form of designation is assigned, generally letters for the blocks and numbers for the rows. Two standard systems are used for labeling plant material within production nurseries. In propagation beds, small field production areas, and in container production nurseries, the most common method of labeling is from left to right and from front to rear (Fig. 5-4). In large field production nurseries, especially when planting is done mechanically, the labeling system conforms to the direction in which the rows were planted (Fig. 5-5).

PLANTING DESIGNS

The organization or design of nursery production areas varies from area to area of the country and from nursery to nursery. The primary designs are the row, square, offset square, rectangle, equilateral triangle, interplanting, or a combination of two or more systems. The determining factor in organizing production areas should be production efficiency. When land is expensive intensive cropping systems may be warranted. When land is relatively inexpensive the use of wider spacing may be justified. However, a balance is desirable, particularly with the use of large equipment currently employed in planting, maintaining, and harvesting nursery stock.

The *row* is the oldest and simplest method of planting nursery stock on level terrain. However, on hilly, well-drained sites, the straight row can still be used, whereas on hilly, poorly drained sites, the row is modified to follow the contour. The row is used primarily in the production of bare-root plants such as herbaceous perennials, roses, shrubs, and small-diameter trees. The spacing between rows is determined by the width of equipment used in planting, maintaining, and harvesting the crops. The standard width between nursery rows in many field production nurseries is 42 in., but this is modified to fit production methods. Long nursery rows can be planted, cultivated, and harvested much more efficiently than a series of short rows, since less time is spent in turning around at the end of the rows.

The *square design* (Fig. 5-6) is commonly used for the field production of B&B material such as large trees and specimen evergreens. It is also used extensively in the placement of containers within the beds of container production nurseries. It allows for cross cultivation in the maintenance of field production nurseries and lends itself to

Figure 5-6   Square design.

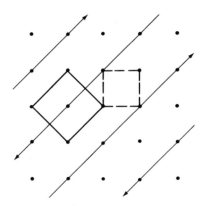

Figure 5-7   Digging on the diagonal.

Figure 5-8   Rectangle design.

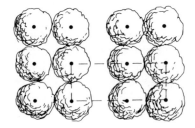

Figure 5-9   Rectangle-square design.

harvesting on the diagonal (Fig. 5-7) for thinning of the field block or container bed when harvesting a crop of small plants for early market. The spacing between plants following harvesting is the diagonal of the former square. This can be calculated by use of the Pythagorean theorem: $c = \sqrt{a^2 + b^2}$. The square design is used where land costs are relatively low because it efficiently utilizes only 78% of the land, but this disadvantage is partially compensated for by its advantages.

The *offset square* is used in some nurseries. This is where the plants in even-numbered rows are offset between the plants in the odd-numbered rows. However, this system gains little advantage over the square, since the distance between plants in the row remains the same. It also sacrifices the advantages of cross cultivation and harvesting on the diagonal. It is used, sometimes, when planning a marketing program, incorporating three times of harvest. When this is done, every other row is dug, followed a year later by every other plant in the remaining row, and finally the widely spaced plants are harvested.

Figure 5-10   Interplanting design.

In the *rectangular design* (Fig. 5-8), the distance between rows is greater than the distance in the row. It is the least efficient in space utilization (less than 78%), but is employed where land is relatively inexpensive or where larger mechanical equipment is utilized in maintaining and harvesting operations.

A modification of the rectangular design is the *rectangle-square system* (Fig. 5-9). It is used to decrease loss of space but still allows for the movement of large digging equipment between every two double rows. Another modification is the *interplanting system* (Fig. 5-10), employed where wide spacing is used for a long-term crop. In this system, a short-term crop is interplanted to gain a quick cash return. However, it has the disadvantage of different cultural requirements, and if not properly cared for and harvested on time it can lead to problems in management. In some situations the interplanted short-term crop could be a quick cash crop (e.g., vegetables). It is desirable to integrate the cultural programs for the two crops prior to planting to assure compatibility.

A variation of the interplanting system that is used in the production of field-grown shade trees requiring large-sized digging equipment for harvest is to plant two rows of rapidly maturing plants between every two, three, or four rows of shade trees. The open alley, produced by early harvest of the interplant crop, allows easy access of the heavy digging machines for harvesting of the large shade trees.

The *equilateral triangle-hexagon design* (Fig. 5-11) should be

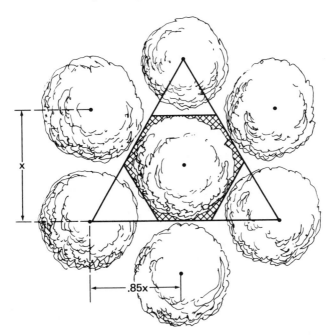

Figure 5-11 Equilateral triangle—hexagon design.

used when it is desired to maximize the utilization of space (Table 5-1). It is most commonly used in container production nurseries where land is expensive and maximum production per unit area is desired, but it can also be used in field production areas where land is expensive. In this design 91% of the space is utilized when the plants reach their maximum size. The rows are offset from the square but the between-the-row distance is 15% less than the spacing between plants in the row. However, plants in the ground cannot be cross-cultivated and harvesting time is critical.

A space efficient design for shade trees which permits easy access of equipment into the blocks, is to plant the trees in four- or five-row units, utilizing the equilateral triangle design, with a wide alley between each unit. This is for access of the large equipment used in maintenance and harvesting. The alley can be seeded to a sod to allow equipment to function during periods when the soil is wet. The area in plants can either be clean-cultivated or sod strips can be established between the rows with clean cultivation in the rows. Herbicides can be used to aid in maintaining the planted areas in a weed-free condition (Fig. 5-12).

Table 5-1 Plant density for various spacings in the nursery

Spacing (feet)	Square feet /plant, $l \times w$	Area/plant, $0.7854d^2$	Number/1000 ft^2	Number/acre	Equilateral Triangle[a]
2 × 2	4	3.14	250	10,890	12,620
2 × 3	6	3.14	167	7,260	
2 × 4	8	3.14	125	5,445	
2.8 × 2.8[b]	8	6.28	125	5,445	
3 × 3	9	7.07	111	4,840	5,600
3 × 4	12	7.07	83.3	3,630	
3 × 6	18	7.07	55.5	2,420	
4.2 × 4.2[b]	18	14.14	55.5	2,420	
4 × 4	16	12.57	62.5	2,722	3,150
4 × 6	24	12.57	41.7	1,815	
4 × 8	32	12.57	31.3	1,361	
5.7 × 5.7[b]	32	25.13	31.3	1,361	
5 × 5	25	19.64	40.0	1,742	2,018
5 × 6	30	19.64	33.3	1,452	
5 × 8	40	19.64	25.0	1,089	
5 × 10	50	19.64	20.0	871	
7.1 × 7.1[b]	50	39.27	20.0	871	
6 × 6	36	28.27	27.8	1,210	1,400
6 × 8	48	28.27	20.8	907	
6 × 10	60	28.27	16.7	726	
8.5 × 8.5[b]	72	56.55	14.1	605	
8 × 8	64	50.27	15.6	680	785
11.3 × 11.3[b]	128	100.53	7.8	340	
10 × 10	100	78.54	10.0	435	500

[a]Distance between rows = 0.85 in-the-row distance.
[b]Spacing resulting from removing diagonal rows.

Figure 5-12 Shade trees growing in a nursery with grass sod between the rows. Rows are treated with a selective herbicide. (Courtesy Manbeck Nursery.)

Economic and Cultural Considerations

The physical organization of the plantings within a nursery will vary with the situation, but the following economic and cultural factors should be considered.

1. *The efficient use of land:* The equilateral triangle produces the most efficient use of space; the square-rectangle is the least efficient.

2. *The size of plant for the market objective:* If the market objective is for small plants, the spacing can be relatively close, but if the objective is to produce large, landscape-sized plants, the spacing must be wide to accommodate the crown of the plant.

3. *The cultivar:* If the cultivar has a narrow, upright habit of growth, the spacing can be close, whereas if the cultivar is wide-spreading or of a weeping habit, the spacing must be wider.

4. *Equipment use in maintaining and harvesting:* When the horse and mule were used for cultivation, the spacing between rows was

fairly narrow. But with modern equipment of high horsepower, it is necessary to increase the spacing between the rows to permit entry and movement of the equipment.

5. *Economic return on investment:* Although many agricultural enterprises, including container production nurseries, measure return on investment per acre of land, it is more appropriate for a field production nursery to evaluate a total production system, including land, spacing, maintenance, and harvesting to maximize return on total investment, not only on land. Land use is one input into the system, and it should be used efficiently. But materials handling is the major cost input in the production of nursery products, and if machines can make labor more effective, it may be necessary to redesign the production areas to obtain the most effective materials-handling system, even though it calls for less efficient use of land.

CONTAINER PRODUCTION AREAS

The design of container production areas is strongly influenced by a number of factors, including irrigation and drainage, materials handling, cultural and maintenance requirements of the plants, size of the containers and the costs involved. *Irrigation* is an absolute requirement in the development of container production nursery areas, since plants in containers are totally dependent upon a supply of water. Container-grown plants should be grouped according to their water requirement to obtain maximum benefit from the irrigation system (Chapter 10).

Drainage is the companion factor to irrigation and must be considered in the development of the container area, since large volumes of water are applied to the plants throughout the growing season, and much of this water falls outside the containers or drains through them. It is necessary to remove this excess water from the area to assure drainage of the media within the containers, and to carry on various plant maintenance and materials-handling operations. If the site is not well drained, it will have to be graded and a drainage system developed. Excess water should not be drained back into a pond used for irrigation of nursery stock, since it may be high in soluble salts or contaminated with weed seeds, herbicides, or spores of various fungi, any of which have the potential of causing plant production problems. In most situations excess water is disposed of via county or municipal drainage facilities. However, in recent years, some communities have enacted ordinances prohibiting the disposal of water contaminated with excess soluble salts into these facilities. This necessitates developing other means to dispose of the excess water. Two alternatives are to construct holding ponds or to install "French" drains at various sites within the area if the soil profile permits. The water collected in the holding ponds might possibly be reused within the nursery if it is of acceptable quality. However, in most situations it is either used to irrigate agronomic crops or is allowed to evaporate into the air. If the water can be reused, the ponds should be constructed fairly deep with a relatively small surface area, whereas if the water cannot be reused, the ponds should be constructed fairly shallow with a large surface area. French drains are simply deep holes or trenches dug through low-porosity topsoils into high-porosity subsoils. The trenches are then filled with rocks or crushed gravel. These drains allow the excess water to percolate into the soil and recharge the underground water supply. The area about the beds is graded to channel the water to the drains.

Materials handling is probably the most significant factor in the development of the area. Plans need to be developed and the area designed to expedite the efficient handling of materials through the various phases of production, including media preparation, potting, setting out of containers, pickup of containers for shipping or rearrangement for overwintering, and loading for shipping. A well-planned design should provide for a logical rotation of crops through the production cycles so that double handling of the containers is kept to a minimum. The design of the area must also provide for the space needs of machines, especially transport equipment, used in the operation of the nursery.

The cultural and maintenance requirements of the plants will also influence the design of the container area. Plants that have special requirements are best grown together in areas where their special needs can be met most efficiently. Also, plant maintenance requirements such as fertilizing, pest control, pruning and training, and spreading for growth increase—must be provided for, although in some situations the planted containers are spaced when set out to meet their spacial needs throughout the production cycle. This is done to minimize handling, but it sacrifices water efficiency if the plants are watered by an overhead means.

In areas of the country where it is necessary to provide winter protection for container-grown plants, overwintering structures (see Chapter 13) must be planned for in the development and organization of the site. When such facilities are to be constructed, they should be designed and located so that plant material can be moved into and out of the facility with efficiency. Also, the structure must be oriented and built in a manner to withstand the force of wind in areas where winds are a problem.

Size of containers is another parameter that affects the overall design of the container area. Containers are best grouped by size to aid in providing for the water requirements, ease of handling, and maintenance. The various areas might include small (1 and 3 gal), medium-sized (5, 7, 15 gal), and large (20 gal or larger) containers. Within each area the containers can be subgrouped into beds by species. The size and arrangement of the beds is influenced by the growth habits of the plants, the rotation program, and the size and physical limitations of the area.

For maximum utilization of space within the beds, containers are set touching one another in offset rows. As the plants grow and require additional space, the containers are spaced and rearranged, commonly utilizing the equilateral triangle-hexagon design. In some situations, the interplanting (understory) design is utilized. In this design shade-tolerant species are grown under the canopy of taller-growing plants. Where space is not a factor or where either physical requirements of the plants or the physiography of the area impose limitations, other designs are utilized.

The cost of developing container production areas should be carefully researched prior to construction. This includes the raw materials for plant production (e.g., ingredients for the medium, water, fertilizers, containers, etc.); the cost of land leveling, irrigation, drainage, and so on; and the costs of operating the facility. In some situations the initial cost of development could be a limiting factor in effecting a successful cash flow except at low interest rates (see Chapter 7), whereas in other situations the development or expansion of a container production facility may be a desirable capital investment for nurseries that are expanding, especially when reinvesting income derived from previous crops.

PRODUCTION PROGRAMING

It is extremely difficult to efficiently produce a wide range of plant material. Growing a wide variety of species, each requiring its special method of propagation and field culture, does not lend itself to production efficiency. In order to gain a greater degree of management control over production, it may be desirable to specialize either by type of plant or by method of production. Limiting production to plant groups that have similar production requirements and are compatible with production capabilities is one means of gaining production efficiency. Also, with increased mechanization of routine production operations there is greater need for standardization of techniques. Specialization and standardization permit managers to

Species _____   Size class _____

Sales or market   Previous sales _____
  information
_____   Projected sales
_____   Garden center _____
_____   Wholesaler   _____
_____   Landscape   _____
                                       Other   _____
Technical data   Projection for planning _____
_____
Propagation: method and times _____
_____

Soil and water _____
_____

Plant requirements _____
_____

Pests _____
_____
_____

Expected growth performance _____
_____
_____

Additional data _____
_____

Resources needed

Space:
  Propagation bench space_____ sq. ft
  Liner beds   _____ sq. ft
  Fields   _____ acres

Materials:
  Fertilizer _____
  Pesticides _____
  Other   _____

Labor inputs _____
_____

Estimated losses:
  Through replacements _____
  Through grade-out   _____
  In-the-field   _____
  In liner beds   _____
  In propagation   _____

Equipment needs _____
_____
_____
_____

Cost estimates _____
_____

Notes _____
_____
_____
_____

Figure 5-13 Nursery production information.

plan and control production, thus ensuring a greater chance of success in the business. But nursery managers must be careful not to become too specialized, since monoculture is very vulnerable to disaster should there be a major change in weather conditions, plant pests, or in market demand. It is seldom desirable that one genus or one class of plant material make up more than 20–25% of the total production effort.

Production programing must begin with a market analysis to determine if there is a market for the product, the potential demand, in what size and form, and how many plants per year would meet the production goal. Information must be obtained on production requirements related to propagation, soil and water requirements, general culture in the nursery, and pest problems. An estimate must be made of the resources that will be needed, the production efficiency or mortality that can be expected, and the costs involved. The production requirements are summarized, in part, in Fig. 5-13.

Up-to-date technical information should be collected and summarized so that the manager, propagator, and the grower will have available, in abstract form, the details needed for planning the best production system and timing of operations. This information should be updated periodically with practical, relevant experience data as they are accumulated within the production nursery.

ESTIMATING PLANT MATERIAL REQUIREMENTS

Once a production quota has been established for the end product, it becomes necessary to calculate the quantity of cuttings to be stuck, grafts to be made, or seeds to be sown in order to produce the transplants and ultimately the liners that will either be field-planted or planted in containers in order to meet production quotas. In each step of the operation there is a mortality that can be expected plus a loss of material at grade-out for some classes of plant material, and a factor for replacements. These data may be available from past records or an estimate can be made based on information obtained from other sources.

Estimates for subsystem quotas are obtained by working backward from the estimated production or sales figure. The calculation is made for each step in the production cycle by dividing the production quota of that phase of production by its estimated return percentage (Table 5-2). This is obtained by subtracting the percent mortality from 100%. For example, if 10,000 is the production goal,

Table 5-2 Estimate of plant material requirements

Species:	*Taxus* 'Hicksi'
Class:	B&B 3–4 ft
Rotations:	Field 5–1; linear 2–1
Propagation:	Evergreen cuttings, Dec.–Apr.

Estimated Goal for:	*Plants*
Sales objective	10,000
Replacements 5%[a]	
First revision	10,530
Grade-out (if applicable)	
(not applicable with B&B material)	
Field mortality 15%	
Second revision (liners needed)	12,400
Liner loss 10%	
Third revision (transplants needed)	13,770
Propagation loss 25%	
Fourth revision (cuttings to stick)	18,350

[a]Percentages must be obtained from past experience. These are for demonstrative purposes only.

10,000 represents 100%; if replacements are 5%, 10,530 plants must be produced to meet sales plus replacements (10,000 ÷ 0.95 = 10,530). Combining percentage loss figures to calculate the material needed to start the production cycle results in a figure less than what is actually needed.

ESTIMATING SPACE REQUIREMENTS

Space requirements can be estimated for propagation, liner production, and either field or container production. When a perpetual production system is designed, it is necessary to know the rotation system that will be employed in addition to the planting densities that will be used in the field or the container production areas, the liner area, and the propagation bench. This information can then be used in planning for and adjusting the space needs for the total operation.

Using this information, the various department heads (propagation, field, container, storage, shipping, etc.), can plan and program their space, labor and material requirements. For example, the propagator can assemble all the production programs for the current season and plan his or her material, space, and labor requirements.

Table 5-3 Propagation space needs and allocation chart

Group	Priority	Space needed (ft^2)	Weeks	Adjusted Square feet	Adjusted Weeks
A	2	500	45-5	—	—
B	3	1000	40-5	B_1: 500	40-5
				B_2: 500	5-17+
C	2	500	5-15	500	10-20+
D	1	1500	42-10	—	—

After the individual species to be propagated have been classified by method of propagation and a priority index assigned (Table 5-3), the space and time requirements can be estimated and adjusted to fit the limitations imposed by the available bench space (Fig. 5-14). In the example here, group D has priority 1 and is plotted first, followed by groups A and C. Group C must be delayed by 5 weeks due to space limitations, but group A is programed according to schedule. Group B, with priority 3, is split into two groups, B_1 stuck on time and B_2 delayed until week 5; the cuttings can be held in storage until space is available. Similar estimates can be made by other department heads, who coordinate their activities with each other under the overall control of the production manager.

Figure 5-14 Propagation space availability diagram.

PRODUCTION LAND UTILIZATION

Field-Grown Crops

Land used in the production of field-grown stock is generally occupied for several years. In addition, the land may be out of production, either lying fallow or in a cover crop, for a period of time that will vary from a few months to a number of years prior to replanting. One saleable acre of nursery crops will require a number of non-saleable acres to support the program. Table 5-4 lists estimated acreage requirements for selected classes of field-grown nursery stock.

Management practices will vary with type of nursery and production objective. Therefore, the estimated acreage requirements should be used only as a guide where individual data are not available. Another land requirement that must be added to these figures is the land needed for turnaround and service areas. It is estimated that these requirements may vary between 5 and 10% of the production requirement.

Table 5-4 Estimated acreage requirements for field-grown nursery stock

Class	Average age at sale	Years in rotation	Land required per acre of annual sale
Broadleaved evergreens	3.5	0.8	4.3
Range[a]	2.6–4.5	0.5–1.4	3.5–5.0
Narrowleaved evergreens	3.5	0.9	4.4
Range	2.4–5.3	0.5–1.3	3.3–5.8
Deciduous shrubs	2.7	1.3	4.0
Range	1.8–4.4	0.5–3.2	2.4–5.8
Ornamental trees	4.4	0.7	5.1
	2.1–8.2	0.2–1.9	3.3–8.8

[a]Range = shortest to longest period reported.
SOURCE: Data from South. Coop. Seri. Bull. 143, 1969.

Container-Grown Crops

Land used in the production of container-grown crops is occupied for only a few months for crops with a rapid production cycle, up to 1-2 years for species with longer production cycles. This is one of the major advantages for container production—shorter rotation time—leading to faster turnover of invested capital. The actual space requirement varies with the market objective, the climate, various cultural practices, and spatial arrangements.

If the market objective is to produce small plants in small containers on a rapid rotation, 1 acre of land may produce two to three crops per year, so that only 0.5 or 0.33 acre of space is required per area of annual sales. However, for large plants on a 2-year rotation, it may take as much as 2 acres of land or as little as 1.5 acres per acre of annual sale. Climate and various cultural operations will influence growth rates, which will affect turnover rates. Nurseries located in southern latitudes have longer growing seasons and are capable of producing crops in a shorter period than nurseries located in northern climates. Also, plants that are produced under optimum cultural conditions of light, nutrition, moisture, and pest control can be produced on a shorter production cycle, which will reduce the time that each container-grown plant occupies space in the nursery. Finally, the space needs will be influenced by the spatial arrangement of the containers through the production cycle.

Container production nurseries that are operated on a profit basis must be cognizant of utilizing space efficiently and minimizing rotation time when planning the development of a production system. By careful planning, many container production nurseries can increase their production efficiency on both an acre basis and on invested capital.

SUMMARY

The organization and development of the land areas within a nursery should be carefully planned prior to development. The best sites should be reserved for plant production. Each unit should be located and developed to produce optimum growth of plants and to maintain their quality following harvest but still permit efficient use of labor in each phase of the production, maintenance, and marketing effort. The time spent in carefully planning the layout and development of the nursery site is well worth the effort in the efficiency that can be gained in the use of the other factors of production.

REFERENCES

DAMBACH, C. A. 1948. A study of the ecology and economic value of crop field borders. Graduate School Stud. Ohio State Univ. Bio. Sci. Ser. 2.

GILFORD, J. C. 1974. Some thoughts on production planning. Proceedings of the 9th Refresher Course for Nurserymen, Pershore College of Horticulture, Pershore, England, pp. 34–43.

STOECKELER, J. H. 1957. Forest nursery practice in the lake states. USDA Agricultural Handbook 110.

WIANT, H. V., JR. 1973. Efficiency of regular spacing planting designs. Tree Planters Notes 24(3):31–31.

Chapter 6

Laws, Regulations, Standards, and Codes

The nursery industry, like other major industries, must comply with certain laws and regulations. The laws and regulations are promulgated by government primarily for the protection of people. Federal laws and regulations, other than tax laws, that are of concern to the nursery industry include (1) Federal Social Security and Unemployment Compensation, (2) Fair Labor Standards Act of 1938 as amended, (3) Occupational Safety and Health Act of 1970, (4) Farm Labor Contractors Registration Act of 1963, (5) Plant Pest Acts and Quarantines, (6) Federal Environmental Pesticide Control Act of 1972, (7) Federal Warranty Act of 1975, (8) Federal Price and Services Act of 1936, (9) Plant Patent Act of 1930 as amended, (10) Workmen's Compensation, and (11) Trade Practice Rules for the Nursery Industry. In addition, various state and local units of government have laws that affect the nursery industry. There are also industry standards for nursery stock.

FEDERAL LAWS AND REGULATIONS

The following is a synopsis of federal laws and regulations as they affect the nursery industry. For specific details and up-to-date information on these laws and regulations, since they are amended periodically, the nursery manager should contact the American Association of Nurserymen or a lawyer. The AAN is in a position to provide member firms with useful information on all federal regulations and legal decisions relative to the nursery industry.

The 1935 *Federal Social Security Act* provided for federal–state cooperation in an old age assistance and unemployment insurance program. The Old Age and Survivors Insurance (OASI) program is designed to provide an income in the worker's old age and to assure some income for dependents after his or her death. The cost of the program is borne by both employers and employees. Every employer who employs one or more persons is liable for this tax. Employers pay a tax on each employee's wages up to a base amount (which changes with time). The employee pays a similar tax. However, the employee's share of the tax is deducted by the employer at the close of each pay period and forwarded to the Director of Internal Revenue. As of January 1, 1980, the wage base was $25,900 and the tax rate was 6.13%, paid equally by employer and employee. The wage base and the tax rate are scheduled to increase over the next 10 years. Current information on OASI and the necessary forms are available from the district director of the Internal Revenue Service.

Federal Unemployment Compensation became effective for agricultural workers January 1, 1978. Under the federal law the tax, paid by the employer, is 3.4% of the first $6000 of wages (percentage and base change with time). If employees are covered by a state unemployment compensation law, the employer receives a credit against the federal tax. Since the wage base and tax percentage vary with the individual states, it is suggested that nurserymen contact their state unemployment compensation agency for specific data. Most states impose substantial penalties for late payment or failure to pay unemployment compensation taxes.

The *Fair Labor Standards Act* of 1938 (referred to as the Federal Wage-Hour Law) established 25 cents as the minimum pay for 1 hr of labor. But the law was limited to firms engaged in interstate commerce, and agriculture was exempted from coverage under the law. Over the years minimum pay has increased and coverage has been extended with fewer exemptions. As of January 1977, the only agricultural exemption was for an employer who used less than 500 worker-days of agricultural labor during the preceding calendar year. Also, overtime (not less than 1.5 times the employee's regular rate) must be paid for hours worked in any week in excess of 40.

For many years agriculture had a seasonal exemption, but as of January 1977 there was no seasonal exemption. Within a nursery organization, the only personnel exempt from the minimum pay and overtime requirements are executive, administrative, or professional employees, each of whom must meet the test for exemptions as required by the latest regulations.

Nurserymen must comply with the Federal Wage-Hour Law's equal-pay provisions. The law requires equal pay, regardless of sex, for equal work on jobs that require equal skill, effort, and responsibility, and are performed under similar conditions. Exceptions to the law are payments made because of a seniority system, a merit system, a system that measures earnings by quantity or quality of production, or a differential based on any factor other than sex.

Employers found in violation of the law can be required to pay the difference in back wages for 2 years as well as increase the pay of the employee(s) who had been paid the lesser amount. An employer cannot reduce the wage of other employees in order to come into compliance with the act.

Time and payroll records must be maintained for 3 years. The records must show daily and weekly hours worked by all nonexempt employees. Also, the records must show overtime payments separately from straight-time payment, total earnings, deductions, and net pay.

The latest amendment to the law also contains a number of new provisions and penalties to the child labor portion. The law prohibits the use of oppressive child labor in interstate commerce or in the production of goods for interstate commerce. The law limits the use of child labor by age group and type of activity.

Individuals 18 years of age or older may be employed in any occupation without regard to the time of day or the number of hours worked. But minors under 18 years of age may not be employed in occupations declared to be hazardous by the Secretary of Labor. Examples of hazardous occupations within the nursery industry are operation of a tractor of over 20 PTO horsepower; operation of power-driven posthole digger or driver; operating or assisting in operation of trencher, earth-moving machine, forklift, power-driven saws; driving a vehicle transporting passengers; working on a ladder or scaffold of over 20 feet; and handling or applying agricultural chemicals classified under the Federal Insecticide, Fungicide or Rodenticide Act as category I and category II.

Minors under 16 years of age may be employed in agricultural occupations, except those which have been declared to be hazardous. But their employment is not permitted during school hours. All minors must be paid minimum wage unless certificates are obtained for the employment of full-time students at 85% of the minimum.

Employers must maintain records on the employment of all individuals under 19 years of age. Such individuals should be required to furnish either an age or employment certificate (obtained from local school authorities) or a copy of their birth certificate as proof of age.

The Williams–Steiger *Occupational Safety and Health Act* (OSHA) of 1970 was enacted by Congress "to assure so far as possible, every working man and woman in the nation safe and healthful working conditions and to preserve our human resources." This act covers all employers with 11 or more employees.

The general duty clause of the act states: "Each employer (1) shall furnish to each of his employees a place of employment free from recognized hazards that are causing or are likely to cause death or serious physical harm to his employees; (2) shall comply with the occupational safety and health standards promulgated under this act." However, the act also places some responsibility on employees. The general duty clause also states: "Each employee shall comply with occupational safety and health standards and all rules, regulations and orders issued pursuant to this Act which are applicable to his own actions and conduct."

Landscape contractors are subject to the general construction safety and health standards, which include first-aid services, provisions for medical care and consultants, wearing of hard hats, eye and face protection, and so on.

If growing horticultural commodities is the primary activity of the establishment, it is considered agriculture; thus most safety and health standards do not apply. However, the general-duty clause is applicable to employees of the establishment. Nurserymen should obtain a copy of subpart J, Regulations 1910.141 through 1910.148, for regulations and standards that apply to nurseries.

As of September 1976, five federal standards apply to nurseries, including SMV emblem, housing in labor camps, anhydrous ammonia, tractor-rollover protection, and PTO guards. The SMV (slow-moving vehicle) emblem must be displayed on all slow-moving equipment operating on public roads. The emblem must be kept clean and be replaced when faded.

Nurserymen who operate labor camps must obtain a license, generally from the department of health in the state where the camp is located. Requirements for licensing are based on a 1968 U.S. Department of Labor standard on housing agricultural workers. The standard covers environmental aspects of temporary housing for employees, such as building construction, sanitation, water, refuse disposal, and so on.

The anhydrous ammonia standard requires that equipment used in applying anhydrous ammonia meet certain standards. Nurserymen should ask suppliers to certify in writing that their equipment meets OSHA standards.

The rollover protection standards as published by OSHA require that all tractors of more than 20 engine horsepower manufactured after October 25, 1976, must be equipped with rollover protective structures and a seat belt. Employers must instruct employees on operation practices and ensure the use of seat belts when operating tractors with rollover protective structures.

Safety standards on guarding of farm equipment, effective October 25, 1976, require power-takeoff (PTO) drives to be guarded. Also, signs must be placed at prominent locations on tractors and PTO-driven equipment specifying that PTO safety shields must be kept in place.

Record-keeping requirements are very specific. They are contained in the booklet entitled "Record Keeping Requirements Under the Williams–Steiger Occupational Safety and Health Act of 1970." Every nurseryman should obtain a copy from a district office of the U.S. Department of Labor. Employers who violate the law can be assessed costly penalties.

OSHA provides that states may develop their own safety and health laws and assume most of the enforcement processes. But the state program must be at least as effective as the federal program. Most states have developed and are enforcing programs in safety and health.

To assure compliance with this far-reaching piece of legislation, nursery managers may wish to organize an OSHA committee within the nursery. The committee, chaired by a key employee, should be responsible for advising the manager on matters pertaining to safety and health, keeping informed on all state and federal requirents, and seeing that nursery employees comply with all applicable standards.

The *Farm Labor Contractors Registration Act* (FLCRA) of 1963 and amendments of 1974 applies to any person, who for a fee . . . recruits, solicits, hires, furnishes, or transports migrant workers (excluding members of his immediate family) for agricultural employment. It requires that a farm labor contractor obtain a certificate of registration, that the certificate be current and in full force and effect, and that it be in such person's possession. The law also requires that the labor contractor inform workers of area of employment, crops and operations on which they may be employed, transportation, housing and insurance, wage rates, and charges to be made by contractor for services. The farm labor contractor must also maintain payroll records for each worker, showing total earnings, all withholding, and net earnings.

Nurserymen engaging the services of a farm labor contractor must be certain that the contractor possesses a current registration certificate from the U.S. Department of Labor. The 1974 amendments require that "any person who is furnished any migrant worker by a farm labor contractor shall maintain all payroll records required to be kept by such persons under Federal law. . . ." Current details of the law can be obtained from the U.S. Department of Labor, *Wage and Hour Division's Field Operations Handbook.*

The *Plant Pest Act of 1912* and the *Plant Pest Act of 1957* are the basic laws of plant quarantines in the United States. Prior to 1912, there were no laws protecting the United States from the entry of foreign pests or to prevent and control their distribution within the country. The 1912 Act, as amended by Congress, gave authority to the Secretary of Agriculture to regulate by quarantine the importation and interstate movement of nursery stock, other plants, and plant products that may be vectors of foreign plant pests.

There are three levels of quarantine that affect nurserymen, depending upon their sources of materials and the geographic distribution of their products:

1. *Foreign quarantines* affect the movement of plants and plant products between nations. But in general, few nurserymen are concerned with foreign quarantines, except as they affect shipments to and from Canada and Mexico. Nurserymen wishing to import or export plants or plant products should obtain a copy of "Foreign Quarantine Notices," Title 7, Chapter III, Part 319, from the Animal and Plant Health Inspection Service (APHIS), USDA, and obtain a special permit, which can be obtained in most states through the state department of agriculture or from APHIS. There are some

plants and plant products that cannot be imported into the United States from certain foreign countries. Details are contained in "Foreign Quarantine Notice," which is updated periodically.

Canadian virus regulations on the genera *Cydonia, Malus, Prunus,* and *Pyrus* became effective July 1, 1976. Nurseries wishing to export plants of these genera into Canada must obtain certification that the plants are free of certain viruses.

2. *Interstate quarantines* are of major concern to nurserymen engaged in interstate shipment of plants. These may be federal or state quarantines. The general policy in the enforcement of interstate quarantines is to permit unrestricted movement of all plant products within the regulated area and to restrict shipments beyond the quarantined area to uninfested products and plants. Examples of domestic quarantines include golden nematode, Mexican fruit fly, citrus blackfly, pink bollworm, imported fire ant, witchweed, and schleroderris canker. A number of states impose exterior quarantine requirements on nursery plants moving in interstate commerce. Nurserymen in states where Japanese beetles are known to exist must have their production land treated so that the plants can be certified as free of Japanese beetles when they are shipped into states imposing the quarantine. Copies of federal regulations may be obtained by writing: Plant Protection and Quarantine Program, APHIS, USDA, Federal Building No. 1, Hyattsville, Maryland 20782.

3. *Intrastate quarantines* or regulations are authorized by state legislation and are imposed and administered by the state agency in charge of plant pest regulation, generally a part of the state's department of agriculture. These regulations are designed to prevent the spread of specific pests within the state and as a means of preventing other states or the USDA from restricting the movement of plants and plant products from the entire state rather than from just the infested portion of the state.

A quarantined area is usually a civil boundary such as national, state, or county. In order to move regulated products out of a quarantined or restricted area, they must be inspected or subjected to some pest-destroying treatment and carry a certificate assuring their freedom from the pest upon which the quarantine is placed. All states have laws pertaining to the inspection and movement of nursery stock. Nurserymen should be familiar with these laws and comply accordingly. The A.A.N. publishes a quarantine wall chart and maps of quarantine areas. All nurserymen shipping nursery stock interstate should have up-to-date copies of the chart and the selected maps to post in the shipping area of the nursery. But nurserymen should invite inspection, since the plant inspector can help identify plant pests and suggest control measures before they become serious problems.

A state license is required in all states of persons, partnerships, or corporations growing and/or desiring to sell nursery stock. The license is obtained from the director of agriculture, but in some states it may be available from the secretary of state. Also, all nursery stock must be inspected and found free of serious pests before it may be sold or moved from place to place. Nurserymen are required to make application for inspection and are often assessed a fee, usually on the acreage of saleable stock. Nurserymen must comply with all federal and state quarantines, rules, and regulations.

Nurserymen shipping nursery stock out of state have been required to file a nursery inspection certificate with the state department of agriculture in the various states into which stock was shipped. However, since 1974 many states have accepted a current list of certified nurseries and nursery stock dealers in lieu of the individual certificates. This change was recommended and adopted by the National Plant Board in 1974. An up-to-date list of states accepting the list in lieu of certificates is generally available through the Department of Agriculture, Plant Industry Division, within each state.

The *Federal Environmental Pesticide Control Act* (FEPCA) of 1972 [amendments to Federal Insecticide, Fungicide and Rodenticide Act (FIFRA)] were enacted to protect people and the environment from the hazards of dangerous pesticides. The act classifies pesticides and pesticide applicators, and it limits the application of pesticides according to the applicator's training and certification. The act is administered by the Environmental Protection Agency (EPA).

Pesticides are classified into two categories: general use and restricted use. General-use pesticides are those which when applied in accordance with directions for use will not generally cause unreasonable adverse effects on the environment. Restricted-use pesticides are those when applied in accordance with directions for use may cause unreasonable adverse effects on the environment, including injury to the applicator. The misuse of pesticides, including use, that is "inconsistent with label directions" is in violation of FIFRA and is subject to a fine.

The EPA is responsible for classifying and updating the classification of pesticides. Anyone can purchase and apply general-use pesticides, but since October 1977, only certified pesticide applicators can purchase and use restricted-use pesticides. The law requires that individuals who use or supervise the use of restricted-use pesticides be certified either as a private applicator or as a commercial applicator. They must keep a record of all restricted-use materials used for 3 years.

A private applicator is an individual who uses or supervises the use of restricted-use pesticides for the purpose of producing an agricultural commodity on property owned or rented by the applicator or his or her employer, or on the property of another person if applied without compensation (other than trading of personal services between producers of agricultural commodities).

A commercial applicator is an individual who uses or supervises the use of any pesticide that is classified for restricted use for any purpose or on any property other than as provided for by the private applicator classification.

To be certified, an individual must be determined to be competent with respect to the use and handling of pesticides. States can develop their own programs for training and certifying applicators, subject to the approval of the federal EPA administrator. In most states, the state department of agriculture administers the certification and licensing of pesticide applicators. Two pesticide applicator manuals are available from the Superintendent of Documents, U.S. Government Printing Office, Washington, D.C. 20402: "A Guide for Private Applicators" for those applying pesticides only on their own or rented crop land; and "A Guide for Commercial Applicators," for those applying pesticides on other people's property for hire. The manuals are helpful to those who wish to become certified as pesticide applicators. For up-to-date details on classification of pesticides, procedures for certification, liabilities, and so on, nurserymen should contact their state department of agriculture or the agriculture agents of their local county Cooperative Extension Service.

The Magnuson–Moss *Warranties Act* of 1975 requires that written warranties on all "consumer products" manufactured after July 4, 1975, and costing more than $10 must be designated either "limited" or "full" and that the warranty designation must be made clearly and conspicuously. A "consumer product" is "any tangible personal property which is to be distributed in commerce and which is normally used for personal, family or household purposes."

The act, administered by the Federal Trade Commission (FTC), does not require the seller to grant warranties, but if a warrant is offered, the law is applicable. To qualify as a "full warrant" under the act, the seller (nurseryman) must warrant that he will remedy (repair, replace, or refund) without charge in a reasonable time in the event of a defect or failure of the product. A full warrant includes the cost of replanting if the plant was planted by the nurseryman. However, a nurseryman is not under obligation to fulfill a warrant if it can be shown that the plant died or was damaged as a result of storms, animals, or by the warrantee's (customer) failure to provide reasonable and necessary maintenance. Nurserymen not wishing to be obligated by the full-warranty requirements may grant a "limited warranty," in which they state the limitations of the warrant.

The FTC, through the publication of regulations, will clarify and particularize the seller's obligations under the act. The act does not regulate state laws related to contracts which also govern laws of warranty. Therefore, nurserymen offering written warranties may wish to consult an attorney familiar with the laws and regulations pertaining to warranties to ensure that their warranty complies with both state and federal laws. Current information on the latest federal regulations on warranties can be obtained by writing to one of the regional offices of the FTC. Information on state laws can be obtained from the office of the state attorney general.

The Robinson–Patman *Price and Services Act* of 1936, an amendment to the antitrust act of 1914, prohibits a seller from discriminating between his or her business customers in price and service and prohibits a buyer from knowingly receiving illegal favors or services. The act applies to the sale of tangible goods in interstate commerce and is enforced by the FTC. In essence, the act requires that a seller treat all commercial customers equally with regard to the price of the same product and service offered. The simplest way for nurserymen to comply with the act is to sell from a price list (catalog) which is uniform for all customers competing for the product, in wholesale units.

The Towsend–Purnell *Plant Patent Act,* an amendment to the general patent law, was passed by Congress in 1930 and amended slightly in 1954. The significant portion of the statute states, "Whoever invents or discovers and asexually reproduces any distinct and new variety of plant, including cultivated sports, mutants, hybrids and newly found seedlings, other than a tuber-propagated plant or plant found in an uncultivated state, may obtain a patent, therefore. . . ." Characteristics that may distinguish a new variety (cultivar) of a plant for patent consideration include, among others, habit of growth; color of stems, leaves, flowers, or fruit; resistance to cold, drought, heat, or disease; productivity or lack of productivity of flowers or fruit; fragrance; storage qualities; and ease of asexual propagation.

The plant patent is a grant by the federal government to the inventor (or his or her heirs or assignee) the right to exclude others from asexually propagating the plant or selling the plant so reproduced for a period of 17 years from the date of issue. Application for a plant patent may be obtained from the Commissioner of Patents, Washington, D.C. 20231. Nurserymen wishing to patent a plant may wish to discuss the topic with a current holder of a plant patent and to contact an attorney or agent registered with the patent office. A copy of "Directory of Registered Patent Attorneys and Agents" is available from the Commissioner of Patents.

Workmen's Compensation Insurance (WCI) must be carried by employers who hire one or more employees that work in a hazardous occupation (listed in section 3, workmen's compensation law) and by all employers who employ three or more employees. If coverage is not required by law, an employer may obtain workmen's compensation insurance on a voluntary basis. The insurance may be obtained from any private insurance company authorized to transact the business of workmen's compensation insurance within each state.

Rates for WCI vary according to the type of employment, the hazards involved, and the personal injury history of the company. Insurance groups working through trade associations (e.g., AAN) offer special WCI savings plans. These plans are designed to provide dividends on WCI premiums, depending upon the claim experience of policyholders within the group. Nurserymen are advised to consult their state or national trade association for details on the plan.

Trade practice rules for the nursery industry as promulgated by the FTC in 1956 and amended in 1979 as *Guides for the Nursery Industry* are designed to foster and promote the maintenance of fair competitive conditions in the interest of protecting industry, trade, and the public. In general, the rules consider it an unfair trade practice to sell, offer for sale, or distribute industry products by any method, or under any circumstance or condition, which has the capacity and tendency or effect of deceiving purchasers or prospective purchasers as to quantity, size, grade, kind, species, age, maturity, condition, vigor, hardiness, number of times transplanted, growth ability, growth characteristics, rate of growth or time required before flowering or fruiting, price, origin or place where grown, or in any other material respect.

Among practices prohibited by the foregoing are direct or indirect representations: (1) that plants have been propagated by grafting or bud selection methods, when such is not the fact; (2) that industry products are healthy, will grow anywhere without the use of fertilizer, or will survive and produce without special care, when such is not the fact; (3) that plants will bloom the year round, or will bear an extraordinary number of blooms of unusual size or quality, when such is not the fact; (4) that an industry product is a new variety, when in fact it is a standard variety to which the industry member has given a new name; (5) that an industry product cannot be purchased through usual retail outlets, or that there are limited stocks available, when such is not the fact; (6) that industry products offered for sale will be delivered in time for the next (or any specified) seasonal planting when the industry member is aware of factors that make such delivery improbable; (7) that the appearance of an industry product as to size, color, contour, foliage, bloom, fruit, or other physical characteristic is normal or usual when the appearance so represented is in fact abnormal or unusual; (8) that the root system of any plant is larger in depth or diameter than that which actually exists, whether accomplished by excessive packing material, or excessive balling, or other deceptive or misleading practice; (9) that bulblets are bulbs; and (10) that an industry product is a rare or unusual item, when such is not the fact.

All commercial nurseries should have a copy and be familiar with the trade practice rules for the nursery industry. Copies of the rules may be obtained from the FTC.

STATE AND LOCAL LAWS

Most states have laws related to (1) environmental pesticides; (2) labor standards; (3) liens; (4) licenses; (5) occupational safety; (6) pest control, including diseases, insects, and vertebrates (deer, rodents, birds, etc.); and (7) sales taxes.

In some states wholesale nurserymen are required to collect a sales tax on gross in-state sales unless they are presented with a copy of a resale certificate, a farmer's exemption certificate, an exempt use certificate, an exempt organization certification, a direct payment permit, or identification of the purchaser as a government agency. Out-of-state customers are exempt from the tax except when the plants are delivered to a point in or picked up in the state of sale.

Municipal laws affecting nurserymen generally relate to licenses, property zoning, and road limitations. Information on these laws and regulations can be obtained, from state nurserymen's associations, the state department of agriculture, and various units of local government, especially the city or township clerk.

STANDARDS

American Standards for Nursery Stock, sponsored by the AAN is the recognized standard for nursery stock in the United States and is designed for the improvement and standardization of nursery products. The standards have been very effective in establishing grades for deciduous shade and flowering trees, deciduous shrubs, coniferous and broadleaved evergreens, roses, vines and ground covers, fruit trees, small fruits, lining-out stock, seedlings, bulbs, corms, and tubers. In addition, they set standards for the minimum size of root system for ornamental plants of all types. The standards are used by most buyers and sellers of nursery stock, but they should be used only for the minimum acceptable size and quality of plants.

Where minimum–maximum size ranges are stated, an average size is required. That is, one hundred 6- to 8-ft trees are ordered, the plants should average about 7 ft, not just make grade at 6 ft. Since it is almost impossible to establish standards for quality, it is necessary to rely on the integrity of the individual nurseryman, and where this is not forthcoming, to seek other sources of supply.

The standards have been changed periodically over the years since they were established in 1923, and undoubtedly they will be modified in the years ahead. The latest edition (Z60.1 1973) has included standards for container-grown stock. Copies of the standards may be obtained from the AAN.

Deciduous Trees

Caliper of the trunk shall be the determining measurement in grading deciduous shade and flowering trees. The measurement should be made 6 in. above ground level for trees up to and including those 4 in. in diameter. Above this size the measurement is to be made 12 in. above the ground (Fig. 6-1). Caliper is stated in $\frac{1}{4}$-in. units up to 2-in. size, in $\frac{1}{2}$-in. units up to 4-in. size, and in 1-in. units above 4 in. (e.g., $1\frac{1}{4}$-$1\frac{1}{2}$ in., 2-$2\frac{1}{2}$ in., 5-6 in.). The standard recognizes four major types (standard shade trees, slow-growth shade trees, small upright trees, and small spreading trees) and suggests optimum and maximum heights and minimum root spread for trees of various caliper within each type. Height is quoted in single-foot units up to 6 ft and in double-foot units over 6 ft (e.g., 5-6 ft, 6-8 ft).

Deciduous Shrubs

Deciduous shrubs are graded by height and number of canes or stems (Fig. 6-2). The height classes for dwarf or semidwarf shrubs should be stated in inches up to 24 in. (3-in. units up to 18 in., 6-in. units between 18 and 24 in.), and $\frac{1}{2}$-ft units over 6 ft (e.g., 12-15 in., 18-24 in., and 2-$2\frac{1}{2}$ ft). Height classes for strong-growing

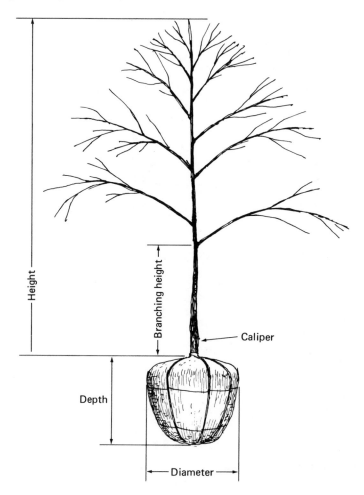

Figure 6-1 Caliper measured 6 in. above ground level if 4 in. or less; if more than 4 in. measure at 12 in.; caliper determines size of rootball (see Table 6-1). (Source: American Standards for Nursery Stock.)

shrubs should be stated in 6-in. series up to 24 in., single-foot units between 2 and 6 ft, and in double-foot units above 6 ft (e.g., 12–18 in., 4–5 ft, and 6–8 ft). The standards suggest a minimum root spread and indicate that the average height of a grade should be close to the mean of the height class (e.g., size of plant, 4–5 ft; minimum root spread, 14 in., and average height, $4\frac{1}{2}$ ft).

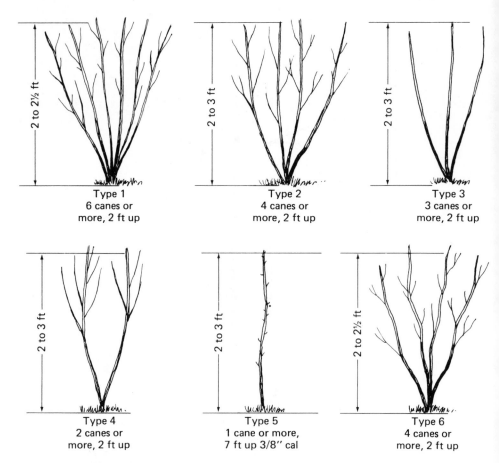

Figure 6-2 Comparisons in the various types of deciduous shrubs. (Source: American Standards for Nursery Stock.)

Evergreens

Evergreens (Fig. 6-3) are divided into conifers and broadleaf, and each group is subdivided into types based on habit of growth. The types include:

Conifer

Creeping or prostrate
Semispreading

Figure 6–3 Cone or pyramidal type evergreen. (Source: American Standards for Nursery Stock.)

Broad spreading, globe, and upright dwarf
Cone (pyramidal)
Broad upright
Columnar

Broadleaf

Spreading
Semispreading
Globe and dwarf
Broad upright
Cone

The height or spread in each group is stated using 3-in., 6-in., 1-ft, and 2-ft intervals. The interval varies with type, but the following intervals are fairly standard.

3-in. intervals up to 18 in.	12–15 in.
6-in. intervals between 18 in. and 4 ft	$2\frac{1}{2}$–3 ft
1-ft intervals from 4 ft up	5–6 ft

Measurement of height is determined from where the branches start, not at ground level, if the plant is leggy. It should also stop where the main part of the plant ends, not at the tip of a shoot.

Christmas Trees

Nurserymen interested in standards for Christmas trees should write to the Consumer and Marketing Service, U.S. Department of Agriculture, Washington, D.C. 20250, and request a copy of "United States Standards for Grades of Christmas Trees."

Rose Grades

Rose standards apply only to 2-year-old field-grown roses when sold either bare-root or individually wrapped and packaged or in cartons. Roses are graded by size, number, and length of canes. Consideration is also given to weight and caliper of canes, depending upon grade and variety. The basic rose grades are No. 1, No. $1\frac{1}{2}$, and No. 2. Each grade must have a minimum number of strong canes, generally 3, of a certain length and in each case branched not higher than 3 in. above the bud union (Fig. 6-4). All No. 1 and No. $1\frac{1}{2}$ grades shall be tied 10 to a bundle and No. 2 grades 20 to a bundle, with two printed variety labels and a grade specification label on each bundle.

Fruit Tree Grades

Caliper is the basic standard for fruit trees and should be taken 2 in. above the collar or bud. It is generally stated in sixteenths of an inch; classes being stated in the odd-number series (e.g., $\frac{5}{16}$ to $\frac{7}{16}$, $\frac{9}{16}$ to $\frac{11}{16}$). In the three West Coast states, 1-year-old standard fruit tree stocks are commonly graded in intervals of $\frac{1}{8}$ in. Trees should have reasonably straight stems, and all grades $\frac{5}{16}$ and larger (except 1-year sweet cherries) should be branched and well rooted. Fruit trees are tied 10 or 20 to a bundle, depending upon size and identified with two printed labels.

18 in.

15 in.

12 in.

Maximum   3 in.

No. 1   No. 1½   No. 2

Figure 6-4 Comparisons in No. 1, No. 1½, and No. 2 Hybrid
Tea, Tea, and Grandiflorce roses. (Source: American Standards
for Nursery Stock.)

Balling and Burlapping

Balling and burlapping (B&B) of trees and shrubs is one means of
packaging plants for market. It is a practice associated with large
trees and with evergreens of various sizes. Although plants can be
successfully transplanted without a large ball of earth, it has become
an accepted practice to transplant large trees B&B.

American Standards for Nursery Stock recommends minimum
sizes of balls for five general plant types (Table 6–1). Although the
recommendations are for plants that have been field-grown under
favorable conditions, it is recognized that the root system of plants
varies with species, soil conditions, and cultural practices, and that
the ultimate size of the ball depends largely upon the integrity of the
nurseryman. However, ball sizes should always be of a diameter and
depth large enough to obtain the fibrous roots necessary to assure

Table 6-1 Recommended balling and burlapping specifications for five general types of plants

Spreading conifer and broadleaved evergreens		Cone and broad upright conifers and broad-leaved evergreens		Columnar evergreens		Shrubs and small trees		Standard shade trees	
Spread (ft)	Diam. (in.)	Height (ft)	Diam. (in.)	Height (ft)	Diam. (in.)	Height (ft)	Diam. (in.)	Caliper (in.)	Diam. (in.)
1½-2	10	1½-2	10	1½-2	10	1½-2	9	1¼-1½	18
2-2½	12	2-3	12	2-3	12	2-3	10	1½-1¾	20
2½-3	14	3-4	14	3-4	13	3-4	12	1¾-2	22
3-3½	16	4-5	16	4-5	14	4-5	14	2-2½	24
3½-4	18	5-6	20	5-6	16	5-6	16	2½-3	28
4-5	21	6-7	22	6-7	18	6-7	18	3-3½	32
5-6	24	7-8	24	7-8	20	7-8	20	3½-4	38
6-7	28	8-9	27	8-9	22	8-9	22	4-4½	42
7-8	32	9-10	30	9-10	24	9-10	24	4½-5	48
8-9	36	10-12	33	10-12	27	10-12	26	5-5½	54
		12-14	38	12-14	30				
		14-16	42	14-16	33				
				16-18	36				
				18-20	40				

SOURCE: American Standards for Nursery Stock.

Table 6-2 Ball diameter/depth ratios for
B&B plants

Diameter of ball (in.)	Depth of ball
Less than 20	Not less than 3/4 of diameter
20–30	Not less than 2/3 of diameter
31–48	Not less than 3/5 of diameter

SOURCE: American Standards for Nursery Stock, 1973.

successful transplanting. The depth of the ball may vary with tree species, soil type, and the area of the country where the tree grows. The diameter/depth ratios in Table 6-2 can be used as a guide in balling plants.

METRIC EQUIVALENTS*

The United States is the one remaining major nation in the world that has neither adopted the metric system nor established a time schedule for conversion. Nevertheless, nurserymen who do business with foreign countries need a conversion table to convert imperial units to metric units or metric units to imperial units. Table 6-3, listing approximate metric units, is suggested for use in grading nursery stock either by caliper, height, spread, or size classes.

CODES

Various codes, including numbers, colors, and letters, are used in the nursery and landscape industry for many purposes.

Numbers are used by many nurseries that use electronic data processing equipment to code the plant material by species, cultivar, and grade, to expedite processing. The order forms of some firms are specially designed to simplify ordering and to speed processing. Prepunched IBM cards can be rapidly assembled into an "order deck" to rapidly and accurately prepare the necessary documents to process the order.

*See Appendix D for metric conversions.

Table 6-3 Metric conversions for nursery stock graded by caliper, height, spread, and size class

			Nursery stock size classes	
Imperial	*Metric*	*Approx. metric*	*Imperial*	*Approx. metric*
Inches	*Centimeters*	*Centimeters*	*Inches*	*Centimeters*
0.5	1.27	1.5	3–6	8–15
1	2.54	2.5	6–9	15–25
1.5	3.81	4.0	9–12	25–30
2	5.08	5.0	12–15	30–40
2.5	6.35	6.0	12–18	30–50
3	7.62	8.0	15–18	40–50
3.5	8.89	9.0	18–24	50–60
4	10.16	10.0		
4.5	11.43	11.0	*Feet*	
5	12.70	13.0	2–2½	60–80
5.5	13.97	14.0	2–3	60–90
6	15.24	15.0	2½–3	80–90
6.5	16.51	16.0	3–3½	90–100
7	17.78	18.0		
8	20.32	20.0		*Meters*
10	25.40	25.0	3½–4	1.00–1.25
12	30.48	30.0	4–5	1.25–1.50
15	38.10	40.0	5–6	1.50–1.75
18	45.72	50.0	6–8	1.75–2.50
			8–10	2.50–3.00
Feet			10–12	3.00–3.50
2	60.98	60.0	12–14	3.50–4.00
2.5	76.20	80.0	14–16	4.00–5.00
3.0	91.44	90.0	16–18	5.00–5.50
			18–20	5.50–6.00
	Meters	*Meters*		
3.5	1.07	1.00		
4	1.22	1.25		
5	1.52	1.50		
6	1.82	1.75		
7	2.13	2.00		
8	2.44	2.50		
9	2.94	2.75		
10	3.05	3.00		
12	3.66	3.50		
14	4.27	4.00		
16	4.88	5.00		
18	5.48	5.50		
20	6.09	6.00		

*See Appendix D for metric conversions.

Climatic zones within the United States and Canada are designed by number (Fig. 6-5). These zone numbers are used by nurserymen to designate areas of the country where their plants are expected to be hardy and where the plants will make optimum growth. The zones are also used in planning shipping schedules for spring and fall deliveries. Zip-code numbers are used by mail-order nurserymen when processing their mailings to gain financial advantages by bulk mailing.

Numbers are also used to identify or code orders, estimates, employees, equipment, and prices. Where orders are identified by number, a convenient practice is to combine the order number and the date received or processed into a date–order number by year, month, day, order (e.g., 78-07-20-333). This not only provides immediate identification of the order but provides a rapid means by which sales or purchases can be analyzed by any desired time period.

Prices can be coded by numbers to fit the needs of the nursery. One effective method is to designate that the last digit of a number series be the number of dimes and all previous digits indicate the number of dollars. For example, a price code number 176 means that the wholesale price is $17.60, and the code 100 means that the wholesale price is $10. Various modifications can be made to this system.

Seedlings and transplants are commonly coded by number to indicate the number of years in a seed or transplant bed (e.g., 2-1 indicates 2 years in seedbed, 1 year in transplant bed; 2-0 indicates 2-year seedling).

Color is used to aid in the rapid identification of items. Colored tapes or flagging are used to identify specific plants in the nursery that have been selected by or for a customer. It is a good practice to reserve one color tape (e.g., red-striped) for use in identifying plants that are to be rogued from the nursery or a landscape planting. This specific tape should never be used for any other purpose. Colored tape is used to identify female plants of a dioecious species (e.g., holly). This aids in identifying female plants when they are not in flower or fruit.

Colored labels can be used to identify size classes to expedite the assembling of orders by inexperienced help. They have also been used by bedding plant growers to identify plants of a certain price. For example, plants priced at $2.50 per flat may have a blue label, whereas plants priced at $3.00 per flat may have a red label, and so on.

Another use for color coding is for the identification of clones, particularly of deciduous species during the dormant period. Color codes can be used to excellent advantage in coding scion wood and

Figure 6-5 The Plant Hardiness Zone Map illustrates the expected minimum temperatures of most of the horticulturally important areas of the United States (excluding Alaska and Hawaii) and Canada. It shows 10 different zones, each of which represents an area of winter hardiness for certain ornamental plants. (Source: USDA—Agricultural Research Service, Misc. Publ. 814.)

APPROXIMATE RANGE OF
AVERAGE ANNUAL MINIMUM
TEMPERATURES FOR EACH ZONE

ZONE 1   BELOW −50°F
ZONE 2   −50° TO −40°
ZONE 3   −40° TO −30°
ZONE 4   −30° TO −20°
ZONE 5   −20° TO −10°
ZONE 6   −10° TO 0°
ZONE 7   0° TO 10°
ZONE 8   10° TO 20°
ZONE 9   20° TO 30°
ZONE 10 30° TO 40°

understocks, especially when a number of different clones are involved, as in the grafting or budding of fruit tree varieties on clonal understocks. Color-coded fruit trees are appreciated by orchardists, who must make large plantings with inexperienced help. The color codes are best applied with spray paint.

Some nurseries, particularly landscape nurseries, use distinctive colors to identify their tools and equipment to avoid loss while working on jobs with other contractors. Distinctive colors are also used to identify special equipment that should be used for only certain jobs, such as sprayers to apply 2,4-D-type herbicides.

Colored forms or tabs can be used to expedite the processing of orders or messages within the office. Many nurseries use specifically designed color-coded order forms for this purpose. The various colored sheets within a set of forms aid in identifying the action to be taken. For example, a wholesale nursery may use a yellow form for the shipping and the receiving copy, a white form for the office copy, pink for order acknowledgment, and green for use by the shipping department. A landscape firm can use various colored forms to control and coordinate landscape sales (e.g., white—sales record, orange—nursery division, green—construction division, pink—record division, etc.).

Certain *abbreviations* are used as standard practice in the nursery industry, although there is some variation between nurseries. Some of the more common abbreviations are:

B	Budded
B&B	Balled-and-burlapped
B&P	Balled-and-potted
BR	Bare-root
C	Cutting
CAL	Caliper
CG	Container-grown
COLL	Collected plants from native stands
DBH	Diameter Breast Height
FP	Field-potted
FR	Field row or field run
G	Grafted
HT	Hybrid tea
PB	Peat-balled
RP	Rose pot or root-pruned
S	Seedling
SPEC	Specimen
Std	Standard

| T, TT | One for each time transplanted |
| X, XX, XXX | Used to designate degree of heavy grades; some nurseries use this symbol to indicate number of times transplanted |

An example: *Picea pungens* Moerheim, G, 10–12, 4 yr, TT. This is a Moerheim blue spruce that was grafted, transplanted twice, is now 4 years old, and averages 10–12 in. in height.

SUMMARY

Nurserymen must comply with a number of federal, state, and local laws and regulations. These have been summarized briefly within the chapter. Since laws and regulations are subject to modification with time, it is desirable that nursery managers keep informed of changes that will affect their nurseries. This is best accomplished by maintaining membership in the AAN as well as in various state and local nursery associations. Nursery standards are used within the industry as a guide to facilitate trading in nursery stock. All buyers and producers of nursery stock should be familiar with the standards. They should obtain copies of the latest editions, which are published by the AAN. Codes, including numbers, colors, and abbreviations, are used within the industry for many reasons. Where standard codes exist, they should be utilized.

REFERENCES

AMERICAN ASSOCIATION OF NURSERYMEN. 1973. American Standards for Nursery Stock. AAN 230 Southern Bldg. Wash. D.C. 20005.

——. 1975. The Federal Warranty Act. ALI 2(4):4.

——. 1975. Buyers and sellers beware. ALI 2(4):16.

ANONYMOUS. 1970. Plant Patents. U.S. Department of Commerce.

FLEMING, W. E. 1972. Preventing Japanese beetle dispersion by farm products and nursery stock. Agric. Res. Serv. USDA Tech. Bull. 1441.

GUIDES FOR THE NURSERY INDUSTRY. Federal Register Vol. 44, No. 40, Feb. 27, 1979, pp. 11177–11179.

LEVERETT, E. J., JR., and J. H. PADGETT. 1972. Complying with the occupational safety and health act. Am. Nurseryman 135(11):10.

MOREFIELD, K. R. 1972. OSHA and Nurseries. Am. Nurserymen 136(4):28.

——.1974. Wage Hour Laws, ALI 1(1):5.

PUBLIC LAWS 1912. An act to regulate the importation of nursery stock. U.S. Statutes at Large. 62nd Congress. Vol 31, part I, pp. 315-319.

PUBLIC LAWS 1930. Plant Patents Act. U.S. Statutes at Large. Vol. 46, part I, Chapter 312, p. 376.

PUBLIC LAWS 1935. Social Security Act. U.S. Statutes at Large. 74th Congress. Vol. 49, part I, pp. 620-648.

PUBLIC LAWS 1938. Fair Labor Standards Act. U.S. Statutes at Large. 75th Congress, 3rd Session. Vol. 52, pp. 1060-1069.

PUBLIC LAWS 775. 1954. Plant Patents. U.S. Statutes at Large. Vol. 68, part I, Chapter 1259, p. 1190.

PUBLIC LAW 85-36. 1957. Federal Plant Pest Act. U.S. Statutes at Large. 85th Congress. Vol. 71, pp. 31-35.

PUBLIC LAW 88-582. 1964. Farm Labor Contractors Registration Act. (PL88-582). U.S. Statutes at Large. Vol. 78, pp. 920-924.

PUBLIC LAW 91-596. 1970. Occupational Safety and Health Act. U.S. Statutes at Large. 91st Congress. Vol. 84, pp. 1590-1620.

PUBLIC LAW 92-516. 1972. Federal Environmental Pesticide Control Act. U.S. Statutes at Large, 92nd Congress. Vol. 86, pp. 973-999.

SIMPSON, R. C. 1973. Understanding quarantine effects. (Reported by H. G. Tilson.) Am. Nurseryman 137(10):74.

Chapter 7

Financial Management

The need for proper management of money and the effective evaluation of sources of money is essential to the life of any business. The growth of a nursery results in increasingly complex financial management. To properly develop and manage the financial aspects of a nursery business, nursery managers should have the services of a lawyer and an accountant and understand the appropriate management use of the information provided by these professionals.

FUNCTION OF FINANCIAL RECORDS

The importance of financial management cannot be overemphasized. Money is used to purchase labor, materials, and in some cases management and technical expertise necessary to start and operate a nursery. Financial statements and records are used to measure the current health and past accomplishments of the nursery firm, to determine the appropriate income tax liability, and to assist in securing the additional financial support needed for a growing business. They may also be used to help predict the growth potential of the nursery and to help identify those divisions of the nursery with the greatest potential for profit. Financial records are one of the major sources of information needed in the management of a nursery. Their accuracy and historical nature, however, can be misleading, and they should not be the only factor in making decisions. Financial records are not a substitute for good judgment and experience in nursery production, marketing, and personnel management.

FINANCING A NURSERY BUSINESS

Money is needed to finance the purchase of equipment, land, structures, supplies, and labor necessary to begin to produce nursery crops. A nursery manager usually has three potential sources of funds needed to establish and operate a nursery business (Fig. 7–1):

1. *The owner's personal savings:* The owner's investment of personal savings demonstrates his or her commitment to the business and ability to earn and save, both of which are important in developing proper personal and business credit ratings needed to obtain future financing.

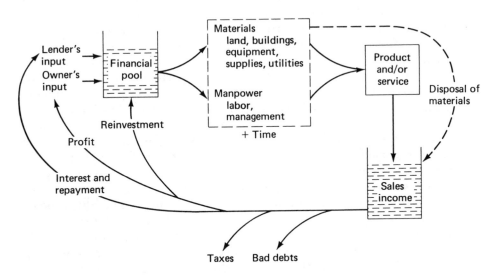

Figure 7-1 Business cash-flow cycle.

2. *Funds generated in the nursery through profit and depreciation accounts:* The sale of products and services in a business produces money needed for general payment of taxes, cost of bad debts, interest and loan repayment, profit, and depreciation. Depreciation allowances are charged against sales income each year to purchase and replace the equipment, buildings, and facilities when they have worn out and are no longer functional. In rapidly expanding and profitable nurseries, capital needs may frequently rise more rapidly each year than can be provided by profits and depreciation allowances from the nursery.

3. *Borrowed funds:* Borrowed funds are used both to initiate and, in most cases, to operate a nursery. There are a variety of sources of borrowed financing available to the nursery manager, including partnerships, contract growing, and loans from a variety of financial institutions.

Partnerships

Partnerships can be developed for the purpose of obtaining additional funds for capital investments. This normally involves sharing management decisions and profits with all full partners. A successful business partnership usually requires that the partners have separate and well-defined management responsibilities. A partner supplying only financial resources may become less desirable when at a later date these financial resources are no longer needed. This problem is alleviated by developing limited partnerships for a specific investment in a crop. Limited partnerships permit the principal partner to retain almost complete management control at all times. Limited partners may invest in a specific crop which the nursery plants, maintains, harvests, and markets for the partnership. The terms of the partnership agreement should specify the yearly investments required of the limited partner, the services provided by the nursery, the terms of marketing, and the distribution of profits. Limited partnerships are difficult to develop for a new firm, because the investor considering a limited partnership is usually relying on the principal partner's demonstrated nursery management ability as partial security for the investment. Certain income tax advantages can be provided to the limited partner, which may make this type of investment appealing to the investor. Limited partnerships may also be developed to allow key employees or individuals with valuable technical expertise to become involved in the financing and management of a division of the firm. In this case the primary purpose of the partnership may be to obtain expertise or to retain and motivate a valuable employee rather than to obtain financing, even though the employee invests funds in the firm and shares in the profits derived from the limited partnership.

Contract Growing

Another source of funds, called *contract growing,* involves using capital obtained from other firms which are marketing nursery stock. A manager may contract to produce a specific crop at a specified price for another firm in return for receiving the financing necessary to produce the crop. In some cases the marketing firm may provide the plants, supplies, and equipment needed to produce the crop. The firm loaning the money receives the benefit of having the entire crop at a specified price (a hedge against inflation) to complete the range of nursery products it markets, whereas the nursery receives the benefit of the financing and a guaranteed market for the crop. Contract growing agreements generally require that the nursery manager producing the crop share some of his management control in return for capital financing.

Borrowing from Financial Institutions

A nursery manager may also borrow money from a number of traditional financial institutions. Borrowing from a financial institution involves obtaining capital to be repaid with interest on a specified schedule in an agreement or note signed by the nursery manager and the creditor. One of the advantages of borrowed funds is that the nursery manager does not share management control with creditors as is usually the case with contract growing or partnerships.

In most cases, buildings, land, nursery stock, equipment, or other assets which are owned either by the nursery or by the owner of the nursery are placed as security or collateral for the loan. If the loan is not repaid as agreed, the ownership of these assets or property is transferred to the financial institution and can be sold to repay the loan. The value of the assets or property identified as collateral must be such that the loan can be repaid even if the assets are under an unfavorable forced-sale condition. Since creditors have a prior claim on the income and assets of the nursery, they will usually accept a relatively lower rate of return in comparison to contract growing agreements. The identification of the amount, duration, and purpose of the loan (Table 7–1) plus a knowledge of the nursery's ability to repay the loan allows for a better understanding and evaluation of the credit status by both the owner and the lender.

Table 7-1 Classification of business loans

I. *Time*

Short-term loans (up to 1 year)

Used to finance working capital during short periods of high expense and low income. Bankers will generally lend up to 80% of accounts receivable.

Intermediate loans (1–5 years)

Used to finance equipment. Bankers may supply up to 90% of the value of the equipment being purchased.

Long-term loans (5 years or more)

Used to finance land, buildings, and other capital improvement or expansion. Bankers may supply up to 60–70% of the assessed value (not market value) of property and real estate.

II. *Security provided*

Real estate

Crop

Stocks and bonds

Equipment

III. *Type of lender*

Banks

Government agencies

Finance companies

Private individuals

Private businesses

IV. *Purpose of loan*

1. Purchase real estate, such as additional land; greenhouses; storage facilities; lath or shade facilities; install drainage for production field; and so on.
2. Purchase lining-out stock, fertilizer spray materials, equipment, and so on.
3. Pay labor and management.

SOURCE: Murray, William G., and Aaron G. Nelson. 1960. Agricultural Finance. Ames, Iowa: Iowa State University Press.

EVALUATION OF ALTERNATIVE INVESTMENTS

The nursery manager must determine the best expenditure for the limited capital available before approaching financial institutions or any other source of funds. Not all of the potential capital investments that can be outlined by a nursery manager can or should be financed. Capital investments must be thoroughly evaluated by the manager to ensure the sound financial management of the nursery. The evaluation procedure has a number of logical steps, each of which is essential if the proper management decisions are to be made.

The initial step is a thorough search within the nursery for all possible profitable investments for the available capital. A nursery manager has alternative crops to produce, requiring different types of production and harvesting equipment, storage and packaging facilities, and labor requirements. These alternative investments must be described in detail. The total capital required and the added earnings expected (cash flow) should be forecast for each alternative investment. Once this information is available, a realistic estimate can be made of the economic benefit of each investment. Profit may not be the only factor considered; the impact of income taxes and other taxes, as well as the future growth and ability to provide a stable future income, may play a major role in the selection of an investment. The actual decision must be based, at least in part, on the economic forecast for each potential investment in a crop, type of equipment, or facility.

There are a number of methods for measuring or comparing the potential economic benefit for alternative nursery investments. These methods of analysis vary considerably in their complexity and reliability. It should be kept in mind, however, that detailed methods of comparison are no substitute for realistic estimates of potential earnings, costs, and a complete consideration of all the alternatives. No decision can be any better than the data used in making that decision.

Urgency Analysis of Alternative Investments

Some nursery managers, particularly in the early stages of the growth of the firm, tend to evaluate a potential investment in a crop or type of equipment only when presented with a crisis deadline. For example, a nursery manager may discover that as a result of overproduction, rooted juniper cuttings must either be sold substantially below cost, planted in the nursery's own production fields, or destroyed. The decision must be made within a few weeks or the sales and planting season will be past and the plants will be worthless. The urgency of the decision and involvement in the sales and planting activities frequently precludes consideration of long-term management goals and alternative crops that might be produced. The decision to plant the rooted cuttings is frequently made even though the manager is aware that they may well be beyond his or her current and projected ability to profitably market them.

Not all investment decisions based on how urgently the investment is needed are unprofitable, nor are they necessarily less profitable than decisions that may be made with other criteria. Some decisions must be faced without taking the time to consider alternatives. For example, if a tree-digging machine breaks down during the digging season and is beyond repair, a replacement must be purchased immediately to allow harvesting to proceed. Making an investment based on how urgently the investment is required is not always undesirable, but may be inappropriate for long-term investments and is an inappropriate substitute for good financial management.

Payback-Period Analysis of Alternative Investments

A second method of capital investment analysis involves the determination of the payback period for alternative investments. The *payback period* is the time it takes for earnings from the investment to pay back the entire initial investment. For example, a nurseryman might have the opportunity to produce and market $4\frac{1}{2}$-in. caliper shade trees. The manager could either buy 2- to $2\frac{1}{2}$-in. caliper trees or buy 6- to 8-ft whips, to begin to produce the trees. Purchasing 6- to 8-ft whips might require a 10-year production period with additional investments each year in cultural care and land cost. The $2\frac{1}{2}$-in. caliper trees might require only a 5- to 6-year production period, with yearly investments for cultural care for only a 5- or 6-year production period. Since no earnings are received until the $4\frac{1}{2}$-in. trees are sold, the planting of $2\frac{1}{2}$-in. caliper trees has the shortest payback period (5 or 6 years versus 10 years). Payback period, however, may be unrelated to the potential profit that could be earned with the alternative investment proposals. Tree whips, might be purchased for $5.00 each, and the same variety at a $2\frac{1}{2}$-in.-caliper size might cost $27.50 each. Not only are the 6- to 8-ft tree whips substantially cheaper to purchase, they would cost less to ship and plant and might have a higher survival rate after planting. The 6- to to 8-ft whips could produce a greater profit even though they require a longer investment period.

The payback period method measures how quickly an investment can be converted to cash and is, therefore, a measure of the firm's liquidity (the relative ability to convert assets into cash) or financial flexibility rather than profit. There may be management advantages in having increased flexibility provided by shorter-term investments as compared to long-term investments, but this advantage should not be confused with the profitability of a potential investment. It is also more difficult to forecast the marketability of a nursery crop many years in the future for a long-term crop investment, increasing the risk involved as compared to short-term crop investments.

Simple-Rate-of-Return Analysis
of Alternative Investments

A third method for analyzing alternative investment opportunities is to compare the *simple rate of return* on an average yearly basis. Consider the following investments. An investment in tree-digging machine A of $25,000 will produce additional earnings (savings in labor) of $7500 per year. The depreciation is $5000 per year over an expected machine life of 5 years. The simple rate of return for machine A is:

$$\frac{\text{additional earnings} - \text{depreciation}}{\text{total investment}} = \text{percentage annual rate of return}$$

$$\frac{7500 - 5000}{25,000} \times 100 = 10\% \text{ rate of return}$$

Ten percent is the average annual rate of return for this particular investment. An alternative investment could be made in a more efficient machine, B, which could only be leased. This machine would cost $6400 per year and provide earnings of $8000 per year. The simple rate of return would be

$$\frac{\$8000 - 6400}{\$6400} \times 100 \quad \text{or} \quad 25\%$$

Therefore, even though machine B would produce only $500 more per year in earnings than machine A, its simple rate of return on invested money would be 25%, as compared to 10% for machine A. The simple rate of return indicates which investment would provide the largest added earnings on a yearly basis.

The simple rate-of-return analysis, however, is not really comparable to interest rates on borrowed funds, because the total investment is not made for the life of the machine. The entire $25,000 investment in machine A is not utilized for the full 5-year period. In fact, during the last (or fifth) year of use, the remaining investment is only $5000 and the additional earnings are $7500.

Discounted-Cash-Flow Analysis
of Alternative Investments

A *discounted-cash-flow analysis* (DCF analysis) accounts for the size of investments, their length, and the date they are made, as well as the amount and date that income occurs. The profit from a potential investment in the nursery is compared by DCF analysis to the profit

131

that could be derived by investing the same sum at a fixed rate of interest in a bank or elsewhere.

DCF analysis allows for the direct comparison of two nursery investments that have different investment schedules, differing rates, and dates of earning income. For example, a $1000 income at the end of 5 years is not comparable to a $200 income per year for 5 years, even though they both provide $1000 in income for a 5-year investment. Incomes and investments can be directly compared only if they all can be adjusted in value to the present time. For example, the present value of a $1000 income to be earned 5 years from now can be viewed as the amount of money that must be invested now in order to grow to $1000 at a compound interest rate (using the current rate of interest offered by banks). The amount of money that must be invested to obtain a specific income in 5 years can be obtained by multiplying the income by a discount factor for compound interest rates (discount factors are available in table form for a variety of interest rates and years, see Appendix K and Aplin and Casler, 1973). The discount factor for 7.5% compound interest for 5 years is $1/(1 + 0.075)^5$, or 0.6964. Multiplying the 5-year 7.5% compound interest discounting factor of 0.6964 times $1000 produces a present value of $696.40. Another way of saying the same thing is that a present investment of $696.40 at an annual 7.5% compound interest will produce $1000 in 5 years. An income of $200 per year for 5 years can be assigned a present value in a similar manner. Each $200 annual income is adjusted to present value by multiplying times the appropriate discounting factor (percent interest and years). These present values are added to determine the present values of the $200 per year for 5 years (Table 7-2). DCF analysis indicates that $808.95 must be invested at 7.5% compound interest in order to provide an income of $200 per year for 5 years.

The present value of $1000 income at the end of 5 years is $696.40, whereas the present value of an income of $200 per year for 5 years is $808.95, indicating the desirability or increased value of the $200 income per year for 5 years.

Investments of varying duration can also be compared by adjusting them to present values. To compare a $1000 investment for 5 years, it is discounted in the same manner used in comparing incomes in Table 7-2. Investments of outflow in a cash-flow table are assigned negative values to distinguish them from income. Therefore, a $1000 investment for 5 years has a present cost (negative value) of -$1000, whereas a $200 per year investment for each of 5 years has a present cost (negative value) of -$808.94.

The DCF analysis shown in Table 7-2 can also be calculated using the present-value-of-annuity formula:

Table 7-2 Discounted-cash-flow analysis of the present value of $200 income per year for 5 years

Year	Income	Discounting factor	Present value
1	$200	0.9302	$186.04
2	200	0.8651	173.02
3	200	0.8045	160.90
4	200	0.7485	149.70
5	200	0.6964	139.28
			$808.94

$$Pv = \frac{a\,[1 - (1 + i)^N]}{i}$$

$$Pv = 200 \times 4.0470 = 808.94$$

where Pv = present value
a = periodic investment
i = interest rate
N = years

Break-Even-Point Analysis

Investment analysis may also be used to answer the question: What is the most efficient rate of production? A *break-even analysis* is based on the fact that in each nursery operation there are fixed costs which do not change (within certain limits) as the volume of production either increases or decreases. These costs might include the cost of capital invested in equipment, buildings, and land. Variable costs, on the other hand, are directly tied to the volume of production and sales, increasing and decreasing in direct proportion to increases or decreases in volume. A break-even analysis requires the graphic display of fixed selling costs, cost of goods sold, variable selling costs, and net sales at two different volumes or rates of operation. Figure 7-2 shows a break-even analysis of a nursery having the following financial data at two different rates of production:

Total sales	$30,000	$95,000
Fixed costs	−15,000	−15,000
Variable costs	−23,000	−70,000
Net profit	−$8,000	+$10,000

The break-even point (intersection of total sales and total costs lines in Fig. 7–2) of these two programs is gross sales of $56,000, which occurs at a production of 2750 units. The assignment of a nursery selling cost as either fixed or variable is to some degree the result of management judgment. The costs illustrated in Fig. 7–2 approximate straight-line functions only for a narrow range of sales volume in a real nursery organization.

Sound financial management requires (1) a thorough search for alternative profitable investment opportunities, (2) an accurate forecast of investments required and potential economic benefit, and (3) the use of an appropriate investment analysis method. The final decision should be based on the investment analysis, as well as the manager's experience in production, marketing, personnel management, growth estimate of the entire nursery industry, and good judgment.

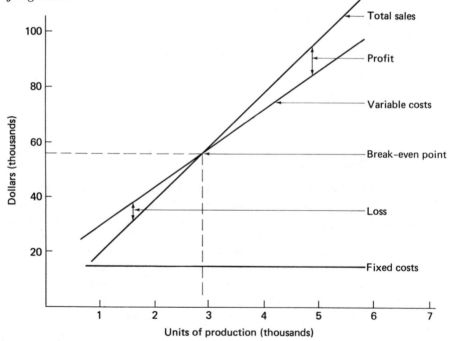

Figure 7-2 Break-even-point analysis.

NEGOTIATING A LOAN

Successful financial management usually requires the borrowing of funds from a variety of potential lending institutions. Most lenders will want financial data from the nursery, audited by a certified public accountant, as well as information concerning the ownership and management and the objectives of the proposed financing. The extent of information required will, in part, depend on the size and nature of the financial commitments.

Lending institutions are interested in the nature of the business organization (e.g., incorporation documents, corporate or business by-laws, lease agreement, and long-term contracts) and the history of the business requesting financing. They will also want to know as much as possible about the management of the firm; their personal and family backgrounds; biographical data, including relevant training and experience; evidence of personal character; and the financial status of owners and management. They will be interested in the possible replacement of key management personnel with other employees should they become incapacitated. The lending institution may be interested in the type of accounting system used, a current balance sheet (Chart 7-1), a profit and loss statement, (Chart 7-2), the relevant financial ratio analysis comparisons (Table 7-5), and the long- and short-range financial outlook of the entire nursery industry. They may also wish to see an audit of the accounts and past financial records of the firm.

The lenders will be interested in the objectives of the loan; the payback schedule; the projected budget, illustrating how the money will be used; and the resulting schedule of the investment. It may be beneficial to indicate alternative payback options that might be available as a result of changing the schedule of production, harvest, and sale of the nursery crop. The proposed budget should indicate the payback options of all other financial commitments in addition to the one being negotiated. The lenders will also be interested in the nature of proposed collateral, particularly an estimate of its forced liquidation value as well as the liquidity of all the assets of the nursery business. Other assets would include the volume and history of accounts receivable, owner's personal assets, value of equipment, vehicles, land, and buildings. The use of nursery stock as security or collateral for a loan requires that the nursery stock in the field be given an estimated forced-liquidation value.

ASSIGNING VALUE TO A NURSERY CROP IN THE FIELD

There are at least three ways to assign value to a nursery crop in the field. One system begins with the wholesale price of nursery stock of a similar size and grade, then subtracting a harvesting and selling cost to arrive at an "in-the-field" value. A manager might estimate that harvesting and marketing a particular nursery crop contributes 25% to the total cost of the crop. The in-the-field value of the crop would be 75% of the wholesale price. This method will include profit in the value assigned to the crop. A second method, based on costs of production, totals all production expenses, including labor, equipment, supplies, cost of land, taxes, and plants involved in developing the nursery crop to its present stage. This method will overestimate the value of the nursery crop when it is very young because the planting and cultural care may be substantial for the first 1 or 2 years, during which relatively little growth occurs (Fig. 7-3). Just before harvest, the crop is growing at a maximum rate and the cultural care tends to be at a minimum, making its sale value greater than production costs. However, if harvest is substantially delayed, the sale value of the crop may not continue to increase, because of reduced growth and quality resulting from crowding. An estimating method based on costs of production does not include profit in the estimated value of the nursery crop in the field, and could be very erroneous for recently planted crops.

A third method for assigning value to a nursery crop uses an outside consultant to provide a professional appraisal of what the spe-

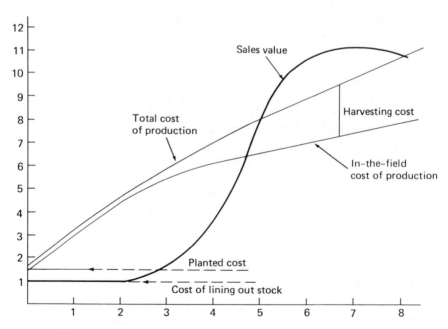

Figure 7-3 Cost of production versus sales value for field-grown nursery crops.

cific nursery crop would sell for in a forced sale. The value would be reduced by the auction sale expenses to develop an in-the-field value for the crop.

A reduction in the value of a nursery crop estimated by any of the foregoing methods may be taken to provide a conservative estimate of what the crop might be worth as a result of a forced sale. Nursery crops or any other item of collateral should be precisely defined, since the nursery would be turning over control of that crop to the lending institution if and when the terms of the loan were not met. Each block of nursery stock to be assigned as collateral should be inventoried and the block described by a surveyed description.

INFORMATION NEEDED ABOUT
THE LENDING INSTITUTION

The successful negotiation of a loan also requires that nurserymen know as much as possible about the lending institution. In many cases, the refusal of a loan has little to do with the quality of the firm and management requesting the loan, but is the result of regulations and limits set by the lending institution. A business manager requesting substantial financing should know the lending institution's loan limits (the maximum loan that can be made to one customer and the maximum length of time it will be loaned). Financial needs exceeding the institution's loan limit or time limit may require that the lender collaborate with other lending institutions.

The board of directors of the lending institution determines the broad guidelines and nature of the loans it will make. Each lending institution has an interest in specific types of business loans and is more inclined to make loans to these types of businesses than to others, because of a lack of confidence. The preparation of information and negotiation of loans is a time-consuming process, particularly for large, long-term, nursery-business loans. It would be desirable to work with a stable lending institution which does not frequently change its loan guidelines and has remained interested in loans to agricultural businesses for a long period of time. Those lending institutions having strong ties with agricultural industries will quite likely be more confident in making nursery-business loans.

It will save time and effort if the nursery manager knows the limits of the loan authority given to the individual representing the lending institution. Lending institutions usually have a loan committee that limits the amounts and length of time of loans granted by its employees. Potential loans beyond the limits, both in time and dollar amount, must be reviewed and authorized by the loan committee. The nursery manager will want to know how frequently the loan committee meets in order to estimate the time necessary to obtain financing beyond the limits of the individual representing the lending institution.

In negotiating a loan, it is usually most productive for the business manager to present the general purpose and nature of the financing needed and the supporting business information and documents. The specific terms of the loan should be negotiated rather than asking the lending institution to accept or reject a single specific proposal.

As in any business transaction, it is well to compare the financial services of competing lending institutions. The effective interest cost of the loan, the amount of collateral required, as well as any other conditions should be compared to the conditions offered by other financial institutions. Lending institutions vary considerably in their willingness to lend money to a specific type of business, and it is well worth the time spent in finding the institution most favorable to your business.

COMPUTING THE FUTURE COST OF A NURSERY CROP

A number of simple formulas can be used to calculate the return of a nursery crop investment. For example, 5000 *Taxus media* 'Hicks' are to be grown for 5 years. Assume that the transplants will cost 35 cents each and that it costs $150 to plant them. The annual cost of caring for these plants will be $500 for labor, $75 for materials, and $500 for overhead. All costs will be financed at 5% per year:*

$$
\begin{aligned}
5000 \text{ plants} \times 35 \text{ cents} &= \$1750 \\
\text{planting cost} \qquad\qquad &= \underline{150} \\
& \ \$1900
\end{aligned}
$$

The future value (in 5 years) of this investment at 5% interest can be calculated using the formula for *future value of invested capital:*

$$Cn = Co(1 + i)^n$$

where Cn = value of the invested capital at year n

Co = invested capital at year 0 (beginning of investment)

*Rates used are for illustrative purposes only. Actual rates vary with time and circumstance.

n = number of years of investment
i = interest rate per year

$$Cn = \$1900 \, (1 + 0.05)^5 = \$1900 \, (1.27628) = \$2420$$

The annual investments in caring for these plants are: labor, $500/year; materials, $75/year; and overhead, $500/year; or $1075/ year for 5 years. Projecting these annual costs forward 5 years with the future-value-of-annuity formula:

$$Fu = \frac{a \, [(1 + i)^n - 1)]}{i}$$

The maintenance costs equal $5940. The total investment in the plants after 5 years is $2420 + $5940 = $8360, or $1.67 per plant.

There is usually little reason to assign all assets of the nursery to the lending institution, even if the loan is substantial. The ratio of assets to loan value should be negotiated to allow for future financial flexibility. As the value of assets changes, increasing as in the case of growing nursery stock, it should be part of the loan agreement that some of the assets can be removed from the loan security. At certain times of the year, a nursery may have the opportunity to invest with the bank for relatively short periods of time when a positive cash flow condition exists. These investment opportunities could be part of the overall loan arrangements with the financial institution.

USING FINANCIAL INFORMATION TO EVALUATE MANAGEMENT

Evaluating the management of most nurseries is a very difficult task because of the complexity of nursery operation. In the United States there are relatively few production nurseries that produce only one product by a single system and sell their product to a single buyer at one time. Therefore, it is extremely difficult to determine the actual cost of production. Management is evaluated on how effectively they have managed all three factors of production and primarily on how much profit is generated. Two of the most valuable financial documents for evaluating management are a balance sheet and a profit and loss statement.

Balance Sheet

Sound financial management of a nursery requires the periodic evaluation of the financial well being or status of the firm. The operation of a nursery results in a constant change in the firm's assets, liabilities, and net worth (the difference between assets and liabilities). A *balance sheet,* prepared periodically by an accountant, is a statement of the financial status of the nursery on the date the balance sheet was prepared. By itself, it does not indicate the rate of change or even the direction of change of any of the assets or liabilities of the firm. Balance sheets are usually issued on a regular basis—monthly, quarterly, or annually—and are of greater significance when compared to similar reports for the same period of previous years.

The assets and liabilities recorded on the balance sheet are divided into current and long-term entries. If the item can be converted into cash within 1 year, it is considered current. This distinction helps to predict the current year's financial position as distinct from the long-range financial position of the firm. An example of the accounts that might be included in a production nursery business balance sheet are shown in Chart 7-1. The accounts shown are a uniform chart of accounts developed by the Horticultural Research Institute (HRI) and suggested for use by the entire nursery industry. The widespread use of a uniform chart of accounts would make the comparison of industry-wide financial ratio analysis (discussed later in the chapter) more reliable and efficient.

Profit-and-Loss Statement

One of the prime concerns of a nursery manager—the potential profit from the operation of the nursery—is not displayed on a balance sheet. An *income statement* or *profit-and-loss statement* combines the total sales over a period of time (month, quarter, or year) and subtracts the total expenses for the same period of time showing the profit or loss developed by the firm (Chart 7-2). This is one of the most important statements provided by an accountant. If the nursery is to survive for any length of time, it must show a profit. Management decisions to expand or change production, as well as the ability to obtain financing, will be influenced substantially by a profit-and-loss statement. To a creditor, the profit-and-loss statement will indicate the potential ability to pay back existing liabilities as well as additional loans.

Since profit, the reward for the risk of operating a commercial enterprise, is a measure by which a commercial nursery is evaluated, it is important to have an understanding of the various concepts of profit. The concept of what constitutes a profit varies with the accounting system, the age of the business, the age of the owner(s), and the legal type of organization of the business.

The interpretation of a profit-and-loss statement as well as other

UNIFORM ACCOUNTS — BALANCE SHEET ITEMS

1000 — CASH ASSETS
(Total of all cash accounts — Total, Series 1000)

1010	CHECKING ACCOUNT	Current balance in checking account
1020	SAVINGS ACCOUNT	Current balance in savings account
1030	PETTY CASH	Cash on hand for small payments

1100 — RECEIVABLES ASSETS
(Total of all receivables — Total, Series 1100)

1101	ACCOUNTS RECEIVABLE	Claims against debtors arising out of every day transactions
1130	NOTES RECEIVABLE — TRADE, CURRENT	Promissory notes held from trade
1150	ACCRUED INTEREST RECEIVABLES	Interest due but not collected
1190	RESERVE FOR BAD DEBTS	Reserve to offset estimated losses due to uncollectable accounts

1200 — INVENTORY ASSETS
(Total cost of inventories on hand — Total, Series 1200)

1201	GREEN GOODS	Cost of green goods on hand
1220	HARD GOODS	Cost of hard goods on hand
1230	CHRISTMAS ITEMS	Cost of Christmas items on hand
1240	FLORIST ITEMS	Cost of Florist items on hand
1250	PRODUCTION DEPARTMENT ITEMS	Cost of production items on hand
1260	SHIPPING & WAREHOUSING DEPARTMENT ITEMS	Cost of shipping & warehouse items on hand
1270	SALES DEPARTMENT ITEMS	Cost of selling items on hand
1280	ADMINISTRATIVE DEPARTMENT ITEMS	Cost of administrative items on hand
1290	RESERVE FOR INVENTORY LOSSES	Reserve to offset estimated losses from damage, obsolescence, pilferage etc.

1300 — PREPAID EXPENSE ASSETS
(Total of all prepaid items — Total, Series 1300)

1301	ADVERTISING	Advertising paid prior to due date
1310	INSURANCE	Paid prior to due date
1320	INTEREST	Paid prior to due date
1330	TAXES	Paid prior to due date

1400 — OTHER ASSETS
(Total of other assets — Total, Series 1400)

1401	NOTES RECEIVABLE - OTHER	All promissory notes held other than those from trade
1420	GOODWILL	Amount paid for a business beyond book value
1430	INVESTMENTS	Investments made in behalf of company
1450	PATENTS	Cost of patents held

1500 — PLANT & EQUIPMENT ASSETS
(Total cost of all plant and equipment — Total, Series 1500)

1501 LAND — Cost of all land owned including cost of improvements if present at time of purchase

1510 LAND IMPROVEMENTS — Cost of land improvements made since purchase

1520 EQUIPMENT, FURNITURE & FIXTURES — Cost of all equipment, furniture and fixtures owned

    1522 Production Items — Equipment, furniture and fixtures utilized in production functions

    1524 Shipping & Warehouse Items — Equipment, furniture and fixtures utilized in shipping and warehousing functions

    1526 Selling Items — Equipment, furniture and fixtures utilized in selling functions

    1528 Administrative Items — Equipment, furniture and fixtures utilized in administrative functions

1530 FACILITY — Cost of all facilities owned

    1532 Production Items — Facilities utilized in production functions

    1534 Shipping & Warehouse Items — Facilities utilized in shipping and warehousing functions

    1536 Selling Items — Facilities utilized in selling functions

    1538 Administrative Items — Facilities utilized in administrative functions

1600 — ALLOWANCE FOR DEPRECIATION (ASSETS)
(Total allowances established for depreciation of property owned — Total, Series 1600)

1601 LAND, IMPROVEMENT — Allowances established for depreciation of improvements on land owned.

1620 EQUIPMENT, FURNITURE & FIXTURES — Total allowances established for depreciation of equipment, furniture and fixtures owned

    1622 Production Items — Allowances established for depreciation of equipment, furniture and fixtures utilized in production functions

    1624 Shipping & Warehouse Items — Allowances established for depreciation of equipment, furniture and fixtures utilized in shipping and warehouse functions

    1626 Selling Items — Allowances established for depreciation of equipment, furniture and fixtures utilized in selling functions

    1628 Administrative Items — Allowances established for depreciation of equipment, furniture and fixtures utilized in administrative functions

1630	FACILITY		Total allowances established for depreciation of facilities owned
	1632	Production Items	Allowances established for depreciation of facilities utilized in production functions
	1634	Shipping & Warehouse Items	Allowances established for depreciation of facilities utilized in shipping and warehousing functions
	1636	Selling Items	Allowances established for depreciation of facilities utilized in selling functions
	1638	Administrative Items	Allowances established for depreciation of facilities utilized in administrative functions

2000 — CURRENT LIABILITIES
(Total of all current liabilities — Total, Series 2000)

2001	ACCOUNTS PAYABLE	Total debts owed arising out of every day transactions
2030	NOTES PAYABLE	Total of promissory notes owed

2100 — ACCRUED LIABILITIES
(Total of debts incurred but not due — Total, Series 2100)

2101	INTEREST PAYABLE	Interest owed but not due
2110	TAXES	Taxes owed but not due other than Federal income taxes
2140	FEDERAL INCOME TAXES	Federal income taxes owed but not due
2170	ROYALTIES	Royalties payments owed but not due

2200 — LONG-TERM LIABILITIES
(Total of long term debt — Total, Series 2200)

2201	MORTGAGES	Total amount of liens against company property
2200	LOANS	Total of promissory notes owed

2300 — EQUITY (LIABILITY)
(Total of all equity — Total, Series 2300)

2301	PREFERRED STOCK	Total received for preferred stock sold
2310	COMMON STOCK	Total received for common stock sold
2320	CAPITAL SURPLUS	Total amount received from sale of stock over the par or stated value
2330	RETAINED EARNINGS	Undistributed profits
2340	OWNERS EQUITY	Total owed owners

SOURCE: Uniform Chart of Accounts for Nursery Production, Landscape, and Retail Operations. Horticultural Research Institute. AAN. Washington, D.C.

Chart 7-2.
Profit-and-Loss Statement Using the Uniform Chart
of Accounts Suggested by HRI

UNIFORM ACCOUNTS — PROFIT AND LOSS ITEMS

3000 — PRODUCTION OPERATIONS REVENUE
(Total of all income — Total, Series 3000 Accounts — LESS refunds Item 3900)

3100	SALES OF GREEN GOODS		All income from sales of green goods
	3125	Sales of Green Goods Produced	All income from sales of green goods produced
	3150	Sales of Green Goods Purchased and Resold	All income from sales of green goods purchased and resold
3200	SALES OF HARD GOODS		All income from sales of hard goods
3400	SALES OF SERVICES OFFERED		All income from sales of services offered
3600	SERVICE CHARGES		All income from service charges
3700	OTHER INCOME		All income generated from sources not elsewhere specified
3900	LESS REFUNDS		Total of all refunds, allowances and adjustments

4000 — COST OF PRODUCTS SOLD
(Total cost of all products sold — Total, Series 4000 Accounts)

4100	COST OF GOODS		Total cost of goods sold
	4105	Depreciation	Cost of writing off goods
	4115	Green Goods	Cost of green goods sold
	4125	Hard Goods	Cost of hard goods sold
	4155	Insurance	Cost of insurance related to products sold
	4165	Taxes	Taxes related to products sold
	4175	Other	Costs related to products sold and not elsewhere specified
4200	EMPLOYEES		Total cost of employees involved in production
	4205	Fringe Benefits	Cost of fringe benefits for production employees
	4210	Insurance	Cost of insurance related to production employees
	4215	Laundry Service	Cost of laundry service for production employees
	4220	Supervisory Salaries	Salaries paid to supervisory production personnel
	4225	Taxes	Taxes related to production employees
	4230	Uniforms	Cost of uniforms for production employees
	4235	Wages	Wages paid production employees
	4240	Other	Costs related to production employees and not elsewhere specified
4300	EQUIPMENT, FURNITURE & FIXTURES		Total cost of equipment, furniture and fixtures utilized in production functions
	4305	Depreciation	Cost of writing off equipment, furniture and fixtures utilized in production functions
	4310	Equipment	Cost of equipment utilized in production functions

4315	Furniture & Fixtures	Cost of furniture and fixtures utilized in production functions
4320	Insurance	Cost of insurance related to equipment, furniture and fixtures utilized in production
4325	Maintenance	Cost of maintaining equipment, furniture and fixtures utilized in production functions
4330	Rental	Cost of renting equipment, furniture and fixtures utilized in production functions
4335	Repairs	Cost of repairing equipment, furniture and fixtures utilized in production functions
4340	Taxes	Taxes related to equipment, furniture and fixtures utilized in production functions
4345	Other	Cost involved in equipment, furniture and fixtures utilized in production functions and not elsewhere specified
4400	FACILITY	Total cost of production facilities
4405	Depreciation	Cost of writing off production facilities
4410	Greenhouse	Cost of greenhouse production facilities
4415	Insurance	Cost of insurance on production facilities
4420	Maintenance	Cost of maintaining production facilities
4425	Rent	Cost of renting production facilities
4430	Repairs	Cost of repairing production facilities
4435	Taxes	Taxes on production facilities
4440	Other	Costs involved in production facilities not elsewhere specified
4600	OPERATIONS	Total cost of operations related to products sold
4624	Fumigation	Cost of fumigation involved in operations of products sold
4628	Labor, Indirect	Cost of labor that is incidental to products sold
4630	Labor, Outside	Cost of labor utilized in production functions that is not employed by company
46321	Labor, Contract	Cost of labor utilized in production functions that is contracted for with other firms
4644	Purchasing	Cost of purchasing functions related to production
4648	Royalties	Royalties paid in connection with products sold
4652	Seed & Stock	Cost of seed and stock for production
4656	Supplies &Materials	Cost of supplies and materials for production
4658	Travel	Cost of travel that is related to production
4660	Other	Costs involved in operations aspect of production and not elsewhere specified
4800	UTILITIES	Total cost of utilities utilized in production functions
4805	Electricity	Cost of electricity utilized in production functions
4810	Gas	Cost of gas utilized in production functions
4815	Heat	Cost of heat utilized in production functions
4820	Telephone	Cost of telephone utilized in production functions
4825	Telegraph	Cost of telegraph utilized in production functions
4830	Water	Cost of water utilized in production functions
4835	Sewer	Cost of sewer utilized in production functions
4840	Other	Cost of other production utilities not elsewhere specified
4900	OTHER COST OF PRODUCTS AND SERVICES SOLD	Costs related to products and services sold and not specified elsewhere

5000 — SHIPPING & WAREHOUSE EXPENSE
(Total cost of shipping and warehousing functions — Total, Series 5000 Accounts)

5200	EMPLOYEES		Total cost of employees involved in shipping and warehousing functions
	5205	Fringe Benefits	Cost of fringe benefits for shipping and warehousing employees
	5210	Insurance	Cost of insurance for shipping and warehousing employees
	5215	Laundry Service	Cost of laundry service for shipping and warehousing employees
	5220	Supervisory Salaries	Salaries paid to supervisory shipping and warehousing employees
	5225	Taxes	Taxes related to shipping and warehousing employees
	5230	Uniforms	Cost of uniforms for shipping and warehousing employees
	5235	Wages	Wages paid shipping and warehousing employees
	5240	Other	Costs involved in shipping and warehousing employees not elsewhere specified
5300	EQUIPMENT, FURNITURE & FIXTURES		Total cost of equipment, furniture and fixtures utilized in shipping and warehousing functions
	5305	Depreciation	Cost of writing off equipment, furniture and fixtures utilized in shipping and warehousing functions
	5310	Equipment	Cost of shipping and warehousing equipment
	5315	Furniture & Fixtures	Cost of shipping and warehousing furniture and fixtures
	5320	Insurance	Cost of insurance related to equipment, furniture and fixtures utilized in selling and warehousing functions
	5325	Maintenance	Cost of maintaining equipment, furniture and fixtures utilized in shipping and warehousing functions
	5330	Rental	Cost of renting equipment, furniture and fixtures utilized in shipping and warehousing functions
	5335	Repairs	Cost of repairing equipment, furniture and fixtures utilized in shipping and warehousing functions
	5340	Taxes	Taxes related to equipment, furniture and fixtures utilized in shipping and warehousing functions
	5345	Other	Cost involved in equipment, furniture and fixtures utilized in shipping and warehousing functions and not elsewhere specified
5400	FACILITIES		Total cost of shipping and warehousing facilities
	5405	Depreciation	Cost of writing off shipping and warehousing facilities
	5415	Insurance	Cost of insurance on shipping and warehousing facilities
	5420	Maintenance	Cost of maintaining shipping and warehousing facilities
	5425	Rent	Cost of renting shipping and warehousing facilities
	5430	Repairs	Cost of repairing shipping and warehousing facilities
	5435	Taxes	Taxes related to shipping and warehousing facilities
	5440	Other	Costs involved in facilities utilized in shipping and warehousing functions and not elsewhere specified
5600	OPERATIONS		Total cost of shipping and warehousing operations

	5604	Automotive	Automotive costs involved in shipping and warehousing operations
	5618	Delivery	Delivery costs involved in shipping and warehousing operations
	5656	Supplies and Materials	Cost of shipping and warehousing supplies and materials
	5660	Other	Costs of operations of shipping and warehousing functions not elsewhere specified
5800		UTILITIES	Total cost of shipping and warehousing utilities
	5805	Electricity	Cost of electricity utilized in shipping and warehousing operations
	5810	Gas	Cost of gas utilized in shipping and warehousing operations
	5815	Heat	Cost of heat utilized in shipping and warehousing operations
	5820	Telephone	Cost of telephone utilized in shipping and warehousing operations
	5825	Telegraph	Cost of telegraph utilized in shipping and warehousing operations
	5830	Water	Cost of water utilized in shipping and warehousing operations
	5835	Sewer	Cost of sewer utilized in shipping and warehousing operations
	5840	Other	Costs of other utilities used in shipping and warehousing operations not elsewhere specified
5900		OTHER SHIPPING & WAREHOUSING COSTS	Costs related to shipping and warehousing functions not elsewhere specified

6000 — SELLING EXPENSES
(Total costs of all selling functions — Total, Series 6000 Accounts)

6200		EMPLOYEES (See 6700 Series for SALESMEN expenses)	Total cost related to employees involved in selling functions
	6205	Fringe Benefits	Cost of fringe benefits to employees involved in selling functions
	6210	Insurance	Cost of insurance related to employees involved in selling functions
	6215	Supervisory Salaries	Salaries paid to supervisory personnel involved in selling functions
	6220	Taxes	Taxes related to employees involved in selling functions
	6225	Wages	Wages paid employees involved in selling functions
	6230	Other	Costs related to employees involved in selling functions and not elsewhere specified
6300		EQUIPMENT, FURNITURE & FIXTURES	Total cost of equipment, furniture and fixtures utilized in selling functions
	6305	Depreciation	Cost of writing off equipment, furniture anf fixtures utilized in selling functions
	6310	Equipment	Cost of equipment used in selling functions
	6315	Furniture & Fixtures	Cost of furniture and fixtures utilized in selling functions
	6320	Insurance	Cost of insurance related to equipment, furniture and fixtures utilized in selling functions

6325	Maintenance	Cost of maintaining furniture, fixtures and equipment utilized in selling functions
6330	Rental	Cost of renting equipment, furniture and fixtures utilized in selling functions
6340	Taxes	Taxes related to equipment, furniture and fixtures utilized in selling functions
6345	Other	Costs related to equipment, furniture and fixtures utilized in selling functions and not elsewhere specified

6400	**FACILITY**	Total cost of sales facilities
	6405 Depreciation	Cost of writing off sales facilities
	6415 Insurance	Cost of insurance for sales facilities
	6420 Maintenance	Cost of maintaining sales facilities
	6425 Rent	Cost of renting sales facilities
	6430 Repair	Cost of repairing sales facilities
	6435 Taxes	Taxes related to sales facilities
	6440 Other	Costs related to sales facilities not elsewhere specified

6600	**OPERATIONS**	Total cost of sales operations
	6606 Advertising	Cost of advertising related to sales
	6608 Brokerage Fees	Cost of brokerage fees related to sales
	6610 Business Promotion	Business promotion expenses related to sales
	6612 Catalogs	Cost of catalogs utilized in sales
	6614 Collection Fees	Cost of collection fees paid to outside firm
	6634 Mailing Pieces	Cost of mailing pieces related to sales
	6638 Postage	Cost of postage utilized in sales
	6642 Public Relations	Cost of public relations utilized in selling functions
	6650 Sales Aids	Cost of sales aids
	6656 Supplies & Materials	Cost of supplies and materials utilized in sales
	6660 Other	Cost of sales operations not elsewhere specified

6700	**SALESMEN**	Total cost of salesmen
	6705 Automobile Expense	Automobile expense of salesmen
	6710 Compensation, Inside	Total compensation paid inside salesmen
	6715 Compensation, Outside	Total compensation paid outside salesmen
	6720 Entertainment	Cost of entertainment incurred by salesmen
	6725 Expenses	Expenses incurred by salesmen
	6730 Fringe Benefits	Cost of fringe benefits to salesmen
	6735 Insurance	Cost of insurance for salesmen
	6740 Taxes	Taxes pertaining to salesmen
	6750 Travel	Cost of salesmen's travel
	6755 Other	Costs related to salesmen and not elsewhere specified

6800	**UTILITIES**	Total costs of utilities utilized by sales
	6805 Electricity	Cost of electricity utilized by selling functions
	6810 Gas	Cost of gas utilized by selling functions
	6815 Heat	Cost of heat utilized by selling functions
	6820 Telephone	Cost of telephone utilized by selling functions
	6825 Telegraph	Cost of telegraph utilized by selling functions
	6830 Water	Cost of water utilized by selling functions

	6835	Sewer	Cost of sewer utilized by selling functions
	6840	Other	Cost of utilities utilized by sales and not elsewhere specified
6900	OTHER SELLING COSTS		Other costs related to selling functions and not elsewhere specified

7000 — ADMINISTRATIVE EXPENSE
(Total cost of administrative functions — Total, Series 7000 Accounts)

7200	EMPLOYEES		Total cost related to administrative employees
	7205	Fringe Benefits	Cost of fringe benefits for administrative employees
	7210	Insurance	Cost of insurance for administrative employees
	7220	Supervisory Salaries	Salaries paid to supervisory administrative personnel
	7225	Taxes	Taxes related to administative employees
	7235	Wages	Wages paid to administrative employees
	7240	Other	Costs related to administrative employees not elsewhere specified
7300	EQUIPMENT, FURNITURE & FIXTURES		Total cost of equipment, furniture and fixtures utilized in administrative functions
	7305	Depreciation	Cost of writing off administrative equipment, furniture and fixtures
	7310	Equipment	Cost of administrative equipment
	7315	Furniture & Fixtures	Cost of administrative furniture and fixtures
	7320	Insurance	Cost of insurance related to administrative equipment
	7325	Maintenance	Cost of maintaining administrative equipment, furniture and fixtures
	7330	Rental	Cost of renting equipment, furniture anf fixtures for administrative functions
	7335	Repair	Cost of repairing administrative equipment, furniture and fixtures
	7340	Taxes	Taxes related to administrative equipment, furniture and fixtures
	7345	Other	Costs related to equipment, furniture and fixtures utilized in administrative functions and not elsewhere specified
7400	FACILITY		Total cost of administrative facilities
	7405	Depreciation	Cost of writing off administrative facilities
	7415	Insurance	Cost of insurance for administrative facilities
	7420	Maintenance	Cost of maintaining administrative facilities
	7425	Rent	Cost of renting administrative facilities
	7430	Repairs	Cost of repairing administrative facilities
	7435	Taxes	Taxes related to administrative facilities
	7440	Other	Costs related to administrative facilities not elsewhere specified
7500	MANAGEMENT		Total cost of administrative management
	7505	Automotive	Automotive cost of management charged to administrative functions
	7510	Directors Fees	Directors fees paid
	7515	Entertainment	Entertainment expenses of management involved in administrative functions
	7520	Fringe Benefits	Cost of fringe benefits for administrative management personnel

	7525	Insurance	Cost of insurance for administrative management personnel
	7530	Owner's Account	All payments to or in behalf of owners of business including salary
	7535	Salaries	Salaries paid management personnel, excluding owners salaries, involved in administrative functions
	7540	Travel	Cost of travel of management personnel involved in administrative functions
	7545	Other	Costs related to management activities utilized in administration functions not elsewhere specified
7600		OPERATIONS	Total cost of administrative operations
	7604	Automotive	Automotive costs charged to administrative functions
	7610	Business Promotion	Business promotion expenses related to administrative functions
	7616	Data Processing	Data processing costs for administration
	7620	Dues	Cost of dues paid by company in behalf of any employee or the company
	7622	Employee Relations	Cost of all employee relations functions
	7626	Insurance	Cost of insurance pertaining to operations activities of administration functions
	7636	Meetings & Seminars	Cost of any employee attending meetings and/or seminars on matters relating to the business
	7638	Postage	Cost of postage utilized by administration
	7640	Professional Services	Cost of outside professional services engaged by the company
	7654	Subscriptions	Cost of subscriptions borne by company
	7656	Supplies & Materials	Cost of supplies and materials utilized by administration
	7658	Travel	Cost of travel related to administrative functions other than that performed by management personnel
	7660	Other	Costs related to administrative functions and not elsewhere specified
7800		UTILITIES	Total cost of utilities utilized by administrative functions
	7805	Electricity	Cost of electricity utilized by administrative functions
	7810	Gas	Cost of gas utilized by administrative functions
	7815	Heat	Cost of heat utilized by administrative functions
	7820	Telephone	Cost of telephone utilized by administrative functions
	7825	Telegraph	Cost of telegraph utilized by administrative functions
	7830	Water	Cost of water utilized by administrative functions
	7835	Sewer	Cost of sewer utilized by administrative functions
	7840	Other	Cost of utilities used by administration and not elsewhere specified
7900		OTHER ADMINISTRATIVE COSTS	Costs related to administrative functions and not elsewhere specified

8000 — OTHER INCOME
(Total of all other income — Total, Series 8000 Income Accounts)

	8010	Gain On Sale of Fixed Assets	Net profits on sales of fixed assets
	8020	Interest Income	All interest earned on savings or investment of company funds

8030	Purchase Income	Discounts resulting from purchase for any reason
8040	Rent Income	Income resulting from renting of lands, property or facilities
8050	Other income	Income resulting from non-business activity and not elsewhere specified

8500 — OTHER EXPENSES
(Total of all other expenses — Total, Series 8500 Expense Accounts)

8510	Bad Debt Losses	Total of debts written off as uncollectable
8520	Donations	Total of donations made by company
8530	Interest Expense	Cost of interest that is not part of product or service cost
8540	Loss On Sale of Fixed Assets	Net losses on sale of fixed assets
8550	Other Expenses	Expenses resulting from non-business activities and not elsewhere specified

9000 — INCOME TAXES
(Total of all income taxes paid)

9100	FEDERAL	Federal income tax paid by company
9200	LOCAL	Local income tax paid by company
9300	STATE	State income tax paid by company
9400	OTHER	Income taxes paid and not elsewhere specified

SOURCE: Uniform Chart of Accounts for Nursery Production, Landscape, and Retail Operations. Horticultural Research Institute. AAN. Washington, D.C.

financial statements depends upon the type of accounting system used by the firm. Most production nursery accounting systems are on a cash basis. Expenses are recorded at the time payment is made, and income is recorded at the time of receipt. The nursery production cycle (the length of time between the initial planting of a crop and the date of harvest) is usually much longer than the accounting period of a balance sheet or profit and loss statement. The accounting period may be quarterly, or more commonly 1 year, whereas the production cycle may range from a few weeks to 6 years. The cash basis system of accounting is misleading if the nursery is changing rapidly by expanding or contracting the volume of nursery crops planted each year. The cash expenses involved in buying the lining-out stock and caring for an increasing volume of nursery stock in the ground could very well be greater than the income from the sale of the relatively small volume of mature harvested nursery stock. In a cash basis accounting system, the inventory of nursery crops in the ground is not assigned a value until it is sold, so the profit-and-loss statement will show little, if any, profit, since income has been used to increase nursery crop inventory. However, this has been a common accounting practice in the nursery industry.

DISCRETIONARY SPENDING

Net receipts in a nursery operation will also vary considerably with discretionary spending. By what amount will expenditures for capital assets (land, buildings) be increased as the nursery grows? What amount will be invested into new growing inventory? What will be invested in new equipment? These decisions will dramatically affect the net profit of a business.

When a nursery business is young, and particularly if the management is young, there is a strong tendency to reinvest profits into land, growing inventory, and related facilities to expand the business. Under the cash system of accounting, the value of the field inventory is not adequately reflected in the standard financial records that are maintained by most nurseries. Also, as the owners of the nursery grow older and to some extent as the business ages, there is a desire to maximize profits. This can be done in a number of ways that will affect net profit. The most common is increased salary and fringe-benefit programs. Another is improved office facilities and modes of transportation. They are all rewards for financial success. However, none of these rewards necessarily reflects a true evaluation of the nursery business. Much of the financial success may be due to an economic increase in land value due to urbanization.

The final version of the 1976 Tax Reform Act requires corporate farms (other than family-held farms and farms with incomes of less than $1,000,000 per year) to use accrual accounting and to assign values to unsold nursery stock inventories. It contains the following exemption: "This section shall not apply to the trade or business of operating a nursery." In an accrual basis of accounting, "changes in resources and obligations including those resulting from the generation of revenues and the occurrence of expense are recorded as they occur (or nearly so)" (Edwards et al., 1974). The inventory of unsold nursery stock in the field or in containers would be assigned a value in an accrual basis of accounting. The increase in value of unsold plants each year would be considered as income in accrual accounting. Production costs including harvesting would be considered expenses only in the year they occur. This dramatically changes potential tax liability. The Internal Revenue Service in 1976 revoked an old rule (IT 1368 issued in 1922) which made it improper for even an accrual-basis taxpayer to inventory growing plants. The American Association of Nurserymen in 1976 maintained that revising this rule would have substantial detrimental impact on the industry and would be in conflict with the 1976 congressional decision against requiring corporate nursery businesses to use accrual accounting and to maintain growing plant inventories. In March 1979 the IRS advised that accrual-basis accounting can be changed to cash bases and that nurseries continuing to use accrual-basis accounting need not maintain inventories.

DETERMINING PROFIT

One of the ways to evaluate the success of an investment in nursery stock is by determining the costs of the various factors of production in a realistic manner and determining the true profit when these costs are deducted from the sales income, true profit being calculated as the effective rate of interest returned on the investment made in the production of the crop or crops during the production period.

When planning the production system for a nursery, after it has been determined what species of plants are going to be produced, it becomes necessary to determine the specific inputs that will be required, some of which are (1) how many plants must be grown to meet a specific market objective; (2) how long the production cycle is and how much land is needed; (3) how much manpower will be required to do the various physical skills required in the production cycle; (4) what facilities, equipment, materials, and supplies will be required; (5) how much money will be invested during the production cycle; and (6) how the various factors (labor, machines, land, and other facilities) can be synchronized to produce the best production system. Once this has been done and the production goal is clearly defined, it will be feasible to evaluate the accomplishments.

COST OF PRODUCTION

Since plants are the marketable product of the nursery which are sold to produce income, a system must be developed to determine the money inputs that are invested to produce the plants. However, most production nurseries produce many species of plants to make up the salable product mix. Each species has its own special input requirements in the way of material and labor skills, so that it becomes almost impossible to accurately determine the dollar inputs into their production. However, if the species are grouped into larger categories, such as shade trees, flowering shrubs, and so on, it does become possible to determine average costs of production.

It is impossible to place a true value on plant material growing in a nursery. This is because the plants gain a true sales value only when a buyer consummates an offer to buy. Up to that point plants in a nursery have only a potential or an estimated value in-the-ground which could be substantially reduced by various economic or climatic factors. A slowdown in the national economy can be quickly reflected in the public demand for plant material; this was dramatically seen in the great depression of the late 1920s and early 1930s.

In the winter of 1873–1874 a severe freeze throughout the Midwest caused the loss of thousands of plants and the failure of many nurseries; and the blizzard of 1890–1891 caused serious financial loss to many nurserymen. A beautiful block of shade trees that might have a potential value of many thousands of dollars could be reduced to a worthless jungle by a brief but devastating hail or sleet storm. Also, a severe drought, such as the one that affected the midwestern United States in the mid-1930s and the one that devastated parts of Europe in 1976, can seriously reduce any potential value that nursery stock might have. But nursery stock either in the ground or in containers does have potential value. Certainly, the nurseryman who owns the stock must place a value on the plants, a value for which he would be willing to sell the plants at a profit, and a forced-sale value which might be the dollar value that he would be willing to accept for the plants, in situ, if he were forced to sell. The forced-sale value most likely would be close to the actual dollar costs that he has invested in the production of the plants, but would not reflect a profit. Therefore, cost-of-production information is needed to determine how much is invested in the plant material in order to estimate an in-the-ground value. Cost-of-production information is helpful in providing nurserymen with factual information to make better mangement decisions relative to production scheduling and pricing. It is also valuable in evaluating changes in cultural methods and productivity of labor. Without production records, including costs, the nursery manager cannot fully evaluate production efficiency. It is very likely that without production cost records, plant material could be priced at a level below the actual total cost of production.

The first step is to determine what data are to be collected, how they are to be collated and processed into usable information, and how much time and money will be budgeted to accomplish the goal. It is pointless to collect data if there are no plans to use the data, and it is poor management if there are no predetermined objectives for the use of the information that is generated upon processing the data.

Nurseries that produced relatively few species or types of plant material or that specialize in a limited product mix can develop and operate relatively simple systems for obtaining production cost data. Nurseries that produce a wide selection of species or a diverse product mix, on the other hand, will need more elaborate systems. However, they need not be complex, and it may be more practical to begin obtaining cost-of-production data within broad plant categories such as outlined in Table 12-1, and later by individual varieties or cultivars.

Systems for Estimating the Cost of Production

Two systems are available for estimating the long-term costs of producing nursery stock. The first system involves obtaining direct costs on labor and material inputs, whereas the second system involves estimating inputs of labor from staffing tables developed over a period of years. In both systems a method is suggested for estimating costs of land, facilities, various overhead expenses, and interest charges. For management purposes it might be desirable to calculate an in the ground cost of production based on field data including direct labor and material inputs only, whereas a price-list cost of production would also include overhead and interest charges. This would represent the average total cost of production (investment) up to a given point in the production cycle.

Planting, Maintaining, and Harvesting Costs

One convenient and meaningful system for production nurseries is to collect and process the data within three categories: planting, maintaining and harvesting, the three primary functions in the production cycle. Figure 7-4 illustrates the system. The dollar values used in the example are for illustrative purposes only. Each manager must collect and process his or her individual data. In year zero, 4000 young shade trees were purchased. Cost includes plants and transportation. The average cost was $6.73/plant. The direct labor and material costs (obtained from daily time sheets and material records) for planting and maintaining the first year were $3720 and $1840, respectively. Unit values can be calculated for comparative analysis if desired. This information is tabulated for both the in-the-ground value and the price-list cost.

Overhead Costs

Overhead is the total of all costs of production that cannot be charged directly to the blocks of plant materials, including such things as rent for use of land and facilities, administrative and management salaries, taxes, and so on. There are various ways of determining overhead and equating it to the various factors of production. One method commonly employed in nurseries is to equate total overhead to total direct labor (DL) and to calculate a percentage factor. This value may vary from a low of 50% DL to a high of 150% DL. In the example, 100% of DL was used throughout. Nurserymen are cautioned to calculate their own value and to include all indirect costs of production.

Interest on invested capital is another factor that should be included, since money invested in plants could have been placed into a bank or other interest earning investment. A standard 7.0% is used in the example. The rate will vary with years, but a fair value prevailing within the community should be used. Note the significant increase in cost of production when overhead and interest on invested capital are included. Maintenance data are collected and processed in a similar manner for the ensuing years, and the average cost of production is calculated. At the end of each year an actual inventory count is taken of the plants within the block, and an average cost-of-production value is calculated.

When plants are sold, harvesting data are collected and processed. All these data are tabulated under price-list cost, since the plants are being removed from the site. No interest is charged to cost of production. However, it may be charged in the sales division if the sale is on credit. Once the plants are sold, their average value must be removed from the ledger. In most cases the records soon reflect a much higher unit cost for maintenance, a lower total value of plants remaining on the site, with a higher individual unit value per plant. At some point this value may exceed the average obtainable selling price, necessitating a decision by management as to the prudence of maintaining the few remaining plants. Hopefully, by keeping up-to-date, accurate records, this type of decision can be avoided; the plants will be marketed in a manner that will enable the plants to be sold according to a market plan, and the number of oversized, unprofitable units can be kept to a minimum.

	Year 0				Year 0+1		
	Units	Cost/unit	In-the-ground cost	Price list cost	Units	Cost/unit	In-the-ground cost
Cost of plants	4000	$6.73	$26,920	$26,920	3950		32,480 ❶
Labor: planting		.42	1,680				
: maintaining		.51	2,040	3720		.24 ❷	960
Materials: planting		.36	1,452	1,840			
: maintaining		.10	388			.13	525
Overhead (100% D.L.)			∑ 32,480	32,480			∑ 33,965
				3720			
				36,200			
Interest (7.0%)				2534			x̄ = 8.69
Total			x̄ = 8.22	∑ 38,734			
Plants lost	-50			9.81	-39		
	3950				3911		
Plants sold							
Labor: harvesting							
Materials: harvesting							
Overhead: harvesting							
Plants remaining/costs outstanding							

Figure 7-4 Example of cost-of-production schedule for field-grown shade trees.

157

Figure 7-4 (continued)

Figure 7-4 (continued)

159

Determining Profitability with a Cost-Sales Analysis

From the estimated cost of production records and from the records for sales, a cost-sales analysis can be prepared to fully evaluate the profitability of having grown the 4000 trees for a period of time extending over 7 years. One method of evaluation is to determine the future value of all inputs and income through the production cycle and to determine if there was a positive cash flow (Fig. 7-5). In the example, with 7% interest rate, a 100% direct overhead, and estimating sales costs at 10% of the selling price, there was a positive cash flow of $15,607.

A somewhat better tool to employ for this evaluation is discounted-cash-flow analysis, equating all finances back to year zero and determining an interest rate that results in a zero (or close to zero) net cash flow. All of the yearly financial inputs, less interest, and all yearly net sales are tabulated and the net cash flow determined by years (Table 7-3). These values are then discounted to year zero by using various interest rates (Table 7-4). This can be done fairly rapidly with the aid of a computer and in a few minutes with the aid of a desk calculator. A partial set of interest rates is tabulated in Appendix K. For more detailed rates, consult interest tables contained in a handbook related to mathematics.

When evaluated at at interest rate of 12%, the example project generated a negative cash flow, but at 10% the cash flow was positive, in excess of $5000, indicating that the project earned a profit in excess of 10% but less than 12%. If outside sources of funding were used to finance the project, it would be necessary to subtract the effective rate of interest from the profit percentage to determine the percentage of net profit in order to truly evaluate management for organizing and directing the enterprise.

Discount analysis of the project points out an important point relative to cash flow. When the discount rate is high, a faster turnover of cash flow is much more desirable, since the present value of long-term future income declines rapidly. Note the rapid drop in discount factors for 12% compared to 10%. Also, depending upon the amount of return on investment that is desired and the rate of turnover in cash flow, the value of the last remaining plants in a block of nursery stock may become a significant factor. In the example, if 12% were desired, it becomes important to sell the last 185 plants, whereas if 10% is a satisfactory rate of return, the last 185 trees could be sacrificed without significantly affecting the rate of return on the investment. Naturally, other factors must be considered, namely, land cost

	Yr.	Production inputs	1 Current value	2	3 7.0% Interest factor	4 Future value 0+6 yrs.
1	0	Plant costs	26920		1.5007	$40400
2						
3		Labor, direct costs				
4	0		3720		1.5007	5583
5	1		960		1.4026	1347
6	2		1118		1.3108	1465
7	3		1521		1.2250	1863
8	4		3738		1.1449	4279
9	5		2209		1.0700	2364
10	6		1000		0	1000
11					Σ	17900
12						
13		Material costs				
14	0		1840		1.5007	2761
15	1		525		1.4026	736
16	2		832		1.3108	1090
17	3		996		1.2250	1220
18	4		2028		1.1449	2322
19	5		1187		1.0700	1270
20	6		700		0	700
21					Σ	10100
22		Overhead costs				
23		(100% direct labor)				17900
24					ΣΣ	86300
25						
26		Sales income		Selling costs		
27	0			(est. 10%)		
28	1					
29	2	100 @ $18.00	1800	– 180	X 1.3108	2123
30	3	450 @ 21.00	9450	– 945	1.2250	10418
31	4	2150 @ 25.00	53760	– 5375	1.1449	55385
32	5	1008 @ 30.00	30240	– 3024	1.0700	29121
33	6	180 @ 30.00	5400	540	0	4860
34						
35					Σ	101907
36						
37						
38		Profit =	101,907	– 86,300	=	$15,607
39						
40						

Figure 7-5 Plant materials cost-income analysis.

Table 7-3 Net cash flow

Year	Input	Net sales	Net cash flow
0	-32,200	0	-32,200
1	- 2,445	0	- 2,445
2	- 3,068	+ 1,620	- 1,448
3	- 3,300	+ 8,505	+ 5,205
4	- 9,504	+48,375	+38,871
5	- 5,605	+27,216	+21,611
6	- 2,700	+ 4,860	+ 2,160
			+67,847
			-36,093
			+31,754

Table 7-4 Discounted-cash-flow analysis

Year	Net cash flow	12%		10%	
		Factor	Value	Factor	Value
0	-36,200	1.0000	-36,200	1.0000	-36,200
1	- 2,445	0.8929	2,181	0.9091	- 2,223
2	- 1,448	0.7972	1,154	0.8264	- 1,197
3	+ 5,205	0.7179	3,737	0.7513	+ 3,911
4	+38,871	0.6355	24,702	0.6830	+26,549
5	+21,611	0.5674	12,262	0.6209	+13,418
6	+ 2,160	0.5066	1,094	0.5645	+ 1,219
			+41,795		+45,097
			-43,272		-39,620
			- 1,477		+ 5,477

and the projected sales income from other uses of the land. In the example, the projected income was relatively low. Also, in the total financial evaluation of the business, the sale of the last remaining plants may become a source of supplementary income rather than direct income from the project, provided that the land cannot be programmed for some more productive use. In many production nurseries, the last remaining plants may not be salable or must be sold at less than full market value.

Another System for Estimating Cost of Production

Another system for estimating the cost of production is a method proportioning the various financial inputs by land, capital assets, direct materials, estimated labor inputs, and overhead expenses. Many of the financial inputs to start a nursery are for land and capital assets, such as propagation structures, storage facilities, and so on. It is difficult to equate a fair cost of the use of these facilities to plant production cost, since they are not direct costs. Nevertheless, they are costs of production and must be included.

One method is to own and develop these facilities under a proprietorship, which then rents them to the nursery, which may be a corporation or a partnership. For example, it may require 10 acres of land at $100 per acre for 7 years to produce 4000 trees. Land costs for the production of the trees would be $1000 per year for 7 years. This would be posted to cost of production as noted in Table 7-5A. Similar estimates can be made for the use of other capital assets. Materials that go directly into the production of the plants can be fairly accurately estimated either on an acre basis (e.g., fertilizer, pesticides, etc.) or on an individual plant or per 1000 plant basis, whichever is most desirable. The data are then converted to the number of plants being costed (in the example, 4000 trees).

Supplies to develop the land and facilities are charged to the owners and are reflected in the rent charges. Equipment charges may either be rent, if owned by a proprietor and leased to the nursery, or they may be calculated as an overhead cost, depending upon which is the most equitable approach to the problem. Over a period of time management should develop production tables that reflect the average productivity for the equipment or for the labor–machine combination used to accomplish the various jobs in the nursery (e.g., digging, planting, packaging, etc; Figs. 3-3 and 3-4).

Labor skills that are directly related to the production of the plants should be charged accordingly. This is best done on a unit basis (generally per 1000); but for large balled and burlapped shade trees the costs may be equated to a single tree, although for some labor skills the actual production may be determined on the number of units produced per hour. Labor skills not directly related to plant production and those that span many categories (supervisors, administrative staff, and management) are best equated as an overhead cost. All overhead costs, those that are not directly related to plant production, can be equated to either direct labor or material costs. In most nurseries, they are equated to direct labor, as noted in the previous example.

Table 7-5 Estimated cost-of-production schedule and cash-flow analysis for 4000 trees

A. Production costs and cash flow

Year	Rent ($100/acre)	Storage facilities $50/1000 ft³	Materials, estimated to nearest $100	Direct labor, estimated to nearest $100	Overhead, 50% of DL	Total yearly investment	Net sales income[a]	Net cash flow
0	$1,000	—	$28,800	3,000	1,500	-34,300	0	-34,300
1	1,000	—	500	1,000	500	- 3,000	0	- 3,000
2	1,000	50	800	1,500	750	- 4,100	+ 1,620	- 2,480
3	1,000	150	1,000	1,500	750	- 4,400	+ 8,500	+ 4,100
4	1,000	100	2,000	4,000	2,000	- 9,100	+47,250	+38,150
5	1,000	50	1,500	2,000	1,000	- 5,550	+27,000	+21,450
6	1,000	50	800	1,000	500	- 3,350	+ 5,000	+ 1,650

B. Sales income

Year	Plants	Price	Income	Sales expense	Net sales income
0	0		0		0
1	0		0		0
2	100	18	1,800	180	1,620
3	450	21	9,450	945	8,500
4	2100	25	52,500	5,250	47,250
5	1000	30	30,000	3,000	27,000
6	200	30	6,000	600	5,400

C. Discounted-cash-flow analysis

Year	Net cash flow	12% Factor	Value	15% Factor	Value
0	-34,300	1.0000	-34,300	1.0000	-34,300
1	- 3,000	0.8929	- 2,680	0.8696	- 2,610
2	- 2,480	0.7972	- 1,987	0.7561	- 1,870
3	+ 4,100	0.7179	+ 2,940	0.6575	+ 2,700
4	+38,150	0.6355	+24,240	0.5718	+21,810
5	+21,450	0.5674	+12,170	0.4972	+10,660
6	+ 1,650	0.5066	+ 840	0.4323	+ 710
			+40,190		+35,880
			-38,960		-38,780
			+ 1,230		- 2,900

[a] From Table B.

It requires money to pay for the materials, the labor skills, and the rent for land and facilities. The money may be obtained from outside sources or from within the nursery organization. But regardless of where it comes from, it should earn a fair rate of interest. This must be reflected in the discount rate as well as the profit due management for the risk involved in producing the nursery stock. If management could put the finances available into low-risk bonds that earn 7.5%, this might be the interest rate that should be charged for the use of the financial input. If management desires an additional 7.5% for risk, the suggested discount rate might be 15%. In the example, it can be seen (Table 7-5-C) that the potential net cash flow earns a positive cash flow at 12%, but a negative cash flow at 15%, making the venture questionable from the start. At the desired 15% discount rate, either the income from sales is delayed too long or is not great enough; or the amount invested the first year is too great. A reevaluation of the production system is warranted.

TOTAL NURSERY PROFITS

Profitability of the nursery must be measured by the cost involved and the sales income generated by the total product mix. An evaluation must be made to determine if the various production systems within the nursery are in balance to maximize productivity of the business. Once the basic assets (land, buildings, equipment, permanent labor force) are assembled, it becomes obligatory that management utilize the assets to its best advantage. Certain fundamental questions must be answered and reevaluated on a continuing, periodic basis: Is the product mix the best for the environment? Are the production facilities being used to optimum capacity? Are the various labor skills being employed most effectively? What changes can be made in the production system to maximize returns on investment?

The product mix is the plants that are being or could be produced by the nursery. Over a number of decades, nursery production has gradually shifted from emphasis on the production of fruit trees to the production of woody ornamental plants. Even within nurseries, there has been a shifting to the production of those species that grow well within a given climate. But once a production nurseryman has determined the primary species of plants that grow best in the environment and has developed the facilities and assembled the labor skills to accomplish the production goals, he or she needs to determine if nursery income could be supplemented by producing selected supplementary species with the facilities and labor skills available. It may be that the current production systems are not fully utilizing the existing facilities, or that at certain times of the year the full-time labor force is not fully productive. All too often the propagation and storage facilities of large production nurseries are empty when they might be used in a supplementary manner. It might be possible to modify current production practices in order to maximize the effective and efficient use of expensive greenhouse space and plant storage facilities.

In some situations the production of supplementary species may require additional inputs in the way of labor. However, the small labor input, coupled with essentially "free" use of existing facilities, may be well worth the investment. Management is evaluated and rewarded on the productive utilization of all three factors of production (materials, personnel, and money). Thus, management must be constantly evaluating all factors of production and trying to put together the most productive and profitable system.

Nursery managers in the future will be in a position to use computers to evaluate their production systems. By programing a computer with data relative to cultural practices, labor productivity, and cost information, the manager will be able to simulate various types of nursery production systems and cycles and test their potential worth by discount analysis. Nursery managers have a very powerful tool at their disposal; it awaits their use.

CASH-FLOW ANALYSIS

One of the financial problems common to all types of nursery businesses is the highly seasonal nature of the annual sales cycle. It is not uncommon to find production nurseries that develop 50% of their annual sales during one quarter of the year. Cash-flow problems result because expenditures precede sales and do not occur in a similar annual cycle. In many cases the major labor input in harvesting nursery stock (which requires substantial cash) occurs almost completely before the nursery stock is paid for by the consumer. Table 7-6 illustrates a typical monthly sales distribution for wholesale nursery growers. A few nursery firms have been partially successful in their efforts to develop other products or services that provide income and productively use labor during the periods of the year when nursery income and labor needs are minimal.

The fluctuation in income and expenses during the year requires short-term financing during the periods of the year when expenses

Table 7-6 Percentage of annual sales[a]

Dec.	4.2%	March	14.9%	June	5.4%	Sept.	6.3%
Jan.	3.9%	April	26.0%	July	3.0%	Oct.	6.4%
Feb.	6.0%	May	13.0%	August	3.7%	Nov.	7.2%
	14.1%		53.9%		12.1%		19.9%

[a]HRI 1971 operating cost study.

exceed income. A projected cash-flow budget should be prepared based on past cash-flow data and the future payment and income projections. The cash-flow analysis should be prepared at least once a year in monthly increments (possibly weekly) and might be required more frequently in cases where projections are altered by dramatic shifts in marketing or production. The total cash expenses and the total income from all sources are tabulated on a monthly basis, and positive or negative cash flow for each month is recorded (Table 7-7). A cumulative positive or negative cash flow developed for each month or week will indicate the necessity for short-term loans well in advance, allowing for proper financing. A cash-flow budget might also indicate opportunities for short-term investment of surplus funds for some periods of the year.

RATIO ANALYSIS

A very useful management tool has been provided by HRI in the publication of an operating cost study for the various segments of the industry. This study and others like it provide average financial data from participating nursery firms that a manager can use as a comparison in evaluating the performance of a nursery. An operation cost study, such as the one provided by HRI, becomes increasingly more useful as the number of participating firms increases and as additional years of data accumulate. A manager can compare financial trends over a number of years in the nursery industry to the trends in the nursery being evaluated.

A number of financial ratios, uniquely suited to the nursery industry, have been developed. G. S. Perkins, working with Florida production nurseries, evaluated nursery production (production area turnover) by dividing the total acreage of nursery crops that were harvested in the nursery each year by the total acreage the nursery had in production. The production-area turnover highlights fast-growing and/or fast-moving crops and illustrates the efficiency resulting from efforts to keep nursery production areas producing and

Table 7-7 A cash-flow statement[a] taken from "A Method of Utilizing

		From January 1 to December 31			
	Jan.	*Feb.*	*March*	*April*	*May*
Cash balance first of month	$2,000	$2,000	$ 1,000	$ 2,400	$ 6,900
Funds provided:					
Receipts from customers	$5,000	$1,000	–	$15,000	$20,000
Bank operating loan		5,000	$10,000		
Total funds provided	$5,000	$6,000	$10,000	$15,000	$20,000
Total funds to be accounted for	$7,000	$8,000	$11,000	$17,400	$26,900
Funds applied:					
Salaries	$1,400	$1,400	$ 1,500	$ 1,500	$ 1,400
Hourly payroll	1,000	1,000	4,000	6,000	4,000
Commissions					1,000
Installment payments	250	250	250	250	250
Purchases for resale					
Freight out					500
Packaging supplies		2,000	1,000		2,500
Purchases of liners					
Manure, peat, and fertilizer					1,000
Rent expense					
Advertising and promotion			500	500	500
Other operating expenses	2,350	2,350	1,350	2,250	1,850
Bank operating loan repayment					5,000
Distribution of profit					
	$5,000	$7,000	$ 8,600	$10,500	$18,000
Cash balance end of month	$2,000	$1,000	$ 2,400	$ 6,900	$ 8,900

[a]Figures are taken from the cash receipts journal and the cash disbursements journal.

SOURCE: Smith, E. M., G. C. Hines, and H. Hollar. 1970. A Method of Utilizing Accounting for Nurseries Producing Field-Grown Stock. Coop. Ext. Serv. Ohio State Univ. Bull. 520.

to eliminate vacant production space. For 1971 Perkins reported an average value of 47.7% production-area turnover for participating Florida nurseries. It should be kept in mind, however, that slow-moving or possibly slow-growing nursery crops may produce low production-area-turnover percentages and high profits.

An additional indication of nursery productivity is provided by the dollar volume of plants sold per acre of nursery production. An average of $28,120 per acre was reported for Florida production nurseries in 1971. HRI, in its 1972 operating cost study, reported an

Accounting for Nurseries Producing Field-Grown Stock"

June	July	August	Sept.	Oct.	Nov.	Dec.	Totals
$ 8,900	$ 5,900	$4,900	$ 1,900	$ 3,900	$ 8,900	$10,000	
$21,000	$ 5,000	$3,000	$10,000	$15,000	$10,000	$ 5,000	$110,000
							15,000
$21,000	$ 5,000	$ 3,000	$10,000	$15,000	$10,000	$ 5,000	$125,000
$29,900	$10,900	$7,900	$11,900	$18,900	$18,900	$15,900	$127,000
$ 1,400	$ 1,400	$1,400	$ 1,400	$ 1,400	$ 1,400	$ 1,400	$ 17,000
3,000	2,000	2,000	3,000	2,000	2,000	1,000	31,000
1,000							2,000
250	250	250	250	250	250	250	3,000
3,000				2,000			5,000
1,500				1,000			3,000
				500	1,000		7,000
2,000							2,000
					1,000		2,000
500						500	1,000
			500				2,000
1,350	2,350	2,350	2,850	2,850	2,350	1,850	26,100
10,000							15,000
						7,000	7,000
$24,000	$ 6,000	$6,000	$ 8,000	$10,000	$ 8,000	$12,000	$123,100
$ 5,900	$ 4,900	$1,900	$ 3,900	$ 8,900	$10,900	$ 3,900	$ 3,900

average of $2000 as nursery crop sales per acre. The higher values reported in Florida ($28,120) probably reflect the difference in sales volume per acre of container production versus field production. Production costs and sales volume per acre are much higher in container-production nurseries than the cost of production and sales volume per acre in field-production nurseries. Ratios and nursery operation cost comparisons are only valid when comparing firms with similar production systems. A high dollar value of nursery crops sold per acre of nursery production indicates productivity but may be unrelated to profitability of the operation.

Ratio analysis can also be used to determine the efficiency and productivity of nursery labor. Perkins reported that an average of

$15,243 of nursery crops were produced per annual full-time employee. An additional labor productivity ratio can be developed by dividing annual production labor cost by the annual volume of crops sold. This percentage is the labor cost per dollar of nursery crop sold, assuming that there is no expansion or contraction in the firm's volume of production. Both labor productivity ratios would illustrate increased labor efficiency through mechanization and alterations of cultural practices as well as more effective motivation and management of nursery labor. Landscape construction and garden center labor efficiency can also be compared by dividing total annual sales by the number of full-time employees. The HRI operating cost study for 1972 reported median ratios of $23,901/employee for landscape construction firms and $39,618/employee for garden centers. Ratio analysis can also be useful in evaluating the productivity of equipment (volume of annual sales/annual equipment depreciation and maintenance costs) and crews (annual landscape sales/landscape crew).

A number of ratios can be used to evaluate various aspects of the financial management of the firm and allow for the comparison of one nursery to others as well as to firms unrelated to the nursery industry. The ratio of goods sold by a garden center to total capital measures the proportion of invested sales that is returned in sales each year. The higher the ratio of sales to invested capital, the sooner the invested capital will be turned over. This factor indicates at least in part how efficiently the capital investments are being utilized in the firm. The solvency of a nursery firm can be approximated by developing the ratio of total debts/total net worth. This ratio indicates the relative amount of money supplied by creditors compared to the amount of money the owners have invested in the firm. The ratio of current assets to current liabilities (current ratio) is of interest, particularly to creditors, because it provides an indication of the firm's ability to meet its current liabilities. The median current ratio reported by the HRI operating cost study in 1972 was 63:1 for production nurseries and 31:1 for landscape firms.

The return the owner receives on the capital invested in the nursery can be evaluated by calculating the ratio of profit (before taxes) to net worth. The 1972 HRI operating cost study indicated that production nurseries reported a median value of 22.3%. Perkins suggested that the goal of production nursery management should be a profit percentage return on capital that is at least twice the current annual interest rate charged for borrowed funds. The usefulness of any ratio analysis or operating cost study involving profit data depends (as was discussed earlier in this chapter) on the type of accounting system, the value assigned to nursery crop inventories, and the manager's discretionary spending of gross profits. Discretionary spending consists of those expenditures which are frequently made by management based on how these expenditures will influence the taxes paid by both the owners and the firm rather than how they will influence gross profits. The common manipulation of discretionary spending by nursery management makes ratio analysis involving profit data of questionable utility.

The use of any ratio analysis is limited to comparisons with similar firms and with ratios of past years' financial data for the same firm. Ratios and operating-cost data, even those most specifically related to the nursery industry, serve only to identify areas where a firm differs from other firms or past years. Ratios do not indicate whether these differences are healthy or unhealthy. The median ratios of the nursery industry are not absolute standards that must be approximated. The goals of the firm (growth, profit, quality of product, stability, etc.) should not include the creation of financial ratios that approximate the median for the industry.

SUMMARY

Financial management makes use of financial records to document the growth potential, profitability, and the value of the assets of a nursery which is needed to obtain capital for operation and expansion of the firm. These records can also be used to help decide what kinds of expansion, production, purchases, and so on, will be most beneficial. The cost of production can be documented by financial records indicating the profitability of various types of nursery products and practices. Financial records and proper financial management are essential to start, manage, and evaluate the success of the nursery. Financial management is the core of the nursery business, and all aspects of the business are affected by it.

REFERENCES

AMERICAN NURSERYMAN. 1976. Tax Bill Exemption. Vol. 144, No. 8, pp. 110–111. American Nursery Publishing Company, Chicago, Ill.

APLIN, R. D., and G. L. CASLER. 1973. Capital investment analysis: using discounted cash flows. Grid Inc., Columbus, Ohio.

EDWARDS, J. D., R. H. HERMANSON, and R. F. SALMANSON. 1974. Accounting I, 3rd ed. Richard D. Irwin, Inc., Homewood, Ill.

MURRAY, W. G., and A. G. NELSON. 1960. Agricultural finance. Iowa State University Press, Ames, Iowa.

OPERATING COST STUDY. 1972. Wholesale Landscape and Retail Horticultural Research Institute, Inc., 230 Southern Building, Washington, D.C. 20005. (1965–66, 1967, 1968, 1969 are also available.)

PERKINS, G. S. 1973. The economics of ornamental nursery management. Fla. Agric. Exp. Sta. Univ. Fla. J. Ser. 5180, pp. 411–415.

SMITH, E. M., G. C. HIMES, and H. HOLLAR. 1970. A method of utilizing accounting for nurseries producing field grown stock. Coop. Ext. Serv. Ohio State Univ. Bull. 520.

TOWER, R. B. 1962. A handbook of small business finance. Small Business Management Series 15. (Small Business Administration). Superintendent of Documents, Washington, D.C.

UNIFORM CHART OF ACCOUNTS FOR NURSERY PRODUCTION, LANDSCAPE, AND RETAIL OPERATIONS. 1971. Horticultural Research Institute, Inc., 230 Southern Building, Washington, D.C. 20005.

UPDATE, a report to the Allied Landscape Industry. American Association of Nurserymen, 230 Southern Building, Washington, D.C. 20005.

Chapter 8

Soil and Nutrition Management for Field-Grown Plants

Soil is the field production nurseryman's number one asset, since it is from the soil that the essential mineral elements and water are obtained for plant growth and development. The soil also provides a medium of support for the plants and is the home for billions of microorganisms that play a vital role in changing the chemical and physical properties of the soil into an ecosystem capable of supporting plant growth. Therefore, it is imperative for a nurseryman to have an appreciation and understanding of this complex system since his livelihood is dependent upon it.

A nurseryman should know (1) the essential mineral elements—how they affect plant growth, their deficiency symptoms, and methods for preventing or correcting deficiencies; (2) the role that soil reaction (pH) plays in the availability of the various mineral elements and ultimately in the growth of plants; (3) the concept of nutrient-element balance and how nutrient-element balance affects the growth of plants; (4) how soils and plants are tested for the various elements; and (5) how to interpret the results of the tests as they relate to the particular situation. To fertilize effectively, a nurseryman should also have a knowledge of cation exchange capacity, fertilizers, soluble salts, the importance of maintaining soil structure, and the organic matter content of soils.

Although there is no unanimity in defining soil, it is commonly thought of as that portion of the earth's surface which has been derived from rock and in some cases organic remains and with which living organisms are usually associated. Rocks that have weathered are broken down by the processes of disintegration and decomposition into smaller particles having a changed physical and chemical state capable of supporting the growth of plants when supplied with water in the proper ambient atmosphere. Soil is the product of the rocks from which it was derived, but is also dependent upon the length of time and the intensity of the chemical, physical, and biological forces that have acted upon it. The soil, in turn, is the source of the essential mineral elements for plant growth.

ESSENTIAL ELEMENTS

The essential mineral elements, often referred to as plant nutrients, may be divided into two groups. The major or *macronutrients* include the elements nitrogen, phosphorus, potassium, calcium, magnesium, and sulfur. Nitrogen or potassium are most commonly deficient in soils of low fertility and commonly need to be added to nursery soils. Under normal conditions, phosphorus, calcium, magnesium, and sulfur are in ample supply in most agricultural soils and therefore seldom limit the growth of woody species.

The second group is called the *micronutrients,* since they are needed in very small quantities. They are also known as the trace or minor elements. They include boron, copper, iron, manganese, molybdenum, zinc, and chlorine. It should be pointed out that although they are needed in only trace or micro quantities, they each perform an essential function in plant growth and development which is not minor.

The function of each of these elements in plant growth and its deficiency symptoms are discussed briefly. For more detailed information, reference should be made to a modern textbook on plant physiology.

Macroelements

Nitrogen (N), as a constituent of protein, is involved in all the physiological processes taking place in plants. A deficiency of nitrogen is expressed in woody plants as a decrease in vigor and a light green to a yellowing of the foliage; the older leaves express the symptoms first. Under a prolonged deficiency, the leaves scorch and drop off. An excess of nitrogen can result in excessive growth and a decreased flowering and fruiting. An excess of nitrogen may also predispose plants to various pathological and physiological disorders, such as fireblight and soft, weak growth.

Phosphorus (P) is needed for root development, flowering, and fruit formation. It is found in large quantities in meristematic tissue and is essential for cell division. A phosphorus deficiency ultimately results in stunted plants. Early indications of inadequate phosphorus within many species of plants are the development of a bronze or purple coloration of the petioles on the underside of the leaves, followed by a yellowing of the leaves, particularly at the time of flowering and fruiting. However, phosphorus deficiency is seldom observed in woody perennial plants growing in a field production nursery or in the landscape. Apparently, the roots, which penetrate throughout a vast volume of soil, are able to absorb enough phosphorus to supply the plant's need.

Potassium (K), although not an integral part of the plant tissue, is important for plants. It modifies the absorption of other nutrient elements, influences the carbohydrate–nitrogen relationship, and is thought to influence the absorption and utilization of water, which in turn affects the drought and possibly the cold-temperature resistance of plants. A lack of potassium in broadleaved plants is first expressed by a marginal yellowing of the older leaves, followed by scorching and leaf drop. In needleleaved plants, an apical brown tip is separated from a green basal portion by a yellow band. There is also a decrease in the number of years that the needles persist on the plants.

Calcium (Ca) is one of the primary elements in the development of woody plants. It is a constituent of the cell walls; it modifies the permeability of membranes and is important for development of roots. Since calcium is relatively immobile within the plant, deficiency symptoms are exhibited first in the apical portions. Although a deficiency is not too common in woody plants, it is manifested by death of the terminal portions, yellowing and necrosis of the adjacent young leaves, plus severe distortion; margins are ragged and often rolled.

Magnesium (Mg) is essential for chlorophyll formation and growth of all green plants. Some form of chlorosis is associated with a magnesium deficiency, but the expression varies considerably with the species. It is reported that dead areas developing suddenly between the veins are an indication of an inadequate supply of magnesium. In advanced stages of magnesium deficiency, shoots defoliate and become devoid of leaves except for a few at the tip.

Sulfur (S) is a constituent of protein and various volatile compounds. When sulfur is deficient, plants are stunted and the leaves are light green or yellow, starting with the young leaves and progressing to the older leaves. Growth is restricted and stems are thin but remain erect. However, sulfur deficiency has not been a problem in the production of nursery crops. Perhaps this is due to its presence in most complete fertilizers as a contaminant and in various forms of nitrogen, phosphorus, and potassium salts that are used in the production of nursery crops. It is also an air pollutant in industrial areas.

Microelements

Iron (Fe) is a catalyst in chlorophyll formation and for oxidation-reduction reactions. Its availability in the soil decreases with high pH, high phosphates, or in high concentrations of heavy metals or carbonates. Young leaves exhibit an interveinal chlorosis with the veins remaining green. Woody perennials exhibit dieback of branches if exposed to iron deficiency for extended periods of time.

Manganese (Mn) is needed for assimilation of carbon dioxide in nitrogen metabolism and for the formation of organic acids and carotene. It may be deficient in soils of high pH or if large quantities of calcareous material have been used as a soil amendment. The deficiency symptoms are similar to those for iron. Manganese deficiency has been reported for red, sugar, and Norway maple, and it can probably occur on other woody species. Manganese toxicity has been observed in some woody species (apple, holly). Early symptoms of Mn toxicity are chlorotic leaves and suppressed growth with smooth, raised pimples (measles) underlain by small dark-brown spots in the young bark of some species. Later the pimples develop sunken areas and the bark begins to crack. In advanced stages, the bark becomes very rough, cracked, and scaly. Manganese toxicity appears to be cultivar-specific and is associated with acid soils, anaerobic conditions, and with some steam-sterilized soils.

Zinc (Zn) functions in cell elongation and in seed development. Zinc deficiency, although not too common in woody ornamentals, is manifested by older leaves having a yellow to bronze color. The leaves are relatively narrow with a wavy margin and rosetted due to reduced internodes. Dieback of shoots can occur where the deficiency is acute.

Boron (B) aids in proper root development, flowering, and fruiting and is necessary for nitrogen and carbohydrate metabolism. The application of excess lime may induce boron deficiency, which is more common in sandy soils than in clays. Death of the growing points, brittleness and dieback of the stems, combined with scorched, curled, and often rosetted leaves are symptoms sometimes associated with boron deficiency.

Copper (Cu) is a catalyst in respiration and is needed for carbohydrate and protein metabolism and in seed formation. Although copper deficiency is not too common in woody perennials, it has been reported in young fruit trees and in azalea plants growing for prolonged periods in containers. In fruit trees, the deficiency is expressed by a withering and death of young shoots in the late spring or early summer. In azaleas the new leaves are smaller than normal and soon become scorched; the early symptoms resemble potassium deficiency.

Molybdenum (Mo) is needed for protein synthesis, but is needed in such minute quantities that it seldom limits growth of woody plants.

SOIL REACTION

The reaction of a soil (pH) is an indication or a measure of the degree of acidity or alkalinity of a soil. Soil reaction can be stated or measured in a number of ways. It is common to speak of a soil as being slightly acid, moderately acid, or very acid; or in other cases, as being slightly alkaline. A more accurate method of expressing soil reaction is to express it in terms of the hydrogen-ion concentration. Therefore, soil reaction is expressed as the logarithm of the reciprocal of the hydrogen-ion concentration, and a pH scale of 0 to 14 is employed with 7 as the neutral point. The "p" indicates a logarithm and the "H" indicated hydrogen-ion concentration. Each pH unit is divided into tenths. It should be remembered that the scale is logarithmic, and with each increase or decrease of one pH unit the change in hydrogen-ion concentration is 10 times as great. Since the values are logarithms, they do not lend themselves to averages.

The soil reaction (pH) can be determined by the use of a pH meter or by the use of dyes and special pH test papers. Test papers, available in handy dispensers, are color-sensitive and practical for making quick tests. Soils should be mixed with buffers of solutions for maximum accuracy when determining the soil reaction. The operator should be familiar with the limitations of each technique and check his results periodically with known standards. A pH meter should be carefully protected and calibrated prior to use.

The soil reaction has a strong influence upon the availability of the various mineral elements needed for plant growth (Fig. 8-1). Also, plants grow better when grown in soil at the optimum pH

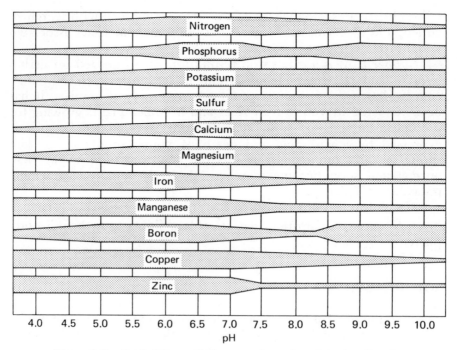

Figure 8-1 Availability of plant nutrients in mineral soil as influenced by pH; the wider the bar, the more available the nutrient is. (Source: Modified from Truog, USDA—Yearbook of Agriculture, 1943-47, p. 570.)

range for the particular species. The macronutrients are readily available within a pH range of 6.0-8.0. But the availability of these elements declines rapidly as the soil reaction becomes more acid. Iron and manganese are readily available at low pH values, but as the pH of the soil solution increases their availability declines. The lack of iron or manganese, due to high pH of the soil, can become a limiting factor in the production of certain woody species.

The most favorable soil reaction for the growth of most plants is between a pH of 5.5 and 7.5. Within this range, the essential mineral elements are readily available, the microorganisms of the soil carry on their beneficial functions, and fortunately, toxicity due to aluminum is minimized. However, some species of plants grow best under acid conditions (e.g., blueberries and rhododendrons) and others under more alkaline conditions. Nurserymen should be familiar with the optimum pH range for their crops and select sites accordingly for their production. For example, pin oak and red oak grow best in soil with a pH range of 4.5-6.0. They tolerate a pH between 6.0 and

6.8, but in soils with a pH greater than 6.8, they are often chlorotic and grow poorly. The soil reaction (pH) preferences for selected plant species are listed in Table 8-1.

MODIFYING SOIL REACTION

Where the soil reaction is too acid for optimum plant growth, it can be modified by the application of limestone. However, the amount of limestone that needs to be applied will vary with the degree of change that is desired, the soil texture, the content of organic matter, and the form of limestone to be used. Where the soil reaction is too alkaline, it can be acidified by the application of sulfur. The amount to be applied will depend upon the soil type and the number of pH units that the soil reaction is to be modified. The best recommendations for the amount of limestone or sulfur to apply are based on soil tests performed by persons trained in the analysis of soils. Production nurserymen should consult with their county agricultural agents or soils specialist for advice on management practices that are best for their soils and environment.

Effecting a pH change of nursery soils is best done when the land is not in crop production and well in advance of planting the nursery crop. The material should be spread evenly over the soil and thoroughly disked into the soil prior to plowing. In some situations it may be desirable to make split or multiple applications. Tables 8-2 and 8-3 can be used as a guide for the amount of sulfur or limestone to use in affecting a pH change. However, these tables are only estimates and do not account for variations in potential acidity, especially exchangeable aluminum. A lime requirement test, known as the SMP or Ohio lime requirement method, is used in a number of states; it measures both the active and the potential acidity. This gives a more precise determination of lime requirement than an estimate from soil pH and soil texture. A comparison of this measurement (Lime Index) and the lime requirement is given in Table 8-4.

The maximum amount of lime that should be applied in any season is 5 tons/acre. Nursery soils should be retested for additional lime needs prior to preparation of the land for a cover crop.

Various forms of limestone have varying abilities to modify the acidity of soils. This difference in ability is referred to as the "neutralizing value" and is equated on the basis of pure calcium carbonate. Pure calcium carbonate has a molecular weight of 100, and soil

Table 8-1 Soil reaction (pH) preferences for selected plants

Common name	Botanical name	\(4\)	\(5\)	\(6\)	\(7\)	\(8\)
Almond, flowering	*Prunus triloba*			xxxxxxx	xxxxxxx	xxxxxxx
Ash, American mountain	*Sorbus americana*		xxxxxxx			
Ash, European mountain	*Sorbus aucuparia*			xxxxxxxxxx	xxxxx	
Ash, white	*Fraxinus americana*			xxxxxxxxx	xxxx	
Beech, American	*Fagus grandifolia*		xxxxxxxxxxxxx	xxxxxx		
Birch, American white	*Betula alba*		xxxxxxxxx	xxxxx		
Birch, cherry	*Betula lenta*		xxxxxxxxxxxxxxxxxx	xxxxx		
Cherry, dwarf flowering	*Prunus glandulosa*			xxxxxxxxx		
Crabapple, plum-leaved	*Malus prunifolia*			xxxxxxxxxxxx	xxxxx	
Crabapple, showy	*Malus floribunda*		xxxxxxxxx	xxxxx		
Dogwood, flowering	*Cornus florida*		xxxxxxxxxxxxx	xxxxx		
Elm, American	*Ulmus americana*			xxxxxxxx	xxxxxxx	
Hawthorn	*Crataegus biltmoreana*			xxxxxxx	xxxxxxx	
Hawthorn, English	*Crataegus laevigata*			xxxxx		
Hickory, shagbark	*Carya ovata*			xxxx		
Holly, American	*Ilex opaca*		xxxxxx			
Holly, English	*Ilex aquifolium*	xxxxxxxxxx				
Honey locust	*Gleditsia triacanthos*			xxxxxxxxxxx	xxxxxxxxxx	x
Kentucky coffee tree	*Gymnocladus dioica*			xxxxxxxxxx	xxxxxxxxx	
Magnolia, saucer	*Magnolia soulangiana*		xxxxxxxx			
Magnolia, southern	*Magnolia grandiflora*		xxxxxxxx			
Magnolia, star	*Magnolia stellata*		xxxxxxxx			
Maidenhair tree	*Ginkgo biloba*			xxxxxxxx		
Maple, sugar	*Acer saccharum*			xxxxxxxxxx	xxx	
Oak, black	*Quercus velutina*			xxxxxxxx	xxx	

Shade and flowering trees

pH preference

Common name	Botanical name	4	5	6	7	8
Oak, English	*Quercus robur*				xxxxxxxxx	xxxxxxxxx
Oak, pin	*Quercus palustris*		xxxxxxxxx			
Oak, red	*Quercus rubra*		xxxxxxxxx			
Oak, southern live	*Quercus virginiana*		xxxxxxxxx			
Oak, white	*Quercus alba*		xxxxxxxxx	xxxx		
Pecan	*Carya illinoinensis*			xxxxxxxx	xxxxxxxxx	xxxxxxxxx
Sour gum	*Nyssa sylvatica*			xxxxxxxx	xxxxxxxx	
Sourwood	*Oxydendrum arboreum*			xxxxxxxx		
Sweet gum	*Liquidambar styraciflua*			xxxxxxxx	xxxxxxxx	xxxx
Sycamore, American	*Platanus occidentalis*			xxxxxxxx	xxxxxxxxx	
Tulip tree	*Liriodendron tulipifera*			xxxxxxxx		
Willow, weeping	*Salix babylonica*		xxxxxxxx			
Witch hazel	*Hammamelis virginiana*			xxxxxxxx	xxxxxxxx	

Ornamental shrubs

				pH preference		
Common name	Botanical name	4	5	6	7	8
Azalea, hiryu	*Rhododendrum obtusum*		xxxxxxxx	xxxxxxxx		
Azalea, pink	*R. periclymenoides*		xxxxxxxx			
Barberry, Japanese	*Berberis thunbergii*			xxxxxxxx	xxxxxxxx	
Bayberry	*Myrica pennsylvanica*		xxxxxxxx			
Beautybush	*Kolkwitzia amabilis*			xxxxxxxx	xxxxxxxx	
Boxwood, common	*Buxus sempervirens*			xxxxxxxx	xxxxxxxx	
Butterfly bush	*Buddleia davidii*			xxxxxxxx	xxxxxxxx	
Buttonbush	*Cephalanthus occidentalis*			xxxxxxxx	xxxxxxxxx	xxxxxxxxx
Chokeberry, black	*Aronia melanocarpa*		xxxxxxxx			
Chokeberry, red	*Aronia arbutifolia*		xxxxxxxx			
Cotoneaster	*Cotoneaster tomentosus*			xxxxxxxx	xxxxxxxxx	xxxxxxxxx

(continued)

181

Table 8-1 (continued)

Common name	Ornamental shrubs — Botanical name	pH preference
Cotoneaster, rock	*Cotoneaster horizontalis*	xxxxxxxxx (≈6.5–7.2)
Daphne, February	*Daphne mezereum*	xxxxxxxxx (≈6.5–7.2)
Daphne, rose	*Daphne cneorum*	xxxxxxxxxxx (≈6.7–7.3)
Deutzia	*Deutzia gracilis*	xxxxxxxxxxx (≈6–7)
Deutzia, Lemoine	*Deutzia lemoinei*	xxxxxxxxxxxxxxxxx (≈6–8)
Dogwood, goldentwig	*Cornus sericea* Flaviramea	xxxxxxxxx (≈6.5–7.2)
Euonymus, winged	*Euonymus alata*	xxxxxxxxxx (≈5.5–6.5)
Fire thorn	*Pyracantha coccinea*	xxxxxxxxxxxxxxxxxxxxxxxx (≈5.5–7.5)
Fringe tree, white	*Chionanthus virginicus*	xxxxxxxxxxxxxx (≈6–8)
Hackberry, nettle tree	*Celtis occidentalis*	xxxxxxxxxx (≈5–6)
Heather, Scotch	*Calluna vulgaris*	xxxxxxxxxxxxxxxx (≈4.5–6)
Hibiscus, Chinese	*Hibiscus rose-sinensis*	xxxxxxxxxx (≈5.5–6.5)
Holly, Japanese	*Ilex crenata*	xxxxxxxxxxxxx (≈5–6)
Hollygrape, Oregon	*Mahonia aquifolium*	xxxxxxxxxxxxxxxxxx (≈6–8)
Honeysuckle, Tatarian	*Lonicera tatarica*	xxxxxxxxxxxxxxxxxx (≈6–8)
Hydrangea, Peegee	*Hydrangea paniculata* Grandiflora	xxxxxxxxx (≈6–6.5)
Lilac, common	*Syringa vulgaris*	xxxxxxxxxxxxxx (≈6–7)
Lilac, Persian	*Syringa persica*	xxxxxxxxxxxxxxxxx (≈6–8)
Mock orange	*Philadelphus coronarius*	xxxxxxxxxxxxxxxxxx (≈5.5–8)
Mountain laurel	*Kalmia latifolia*	xxxxxxxxxxxxx (≈4.5–6)
Oleander	*Nerium oleander*	xxxxxxxxxx (≈6–7)
Rhododendron	*R. mucronulatum*	xxxxxxxxxxxxx (≈4.5–6)
Rhododendron, alpine	*R. hirsutum*	xxxxxxxxx (≈6–7)
Rhododendron, Carolina	*R. carolinianum*	xxxxxxxxxxxxxxxxx (≈4.5–6.5)
Rose, hybrid tea	*Rose* sp.	xxxxxxxxxxxxxxxxxxxxxxxxxx (≈4.5–8)

Common name	Botanical name	4	5	6	7	8
Rose, Japanese	*Rosa rugosa*			xxxx	xxxx	
Rose, memorial	*Rosa wichuriana*			xxxx	xxxx	
Rosebay, mountain	*Rhododendron catawbiense*		xxxxxxxx		xxxxxxxxxxxx	
Rose-of-sharon	*Hibiscus syriacus*		xxxxxxxx		xxxxxxxx	
Serviceberry	*Amelanchier canadensis*		xxxxxxxx		xxxxxxxx	
Spirea	*Spirea vanhouttei*		xxxxxxxx			
Sumac, smooth	*Rhus glabra*		xxxxxxxx			
Sumac, staghorn	*Rhus typhina*		xxxxxxxx			
Viburnum, double-file	*Viburnum plicatum* Tomentosum			xxxxxxxx		
Viburnum, maple-leaved	*Viburnum acerifolium*	xxxxxxxx				
Wayfaring tree	*Viburnum lantana*		xxxxxxxx	xxxxxxxx	xxxxxxxx	

Evergreens

Common name	Botanical name	4	5	6	7	8
				pH preference		
Arborvitae, American	*Thuja occidentalis*			xxxxxxxx	xxxxxxxxxxxx	
Fir, balsam	*Abies balsamea*		xxxxxxxx	xxxxxx		
Fir, Douglas	*Pseudotsuga menziesii*			xxxxxx		
Fir, Fraser	*Abies fraseri*	xxxxx				
Hemlock, Canada	*Tsuga canadensis*		xxxxxxxx	xxxxxxxx		
Hemlock, Carolina	*Tsuga caroliniana*		xxxxxxxx	xxxxxxxx		
Juniper, creeping	*Juniperus horizontalis*		xxxxxxxx			
Pine, mugho	*Pinus mugo*		xxxxxxxxxxxx			
Pine, red	*Pinus resinosa*		xxxxxxxx			
Pine, Scots	*Pinus sylvestris*		xxxxxxxxxxxx			
Pine, white	*Pinus strobus*	xxxxxxxxxxxx				
Spruce, Colorado	*Picea pungens*		xxxxxxxx	xxxxxxxx		
Spruce, Norway	*Picea abies*		xxxxxxxx			

(continued)

183

Table 8-1 (Continued)

Evergreens

Common name	Botanical name	pH preference				
		4	5	6	7	8
Spruce, white	*Picea glauca*		xxxxxxx			
Yew, Japanese	*Taxus cuspidata*			xxxxxxxx		

Vines

Common name	Botanical name	pH preference				
		4	5	6	7	8
Bittersweet, American	*Celastrus scandens*	xxxxxxxxx				
Clematis, Jackman's	*Clematis jackmanii*			xxxxxxxxx		
Dutchman's pipe	*Aristolochia durior*			xxxxxxxxxxxxxxxxxxxxx		
Honeysuckle, trumpet	*Lonicera sempervirens*			xxxxxxxxxxxxxxxxxxxxx		
Ivy, Boston	*Parthenocissus tricuspidata*			xxxxxxxxxxxxxxxxxxxxx		
Ivy, English	*Hedera helix*			xxxxxxxxxxxxxxxxxxxxx		
Virgin's bower	*Clematis paniculata*			xxxxxxxxxxxxx		
Wisteria, Japanese	*Wisteria floribunda*			xxxxxxxxxxxxxxxxxxxxx		

Fruit plants

Common name	Botanical name	pH preference				
		4	5	6	7	8
Apple, common	*Malus pumila*		xxxxxxxxxxxxx			
Apricot	*Prunus armeniaca*			xxxxxxxx		
Blueberry, high bush	*Vaccinium corymbosum*	xxxxxxxx				
Cherry, sweet	*Prunus avium*			xxxxxxxxxxxxx		
Grapefruit	*Citrus paradisi*			xxxxxxxxxxxxx		
Orange, sweet	*Citrus sinensis*			xxxxxxxxxxxxx		
Peach	*Prunus persica*			xxxxxxxxxxxxx		

Common name	Botanical name	4	5	6	7	8
Pear, common	*Pyrus communis*				xxxxxxxxxx	
Plum, American	*Prunus americana*				xxxxxxxxxxxxxxx	xxxxx
Raspberry, black	*Rubus occidentalis*			xxxxxxxxxxxxx		
Raspberry, red	*Rubus idaeus*			xxxxxxxxxxxxxxxxx		

Grass

Common name	Botanical name	4	5	6	7	8
				pH preference		
Bluegrass, annual	*Poa annua*				xxxxxxxx	
Bluegrass, Canada	*Poa compressa*				xxxxxxxxxxxx	x
Bluegrass, Kentucky	*Poa pratensis*			xxxxxxxxxxxxxxxxx		x
Fescue, chewing	*Festuca rubra* var. *commutata*			xxxxxxxxx		
Fescue, red	*Festuca rubra*			xxxxxxx		

Ground covers

Common name	Botanical name	4	5	6	7	8
				pH preference		
Bearberry, common	*Arctostaphylos uva-ursi*		xxxxxxxxxxxxxxx			
Bugleweed, carpet	*Ajuga reptans*				xxxxxxxxxxxxx	

SOURCE: Spurway 1944.

Table 8-2 Materials and rate to decrease the soil pH by 1 unit below pH 6.0

	Sandy loam	Loam	Clay loam or peat
Materials		*lb/100 ft^2*	
Aluminum sulfate	2.5	5	7
Iron sulfate	2.5	5	7
Sulfur	0.5	1	1.5

Table 8-3 Recommended tons of limestone per acre,[a] estimated from soil pH and texture, to raise the pH of a 6⅔-inch plow layer of different soils to pH 6.5

Texture of plow layer	pH range			
	4.5–4.9	*5.0–5.4*	*5.5–5.9*	*6.0–6.4*
Clay and silty clay	6	5	4	2½
Clay loams or loams	5	4	3	2
Sandy loams	4	3	2½	1½[b]
Loamy sands	3	2½	2	1[b]
Sands	2½	2	1½[b]	½[b]

[a]Lime recommendations based on a liming material having 25% passing through a 100-mesh sieve and having a neutralizing value of 90%.

[b]It is preferable to recommend 2 tons/acre so as to obtain uniform application and to justify the expense of application.

SOURCE: Coop. Ext. Serv. Mich. State Univ. Ext. Bull. 471.

scientists use it as the basis to equate the neutralizing value of other forms of limestone. For example, the molecular weight of pure calcium hydrate is 74. By dividing 100 by 74, the percent value is 135. This indicates that 1 lb of calcium hydroxide is equal to 1.35 lb of calcium carbonate, or when equated on the basis of 1 ton of pure calcium carbonate, 1480 lb of calcium hydroxide is equally effective. The relative neutralizing value of several liming materials is tabulated in Table 8-5. Most limestone quarries can supply an analysis of the calcium carbonate equivalent of their product. This is required by law in some states.

The lime recommendations given in Table 8-4 are for limestone with a neutralizing value of 90. If the material to be used has a neutralizing value significantly different from 90, the amount should be adjusted. Figure 8-2 can be used for this purpose. For example, a material with a neutralizing value of 135 would require 0.65 ton

Table 8-4 Tons of limestone needed to raise soil pH of mineral soils to pH 6.0, 6.5 or 6.8, as determined by the Lime Index method

Lime index	Tons lime per acre (9-in. plow depth)[a]		
	to pH 6.0	to pH 6.5	to pH 6.8
7.0	—	—	0.5
6.9	—	0.5	1.0
6.8	1.1	1.5	1.8
6.7	1.9	2.4	2.6
6.6	2.7	3.3	3.6
6.5	3.5	4.3	4.7
6.4	4.3	5.3[b]	5.7[b]
6.3	5.1[b]	6.2	6.7
6.2	5.8	7.2	7.8
6.1	6.6	8.1	8.9
6.0	7.4	9.1	10.0

[a]To convert lime recommendations to depth of plowing other than 9 in., divide above rates by 9 and multiply by the depth of plowing.

[b]The maximum lime recommendation for one season is 5 tons. Retest soil in 2 years for additional lime needs.

SOURCE: Coop. Ext. Serv. Mich. State Univ. Ext. Bull. E-550, 1976.

Table 8-5 Neutralizing value (percent calcium carbonate equivalent) of various liming materials

Material	Neutralizing value
Calcium carbonate (pure)	100
Magnesium carbonate (pure)	119
Calcium hydrate (pure)	135
Magnesium hydrate (pure)	172
Calcic limestone	<100
Dolomitic limestone	<108
Calcic hydrated lime	<135
Dolomitic hydrated lime	<170

SOURCE: Coop. Ext. Serv. Mich. State Univ. Ext. Bull. 471.

to equal 1 ton of the 90% material. The values in Table 8-4 are multiplied by the factor, in this case 0.65. Liming materials react at different rates because of their chemical composition, coarseness, and hardness. The finer a limestone is ground, the more quickly it will react. Also, the more porous calcite materials will react more quickly than harder dolomitic materials.

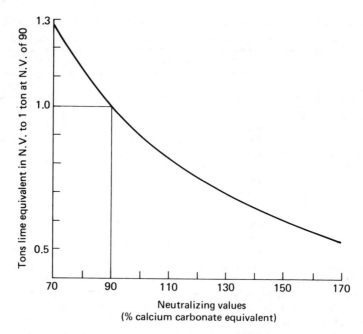

Figure 8-2 Conversion chart to determine amounts of limestone of various neutralizing values (N.V.) that are equivalent to 1 ton lime with N.V. of 90. (Source: Coop. Ext. Serv. Mich. State Univ. Ext. Bull. 471.)

CATION EXCHANGE CAPACITY

One of the interesting phenomena of nature is the ability of soil to adsorb various mineral nutrients when applied as fertilizers and then to release them to be absorbed by plants for use in their metabolism. The ability of the soil to hold certain minerals is known as cation exchange capacity (CEC). The exchange capacity of soil developed as a result of the weathering of rocks into small clay particles which possess negatively charged crystal surfaces. The negative charge is due to the dissociation of hydrogen from the exposed hydroxyl (OH^-) radical leaving the attached oxygen with the charge and from charges in the structure of the clay upon weathering. Clay particles adsorb thousands of hydrogen ions (H^+) and other exchangeable cations, such as Ca^{2+}, Mg^{2+}, K^+, and Na^+, upon their surfaces. The force with which these ions are attracted to the clay particles also influences the ease by which they may be exchanged. It is dependent upon the nature of the exchange complex, the size of the ions, the number of valence electrons, the degree of hydration, and the concentration of salts. The smaller the ion and the greater the charge per unit of mass, the tighter it will be held and accordingly the more difficult to replace. On the other hand, ions that are highly hydrated are more easily replaced. The common soil cations Na^+, K^+, Mg^{2+}, Ca^{2+}, and H^+ are listed in order of decreasing hydration. This explains, in part, why hydrogen ions play such an important role in soil, why calcium is the predominant mineral ion in most inorganic soils, and why potassium might be expected to be replaced and leached from a soil by improper fertilizer practices.

Anions, such as $H_2PO_4^-$, NO_3^-, and SO_4^- are absorbed primarily in the organic matter within the soil. They are made available to plants through the decomposition of the organic matter by various microorganisms within the soil. The anions then become part of the soil solution and can be adsorbed by the roots of plants.

Cation exchange takes place when a plant makes contact with a clay particle. The root exchanges one or more hydrogen ions for an exchangeable cation which is absorbed by the plant and used in its metabolism (Fig. 8-3). A knowledge of CEC can be of value to a nurseryman planning a soil management program.

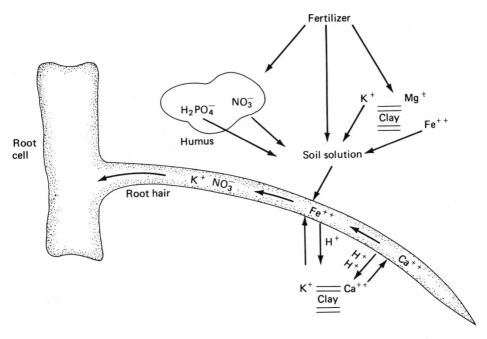

Figure 8-3 Diagrammatic representation of ion absorption from clay particle, humus particle, and the soil solution.

Most plants grow best on a specific soil type and under a specific set of environmental conditions. But it is impractical to provide all the ecological conditions required of plants in any one nursery. Therefore, it is desirable to classify the soils of a field production nursery into soil management groups on the basis of their CEC or pH, to develop a soil management program for each group, and to grow within each group those plants that lend themselves to the program (see Table 8–7).

A knowledge of CEC and levels of fertility are also valuable in developing fertilizer programs for nurseries and landscape plantings. Soils of low CEC should be fertilized more frequently at relatively low rates, since they do not have the physiochemical ability to hold large quantities of nutrient on their exchange complex. Thus, to ensure an adequate supply of nutrients for optimum plant growth, the fertilizer should be applied more often. On sites with a high CEC, the fertilizer may be applied less often and at a higher rate if needed. However, all fertilizer applications should be made on the basis of need, as indicated by a soil test.

NUTRIENT-ELEMENT BALANCE IN PLANTS

Nutrient-element balance is a fundamental concept in plant nutrition. The concept is that plant growth is a function of two variables of nutrition, intensity and balance. The intensity and balance are reflected in the chemical composition of the leaves when the plants are in the same stage of growth or development, all other factors being constant. Maximum growth and yield occur only upon the coincidence of optimum intensity and balance. An imbalance of elements can result in toxicity or deficiency which can limit growth. For example, boron toxicity can be induced by a high ratio of $(Ca + K)/Mg$ or $(Ca + Mg)/K$ but not by a high ratio of $(K + Mg)/Ca$. A ratio of less than four for $(Ca + Mg)/K$ is desirable for optimum growth of apples and less than three and one-half for alfalfa and corn. Calculations are based on milliequivalents per 100 g. A deficiency of manganese can be induced by a high accumulation of one or all three major bases (Ca, Mg, K) in proportion to manganese. There may be little or no response to increases in nitrogen fertility unless phosphorus levels are in balance with nitrogen. Heavy phosphorus fertilization of soils can induce deficiencies of iron, copper, manganese, and zinc.

LEAF ANALYSIS

The chemical composition of leaves can be determined by chemical analysis. This analysis, made with the aid of a spectrograph and other supporting equipment, provides valuable data on the mineral composition of the plant. But like a financial statement that reflects the financial status of a business as of a particular day, leaf analysis reflects the nutritional status of the plant as of the day the samples were collected.

The nutritional status of plants changes constantly throughout the growing season. For most plants, growing under optimal levels of nutrition, the concentrations of nitrogen and potassium decrease with time: calcium, magnesium, iron, and manganese increase, while phosphorus, boron, and copper remain relatively unchanged. Therefore, to interpret leaf analysis data intelligently, it is necessary to establish a standard method, including when to sample, the part of the plant to sample, and standards to compare the data. Since the nutrition of leaves is fairly well stabilized by the end of the growing season, this is the time that is recommended that samples be collected; with evergreens they may be collected through the end of December. The portion of the plant to be sampled varies with plant type. For deciduous species and evergreens such as pine, the middle foliage from the current year's growth is suggested; for evergreens such as juniper and arborvitae, the current year's growth is sampled. Leaves or shoots should be collected at random and combined into a composite sample for analysis. The data can then be compared with standard values to determine the relative nutritional status. Table 8-6 lists some suggested standards for deciduous and evergreen species; more exact values are available at laboratories that conduct chemical analysis of plants. Although exact fertilizer recommendations cannot be made based solely on leaf analysis data, a trained horticulturist with a knowledge of the crop and the site where the plants are growing, plus a current soil test, supplemented with information on past fertilizer and cultural practices can usually suggest a cultural program that will improve the quality of growth.

SOIL TESTS

Soil tests made on representative samples of a nursery or landscape soil can provide a nurseryman with considerable information to arrive at soil management decisions. However, it is important to know what testing procedures were used in order to make a meaning-

Table 8-6 Suggested foliar, nutrient-element standards for deciduous and evergreen plants (fall analysis)

Element	Deciduous	Evergreen
	Percent dry weight	
Nitrogen	1.50–3.00	2.00–2.35
Phosphorus	0.15–0.26	0.25–0.40
Potassium	0.80–1.60	1.00–1.20
Calcium	1.40–3.00	0.50–1.25
Magnesium	0.30–0.45	0.20–0.35
	Parts per million	
Iron	150–300	200–300
Copper	25–35	25–40
Manganese	50–200	25–50
Boron	25–50	25–50
Zinc	25–50	25–50
Molybdeum	1–5	1–5

ful interpretation of the data. Since different extraction techniques are used by soil testing laboratories, it is not always possible to compare test results between laboratories. Soil samples must be taken with care to ensure that the results of the test and the fertilizer recommendations developed from them are meaningful. Soil tests are performed on a very small sample of the greater mass, and if the sample is not representative of the whole, the results are not meaningful. Samples taken from the upper 6–8 in. of soil, which may be satisfactory for annual crops, have only limited value for deep-rooted perennial crops, since they do not reflect the true nutrient status of the soil-root zone from which the plant is absorbing its nutrients. Soil samples taken to develop recommendations for long-term nursery crops or for woody perennials in the nursery or landscape should be taken from various depths in the soil (0–6 in., 6 in.–1 ft, etc.) and locations in the nursery to be representative of the overall soil profile.

Most soil testing centers provide information on the cation exchange capacity or the soil group, soil reaction (pH), the availability of the macroelements except nitrogen and sulfur, and when requested, the availability of selected microelements, total nitrogen, organic matter content, and soluble salts. For many years phosphorus and potassium were reported as oxides, P_2O_5 and K_2O, respectively, since this is the form that they are found in fertilizer.

Currently, most soil testing laboratories report P and K on the elemental basis. P and K are normally in pounds per acre, Ca and Mg are reported either as milliequivalents per 100 grams or in pounds per acre, and the microelements are expressed as parts per million (ppm). To convert P and K to the oxide form, multiply by 2.3 and 1.2, respectively. To convert P_2O_5 and K_2O to the elemental form, multiply by 0.44 and 0.83, respectively.

Very little information is available on soil fertility standards for ornamental plants. The data in Table 8-7 are provided as suggested standards until more definitive data are available.

Table 8-7 Suggested standards of soil fertility for growing woody perennials in field production nurseries

Group	CEC	Available P^a	Available K^a	Exchangeable Ca^b	Exchangeable Mg^b
		lb/acre		mEq/100 g	
1. Silt loam to loam	12–16	35–70	150–200	5.0–10.0	2
2. Sandy loam	5–10	25–35	100–150	2.5–4.0	1
3. Loamy sand to sand	2–4	15–25	60–100	1.5–2.0	0.5

^{a}P $\times$ 2.3 = P_2O_5; K $\times$ 1.2 = K_2O.
^{b}1 mEq/100 g Ca = 400 lb/acre; 1 mEq/100 g Mg = 240 lb/acre.

TYPES OF FERTILIZERS

Nurserymen have a vast array of fertilizer materials from which to select in order to meet their individual requirements and preferences. There are many ways to classify fertilizers, but one way is to classify them according to their chemical and physical properties (Table 8-8).

Organic fertilizers are carbonaceous compounds which are either natural (Table 8-9) or synthetic. Most of the natural organic materials are multielement compounds, but the essential elements are present in small quantities, necessitating high application rates to obtain significant amounts of the needed nutrients. They are slowly soluble and can be used with a high degree of safety. The *synthetic organic fertilizers* are manufactured products. Urea, for example, is produced under high pressure from carbon dioxide (CO_2) and ammonia (NH_3), and urea-formaldehyde (UF) is a reaction product of

Table 8–8 Chemical and physical properties of fertilizers

Chemical properties	Physical properties
A. State	A. State
1. Organic	1. Dry
a. Natural	a. Pulverized
b. Synthetic	b. Granular (prills)
2. Inorganic	c. Tablet
a. Natural	d. Packet
b. Synthetic	e. Encapsulated
B. Element	2. Liquid
1. Single	a. Water-soluble
2. Double	b. Suspension
3. Triple (complete)	B. Release rate
4. Multi	1. Rapid
C. Long-term effect on soil pH	2. Slow (controlled)
1. Acidic (lowers pH)	
2. Neutral	
3. Basic (raises pH)	

urea and formaldehyde. Urea is highly soluble and must be used with caution, whereas UF is slowly soluble. IBDU is a reaction product between isobutylidene and urea producing a slow-release nitrogenous fertilizer.

Inorganic materials provide the most available source of supply for the essential elements. They are either natural compounds that have been mined and processed into fertilizer, or they are reaction products synthesized for a specific purpose. They are available in dry or liquid formulations and vary greatly in chemical composition and solubility (Table 8–10).

Since the mid-1950s, a number of slow- or controlled-release products have been introduced as fertilizers. Magamp is an improved formulation of magnesium ammonium phosphate with the addition of nitrogen and potassium. It is a granular formulation which releases nitrogen slowly due to its solubility in water.

Osmocote is a controlled-release fertilizer. It is a homogenous prill of water-soluble fertilizer covered with a plastic resin. The prills do not dissolve in water, but become hydrated and release the nutrients as a result of osmotic pressure. The process is moisture- and temperature-dependent. Therefore, the nutrients are not readily available when soils are dry or cold.

Slow- or controlled-release fertilizers are best utilized in the production of container-grown plants. They are relatively more

Table 8-9 Natural organic fertilizers

Fertilizer	Approximate analysis			Rate (lb/100 ft²)	Comments
	N	P_2O_5	K_2O		
Blood, dried	12	1.5	0.5	3–4	Rapidly available source of nitrogen
Guano					
Bat	6	9	3	3–4	Partially decomposed bat manure from caves in southwest United States
Bird	13	11	2	2–3	Partially decomposed bird manure from islands off coast of South America
Kelp or seaweed	1	0.5	9	5	Good source of K
Manure					
Cattle	0.5	0.3	0.5		Manures are generally low in nutrients, but when used in larger amounts, as a soil conditioner, they do add fertilizer. Avoid use of fresh manure or use too soon after steaming. Nutrient content variable, particularly with bedding materials used. Uncomposted animal manure often contains weed seed.
Chicken	1.0	0.5	0.8		
Horse	0.6	0.3	0.6		
Mushroom, spent	1.0	1.0	1.0		
Sheep	0.9	0.5	0.8		
Swine	0.6	0.5	1.0		
Meal					
Bone, raw	4	20	0	5	Phosphorus very slowly soluble
Bone, steamed	2	27	0	5	Phosphorus is soluble, some nitrogen lost by steaming
Cotton seed	6	2.5	2.0	3–4	Acid in reaction, good for azaleas, rhododendrons, blueberries
Hoof and horn	14	0	0	2	Good source of organic nitrogen
Peanut hulls	1	0	1	5	Low in nutrients
Sludge					
Sewage	2.0	1.0	0.5	5	Variable. Check source. Avoid those possibly contaminated with heavy metals.
Activated	6.0	3.0	0.5	3–4	Microorganisms added
Tobacco stems	1.5	1.0	6.0	5	Good source of K_2O, alkaline reaction
Wood ashes	0	2.0	6.0	5	Source of K_2O, very alkaline

Table 8–10 Inorganic fertilizers, nutrient content, reaction, and solubility

Sources		Total N	Percent availability					Long-term reaction effect	Solubility
			NO_3	P_2O_5	K_2O	Ca	S		
Nitrogen sources									
Ammonium nitrate	NH_4NO_3	33	17					Acid	High
Ammonium sulfate	$(NH_4)_2SO_4$	20.5					24	Very acid	Medium
Calcium nitrate	$Ca(NO_3)_2$	17	15			20		Base	Medium
Sodium nitrate	$NaNO_3$	16	16					Base	High
Potassium nitrate	KNO_3	13	13		44			Base	Medium
Phosphorus sources									
Monoammonium phosphate	$NH_4H_2PO_4$	11		48				Acid	Low
Diammonium phosphate	$(NH_4)_2HPO_4$	21		54				Acid	Low
Superphosphate	$CaH_4(PO_4)_2 \cdot H_2O \cdot CaSO_4$			20		20	12		Very low
Double (triple) superphosphate	$CaH_4(PO_4)_2 \cdot H_2O$			40–50		15			Very low
Magnesium sources									
Magnesium ammonium phosphate	$MgNH_4PO_4 \cdot 6H_2O$	6		29			Mg16	Acid	Low
Magnesium sulfate	$MgSO_4 7H_2O$						Mg20		High
Potassium sources									
Potassium chloride	KCl				48–62				High
Potassium sulfate	K_2SO_4				48		18		Medium

expensive, per unit of plant food, than the natural inorganic fertilizers, but because of their release rate, they have a number of advantages. They can be applied at the time of planting and supply the needed nutrients for a full growing season, thus eliminating the need for additional applications of fertilizer. This can result in a considerable saving in labor. They can supply nutrients at a fairly uniform rate; thus plant growth is not limited by excess soluble salts or by leaching. Their use can reduce the loss of soluble materials through leaching and runoff, resulting in a substantial savings, and at the same time minimize contamination of the environment.

When fertilizer is manufactured and packaged for sale, the product label will indicate the chemical analysis. It is industry practice to list fertilizer analysis in the order of the three primary elements, as % elemental N, % P_2O_5, and % K_2O. Fertilizers that contain nitrogen, phosphorus, and potassium are known as complete fertilizers. However, it should be noted that a complete fertilizer does not contain all the essential elements, although some calcium, magnesium, sulfur, and microelements are commonly present in the product as carriers or as contaminants.

Fertilizers may have an acid, alkaline, or neutral reaction, depending upon the materials contained in the product. Complete fertilizers, as blended, are neutral but many will produce an acid reaction upon the soil following chemical breakdown. The reaction of various fertilizers is listed in Table 8-10.

SOLUBLE SALTS

Another characteristic of fertilizers is their solubility. When fertilizer is applied to soil, it comes in contact with water, which causes the material to solubilize. The degree of solubility is a function of the fertilizer carrier (Table 8-10).

Soluble salts when present in the soil solution in excess quantities limits the availability of water to the plant or can reach excessive levels in plant tissue, which restricts growth and can result in death of the plant when the concentration reaches the toxic level for the species. Excess soluble salts are a potential problem to all plantsmen who use highly soluble fertilizers. When a soluble salts problem is suspected, a soil salinity test should be made with the aid of a Solubridge. A sample of soil is mixed with distilled water, and the solution is tested for its ability to conduct electricity. Some laboratories use the saturated paste technique, while others use a 2:1 or 5:1 distilled water/soil dilution method. The former has the advantage of being more accurate, especially with sandy soils or with soils to which gypsum or aluminum sulfate has been added. However, the latter is more rapid and less expensive, and if total accuracy is not important, the results can be of practical diagnostic value.

Soluble salts dissociate into ions which have the ability to conduct an electric current. As the concentration of soluble salts increases in the solution, conductance increases. This conductance of electricity can be measured by a Solu-bridge which has been calibrated in units called mhos. The decimal units are converted to whole numbers by employing negative exponents. For example, 0.00300 mho converts to 300×10^{-5} mhos. This is sometimes stated as 3 millimhos or 3000 micromhos. (Some laboratories report conductance in K values, which are millimhos $\times$ 100.) Table 8–11 provides some guidelines for levels of soluble salts and anticipated plant responses for plants growing in field production nursery or in a landscape.

Although there is little information available on the tolerance of ornamental plants to soluble salts, there are enough data to indicate that a reading of 3000 micromhos/cm (saturated paste extract) or slightly less should be satisfactory for most plants. Some plants, such

Table 8–11 Interpretation of solu-bridge data as related to field-grown plants

Conductivity, $EC \times 10^6$ at $25°C$ (micromhos/cm)			
2:1	*5:1*	*Saturated paste extract*	*Interpretation*
<150	<80–300		Satisfactory for seed experimentation, but too low for good plant growth. Soil needs fertilizer.
150–500		<2000[a]	Satisfactory if soil is high in organic matter.
500–1800	300–800	2000–3000	Satisfactory for established plants. Upper range too high for seedlings and salt-intolerant species.
1800–2250	800–1000	4000–8000	Toxic levels, reduced growth. Do not fertilize.
2250–3400	1000–1500	8000–16,000	Many species will be stunted. Suggest leaching if possible.
>3400	>1500	>16,000	Too high for most species of plants.

[a]2000 micromhos = 2 millimhos = 0.002 mho. To convert micromhos/cm to parts per million (approx.), multiply by 0.7.

as arborvitae, juniper, and bottle bush, are very salt-tolerant and can withstand a salt concentration as high as 8000–10,000 micromhos/cm, while others, such as roses and viburnums, will be killed if the salts level is greater than 3000 micromhos/cm.

FERTILIZER RECOMMENDATIONS

Fertilizer recommendations for woody plants, and for ornamental species in particular, vary considerably. Most recommendations for fertilizing woody species growing in the ground have been developed from a limited number of studies utilizing mature trees. Some of the recommendations come from fertilizer studies conducted on plants growing in nurseries. Most of the studies were concerned with the three primary elements: nitrogen, phosphorus, and potassium, and with the trace element iron. The studies centered around rates and methods of application. From the results of these fertilizer studies, there is total agreement that the greatest growth response of trees was due to the addition of nitrogen to the soil. Only a few of the studies reported significant increases in growth due to the application of phosphorus or potassium. Chlorosis of oak, plus a few other species, was commonly associated with lack of iron.

Nitrogen

Current fertilizer recommendations for woody species growing in the ground indicate that surface application is most desirable for nitrogen. Rates of application vary with tree size and with the type of fertilizer. The most common practice is to state the rate in pounds of fertilizer or pounds of nitrogen per 1000 ft^2. A second is to equate the rate of application to the size of the tree: pounds of fertilizer or pounds of nitrogen contained in the fertilizer per inch of trunk diameter. Fertilizer recommendations for trees based on trunk diameter can result in considerable variation in concentration of nitrogen applied per 1000 ft^2 and per plant. Since the greatest growth response in woody species is related to nitrogen, the best recommendation for rate of application is to base the rate on pounds of nitrogen per 1000 ft^2. Then regardless of the size of the tree or the fertilizer analysis, the soil will be enriched with nitrogen at a uniform concentration. The actual rate of application will vary with the amount available in the soil, the soil environment and type of fertilizer, the species to be fertilized, and the objective of the nursery manager.

The amount of nitrogen in the soil available for plant growth is a function of a number of interacting factors. Nitrogen is made available from organic materials by the activity of various microorganisms within the soil, by biological fixation of atmospheric nitrogen, and by decomposition of organic matter. It is removed from the soil by cropping and leaching and is made unavailable to plants by the activities of various soil organisms. The actual level of available nitrogen in the soil is the net result of the positive and negative forces acting at any given moment in time.

Soil microorganisms are most active during periods of warm temperature and least active when the soil is cold or is either very wet or very dry. Leaching takes place during periods of heavy rain and as a result of excessive irrigation. Nitrogen is made unavailable following application of low-N organic matter, such as sawdust. Therefore, tests for available nitrogen must be interpreted with these considerations in mind, since the actual level of available nitrogen is influenced by all these factors.

Since there are many forms of nitrogenous fertilizer available for use by nurserymen, it is important to understand the advantages and disadvantages of the most commonly used nitrogenous fertilizers. Inorganic fertilizers contain either nitrate nitrogen or ammonium nitrogen. Both the ammonium ion (NH_4^+) and the nitrate ion (NO_3^-) can be absorbed and utilized by plants. However, most plants exhibit a preference for the nitrate form.

These two forms of nitrogen react differently in the soil, since NH_4^+ is a cation and the other NO_3^- is an anion. Because nitrate fertilizers are highly soluble and readily absorbed by plant roots, they are the most desirable for use on cold or wet soils. But because of its solubility, it can also be readily leached from soils. On the other hand, the positively charged ammonium ion becomes adsorbed to negatively charged clay or organic colloids, and leaching is retarded. The ammonium ion is converted to nitrate nitrogen by microorganisms under the conditions of warm temperature, available moisture, and good aeration.

Organic forms of nitrogen, with the exception of urea, are generally unavailable for use by plants and must be converted either to ammonium or nitrate nitrogen before they are available for absorption by plants. Urea, however, is water-soluble and can be used directly by plants or can be rapidly converted to NO_3 in warm moist soils. Slow- or controlled-release fertilizers, discussed previously, are also a source of nitrogen for the production of nursery crops.

Although rates of fertilizer application should be set primarily on the basis of a soil test (Table 8–12) or foliage analysis, they should be modified on the basis of plant growth and species response. Plants

Table 8-12 Nitrogen fertilizer guide for woody
plants in field production nurseries
on mineral soils

Previous crop or manure application	*Nitrogen (lb/acre)*[a]
Legume and manure, 10 tons/acre	25
Legume	50
Manure, 10 tons/acre	60
No legume, no manure	100

[a]If the season is cool and wet or the field is
poorly drained, additional quantities of nitrate nitrogen may be necessary. Plantings on wide spacing may
be fertilized by banding nitrogen at lower rates.

that have good foliage color and are making good growth may not
require additional fertilizer for a year or two, whereas plants that are
chlorotic and making poor growth may need an application of fertilizer. In previous studies, deciduous trees have responded with a significant increase in diameter growth when fertilized at a rate of 6 lb
nitrogen/1000 ft^2, whereas in another study, field-grown evergreens
(yews) produced their best growth at a rate of 3 lb nitrogen/1000 ft^2.
Rates in excess of 4 lb nitrogen/1000 ft^2 resulted in a decline in
growth.

Nurserymen wishing to accelerate growth should maintain fairly
high levels of available nitrogen in the soil, whereas those desiring to
slow down growth should withhold nitrogen. It is possible to deprive
the nursery crop of part of its nitrogen source by leaching the soil
or by sowing a cover crop. The data in Table 8-12 provide a guide to
nitrogen application for the production of woody plants in field
production nurseries on mineral soils.

Phosphorus

The application of phosphate fertilizers is seldom necessary on field
production nursery soils. When it has been determined that phosphorus in the soil is below some "critical" level (Table 8-7), it is best
to apply the fertilizer to a sod or green manure crop grown prior to
planting of the nursery crop. This practice ensures better distribution
of the phosphorus throughout the soil. Either superphosphate
(0-20-0) or triple superphosphate (0-46-0) can be used effectively
(Table 8-13). In field production areas where sod or green manure

Table 8-13 Phosphate-phosphorus fertilizer guide
for woody plants in field production
nurseries on mineral soils[a]

Available phosphorus (lb/acre)	Pounds per acre[b]	
	P_2O_5	P
0–19	100	44
20–39	75	33
40–59	50	22
60–79	25	11
80+	0	0

[a]Data based on the Bray P_1 (absorbed) method.

[b]Applied to sod or green manure crop prior to planting nursery crop.

crops are not employed in the rotation with the nursery crop, phosphate fertilizers can be applied by banding or by the use of a pelletized fertilizer thoroughly incorporated into the soil prior to planting.

Potassium

Potassium ions on the surface of the exchange complex are available for plant growth. Those in the interior of the soil complex, colloidal clay particles, sometimes known as the stored form, are capable of being released slowly to replace the adsorbed ions. Potassium deficiency is not a common problem on most nursery soils, although it can be in sandy soils. Nurserymen who suspect that their soil might be deficient in potassium should have it tested, and if potassium is needed, apply it to the soil prior to planting (Table 8-14). Potassium fertilizers should be worked into the soil to be most effective.

The two common forms of potassium fertilizers are the chloride form, called muriate of potash, and the sulfate form. Muriate of potash contains approximately 60% K_2O, is the least expensive, and is the most commonly used form. The sulfate form contains 48% K_2O and is used on those crops sensitive to chlorides or in places where large quantities of chlorides are present in irrigation water.

Potassium nitrate (KNO_3), which contains 44% K_2O, also contains about 13% nitrates and has a medium salt index (Table 8-10) per unit of plant food. This material is used extensively in fertilizing container-grown plants. It can be used as a foliar spray (5–10 lb/100 gal water), applied with a spreader-sticker as a transitory means of correcting a potassium deficiency on a nursery crop. This should be

Table 8-14   Potash–potassium fertilizer guide for woody ornamental plants in field production nurseries on mineral soils[a]

| Available soil potassium (lb/acre) | | Pounds per acre[b] | |
Sandy loams and loamy sands	Loams and clay loams	K_2O	K
	0–59	200	166
	60–119	150	125
0–59	120–159	100	83
60–119	160–179	75	62
120–169	180–199	50	42
170–209	200–239	25	21
210+	240+	0	0

[a]Data based on 1.0 N neutral ammonium acetate extraction method.
[b]Applied to sod or green manure prior to planting nursery crop.

followed by a good soil development program prior to planting another nursery crop.

Calcium

Although most soils contain adequate amounts of calcium to support plant growth, nurserymen should be aware that they are removing relatively large amounts with the sale of their product. Liming of soils to maintain an optimum pH adds large quantitites of calcium and may be sufficient to make up for the loss. It should also be noted that calcium plays an important role in the aggregation of soil particles. Soils with adequate calcium are well aggregated, permitting adequate aeration and drainage, which aid in the production of quality plants. Excess calcium in a soil can produce an imbalance of the cations and could induce either a potassium, iron, or manganese deficiency, especially on soils low in these elements.

Magnesium

Magnesium is not commonly deficient in most soils. But a magnesium deficiency can be induced by applying high rates of potassium. The ratio of exchangeable potassium to exchangeable magnesium should not be greater than 3:1 for most crops. Magnesium fertilizer should not be added if the soil magnesium exceeds 3% of the total bases.

A quick, temporary source of magnesium for growing plants is to spray the foliage with a solution of magnesium sulfate, Epsom salt, (20 lb/100 gal water). Dolomitic limestone applied at the rate of 2 tons/acre where the soil pH is below 5.5 will supply adequate amounts of magnesium for most nursery crops.

Microelements

Iron deficiency is commonly associated with iron-sensitive species (oaks, holly, rhododendron) when they are grown on alkaline soils. Iron deficiency is relatively difficult to correct in plants growing in the ground. The best corrective measure for woody plants has been soil applications of iron chelate just prior to spring growth, although trunk implants of encapsulated iron are also effective on shade trees. Foliar sprays of iron have only a transitory effect on woody plants.

Manganese deficiency may be corrected by acidification of the soil to pH 6.0. The use of water-soluble manganese sulfate (5 lb/100 gal water) or a chelated manganese foliar spray, with a spreader-sticker, can be used to correct the deficiency. However, they must be applied annually or even twice a year to assure satisfactory results. Trees exhibiting chlorosis should be carefully diagnosed prior to treating, since an application of iron to effect a cure of a manganese deficiency would further upset the Fe–Mn balance in the soil and within the plant.

Boron deficiency can be corrected by borax applied to the soil (1 lb/1000 ft^2) or by foliar spray of polyborate (2 lb/100 gal water). An excess application to the foliage can cause defoliation; therefore, a fritted formulation applied to the soil is safer.

Copper deficiency can be corrected readily. Bordeaux mixture applied to the foliage will alleviate the problem. Since most peat used in container culture has little or no copper, it should be incorporated into the medium prior to planting or incorporated into the fertilizer program. Copper sulfate spray applied at 3–6 oz/100 gal water can correct the problem.

METHOD OF APPLICATION

Nutrient elements can enter plants through the roots, the foliage, and in some cases through the bark. When fertilizers are applied to the foliage, they must be in liquid form and be applied in dilute solutions. When applied to the soil to be absorbed by the roots, fertilizer can be in either the liquid or dry state and can be a surface application or injected into the root zone. When applied through the bark, they can be in the dry or liquid state, but most often they are encapsulated and implanted into the trunks of trees. When selecting the method to apply fertilizers to nursery crops, nurserymen should consider the nutrients, their ability to be effectively absorbed, the effect of the soil or the environment, equipment availability, the relative cost, and the effects of fertilizer salts on application equipment and the environment.

Surface Application

Band placement along the rows is most commonly used by nurserymen. It is an effective and efficient method for the application of nitrogen, since nitrogenous fertilizers move into the root zone with the downward movement of water. However, direct surface application is not suggested for applying phosphorus, potassium, and other nutrients that become fixed on the exchange complex. These are better applied by incorporation into nursery soils prior to planting.

Fertilizers can be applied to the soil surface with the aid of various types of spreaders. Band application on either side of the row is a satisfactory means, although the fertilizer can be spread evenly over the entire area. Where large acreages are to be fertilized, an airplane can be economically employed.

Fertilizer spreaders should be calibrated to ensure accurate and uniform distribution of the material. Calibration should be done for each fertilizer, field condition, and each individual spreader. Fertilizers vary in their chemical and physical properties; therefore, one calibration of a spreader does not apply to all fertilizers. Also, fields vary from site to site, which has an effect upon rate of travel and distribution rate. The equipment should be recalibrated whenever there is a significant change in surface conditions. Also, rate of application will vary between spreaders and the individual spreader as a result of use. It is a good practice to recalibrate spreaders and to check the rate of distribution periodically to avoid overapplication of fertilizer.

In some situations it may be more economical to contract fertilizer application to a company that specializes in application of fertilizers and pesticides to agricultural crops.

Surface application rates are stated in pounds per acre (lb/acre) or pounds per thousand square feet (lb/1000 ft^2). The two nomographs of Appendices E and F will accomplish the conversion of lb/acre to lb/1000 ft^2 or lb/1000 ft^2 to lb/acre without calculations.

Subsurface Injection

Incorporation into the soil by subsurface application is the most effective means of applying nutrients that become fixed on the exchange complex or are slow to move into the soil solution. Nurserymen can best incorporate these materials into the soil prior to planting the nursery crop. Also, when affecting a pH change, the lime or sulfur should be thoroughly incorporated into the soil. When a few trees in a block of nursery stock require the addition of potassium or one of the trace elements, these can be injected into the root zone with the aid of a punch bar or soil auger. If anhydrous ammonia is used as a source of nitrogen, this has to be chiseled into the soil.

Foliage Application

Fertilizers can be applied to the leaves of plants, since leaves can effectively absorb the applied nutrients. The actual mechanism of foliar absorption is not fully understood. The nutrient ions apparently penetrate the cuticle either directly or through thin permeable areas associated with guard cells and tricome bases. The process is most active when the leaves are warm, and the leaf surfaces remain wet for fairly long periods. Wetting of the leaf surface is enhanced by the addition of a wetting agent to the spray solution. Nitrogen is absorbed very rapidly, within a few hr when applied to the foliage. Potassium, calcium, magnesium, manganese, and zinc are absorbed fairly rapidly, in less than 24 hr, whereas it can take days for sulfur, iron, and molybdenum to be absorbed. Urea sprays are a convenient means for correcting nitrogen deficiency in nursery plantings during periods when the soil is cold and wet. It is generally not economical as a regular nursery practice. Calcium, magnesium, manganese, and zinc deficiency can be readily corrected with one or two sprays during the growing season.

Copper, boron, and molybdenum deficiencies can be corrected very easily by adding small amounts of these minor element fertilizers to spray solution. Copper deficiency is uncommon in nurseries that use Bordeaux mixture in the spray program.

The leaves of most plants will respond to foliar sprays of iron, but the new growth that develops after spraying will remain chlorotic. This is due to the lack of translocation of the iron within the plant. Therefore, if foliage sprays are used to correct iron deficiency, repeat applications will be necessary. Problems with iron deficiency in a nursery should be avoided by proper site selection. Correction of a deficiency might better be accomplished through the use of iron chelates injected into the soil or encapsulated iron implanted into the trunk of trees where this is practical.

Bark Application

Applying fertilizer solutions to the bark of trees has not proven to be too effective as a means of fertilizing trees in nurseries.

TIME OF APPLICATION

The question of when is the best time to apply fertilizer has been discussed for years. Various authorities on the topic of nutrition have recommended fall feeding of trees and others have indicated that spring applications of nitrogen are more effective than summer or fall applications. In a 7-year study on the growth of pin oaks, the variation of the individual growing season was reported to be the most important factor affecting tree growth. Also, it is important that ample moisture be available and favorable temperature conditions prevail following the application of fertilizer.

For nursery crops the best time to apply fertilizer, other than nitrogenous materials, is prior to planting, since these materials should be incorporated into the soil. Nitrogenous materials should be applied annually for best results and at a time when growth will be favorably affected. Nitrogenous fertilizer should not be applied when there is a strong possibility of producing growth that will be injured due to either environmental conditions or cultural practices. There are reports in horticultural journals which attribute some forms of winter injury to late application of nitrogenous fertilizer, whereas other reports indicate that plants that receive a fall application of nitrogen survive exposure to cold better than do nonfertilized plants. There are also reports of plants failing to respond with increased growth following fertilizer application, while other reports indicate excellent response.

To explain and justify all these different responses, it is important for nurserymen to understand growth patterns of woody plants and the ecological factors that affect growth. All plants do not respond the same to light, temperature, and moisture. Some plants grow better under long days than others (Table 11-3). Some stop growth and go dormant under short days. Some plants prefer warm temperature, whereas others grow better at lower temperatures. The same is true for moisture. The plant's growth pattern is a response to many factors, interacting simultaneously.

Woody plants can be classified by growth pattern into two types: (1) heterophyllus (indeterminate growth) types develop two types of leaves during the growing season, those preformed within the bud and those initiated during the current season of growth (e.g., birch, juniper, willow); and (2) homophyllus (determinate growth) types develop one type of leaf during the growing season, preformed within the shoot (e.g., pine, rhododendron, oak).

Heterophyllus plants respond quickly to an application of fertilizer. They continue to grow late into the season as long as the ecological conditions are favorable. However, homophyllus plants do not respond immediately by increased growth, but rather the plant builds up its nutrient reserves and expresses it in a massive growth response the following spring. Under certain artificially produced conditions (long days and warm temperature), these plants can express a growth response during the season shortly after fertilizer application. Therefore, species that are of the heterophyllus type respond best to spring and early summer applications of fertilizer. They might, however, be subject to winter injury if ecological conditions were right and the plants were given a late summer application of fertilizer. Species of the homophyllus type may not exhibit an immediate response to a late spring application of fertilizer, but will build up nutrient reserves from fertilizer applied one year for massive growth response the following year. Plants will absorb and translocate nutrients as long as air and soil temperatures remain favorable. Fall application of fertilizer to homophyllus species could result in a significant increase in growth the following spring, whereas fall applications of fertilizer to heterophyllus species may be less effective.

ORGANIC MATTER

The maintenance of organic matter in nursery soils is an important soil management consideration for field production nurserymen committed to a sustained yield program. With the removal of top soil with many nursery products and with the use of clean cultivation practices, particularly the use of herbicides, the organic-matter content in many nurseries is gradually being depleted. This reduction in organic-matter content will ultimately result in soils of poor tilth, leading to poor plant quality and increased production costs.

Organic matter is of value because it directly influences the physical and biological properties of the soil and because some forms of organic matter serve as a source of nutrients. Organic matter that has been converted to humus improves tilth and soil structure. It reduces the tendency of clay soils to become sticky when wet or to "bake and cake" when dry.

Organic matter also improves aeration, water penetration rates in clay soils, and the water- and nutrient-holding capacity in sandy soils, all of which improve root distribution patterns and plant quality. Organic matter serves as a source of energy for microorganisms that are responsible for the conversion of mineral elements into forms available for plant growth. Organic matter may be either grown as a sod or green manure and plowed under, or it may be added by application of either animal manures or various plant products.

Animal Manures

Animal manures have long been used as a source of organic matter and plant nutrients. Although manures contain relatively low concentrations of plant nutrients on a percentage basis, 0.5-1.5% N, 0.1-0.4% P, and 0.35-1.0% K, they supply appreciable quantities when applied at relatively high rates per acre. The actual composition of manure varies considerably (Table 8-15).

Stable manure may be applied at rates as high as 30 tons/acre, although more frequent smaller applications (5-10 tons/acre) are more effective. The manure can best be applied in late winter when the soil is still frozen and cultivated into the soil as soon as it can be worked in the spring. Poultry manure contains two to three times as much nitrogen as other manures and decays rapidly, releasing ammonia, which can cause plant injury. If the poultry manure is thoroughly mixed with soil or sawdust, it is less likely to cause injury. The primary objections to the use of animal manures is the weed problem that follows application and the cost of handling. The weed problem can be minimized either by using manure obtained from confinement feeding operations or by composting the manure prior to use. Handling cost is offset by improved growth. Animal manure is an excellent organic source of slow-release nutrients. They can be used to good advantage on soils that have been subjected to poor management or have been disturbed as a result of some type of land-forming operation.

Sod and Green Manure

Sod and green manure crops are grown in rotation with nursery crops to improve soil structure and add organic matter. Grasses in combination with legumes are excellent crops for improving nursery soils. Grasses supply organic matter, especially by their dense root system, while taprooted legumes (e.g., alfalfa) improve the internal drainage. For maximum production of organic matter, sods should be grown for 2 years. In situations where a sod crop cannot be used in rotation

Table 8-15 Average nutrient composition of manure from selected farm animals

Kind of manure	Percent water	N	P	K	Ca	Mg	S	Cu	Fe	Mn	Mo
						Pounds per ton of manure					
Chicken	55	31.2	8.0	7.0	74.0	5.8	6.2	0.03	0.93	0.18	0.011
Dairy cattle	80	11.2	2.0	10.0	5.6	2.2	1.0	0.01	0.08	0.02	0.002
Hog	75	10.0	2.8	7.6	11.4	1.6	2.7	0.01	0.56	0.04	0.002
Horse	65	13.8	2.0	12.0	15.7	2.8	1.4	0.01	0.27	0.02	0.002
Sheep	65	28.0	4.2	20.0	11.7	3.7	1.8	0.01	0.32	0.02	0.002

with nursery crops, green manure crops can often be used to advantage. They are grown for less than a growing season and are plowed under while in a succulent state and before they set seed. Tall-growing crops are usually chopped to aid incorporation. Some crops that are used as green manure include (1) annual ryegrass, (2) alfalfa, (3) field corn, (4) foxtail millet, (5) soybeans, (6) sorghum, (7) sudan grass, (8) sudan-sorghum hybrids, and (9) in some areas wheat over-seeded in the spring with clover.

Sudan grass and sudan-sorghum hybrids produce organic matter yields at rates equal to or greater than thickly planted corn. They are more drought-resistant than corn and can be worked into the soil with greater ease. In the cooler parts of the country (climatic zones 3 and 4), foxtail or pearl millet may be preferred, since they grow better under cooler growing conditions (Fig. 6-5). Sudan grass, sudan-sorghum hybrids, and millet can be mowed when they start to head out, causing them to grow more thickly. Several cycles of growth and mowing can be repeated during the year, greatly increasing yield. Fertilizing green manure and cover crops is an excellent way to improve soil fertility, soil structure, and to reduce weed populations.

Cover Crops

Cover crops are grown to protect the soil against the forces of erosion, and aid in maintaining the organic matter content of the soil. It is a common practice in production nurseries located in the northern part of the country (climatic zones 3, 4, and 5) to sow a crop of oats (*Avena sativa*) or buckwheat (*Fagopyrum esculentum*) between the nursery rows in late August or early September to help harden-off the nursery stock for winter by taking up nitrogen. When the ground freezes, the plants die, but a mulch is left to protect the soil over winter and in the early spring. The light mulch also aids in retaining moisture in the spring, enhancing digging operations. In those areas of the nursery where nursery stock has recently been removed or where it is too late to sow a green manure crop, it may be desirable to sow a winter annual such as winter rye (*Secale cereale*) or ryegrass (*Lolium* spp.) in the late summer or early fall. The crop is plowed under in the spring before it goes to seed. However, where land costs are high, a cash crop such as wheat or field corn may be grown. The grain provides a financial return from the land and at the same time the stubble adds organic matter to the soil, improving the tilth for the next nursery crop. Table 8-16 provides some guidelines for the seeding of green manure or cover crops for nursery plantings.

Table 8-16 Suggested seeding rates, planting depth, and planting dates for selected green manures and cover crops[a]

Crop	Seeding rate (lb/acre)	Planting depth (in.)	Planting date
Alfalfa	6-10	½	Spring or summer
Buckwheat	40-60	1-2	Late spring
Corn (field)	1-2 bushels	2	Spring
Kentucky bluegrass	15-30	½	Late summer, very early spring
Millet	10-15	½-1	Late spring
Oats	60-80	1-2	Late summer
Ryegrass	10	½	Fall
Sorghum	5-8	½	Late spring
Sorghum-sudan hybrids	40	1	Late spring

[a]See county agricultural agent for local recommendations.
SOURCE: After Hildebrand and Copeland, 1977.

Table 8-17 Percent of dry weight of carbon and nitrogen and the C/N ratio of selected organic materials

Material	% C	% N	C/N
Alfalfa	39	3.0	13:1
Legume-grass hay	40	1.6	80:1
Oat straw	40	0.5	80:1
Sawdust	50	0.2	250:1

Organic Amendments

Bark or sawdust have been found to be economical soil amendments in some situations when supplemented with nitrogen. When bark or sawdust or other similar materials are applied to or mixed with soil in which plants are growing, nitrogen deficiency can and often does develop. Microorganisms, which multiply due to the presence of the carbonaceous substrate, require nitrogen for growth. They compete more successfully for available nitrogen than do the economic crops resulting in nitrogen deficiency. However, a supplemental application of approximately 2% available nitrogen per unit weight of sawdust will minimize this problem. A C/N ratio of 20:1 or less is needed to avoid the necessity of adding supplemental nitrogen (Table 8-17). In some soils, low in available P_2O_5, supplemental applications of superphosphate may be needed to avoid phosphorus deficiency. Sawdust has a tendency to lower the pH of soils slightly. Where crops requiring an alkaline soil reaction are to be grown, it may be necessary to apply lime to modify this effect.

Peat moss is used to improve many types of landscape soils, but because of its high cost, it is used only in limited ways in the field production of nursery stock. It is used as a medium in container production of plants, as a propagation medium for some species, and as a packaging material.

In preparing land to be planted with a long-term nursery crop, it is highly desirable to incorporate a liberal quantity of organic matter to replace that removed with the previous crop and ensure a long-range supply, since additional application of organic matter is seldom made while the crop is on the land. The land should be plowed to a depth of 8 in. or more to incorporate and distribute the organic matter into the root zone. Following plowing, the land should be disked and, if necessary, smoothed with a harrow.

SOIL CONSERVATION

Soil conservation is another area in a field production nursery to which management must direct its attention if the nursery is to remain productive. Soil conservation is managing the soil so that its productivity can be optimized for both current and future plantings. Unfortunately, many nursery practices contribute to loss of soil productivity; these include (1) loss of soil by digging operations and erosion, (2) long periods of clean cultivation, and (3) performing nursery operations when the soil is wet.

The *loss of soil by digging* B&B or balled and potted nursery stock is considerable. Digging an acre of 5-year B&B evergreens removes about 165 tons of soil, representing an average loss of 33 tons per year. Digging shade trees with a 44-in.-diameter ball removes 1.3 tons of soil, or about 470 tons of soil per acre. This is an average of 67 tons per year for a 7-year rotation. In addition to "mining" of soil, with the sale of plants, nurserymen can also lose a substantial amount by erosion. Under conditions of clean tillage, the loss of soil by erosion varies from 19 to 69 tons/acre/year, depending upon slope, soil type, and environmental conditions. When the average annual "mining" loss of soil for shade tree production is combined with the average annual loss of soil by erosion (44 tons/acre), the amount averages 100 tons of soil per year. At this rate, there would be a loss of 4.2 in. of top soil every 7 years.

Clean cultivation of nursery stock contributes to the loss of soil by erosion and to degradation of soil structure. Allowing the soil surface to remain "naked" following plowing, disking, and cultivating exposes it to erosion. Also, the extensive use of herbicides removes the protective cover of weeds, leaving soil in a prime condition for erosion. The effect of raindrops or sprinkler irrigation water hitting the soil (splash erosion) is the first step in water erosion. Splash erosion breaks down the natural structure of the soil. This breakdown of the soil aggregates results in crusting of the surface and reduced soil porosity. These, in turn, reduce water infiltration, causing more runoff, and increasing the potential for more serious forms of erosion, especially on nonlevel sites.

Performing field operation when the soil is wet is often necessary in field production nurseries, especially in the spring. This practice will compact the soil and reduce its porosity. The overall effect is to reduce its production potential and add to the cost of production. If the soil can be rolled into a "ball" or a "snake," it is too wet for field operations.

SOIL CONSERVATION PRACTICES

Little can be done to prevent the loss of nursery soil that is sold as part of the product, other than to change to a container production system or to produce bare-root plants. However, much can be done to minimize the loss of nursery soils by erosion and to maintain or improve soil structure.

Protecting the soil surface with a canopy of vegetation or with mulches will reduce the effect of rain or irrigation water. Anything that can be done to promote the rapid establishment of the nursery crop is likely to reduce the amount of erosion. Planting a sod crop between the rows (Fig. 5–12) is a desirable conservation practice, where it is a viable option. The planting of green manure or cover crops, discussed previously, is also a desirable soil conservation practice as well as a means of increasing organic matter and improving soil structure. The application of mulches, such as bark or animal manure, to the soil or allowing crop residues to remain on the soil following harvest can also protect the soil surface from splash and wind erosion.

The use of heavy equipment on the land, particularly when the soil is wet, should be minimized. Where feasible, "minimum tillage" should be practiced to reduce the frequency that heavy equipment is upon the land. Prior to tilling the soil, consideration should be given to using a chisel plow in place of the standard moldboard plow. The chisel plow leaves crop residue on the surface, which aids in reducing erosion. Also, when possible, fall plowing should be avoided or confined to level fields, since fall plowing leaves soils exposed to erosion for extended periods.

Across-the-slope tillage or planting nursery rows on the contour will produce small dams that will slow the flow of water and minimize gully erosion on hilly sites. In areas where the terrain is composed of short, irregular slopes, this type of tillage may not be possible.

Strip-cropping uses the concept of growing clean-cultivated crops in alternate strips with close growing or sod crops. Strip-cropping is most effective in areas where the slopes are too steep to control water erosion by contour tillage alone, but not steep enough to require the construction of terraces. Strip-cropping is useful for nurseries situated on long sloping sites, since it permits a rotation to be developed between nursery crops and sod.

Various water disposal systems can be developed in nurseries to minimize soil losses by erosion, including the construction of terraces, grass waterways, and subsurface drainage systems. Terraces are earth ridges, constructed on the contour, to form a damlike channel for the interception of water, which is then slowly conducted from the field by a grassed waterway or underground drains. The shape, width, and length of waterways will vary with size of the watershed area. The driving of cars and trucks should never be permitted on terraces and waterways if they are to remain functional for the purpose for which they were designed.

The success of conservation practices depends upon good design, construction, proper use, and maintenance. Assistance in design and construction can be obtained from local Soil Conservation District engineers and from the USDA Soil Conservation Service. Proper use and maintenance of soil conservation systems is the responsibility of management.

SUMMARY

Field production is a major method for the production of nursery stock. If fields are to be productive for current and future generations, they must be well managed. By developing and practicing good soil-management methods, it is possible to maintain nursery soil productivity at relatively high levels.

REFERENCES

ALLISON, F. E., and M. S. ANDERSON. 1951. The use of sawdust for mulches and soil improvement. USDA Cir. 891.

ANONYMOUS. 1948. Your nursery and soil conservation. American Association of Nurserymen, 230 Southern Building, Washington, D.C. 20005.

BENJAMIN, L. P., L. C. CHADWICK, and K. W. REISCH. 1964. The effectiveness of ureaformaldehyde as a source of nitrogen for container-grown woody ornamental plants. Proc. Am. Soc. Hort. Sci. 84:636–647.

BERG, A., G. CLULO, and C. R. ORTON. 1958. Internal bark necrosis of apple resulting from manganese toxicity. W. Va. Agric. Exp. Sta. Bull. 414T.

BERNSTEIN, L. 1964. Reducing salt injury to ornamental shrubs in the West. USDA Home Garden Bull. 95.

____. 1965. Salt tolerance of fruit crops. USDA Inf. Bull. 292.

BOONSTRA, R., A. L. KENWORTHY, and D. P. WATSON. 1957. Nutritional status of selected plantings of *Taxus media* "Hicksi." Proc. Am. Soc. Hort. Sci. 70:432–436.

BOWER, C. A. 1963. Diagnosing soil salinity. USDA Agric. Inf. Bull. 279.

BRADLEY, G. A. and D. SMITTLE. 1965. Media pH and extractable Fe, Al and Mn in relation to growth of ericaeous plants. Proc. Am. Soc. Hort. Sci. 87:486–493.

CANNON, T. F., L. C. CHADWICK, and K. W. REISCH. 1960. Nitrogen and potassium nutritional studies of *Gleditisia triacanthos Inermis* "Moraine." Proc. Am. Soc. Hort. Sci. 75:693–699.

____, L. C. CHADWICK, and K. W. REISCH. 1960. Nutrient element status of some ornamental trees. Proc. Am. Soc. Hort. Sci. 76:661–666.

CHADWICK, L. C. 1934. The fertilization of shade trees in the nursery. Proc. Am. Soc. Hort. Sci. 32:357–360.

DAVIDSON, H. 1960. Nutrient-element composition of leaves from selected species of woody ornamental plants. Proc. Am. Soc. Hort. Sci. 76:667–672.

____, and W. BARRICK. 1975. Fertilizer practices and vegetation control on highway landscape plantings. Agric. Exp. Sta. Mich. State Univ. Res. Rep. 262.

____, and W. MCCALL. 1959. Fertilizer studies on *Taxus*. Quar. Bull. Mich. Agric. Exp. Sta. 42(2):317–322.

DICKEY, R. D. 1968. Identification and correction of copper deficiency. Am. Nurseryman 128(8):10.

DUNHAM, C.W., and D. V. TATNALL. 1961. Mineral composition of leaves of

216

three holly species grown in nutrient sand cultures. Proc. Am. Soc. Hort. Sci. 78:564–571.

FENN, P., and R. D. DURBIN. 1974. A nutritional disorder of red oak seedlings. HortScience 9(3):240–241.

FURUTA, T., and W. C. MARTIN. 1961. Effect of fertilizer application rate and method on plant growth. Proc. Am. Soc. Hort. Sci. 77:637–642.

GOOD, G. L., and H. B. TUKEY, JR. 1969. Root growth and nutrient uptake by dormant *Ligustrum ibolium* and *Euonymus atatus* "Compactus." J. Am. Soc. Hort. Sci. 94(3): 324–326.

GOUIN, F. R., and C. B. LINK. 1966. The effects of various levels of nitrogen, phosphorus and potassium on the growth and chemical composition of *Taxus media* "Hatfieldi." Proc. Am. Soc. Hort. Sci. 89:702–705.

HAMILTON, C. L. Terraced outlets and form drainways. USDA Farmers' Bull. 1814, July 1939.

HILDEBRAND, S. C. and L. O. COPELAND. 1977. Coop Ext. Serv. Mich. State Univ. Ext. Bull. E-489.

HIMELICH, E. B., D. NEELY, and W. R. CROWLER, JR. 1965. Experimental field studies on shade tree fertilization. Ill. Nat. Hist. Surv. Biol. Notes 53.

JACOBSON, P., and W. WEISS. Farming terraced land, USDA Soil Conserv. Serv. Leaflet 335, November 1952.

KELLEY, J. D. 1972. Nitrogen and potassium rate effects on growth, leaf nitrogen and winter hardiness of *Pyracantha coccinia* "Lalandi" and *Ilex crenata* "Rotundifolia." J. Am. Soc. Hort. Sci. 97(4):446–448.

____, and R. W. SHIER. 1965. Seasonal changes in the macronutrient composition of the leaves and stems of *Taxus media*. Proc. Am. Soc. Hort. Sci. 86:809–814.

____, and R. W. SHIER. 1965. Seasonal changes in the micronutrient composition of leaves and stems of *Taxus media*. Proc. Am. Soc. Hort. Sci. 87: 545–550.

KIELBASO, J. J., and K. OTTMAN. 1976. Manganese deficiency contributory to maple decline. J. Arboriculture:27–32.

LUNT, H. A., A. M. KOFRANEK, and J. J. OERTLI. 1961. Coated fertilizers: general description and applications. Calif. Agric. 15(12):2–3.

____, and J. J. OERTLI. 1962. Controlled release of fertilizer minerals by incapsulating membranes: II. Efficiency of recovery influence of soil moisture, mode of application and other considerations related to use. Soil Sci. Soc. Am. Proc. 26(6):584–587.

MEYER, M. M., JR. 1969. External and internal nutrition and spring growth of woody ornamental plants. Proc. Int. Plant Propag. Soc. 19:300–305.

_____. 1971. Phosphorus utilization from internal and external sources in the growth of woody ornamental plants. J. Am. Soc. Hort. Sci. 96(2):209–212.

_____, and H. B. TUKEY, JR. 1965. Nitrogen, phosphorus and potassium plant reserves and spring growth of *Taxus* and *Forsythia*. Proc. Am. Soc. Hort. Sci. 87:537–544.

_____, and H. B. TUKEY, JR. 1967. Influence of root temperature and nutrient applications on root growth and mineral content of *Taxus* and *Forsythia* plants during the dormant season. Proc. Am. Soc. Hort. Sci. 90:440–446.

MILLER, R. O., and D. C. KIPLINGER, and H. K. TAYAMA. 1967. Soluble salts. Florists Rev., November 2, p. 49.

NEELY, D., E. B. HIMELICK, and W. R. CROWLEY, JR. 1970. Ill. Nat. Hist. Surv. Bull. 30, Art. 4, pp. 235–266.

OERTLI, J., and O. R. LUNT. 1962. Controlled release of fertilizer minerals by incapsulating membranes: 1. Factors influencing the rate of release. Soil Sci. Soc. Am. Proc. 26(6):579–583.

RADER, L. F., L. M. WHITE, and C. W. WHITTAKER. 1943. The salt index—a measure of the effect of fertilizers on the concentration of the soil solution. Soil Sci. 55:201–218.

ROBERTSON, L. S., D. L. MOKMA, and D. L. QUINSENBERRY. 1977. Soil erosion by water. Coop. Ext. Serv. Mich. State Univ. Ext. Bull. E–1169.

ROGERS, B. L., A. H. THOMPSON, and L. E. SCOTT. 1965. Internal bark necrosis (measles) on Delicious apple trees under field conditions. Proc. Am. Soc. Hort. Sci. 86:46–54.

SCHOENEWEISS, D. F. 1973. Correction of lime-induced chlorosis of pin oak by liquid soil injection. HortScience 8(4):333–334.

SHEAR, C. B., H. L. CRANE, and A. T. MYERS. 1946. Nutrient element balance: a fundamental concept in plant nutrition. Proc. Am. Soc. Hort. Sci. 47:239–248.

_____, H. L. CRANE, and A. T. MYERS. 1950. Nutrient element balance: application of the concept to the interpretation of foliar analysis. Proc. Am. Soc. Hort. Sci. 51:319–326.

SMITH, E. M. 1975. Fertilizing field-grown evergreens and shrubs. Am. Nurseryman 142(10):10.

_____. 1975. Growth response of fertilized trees. Am. Nurseryman 143(1):11.

SPURWAY, C. H. 1944. Soil reaction (pH) preferences of plants Mich. State Col., Agric. Exp. Sta. Special Bul. 306.

_____, and K. LAWTON. 1949. Soil testing, a practical system of fertility diagnosis. Mich. State Univ. Agric. Exp. Sta. Tech. Bull. 132 (4th revision).

TATNALL, D. V., and C. W. DUNHAM. 1961. Nutrient deficiency symptoms in American, Japanese and Chinese hollies. Proc. Am. Soc. Hort. Sci. 78: 560–563.

WIKLE, J. 1963. Some comments and questions on soil improvement and fertilization for shade trees. Arborist News:61–69.

WILDE, S. A. 1938. Soil fertility standards for growing northern conifers in forest nurseries. J. Agric. Res. 57:945–952.

____. 1946. Soil fertility standards for game food plants. J. Wildl. Manage. 10:77–81.

____, and W. E. PATZER. 1940. Soil fertility standards for growing northern hardwoods in forest nurseries. J. Agric. Res. 61:215–221.

WITTWER, S. H. 1963. Foliar application of fertilizer. New Horizons in the Fertilizer World. Tennessee Valley Authority.

YOUNGBERG, C. T., and R. C. AUSTIN. 1954. Fertility standards for raising Douglas fir in forest nurseries. J. For. 52:4–6.

____, and R. C. AUSTIN. 1958. The uptake of nutrients by western conifers in forest nurseries. J. For. 56(5):337–340.

ZIMMERMAN, R. H. 1959. Visual symptoms of plant nutrient deficiencies. Proc. Int. Plant Propag. Soc. 9:131–135.

SUGGESTED READING

DIRR, M. A. 1975. Plant nutrition and woody ornamental growth and quality. HortScience 10(1):43–45.

DONAHUE, R. L., R. W. MILLER, and J. C. SHICKLUNA. 1977. Soils: an introduction to soils and plant growth. Prentice-Hall, Inc., Englewood Cliffs, N.J.

MENGEL, K., and E. A. KIRKBY. 1978. Principles of plant nutrition. International Potash Institute, Worblaufen-Bern, Switzerland.

METHODS OF SOIL ANALYSIS, Parts 1 & 2. 1965. Amer. Soc. of Agronomy, 677 South Segoe Rd. Madison, Wisc. 53711.

U.S.D.A. SOIL, THE YEARBOOK OF AGRICULTURE. 1957. Superintendent of Documents, Washington, D.C.

Chapter 9

Media and Nutrition Management for Container-Grown Plants

Producing plants in containers has become a permanent part of the nursery industry and in some parts of the country the practice has replaced field culture as the primary method of production. In contrast to field culture, the volume of medium available per plant is greatly reduced. Also, the root environment is significantly affected by the physical and chemical composition of the medium, the size and shape of the container, the surface upon which it is placed to grow, and the ambient atmosphere surrounding the containers. Therefore, good container-media management is basic to the production of quality container-grown plants. It is necessary to (1) understand the primary functions and establish some basic criteria for container media, (2) be familiar with the physical and chemical properties of some of the more commonly used ingredients and mixes, (3) understand the need for chemical supplements and method of testing and controlling their availability, and (4) understand the need for and methods of media sterilization.

FUNCTIONS AND CRITERIA

In developing a medium for the production of container-grown plants, the functions of the medium in plant growth and development must be understood and criteria determined to produce the most functional medium for the climate and for the nursery objective. The two basic functions of the medium are (1) to serve as a means of anchorage and support for the plant and (2) to serve as a reservoir for water and the mineral nutrients for plant growth and development. In addition, the medium must have a pH conducive to plant growth, a structure that will permit gaseous exchange to provide aeration for the roots and permit water infiltration and movement.

Anchorage and Support

The roots of plants serve to anchor them to the soil, which in turn serves to support the plant. In field production this works, since the roots can grow unrestricted. However, in container culture the roots are restricted to the confines of the container. Therefore, a medium for container production of plants in a nursery must be heavy enough to provide ballast for the species of plant it will support, unless other forms of artificial support are provided, particularly for larger trees and shrubs. Small plants produced in 1- to 5-gal containers and spaced pot to pot can be grown in a medium of low bulk density (BD)—weight per unit of volume—whereas larger plants grown on wider spacings require a medium of higher BD. Where the plants are large and the BD of the medium is low, some other form of support is necessary, such as staking or tying to a wire.

Nutrients

Plants produced in containers require the same essential elements as plants produced in field culture. The total supply of minerals available for plant growth is limited by the size of the container. This makes it desirable that the medium used for container production have a relatively high cation exchange capacity (CEC) to serve as a reservoir for mineral elements other than nitrogen or those that will be supplied by other means. Most of the organic ingredients provide this even though at a low level. The CEC for medium mixtures used in container production of plants should be reported on a volume basis, which is expressed as milliequivalents per 100 cubic centimeters (e.g., sand approximately 1 mEq/100 cc, bark approximately 11-13 mEq/100 cc). Maintaining optimum levels of nitrogen during the growing season may be done through the use of slow-release fertilizers (page 194) or by the use of soluble fertilizers applied through the irrigation system (Table 8-10).

Soil (Medium) Reaction (pH)

The optimum pH for organic mixes (Fig. 9-1) tends to be 1-1.5 units lower than those generally considered to be desirable for mineral soils (Fig. 8-1). Liming organic soils with a pH above 5.8 is undesirable because of the reduced availability of P, Mn, B, Cu, and Zn.

Moisture-Holding Capacity and Porosity

Growing plants require large quantities of water for metabolic purposes and to replace that which is lost by transpiration. Therefore, one of the important functions of a good container medium is to store and supply the moisture needed for plant growth. However, for the moisture to be available to the plants requires that the roots must have a supply of oxygen, necessitating that the container medium have good aeration porosity so that the roots can carry on respiration and allow for the removal of the carbon dioxide (CO_2) that is generated in the process. This presents somewhat of a problem with containers, since they are relatively shallow and develop a perched water table at the bottom of the container. The shallower the container and the finer the texture, the greater the moisture-holding capacity but the poorer the aeration porosity. On the other hand, deep containers and coarse-textured materials improve the aeration porosity but reduce the moisture-holding capacity.

The effect of shallowness can be partially avoided by incorporating coarse-textured ingredients (sand, bark, perlite) into the container medium. However, sufficient coarse material must be blended into an ingredient of fine texture so that the threshold proportion is exceeded. This is the blend or mix at which pore space is minimized; as the proportion of the coarse texture ingredient is increased beyond the threshold proportion, porosity is increased (Fig. 9-2). Improvement of the porosity of a fine-textured medium requires a substantial addition (80-90% of the total bulk volume) of the coarse-texture ingredient. A medium for the production of container-grown plants should be blended to produce a mix that has good water-holding capacity and also good porosity. This is dependent upon the texture of the various ingredients and the relative proportions within the mix.

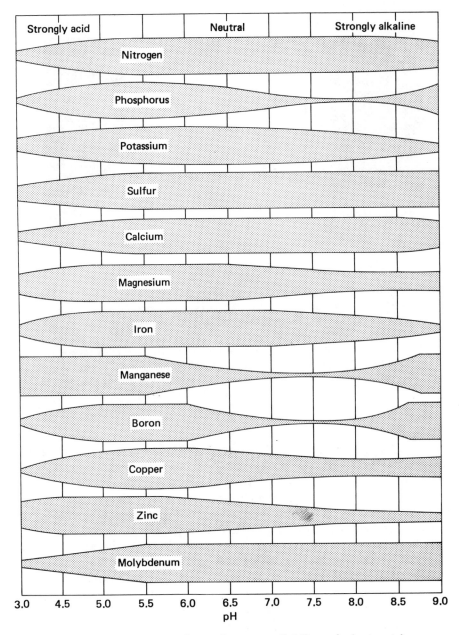

Figure 9-1 Influence of reaction on availability of plant nutrients (organic soils). Widest part of bar indicates maximum availability. (Source: Lucas and Davis,1961.)

Figure 9-2 Modifying aeration and water-holding capacity of container soil. Starting with 100 percent soil, additions of perlite up to about 70 percent (critical proportion) reduce total pore space without increasing the number of larger pores. Starting with 100 percent perlite, additions of soil up to about 30 percent reduce total pore space by filling in the larger pores. The critical proportion of amendment to soil varies with the kind of amendment and the kind of soil. (Source: Spomer, 1973.)

Porosity determines the volume of the container, when filled with a medium, that is potentially available for water, air, and for root growth. Pore size determines the actual volume of water and air that remains in a container medium following irrigation and drainage; the small pores function as water-retention pores, whereas large pores function as aeration pores (aeration porosity).

Aeration porosity and water retention of a container medium are also influenced by the depth of the container. A medium in a shallower container will hold a greater volume of water than the same volume of medium in a deeper container. Therefore, when characterizing water retention and aeration porosity of a container medium, it is necessary to consider container depth.

Although it is not possible, owing to the lack of data, to provide specific recommendations as to the aeration porosity requirements for the optimal growth of plants grown in containers, it is suggested that a value less than 10 be considered low and a value greater than 25 be considered high.

Nurserymen can estimate the total porosity, aeration porosity, and water-retention porosity of a container medium by a simple technique. The only necessary equipment includes the container, a plug for the drainage hole at the bottom of the container, and a graduated cylinder or some other method for measuring water volume.

1. Plug the drain hole and fill the container with water. Measure the volume of water it contains (= container volume).

2. Empty the container and fill it with dry soil mix. Very slowly and very thoroughly saturate the mix in the container by carefully pouring water onto the surface at one edge of the container. Keep track of the volume of water you are adding (= pore volume).

3. Unplug the drain and catch the water that drains out of the container and measure its volume (= aeration pore volume).

4. Porosity is obtained by dividing pore volume (step 2) by container volume (step 1) and multiplying by 100%.

5. Aeration porosity is obtained by dividing aeration pore volume (step 3) by container volume (step 1) and multiplying by 100%.

6. Water retention porosity is obtained by subtracting aeration porosity (step 5) from porosity (step 4).

In summary:

$$\text{Porosity} = \frac{\text{container mix pore volume}}{\text{container volume}} \times 100\%$$

$$\text{Aeration porosity} = \frac{\text{aeration pore volume}}{\text{container volume}} \times 100\%$$

$$\text{Water-retention porosity} = \text{porosity} - \text{aeration porosity}$$

SOURCE: Spomer, 1977.

INGREDIENTS

The two most commonly used ingredients in the production of media for container growing of woody plants have been sand and peat moss. However, soil is used in some mixes and various wood-waste products are being used to replace peat moss. Composted hardwood bark is used fairly extensively in the Midwest, pine and Douglas fir bark is used where it is readily available, and redwood sawdust is used in California.

The following information briefly summarizes some of the properties of the most commonly used ingredients as they pertain to the production of container-grown plants.

Sand consists of weathered mineral particles between 0.05 and

2.0 mm in diameter. But for container-soil mixes, the size range should be between 0.05 and 1.0 mm with less than 10% of the sand in the coarse-sized classification, between 0.5 and 1.0 mm. The mineral composition of the sand is related to the rocks from which it was formed, but for horticultural purposes sand contains few, if any, mineral elements, and has no significant buffering or cation exchange capacity. Sand may or may not be sterile, depending upon the source.

Peats used in media for the production of container-grown plants are commonly classified into three types: moss peat, reed-sedge peat, and peat humus.

Moss peat is composed principally of sphagnum, hypnum, and other mosses. Sphagnum is the least decomposed of the three types. It is light tan to dark brown in color, lightweight, high in moisture-holding capacity, and high in acidity. Moss peat will hold 10 times its dry weight in moisture, and because of its high acidity it is slow to decompose. Moss peat should not be confused with sphagnum moss, which is the live portion or the young, nondecomposed residue of sphagnum. Sphagnum moss is used by nurserymen in packaging and shipping of tender plants and as a propagation medium.

Reed-sedge peat is formed principally of reeds, sedges, marsh grasses, and other swamp plants. It varies considerably in its degree of decomposition and acidity. The partially decomposed reed-sedge peats are brown to reddish brown in color, whereas the more decomposed types are almost black. They have a pH between 4.5 and 7.0 and a medium water-holding capacity.

Peat humus is derived from either reed-sedge or hypnum moss peat in an advanced stage of decomposition. It is dark brown to black in color, has a low water-holding capacity, but is more resistant to decomposition than is moss or reed-sedge peat.

Wood products of various types, including sawdust, wood chips, shredded bark, and wood shavings, are an excellent source of organic material for soil mixtures in the production of container-grown plants. For many years nurserymen declined to use wood products as a soil amendment because it was thought they contained materials that were toxic to plant growth. However, present evidence indicates that sawdust and most other woodwaste products contain relatively few compounds that are toxic to plant growth.

The reason for the "toxic" effect, a stunting and chlorosis of the plant, is related to the carbon–nitrogen ratio of the sawdust and its effect upon the soil–plant nitrogen relationship. When undecomposed wood products, such as sawdust or wood chips, are mixed with soil under favorable conditions of warm temperature and available moisture, they start to decompose. The decomposition is aided by various forms of microflora. These microorganisms require a source of energy carbon, which is supplied by the wood, and a source of nitrogen, which the wood does not supply except in trace quantities. Therefore, the microflora obtain the needed nitrogen from the only other available source, the soil. If there are plants present, the microorganisms compete with them for the available nitrogen, and unless there is enough for both, the plants will exhibit nitrogen deficiency. This problem can be avoided by the addition of nitrogen to the sawdust–soil mixture. If the nitrogen content of the mixture, on a weight basis, is about 1.2–1.5% and optimum conditions for biological activity are present, decomposition will proceed without depleting the supply of available nitrogen to the growing crop. Since sawdust contains about 0.2% nitrogen, the addition of 25–30 lb nitrogen/ton of sawdust are required.

Aged sawdust makes an excellent ingredient for container production of nursery stock. It is lightweight, has good water-holding capacity, and good aeration porosity. It does not require the addition of large quantities of nitrogen to support microbial development, and it is relatively sterile.

Hardwood bark is a lightweight, woodwaste product which when supplemented with nitrogen makes an excellent organic ingredient for the production of container-grown plants. It may be used alone or in combination with sand. It is lightweight, easy to handle, and the CEC exceeds that of peat. Bark contains all the trace elements and significant amounts of the major elements. Some hardwood barks may contain phytotoxic substances that are harmful to plant growth. But by composting for a period of at least 30 days, most of these compounds are eliminated. The material is readily available in many parts of the country and is relatively inexpensive.

Pine and Douglas fir bark is an excellent medium for the production of plants that prefer an acid root environment such as rhododendrons. It is also used either alone or in combination with sand, after the pH has been adjusted, for the production of all types of container-grown plants. Softwood bark has a low bulk density and a fairly good CEC (11–13 mEq/100 cc). It is somewhat difficult to wet, but upon wetting it possesses a good water-holding capacity, together with good aeration. Some barks, such as Douglas fir, contain sharp slivers, which necessitates the use of leather gloves when handling the material.

Perlite is a lightweight, granular material obtained by heat-treating crushed lava. It weighs less than 8 lb/ft^3. It is sterile, has a pH close to neutral, and a water-holding capacity, on the surface of the particles, equal to three to four times its weight. The material is without either buffering or cation exchange capacity. Perlite is a good propagation medium or an amendment to decrease weight and improve aeration of container mixes.

Vermiculite is a very lightweight, platelike material obtained by heat-treating mica. It weighs about the same as perlite, 6–10 lb/ft^3, depending upon the grade; has a good water-holding capacity, equal to three to four times its weight; and a good CEC. Since the material is produced by heat treatment, it is sterile. Vermiculite makes an excellent propagation medium and a media amendment for producing small container-grown plants. It must be handled with care when wet to avoid compressing the particles. Compressed vermiculite is an undesirable media amendment, since it results in poor drainage and poor aeration porosity.

Turface is a calcined clay that is excellent for improving the aeration porosity of soils or container mixes. Its bulk density is greater than perlite or vermiculite, but it has good internal capacity for holding nutrients and water.

CONTAINER MEDIA

A good container medium must possess the criteria and perform the various functions discussed previously. In addition, it should be: (1) readily available; (2) relatively inexpensive; (3) light enough to be handled conveniently within the nursery and to be transported economically to market; (4) free of pests (weed seeds, disease organisms, insects, nematodes, herbicide residue, etc.) or be capable of being sterilized without the production of toxic substances (e.g., soluble salts, ammonia, biuret, or other phytoxins); (5) economically blended into a uniform, relatively stable medium; and (6) capable of being stored for short periods of time without significant changes in the physical and chemical properties.

Mixes

The early container mixes, prior to 1940, incorporated a loam soil; a clean, sharp sand; and peat in various proportions. This was supplemented with lime, superphosphate, and various fertilizers, which generally included an organic source of nitrogen. But these mixes were not satisfactory because they lacked uniformity and plant performance was highly variable. Soil and sand have a high bulk density (100 lb/ft^3), making them difficult to handle and costly to transport to market.

John Innes Composts

In 1939 researchers at the John Innes Institute in England published recommendations on the development of two standardized composts that could be used for all kinds of plants. Since that time, they have modified their recommendations only slightly. The basic ingredients of the John Innes composts are a medium loam, containing little or no sand; fibrous or granular, relatively undecomposed peat; and coarse sand. The loam used in the John Innes mixes is the primary ingredient. Its functions are to supply the nutrient-holding capacity for the medium and the actively decomposing humus, which furnishes the microflora needed in a good biologically active soil mixture. The ingredients are blended by volume, according to a strict formula, composted for a period of time, and then sterilized and fortified with various soil amendments to adjust the pH and supplement the nutritive condition of the compost. The basic principles relating to compost development, as stated in the first edition of *Seed and Potting Composts,* are still in use today and have served as the basis for the development of soil mixes and container-culture programs in other countries.

The U.C.-Type Soil Mixes

The U.C. system for producing healthy container-grown plants was developed at the University of California, Los Angeles, in the 1940s and early 1950s. The primary objective of the system was to reduce cost of production by reducing plant losses and by lowering labor costs through mechanization. One part of the system was the development of the U.C.-type soil mixes, which have the qualities of reproducibility and reliability. The physical and chemical properties can be reproduced with a high degree of consistency, and the various mixes will function in a consistent manner under similar production programs.

The basic ingredients for the mixes are fine sand (0.5–0.05 mm) and peat moss of the sphagnum type. However, redwood shavings, sawdust, or rice hulls can substitute for all or part of the peat moss. If rice hulls are used, they should be sterilized to avoid having rice as a weed problem. The ingredients are blended on a percent by volume basis, producing five basic mixes when blended in 25% increments of fine sand to peat moss. The two most commonly used mixes were 75% fine sand plus 25% peat moss, and 50% fine sand plus 50% peat moss.

The U.C. mixes are fortified with various fertilizers to provide an available supply of the major nutrients: N, P, K, Ca, and Mg. The peat moss and fine sand contain a sufficient supply of the micro-elements to meet the needs of most container-grown plants. How-ever, some acid-requiring plants (e.g., rhododendron, blueberry) and plants grown in containers for long periods of time may require a supplemental application of iron chelate or a minor element fertilizer which contains a mixture of the microelements.

The type of fertilizer to be added varies with the medium, the storage requirement prior to planting, soil salinity problems, and the supplemental fertilizer practices to be followed after planting. Six fertilizer programs are suggested for each of the five mixes, produc-ing a total of 30 container-production media programs.

Prior to mixing the various ingredients, the peat moss should be thoroughly moistened to ensure uniform mixing. The fertilizer materials must be carefully weighed and mixed together, preferably in a small quantity of sand, prior to mixing with the various ingre-dients of the mix. This will aid in obtaining uniform distribution of the chemical materials throughout the mix and ensure that every cubic yard of mix is the same, both physically and chemically. The U.C. mixes can be sterilized, after blending, with a high degree of assurance that there will be no salinity problems and no detrimental effects upon plants due to soil salinity.

Cornell Peat-Lite Mixes

The Cornell Peat-Lite mixes were developed at Cornell University in the 1960s primarily for seed propagation and production of spring annuals and bedding plants. The basic ingredients of the Peat-Lite mix are sphagnum moss and either vermiculite or perlite, to which is added specific quantities of dolomitic limestone, superphosphate, and a complete fertilizer with a ratio of 1:2:1. To make a cubic yard of these mixes, the ingredients are blended as follows:

Peat-Lite Mix A

11 bushels	Sphagnum peat moss
11 bushels	Horticultural grade 2 or 4 vermiculite
5 lb	Dolomitic lime
1 lb	Single superphosphate (fine)
2–12 lb	5-10-5 fertilizer; 12 lb will supply the nutrient needs of annual plants for about 6 weeks. If less than 12 lb is used, a supplemental fertilizer pro-gram is necessary.

Peat-Lite Mix B
Substitute horticultural-grade perlite for the vermiculite.

The Peat-Lite mixes have several advantages for growers of bedding plants: they are light in weight, the ingredients are uniform, readily available, and sterile. But they have limited use in nursery production, since the medium provides no ballast to support the relatively heavy crowns of woody plants. They are used most successfully for starting seedlings and in the potting of roses and small shrubs for short periods of time (i.e., potting roses in late winter and growing for 1 to 2 months for spring sale). When they are used for larger plants, it is necessary to provide some artificial means of plant support, such as staking or tying to a wire trellis. Peat-Lite mixes must be thoroughly moistened prior to use and firmly compacted about the roots of plants to assure satisfactory results.

Hardwood Bark

Hardwood bark, a woodwaste by-product from various forest industries throughout the United States, especially in the Midwest and eastern states, is an excellent material, either alone or in combination with sand for use as a medium for the production of container-grown plants. It is desirable to hammermill and essential to compost the bark prior to use as a plant-growth medium. The optimum particle size is between $\frac{1}{8}$ and $\frac{1}{32}$ in. Approximately 35% of the particles should be smaller than $\frac{1}{32}$ in. and approximately 10% should be larger than $\frac{1}{8}$ in. to assure good drainage and aeration.

Hardwood bark has a C/N ratio of 150:1, whereas a ratio of 20:1 is most desirable when it is used as a medium for plant growth. To reduce the C/N ratio, the bark is composted with 2 lb of actual nitrogen (6 lb of ammonium nitrate) per cubic yard. Freshly harvested bark has a pH close to 5.2, but this increases as it ages. To keep the pH in the desirable range for good plant growth, 1 lb each of elemental sulfur and iron sulfate is added per cubic yard of bark at the time of composting. It is not necessary to add calcium or magnesium, since there is an adequate supply of these elements in the bark. Phosphorus (2.5 lb of treble superphosphate per cubic yard) is also added at the time of composting. Potassium (2 lb/yd^3) should be added at time of composting if it is omitted from the fertilizer program during the production phase. All the chemical supplements must be uniformly mixed with the bark prior to composting.

The compost pile should be constructed on a well-drained site to assure good drainage. After thorough wetting, the ingredients are formed into a pile 6–8 ft high, 6–8 ft wide, but of any convenient length, to assure that heating and composting will take place. During composting the temperature within the pile will reach 140°F, plus or minus a few degrees. After the temperature reaches its peak within 30 to 60 days and cools by 10–15°F, the pile should be remixed and piled for another period of composting. After the temperature in the pile reaches its second maximum and declines, the material is ready for use as a medium for container-grown plants. The bottom 1 ft of compost should be mixed with some of the upper portions to minimize injury from soluble salts. The postcomposting fertilizer program for plants growing in hardwood bark is dependent upon how the compost is prepared, the amount used in the container mix, and the market objective.

Composted hardwood bark is reported to suppress nematode populations and some parasitic diseases of plants. But it can contain high levels of manganese, which may be toxic to some plants; levels as high as 992–1125 ppm were associated with chlorotic, stunted Japanese holly plants grown in composted hardwood bark.

Softwood Bark

Pine and Douglas fir bark, alone or blended with fine sand, peat moss, and perlite, is used in many parts of the country in the production of container-grown plants. Pine bark is the most commonly used softwood bark. It should be hammermilled to pass through a ½-in. mesh screen. Because of the lack of uniformity of the bark, it is desirable to have a chemical and physical analysis made on the material as it is obtained from the mill and to adjust the physical and chemical amendments accordingly. Pine bark dries out fairly rapidly requiring frequent watering. To increase the water-holding capacity, ingredients, such as fine sand or peat moss, can be added.

Pine bark has a low pH and is an excellent medium for growing plants that like an acid soil reaction. When used to grow species that respond to a higher pH level, it should be supplemented with 5 lb of limestone per cubic yard. Since pine bark has a high C/N ratio (about 300:1), it must be supplemented with nitrogen. Pine bark that has aged for a couple of years is more desirable than is freshly milled bark.

Municipal Compost

Municipal compost has also been used as the organic ingredient in soil mixes for the production of container-grown plants. It consists of garbage or leaf mold that has been ground in a hammermill, sprayed with sewage, and composted in windrows for 12–16 weeks. A mixture of soil–perlite–municipal compost on a 1:1:1 volume basis has produced quality plants when fertilized with a water-soluble, inorganic fertilizer used as either a constant or biweekly liquid feed. If municipal compost or sewage is to be used as a container medium, it should be subjected to a chemical analysis, especially for heavy metals which can produce undesirable effects upon plant growth. Also, in some communities there may be laws that prohibit its use because of various environmental concerns.

Other Materials

A great diversity of other materials, such as stones, ground corncobs, spent hops, and so on, are or can be used as media amendments. However, prior to use they should be checked for their chemical and physical properties and tested on a trial basis prior to extensive use. There are also prepared ready-to-use mixes that can be purchased commercially. These, too, should be tested prior to use and monitored periodically during the growing season to minimize potential problems and assure optimum growth.

CHEMICAL SUPPLEMENTS

Most media manufactured for the production of container-grown plants will require some form of chemical supplement to adjust the pH and to augment the available nutrients. A chemical analysis of the medium and its components should be obtained, unless this information is known.

Peat moss and softwood bark tend to be acidic and may require the addition of limestone to raise the pH if it is below 5.8. However, liming organic soils with a pH above 5.8 is undesirable because of reduced availability of a number of the essential elements. Some sources of peat and hardwood bark are alkaline and sulfur or iron sulfate should be added to lower the pH. Table 9-1 suggests the pounds of limestone or sulfur needed per cubic yard of peat to affect the desired pH change.

Some of the ingredients used for producing artificial soil mixes are low in available P, Ca, Mg, Fe, and various micro elements. Therefore, it is necessary to supplement the medium with an available supply of these nutrients either during composting or just prior to planting. Peat is naturally low in micro elements. Manganese may be needed for naturally well-limed reed-sedge peat, whereas copper, molybdenum, and iron are needed for sphagnum moss peat and fibrous acid sedge peat. If plant deficiency problems appear, the

Table 9-1 Pounds of dolomitic limestone[a] or sulfur needed per cubic yard of peat

Original pH of peat	Desired pH of peat	
	pH 4.5–5.2[b]	pH 5.3–6.2[c]
3.4–3.9	8 lb limestone	14 lb limestone
4.0–4.4	4 lb limestone	10 lb limestone
4.5–5.2	None	5 lb limestone
5.3–6.2	2 lb sulfur	None
6.3–7.0	4 lb sulfur	2 lb sulfur

[a]If obtainable, a mixture of equal parts of dolomitic and calcic limestone is preferred to all-dolomitic limestone.
[b]Desirable pH for rhododendrons, many conifers, and tropical plants.
[c]Desirable pH for most bedding plants and tree nurseries.
SOURCE: Lucas et al., 1971.

Table 9-2 Suggested micronutrient mixtures for 1 cubic yard of peat

Compound	Weight needed
Iron chelate or ferrous sulfate	50 g (2 oz)
Manganese sulfate	30 g (1 oz)
Copper sulfate	10 g (0.3 oz)
Zinc sulfate	6 g (0.2 oz)
Sodium borate (borax)	3 g (0.1 oz)
Sodium molybdate	1 g (0.03 oz)
Total mix	100 g (3.6 oz)

SOURCE: Lucas et al., 1971.

micronutrient mixture in Table 9-2 is suggested for each cubic yard of peat in the mixture. Use only powdered or fine crystalline materials and mix gradually as the mix is blended.

Additional amounts of fertilizer may be needed, depending upon the mix and the length of time that the plants are to be grown in the container. Plants growing in mixes other than the John Innes and the U.C. mixes will require supplemental nitrogen and potassium shortly after planting. This can be accomplished, most satisfactorily, by the addition of one of the slow- or controlled-release fertilizers at the time of planting. The rate of application will vary with the mix and the fertility program of the nursery. If a 1:1 sand/peat medium is used, a rate of application that supplies nitrogen at 300 ppm is satisfactory to supply the nutrient requirements of the plants for about 4 months.

Plants that are to be grown for extended periods of time will require further applications of nitrogen and possibly potassium. This can be applied either as a dry surface application or as a water-soluble fertilizer. The latter can be done most effectively by proportioning a water-soluble fertilizer concentrate solution into the irrigation system (see Chapter 10). A commercial water-soluble fertilizer can be used or a mixture of equal parts of ammonium nitrate and potassium nitrate (23-0-22). An application rate that supplies nitrogen at 100-150 ppm at each watering is used for most media. But a rate of 200-300 ppm N is suggested for hardwood bark, except when the bark has been supplemented with a slow-release fertilizer prior to planting.

TESTING AND MODIFYING

To assure uniformity of production, the media should be tested periodically to assure proper blending prior to planting and that optimum levels of nutrition are maintained during the growing season. Media samples should be tested by a reputable soil testing service for pH, soluble salts, and total available N, P, K, Ca, and Mg. If the blending is being done correctly and the raw materials are uniformly consistent, the values for the various parameters should remain relatively constant. If there is a significant change in any of the values, measures can be taken to correct the situation before it becomes a serious problem.

Soil-testing procedures vary considerably among laboratories. However, efforts are being made to standardize methods, and at some future date one set of standards may apply. Until that time two standards are provided; one as guide to growers who use or subscribe to a service that employs the saturated-soil-extract method (Table 9-3) and the other as a guide to those who use a soil–water ratio method (Table 9-4) of soil testing.

Saturated-Soil-Extract Method

Nitrate–nitrogen levels will vary with the age and species of the crop. Seedlings and newly propagated plants function better at lower levels than do more mature plants. Values above 200 ppm are unnecessarily high, and above 300 ppm may cause nutritional problems. Nitrogen fertilizer should be applied when the level in the saturated

Table 9-3 Suggested nutrient levels in saturated soil extracts for container mixes

	Concentration	
	Acceptable[a]	*Optimum*
Nutrient	*ppm in saturated extract*	
Nitrate-nitrogen (NO_3-N)	40–100	125–175
Phosphorus (P)	5–10	10–15
Potassium (K)	60–140	150–250
Calcium (Ca)	80–200	200–350
Magnesium (Mg)	35–60	75–100
	Micromhos	
Soluble salts	750–2000	2000–3500

[a]Acceptable for most plants when optimal growth is not the primary concern.
SOURCE: Coop. Ext. Serv. Mich. State Univ. Ext. Bull. E-1275, 1978.

Table 9-4 Nitrogen fertilizer needed to increase soil saturation extract test by approximately 10 ppm

Percent N in fertilizer	*Ounces of nitrogen fertilizer per cubic yard of soil*
10	4.0
16	2.4
20	2.0
33	1.2
45	0.8

extract approaches the lower level. The rates given in Table 9-4 will increase soil nitrate tests about 10 ppm in the soil saturation extract.

Phosphate fertilizers can be applied at liberal rates to a container mix without serious problems from excess soluble salts. Generally, superphosphate (0-20-0) is preferred for container mixes because it contains calcium and sulfur. Two pounds of 0-20-0 fertilizer per cubic yard will raise the saturated soil extract test approximately 5 ppm. For most mixes testing low in phosphorus, 2-3 lb of 0-20-0 per cubic yard will provide an adequate level for the growth of most plants without causing other nutritional problems.

Potassium is commonly deficient in sand, peats, and perlite. It must be added to mixes composed of these materials. Most potassium fertilizers have a high salt index (see Table 8-10); therefore, care must be used in applying them. Carriers such as potassium nitrate, potassium sulfate, or potassium phosphate are preferred for container mixes. The level of potassium in the soil mix, as indexed by the saturated-soil extract test, should be relatively low for young plants and seedlings compared to more mature plants. The levels listed in Table 9-3 are suggested levels until exact levels are established for a specific crop in a specific stage of production. Values in excess of 250 ppm are unnecessarily high and may induce nutritional problems, especially if Ca and/or Mg levels test low. The K level in the soil extract can be increased approximately 50 ppm by mixing 2 oz of 60% K_2O fertilizer into a cubic yard of mix.

Calcium is generally adequate in container mixes with a pH of 5.5 or above. Values above 500 ppm are very high and can result in nutritional problems if Mg and/or K are low. The balance of the cations Ca, K, Mg, and to some degree ammonium and sodium is more important than the actual level. Calcium should represent about 15% of the total salts.

Magnesium in the saturated-soil extract should be less than one-half that for calcium, but should exceed one-half that for potassium. A minimum test regardless of the Ca and K levels is about 25 ppm Mg. Finely ground dolomitic limestone is a good source of Mg for container-soil mixes; 2 lb/yd^3 of mix will normally supply ample magnesium. Magnesium sulfate can also be used.

Soil–Water Ratio Method

Nitrate nitrogen will vary considerably, since nitrate availability is a function of temperature and moisture. Also, nitrates can be readily leached. If the recommended range for nitrates for a specific crop is 20-60 ppm in the soil, nitrogen should be applied when the test drops below 20 ppm. On the other end, as the test approaches 100 ppm, growth may be adversely affected; thus, the soil should be leached.

Phosphorus levels are seldom too low or too high to be dangerous. However, levels below 20 ppm are approaching a deficient level and may limit nitrogen metabolism in some species. And levels in excess of 200 ppm may limit the availability of micronutrients.

Potassium tests over 300 ppm may indicate a soluble-salts problem when chloride carriers are being used. If soluble salts are low, soils may test up to 1000 ppm K without difficulty, depending upon the crop and soil density. On very sandy or porous soils (except those containing vermiculite in the soil mix), more frequent potas-

Table 9-5 Suggested nutrient standards for soil mixes having different soil densities and extracted at different ratios

	Soil densities (g/ml)		
	0.8–1.3 (mineral soil)	0.5–0.8	0.2–0.5 (organic soil)
Soil extractant ratio:	1:8	1:12	1:24
Nutrient	*Parts per million in soil*		
Nitrate-nitrogen (NO$_3$-N)[a]	15–40	20–60	40–120
Phosphorus (P)[b]	20–60	30–90	60–180
Potassium (K)[c]	180–300	270–450	540–900
Calcium (Ca)[c]	Above 500	Above 750	Above 1500
Magnesium (Mg)[c]	Above 60	Above 90	Above 180
	Micromhos		
Soluble salts	Below 800	Below 1000	Below 1250

[a]Water-soluble extract.
[b]Extracted with 0.018 N acetic acid (Spurway active).
[c]Extracted with neutral, normal ammonium acetate.

sium application is desirable. Where chlorides are a problem, the sulfate form is suggested.

Calcium is very closely related to the medium pH. If the pH is above 5.5, calcium will be adequate in most mixes. However, excess levels of calcium may induce potassium deficiency and affect the uptake of micronutrients.

Magnesium availability is closely associated with calcium but at a lower magnitude. The ratio of potassium to magnesium should not exceed 3:1 or a magnesium deficiency could be induced.

Micronutrients

Since micronutrients are found in trace amounts, soil tests are not too reliable or are too expensive for routine soil testing. Plant analysis is commonly used to detect deficiency or excess levels. Chlorosis is probably the most common physiological problem related to microelement nutrition and is commonly related to iron deficiency or manganese toxicity. Conditions favoring deficiency include high soil pH, very high phosphorus levels, or excess moisture.

Table 9-6 Readings and interpretation of soluble-salt data for container-grown plants

Conductivity,[a] EC × 10^6 at 25°C (micromhos/cm)			
2:1	5:1	Saturated paste extract	
Mineral soils	Organic soils	All soils	Interpretation
Below 500	Below 350	Below 2000	Low nutrient status for growing plants
500–1000	350–650	2000–3500	Desirable range for most growing plants; upper range may be high for some species
1000–1500	650–900	3500–5000	Higher than desirable for most species
Greater than 1500	Greater than 900	Greater than 5000	Excess soluble salts, wilting or death of plants

[a]To convert micromhos to parts per million (approx.), multiply by 0.7.

SOURCE: Modified slightly from Coop. Ext. Serv. Mich. State Univ. Ext. Bull. 1275, 1978.

Soluble Salts

During the growing season the container medium should be tested monthly for soluble salts. The reading should be in the desirable range for the test method (Table 9-6). Readings below optimum indicate low levels of nutrition, which will result in reduced plant growth. A more complete medium test may be needed to determine the proper fertilizer to apply. This can often be determined by checking fertilizer records or by questioning those responsible for the fertilizer program.

MEDIA STERILIZATION

Another important factor in the successful production of container-grown plants is that the medium be free of organisms harmful to plant growth. Newly mined sand is relatively free of harmful organisms and can be used without sterilization. However, most soil and some sand and peat moss that have become contaminated will contain harmful organisms, such as bacteria, fungi, insects, and weed seeds. These organisms can cause serious problems if they are not eliminated from the medium prior to planting.

Various species of fungi, especially *Rhizoctonia* and *Pythium,* have caused the needless loss of thousands of plants in nurseries as a result of root rots. Grubs of insects chewing upon the roots have resulted in many plants being dwarfed, malformed, or destroyed. And weeds competing for available nutrients, moisture, and light reduce growth rates as well as decrease customer acceptance of the product. All of these problems and others can be minimized or eliminated by composting, sterilizing, pasteurizing, or fumigating. Composting was discussed previously under hardwood bark.

Heat Treatment

Although plantsmen use the term "sterilization" in reference to heat treatment of soil to rid it of harmful organisms, a more correct term is "pasteurization," since the temperatures used (140–180°F) destroy only certain of the harmful organisms. Various means of heat treatment can be employed, but it is desirable to obtain a soil temperature of 140–150°F and to maintain the temperature for at least 10 min but no more than 30 min to destroy most plant pathogenic fungi and bacteria (Fig. 9-3). This temperature regime will allow certain beneficial organisms to survive, especially nitrifying bacteria, which aid in the nitrification of ammonia. The lower temperature also minimizes the problem of excess ammonia release encountered with temperatures above 160°F. Aerated steam has been used effectively to obtain the 140°F temperature. The necessary equipment can be obtained from agricultural engineering firms specializing in soil sterilization. The heat treatment of nursery soils is thoroughly discussed in the "U.C. System for Producing Healthy Container-Grown Plants."

Fumigation

Chemicals can also be used to rid soil of   rmful organisms. In general, they are less destructive of the physical properties of the soil, but they are more costly. Also, many chemicals are very specific as to the organisms that they will control. Therefore, chemicals for treating soil must be carefully selected and applied at the proper concentration to a soil mass that is in the proper physical condition.

Media to be fumigated should be warm, damp, and well aerated.

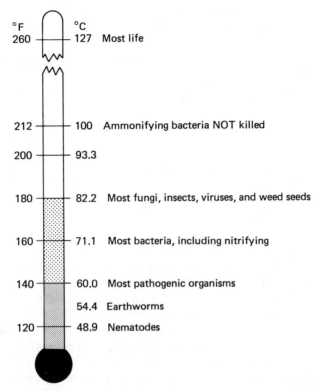

Figure 9-3 Temperatures maintained for 15 minutes will destroy most organisms listed.

The optimum media temperature for best results is close to 70° F. When media are cold, wet, and poorly aerated, chemical treatments are ineffective. Following treatment, the media should be aerated for a period of from 2 days to 2 weeks to allow the chemical to dissipate prior to planting. Warm, sandy media need less time to aerate than do damp media. A number of fumigants, available to nurserymen, will effectively sterilize media, including methyl bromide, formaldehyde, vapam, and chloropicrin.

*Methylbromide** is the most commonly used all-purpose nursery soil fumigant. It will destroy most of the common fungi that cause plant disease problems, except verticillium wilt. It is effective against most weed seeds and nematodes. It is easy to use and has a short treatment and post-treatment aeration-time requirement. However, the material is very toxic to people and animals and must be used

*Methylbromide is a restricted-use pesticide.

with caution. If it is handled with reasonable care, it can be a very effective tool for nurserymen in the preplanting control of harmful organisms.

Media and other material to be fumigated must be enclosed in a gasproof chamber, and the methylbromide gas injected into the chamber at a concentration at 2 lb/100 ft^3 for nematode and weed control or at 4 lb/100 ft^3 for fungus control. A treatment period of from 24 to 48 hr is desirable followed by an aeration period of 48 hr.

A polyethylene tarp free of holes makes an excellent gasproof enclosure. However, the tarp must cover the material to be fumigated in such a way as to ensure free distribution of the gas within and at the same time prevent the gas from escaping, either through holes or cracks along the edges. A special dispenser is provided for injecting the gas into the chamber.

Formaldehyde is an excellent fungicide that has been used by plantsmen for many years, both as fumigant for inorganic soils and as a surface sterilant for propagation benches and storage facilities. It is very water-soluble and will penetrate a soil mass to the depth of wetting, where it volatilizes and becomes an effective media fumigant. Treated media should be covered for at least 24 hr with a gasproof cover. This must be followed by an aeration period of from 10 to 14 days to permit the gas an opportunity to fully dissipate. Any residual gas can be harmful to young plants. Formaldehyde is very irritating to the eyes and nasal passages and is toxic to plants; it must be used with caution.

Vapam (sodium *N*-methyl dithiocarbamate dihydrate) is also an effective media fumigant. It can be used to control most fungi, insects, nematodes, and weeds. It is water-soluble and can be applied in water either to the medium surface or by injection into the media. The chemical should be sealed into the media with an additional application of water. Vapam is most effective when the medium is at a temperature of 60–70°F. The media should be aerated either by cultivation or turning it in a pile 5–7 days following treatment. The media may be safely planted about 2 weeks following treatment provided that there was adequate aeration to rid the soil of chemical residue.

Chloropicrin, commonly known as tear gas, is another excellent media fumigant. The medium must be treated in an airtight chamber, as the material is very volatile. It should be slightly damp but well aerated and at a temperature of 65–70°F for best results. The exposure period should last for at least 24 hr, preferably for 48 hr or more if the medium is not well aerated. Plantings may be made when there is no longer any trace of gas, approximately 7 days.

Chloropicrin is a very effective fumigant and herbicide. But it is also a potent tear gas and is corrosive of most metals; therefore, it must be used with caution. Small quantities are added to methylbromide as a warning agent. It should not be used in areas where people will be exposed to its irritating property. The treatment area should be free of valuable plants and metal objects. Any metal that is exposed to the gas should be washed with kerosene to prevent corrosion.

POST-TREATMENT

Following treatment, sterilized or pasteurized media should be placed into clean, sterile containers for use or stored in an area that has also been thoroughly sterilized. It is a poor plantsman who would go to considerable effort to rid media of harmful organisms and then expose them immediately to reinoculation by handling it with contaminated equipment or by placing it into contaminated containers or storage bins. Media sterilization is only a part of a total program of good plant culture. All people in the production cycle must be cognizant of maintaining sanitary conditions in plant propagation facilities, growing areas, storage facilities, and in the packaging and shipping areas.

SUMMARY

Producing and marketing of quality plants in containers requires careful planning and constant monitoring of each phase of production to assure attainment of production objectives. Blending of the media mixture and maintaining nutrients at the proper intensity and balance is one part of the total production effort. However, it has been the weakest link in the production cycle at many container production nurseries. By practicing good sanitation and maintaining suggested nutritional standards, growers can grow quality plants and obtain a good economic return on their investment.

REFERENCES

BODDY, R. M. 1976. Container-grown rhododendrons. Proc. Int. Plant Propag. Soc. 26:87–93.

BOODLEY, J. W., and R. SHELDRAKE, JR. 1972. Cornell Peat-Lite mixes for commercial plant growing. N.Y. State Coll. Agric. Cornell Univ. Inf. Bull. 43.

BOSLEY, R. W. 1967. Ground bark—a container growing medium. Proc. Int. Plant Propag. Soc. 17:366-370.

BROWN, E. F., and F. A. POKORNY. 1975. Physical and chemical properties of media composed of milled pine bark and sand. J. Am. Soc. Hort. Sci. 100 (2):119-121.

DAVIDSON, H., and W. MCCALL. 1964. Metal ammonium phosphate fertilizers for container-grown plants. Quart. Bull. Mich. Agric. Exp. Sta. 46(3):416-419.

DEWERTH, A. F. 1961. Horticultural Perlite for Texas gardens. Texas Agric. Prog. 7(6):3-6.

FLINT, H. L., and J. G. MCGUIRE. 1961. Effects of different soil levels of nitrogen and potassium on growth of *Forsythia intermedia* and *Viburnum plicatum tomentosum* in containers. Proc. Am. Soc. Hort. Sci. 78:553-559.

_____, and J. G. MCGUIRE. 1962. Nitrogen range for optimum growth of some woody ornamental species grown in containers. Proc. Am. Soc. Hort. Sci. 80:622-624.

GARTNER, J. B., D. C. SAUPE, J. E. KLETT, and T. R. YOCOM. 1970. Hardwood bark as a medium for container growing. Am. Nurseryman 131(8):11.

_____, T. D. HUGHES, and J. E. KLETT. 1972. Using hardwood bark in container grown woody ornamentals to slow-release fertilizers. Am. Nurseryman 135(12):10.

_____, S. M. STILL, and J. E. KLETT. 1973. The use of hardwood bark as a growth medium. Proc. Int. Plant Propag. Soc. 23:222-231.

GOUIN, F. R., and C. B. LINK. 1973. Growth responses of container-grown woody ornamentals to slow-release fertilizers. HortScience 8(3):208-209.

KELLEY, J. D. 1962. Response of container-grown woody ornamentals to fertilization with urea-formaldehyde and potassium frit. Proc. Am. Soc. Hort. Sci. 81:544-551.

KLETT, J. E., J. B. GARTNER, and T. D. HUGHES. 1972. Utilization of hardwood bark media for growing woody ornamental plants in containers. J. Am. Soc. Hort. Sci. 97(4):448-450.

LUCAS, R. E., and J. K. DAVIS. 1961. Relationships between pH values of organic soils and availabilities of 12 plant nutrients. Soil Sci. 92:177-182.

_____, P. E. RIEKE, and R. S. FARNHAM. 1971. Peats for soil improvement and soil mixes. Farm Sci. Ser. Coop. Ext. Serv. Mich. State Univ. Ext. Bull. 516.

MALEK, R. B., and J. B. GARTNER. 1975. Hardwood bark as a soil amendment for suppression of plant parasitic nematodes on container-grown plants. HortScience 10(1):33-34.

MATKIN, O. A. 1971. Soil mixes today. Proc. Int. Plant Propag. Soc. 21:162–164.

_____, and P. A. CHANDLER. 1957. The U.C. type soil mixes. In U.S. system for producing healthy container-grown plants, Sec. 5, Agric. Exp. Sta., Univ. Calif. Manual 23.

MONTANO, J. M., J. T. FISHER, and D. J. COTTER. 1977. Sawdust for growing containerized forest tree seedlings. Tree Planter's Notes 28(2):6–9.

MORRIS, W. C., and D. C. MILBACKER. 1972. Repressed growth and leaf chlorosis of Japanese holly grown in hardwood bark. HortScience 7(5):486–487.

RICHARDSON, T. 1976. Rhododendron production. Proc. Int. Plant Propag. Soc. 26:301–303.

RIEKE, P. E., and R. E. LUCAS. 1968. Greenhouse soil notes. Soil Science Dept., Mich. State Univ.

RIGBY, F. A. 1963. Ground bark as a growing medium for container nursery stock. Proc. Int. Plant Propag. Soc. 13:288–291.

SANDERSON, K. C., and W. C. MARTIN, JR. 1974. Performance of woody ornamentals in municipal compost medium under nine fertilizer regimes. HortScience 9(3):242–243.

SPOMER, L. A. 1973. Soils in plant containers: soil amendment, air and water relationships. Ill. Res. 15(3):16–17.

_____. 1975. Principles of nursery container soil amendment. Am. Nurseryman 142(3):12.

_____. 1977. How much total water retention and aeration porosity in my container mix? Ill. State Florists Assoc. Bull. 369:13–15.

STILL, S. M., M. A. DIRR, and J. B. GARTNER. 1976. Phytotoxic effects of several bark extracts on mung bean and cucumber growth. J. Am. Soc. Hort Sci. 101(1):34–37.

WARNCKE, D. C. 1977. General guidelines for greenhouse soil tests nutrient levels and their interpretation for the saturated soil extract method. Mimeograph, Dept. of Crop and Soil Sciences, Mich. State Univ.

_____, R. E. LUCAS, P. E. RIEKE, and W. H. CARLSON. 1973. Interpreting saturated paste soil tests for flowers, bedding plants and greenhouse vegetables. Mimeograph, Dept. of Crop and Soil Sciences, Mich. State Univ.

WHITE, J. W., and J. W. MASTALERZ. 1966. Soil moisture as related to "container capacity." Proc. Am. Soc. Hort. Sci. 89:758–765.

SUGGESTED READING

BAKER, F., ed. 1957. The U.C. system for producing healthy container-grown plants. Agric. Exp. Sta. Univ. Calif. Manual 23.

BUNT, A. C. 1976. Modern potting composts. Pennsylvania State Univ. Press, University Park, Pa.

LAWRENCE, W. J. C., and J. NEWELL. 1962. Seed and potting composts, 5th ed. George Allen & Unwin Ltd., London.

PATTERSON, J. M. 1975. Container growing. American Nurserymen Publishing Co., Chicago.

Chapter

Irrigation of Nursery Crops

Nursery crops, like other agricultural crops, require water if they are to develop into healthy, salable plants. Water is an important nutrient required by all plants. It functions in plants as a solvent, a heat regulator, and as a biochemical reagent in photosynthesis. It is a major modifier of growth; its availability or nonavailability during certain phases of growth can seriously affect survival, growth rate, and the ultimate size of the plants. Properly irrigated stock will be larger and more vigorous. Therefore, an understanding of irrigation practices is essential to nurserymen, particularly those who produce plants in containers.

Nurserymen who produce plants by field culture require or use water for two primary reasons: either to assure a higher survival rate following transplanting or to increase growth, whereas nurserymen committed to container culture require water not only to increase survival rates following potting and to increase growth, but they have an absolute requirement for water, almost on a daily basis. Container-grown plants have limited soil-moisture reservoirs, defined by container size and the moisture-holding capacity of the medium, which must be resupplied at short, periodic intervals to assure continued survival. The method of growing is the basis for determining the amount of water, type of equipment, and labor that is needed to meet the irrigation requirements within nurseries.

In addition to providing moisture for survival and growth of the nursery crops, the irrigation system can also be used to apply water-soluble fertilizers, to protect some crops from damage due to late spring frost, to moisten the soil to aid digging and transplanting operations during dry periods, and to seal in volatile soil sterilants and herbicides.

SOURCES OF WATER

A reliable source of clean water is a fundamental requirement for irrigation. Rivers, streams, drainage ditches, lakes, ponds, reservoirs, and wells are the common sources of water. Nurserymen who plan to use water from rivers, streams, drainage ditches, lakes, and ponds that have a multiple or public ownership should be familiar with the state and local riparian (water rights) laws, as they may face possible injunctions prohibiting or limiting their use of public water. States located in arid or semiarid areas of the country have strict laws pertaining to water rights. In other parts of the country, riparian laws are not as well defined. A new irrigator upstream can seriously reduce the amount of water available downstream, as can another irrigator drawing from the same lake or reservoir. Complete ownership of the water rights or purchase of water from a dependable supply is usually preferable. Should it become necessary to sink wells for a source of water, it is suggested that information on underground water be obtained from the state geologist and that a reliable well driller, who is familiar with the area, be employed to do the drilling, develop the well, and conduct a pumping test. Nurserymen producing container-grown nursery stock should have, if possible, an alternative source of water to assure a reserve supply in the event of an emergency.

WATER QUALITY

In addition to sources of supply, water quality should also be investigated. Water high in soluble salts or contaminated with industrial wastes, particularly heavy metals or polluted with herbicides, must be avoided. Most nursery plants will not tolerate saline conditions, and some are injured by high levels of sodium, boron, or chlorides found in some water.

Water quality (levels of salinity) is characterized by electrical conductivity (EC). The unit of measurement for EC is mhos per centimeter, at 25°C, which is the reciprocal of ohms, the unit of measurement for electrical resistivity (ER). Since the unit of measurement is very small for most natural water samples, it is commonly expressed as millimhos/cm (EC $\times$ 10^3) or even more commonly as micromhos/cm (EC $\times$ 10^6). Water for irrigation purposes should have an EC value of less than 250 micromhos/cm (Table 10-1). Water that has an EC in excess of 750 micromhos/cm is high in soluble salts and should be used with caution. Water used on container-grown plants can have levels somewhat higher than average, but it is desirable to apply a sufficient quantity at each irrigation to leach the soil.

High levels of sodium (Na) in irrigation water can also be detrimental to some plants. However, its relationship to the cations calcium (Ca) and magnesium (Mg) is important in determining its toxic effects. This is known as the sodium-absorption ratio (SAR) and can be calculated from the formula

$$SAR = \sqrt{\frac{Na}{\frac{Ca^{2+} + Mg^{2+}}{2}}}$$

The concentration of each element is expressed in milliequivalents per liter. An SAR value of 10 or less is considered safe for most nursery situations. But levels between 11 and 18 could present problems on soils with a high cation exchange capacity (fine-textured soils).

Boron, a constituent of all natural waters, is found in toxic concentrations in irrigation water in limited areas of the United States, primarily in the Southwest. Since plants vary in their tolerance to boron in the soil solutions, no exact value can be stated. Nevertheless, relatively low concentrations, in the order of 0.03-0.05 ppm, are needed for normal growth, and relatively high levels (0.5 ppm or greater) should be avoided.

Water containing more than 2.5 mEq/liter of residual sodium carbonate (RSC) is not suitable for irrigation. Water that contains less than 1.25 mEq/liter RSC is probably safe, and those with levels in between are considered marginal.

Appraising water quality for use in irrigation of nursery stock need not be complex. With an understanding of some general chemis-

Table 10-1 Classification of water for irrigation

Micromhos/cm (EC × 10⁶) at 25°C	Salinity level	Irrigation value
<250	Low	Excellent for irrigation on most soils. Normal leaching suggested.
250–750	Moderate	Satisfactory for irrigation. Moderate leaching suggested.
750–2250	High	Avoid use on soil with poor drainage. Plant salt-tolerant crops. Leaching necessary.
>2250	Very high	Not recommended for irrigation purposes. A few salt-tolerant crops can be grown under special salinity culture.

SOURCE: USDA Circ. 969.

try, making a few chemical determinations and some calculations, it is possible to avoid the hazards associated with using poor-quality water. Some states have either private or state-supported laboratories where these tests are made for a fee. Details on the analysis of irrigation water are contained in USDA Agricultural Handbook 60.

In areas where high-soluble salts are a problem, it is desirable to construct large, shallow settling ponds to allow the alkali salts to settle out prior to using the water for irrigation or misting. In some situations distilling or even deionizing the water may be desirable prior to using it on sensitive, high-value crops (e.g., azaleas). Sediment and organic debris, harmful to pumps and sprinkler heads, should be screened out. If it is not, the irrigation equipment can be expected to malfunction; nozzle orifices can become plugged or changed in size, but even more serious, the pump may malfunction, which could result in damage to either equipment or to the plant material.

SOIL MOISTURE DETERMINATION

Crops should be irrigated when the soil moisture in the root zone drops to a predetermined level. Soil moisture levels can be determined by feel of the soil, by calculation, or by the use of various types of soil moisture meters. Experienced plantsmen estimate the appropriate time to irrigate nursery stock by knowing the stress symptoms of plants, by the feel of the soil or by the length of time since the last rain or irrigation. To estimate soil moisture by the feel of the soil, samples are collected from various depths in the root zone and the moisture level is estimated by feel (Table 10-2). To calculate soil moisture, a soil sample collected from a depth of 8-12 in. is placed in a tight container, weighed, dried in an oven (12-24 hours at 100°C), and reweighed. Total moisture (TM) in percent is calculated by the formula

$$TM\% = \frac{(\text{original wt of soil}) - (\text{dry wt of soil}) \times 100}{\text{dry wt of soil}}$$

Available moisture is then estimated by subtracting the wilting coefficient of the soil (data available from soils reference manual or county agriculture agent) from the percent TM.

For sandy soils low in organic matter (<11%), a quick technique is to place the soil sample, about 20-25 g, in a screen-bottom metal

Table 10-2 Soil feel chart

Percentage of remaining available water	Feel or appearance of soils		
	Course textured	Medium textured	Fine or very fine textured
0% (dry)	Dry, loose, flows through fingers	Powder-dry; sometimes slightly crusted but easily breaks down into powdery condition	Hard, baked, cracked; sometimes has loose crumbs on surface
50% or less (low)	Still appears to be dry; will not form a ball with pressure	Somewhat crumbly, but will hold together with pressure	Somewhat pliable, will ball under pressure
50-100% (good to excellent)	Forms weak ball, breaks easily, will not stick	Forms a ball and is very pliable; sticks readily if relatively high in clay	Easily ribbons out between fingers; has a slick feeling
Above field capacity (over-irrigated)	Free water will be released with kneading	Can squeeze out free water	Puddles and free water forms on surface

SOURCE: "Irrigating Small Acreages," Coop. Ext. Serv. Mich. State Univ. Ext. Bull. 320.

container set in a metal cap and obtain the weight. Gradually, pour a small quantity (25 cc) of methyl alcohol over the soil and ignite to drive off the moisture. The sample is reweighed and the available moisture calculated by the previous formula.

Various instruments have been developed to provide a measure of soil moisture. The soil moisture meter is well adapted for use in most field production nurseries. It consists of special plaster of paris blocks that are buried in the soil at the desired depth and location, and then electrical resistance is measured with a moisture meter. The dial of the meter reads in relative soil moisture, 100 representing a fully saturated soil and 50 or less indicating a need for irrigation. A large variety of soil moisture tensiometers are available. However, most of these instruments* are too sophisticated for the needs of most nurserymen.

Leaf temperature has been used to a limited extent to determine when to irrigate ornamental plants in the landscape. Since leaf temperature is generally higher for plants exhibiting moisture stress, it is possible to relate leaf temperature to the need to irrigate. Leaf temperatures can be quickly estimated with the aid of a portable infrared radiometer. It could possibly be used to determine irrigation needs in a nursery.

PUMPS AND POWER

After it has been determined that an adequate source of good quality water is available, the next decision is what type of system will be used to distribute the water; this includes pump(s), power source, water distribution system, and sprinkler units. At this point it is advisable to seek the services of an irrigation specialist who can provide the detailed information. But it is desirable for nurserymen to have a basic understanding of the various systems.

Although there are many types of pumps to select from, the horizontal centrifugal and deep-well turbine pumps are fairly standard for irrigation purposes. The horizontal centrifugal pump is easy to operate, is highly efficient, but is limited to a suction lift of about 22 ft or less and must be primed. Turbine pumps, although more costly than centrifugal pumps and generally more difficult to inspect and repair, are not limited to the 22 ft depth and do not require priming.

*See McDonald and Running, 1979.

The actual selection will depend upon (1) the volume of water to be pumped during the peak use period and (2) the total head in feet** (dynamic pumping head), which is the sum of:

1. The total rise in feet from the pumping level to the elevation of the highest point in the irrigation system.

2. The friction head in feet for the main line plus the longest lateral. (Information available from manufacturer.)

3. The average sprinkler operating pressure, expressed as friction head in feet. (Information available from manufacturer.)

4. Various miscellaneous friction losses (valves, fittings, etc.) estimated to be 10% of the total head in feet.

Power to operate the pump is generally supplied by gasoline, propane, or diesel engines, or by electric motors. If an electric motor is to be employed as a power source, the power company should be contacted prior to purchase to determine availability and cost of electric power and to coordinate installation activities.

Energy is expressed in horsepower; 1 horsepower is equivalent to 33,000 foot-pounds per minute, or 0.746 kilowatt. The horsepower rating of an engine or motor is the amount of power that the engine or motor will develop when operated at full load for short periods of time. Brake horsepower is the effective horsepower that the machine is capable of producing over extended periods at the power shaft. The brake horsepower (BHP) requirement can be calculated by the formula (1 gal water = 8.35 lb):

$$BHP = \frac{GPM \times 8.35 \times total\ head\ (in\ feet)}{33,000 \times pump\ efficiency}$$

For example, the brake horsepower needed for a pump required to deliver 300 GPM against a total head of 200 ft with a pump efficiency of 75% would be 20:

$$BHP = \frac{300 \times 8.35 \times 200}{33,000 \times 0.75} = 20$$

For most portable irrigation systems, a gasoline engine may be the best choice. An electric motor or diesel engine is more desirable

**The total head in feet may be converted to pounds per square inch (psi) by dividing by 2.31, which is the height in feet of a column of water 1 square inch in area that weighs 1 pound.

for permanent systems. When using gasoline or diesel engines, it is desirable to increase the BHP requirement by 25–30%, since the engine is not as efficient over extended periods of use as it is for brief periods of operation under ideal conditions. Also, if the engine were designed to operate on a moving vehicle, the cooling system might have to be modified (e.g., larger radiator and possibly a shroud around the fan) or irrigation water can be run through the radiator. The pump and power sources used in portable systems can be mounted as a unit on a skid, a wheeled trailer, or a truck-bed. An estimate of fuel consumption may be made if one assumes that a well-tuned gasoline engine used for pumping consumes 0.1 gal (U.S.)/hp/hr and for a diesel engine 0.07–0.08 gal (U.S.)/hp/hr.

Tractor power can be used to provide the necessary horsepower to drive power-take-off-driven pumps. But when tractors are used for this purpose, nurserymen should check with the farm equipment dealer as to the maximum continuous dependable power that the tractor engine should deliver at the PTO shaft to drive the pump. In addition, when such units are employed, care must be taken to properly connect and align the PTO shaft. Improper connection or alignment results in excessive wearing of parts and could result in breakage.

Stationary units should be located close to the water source and mounted on a level, solid foundation. Since engines used to power irrigation pumps are often left running unattended for long periods, it is desirable to provide certain safety devices to shut off the engine in the event of a mechanical failure and to prevent bodily injury. Three common failures are: (1) the pump overheats, (2) it loses oil pressure, and (3) it loses prime. If possible, the power unit should be enclosed in a locked building or a fenced area. In addition, container production nurseries should have both an auxiliary source of power and a pump to substitute in the event the primary source fails.

A few points to consider that may aid in the proper functioning of the pump are: (1) the pipe or hose on the suction side of the pump should be one size larger than the discharge side in order to reduce friction and improve efficiency of the pump; (2) the intake should be placed low enough into the water to assure that an air swirl does not develop over the intake screen, allowing air to be drawn into the system causing a loss of suction; (3) it should also be placed a few inches above the bottom to reduce the intake of sediment; and (4) where a surface source of water is used, a strainer should be used to prevent various forms of debris from being drawn into the pump and causing trouble. In some water sources, a debris barrier may need to be constructed in addition to the strainer to prevent plugging of the intake.

Centrifugal pumps must be primed. There are a number of devices that can be connected to the pump to accomplish this, but a simple method is to keep a barrel or tank of water close by, which is used to fill the suction pipe and pump chamber.

DISTRIBUTION SYSTEMS

Distribution systems for irrigation may be classified by the method of conveying water or by the degree of permanence of the system. Surface irrigation methods are adapted to relatively flat areas with medium- to heavy-textured soils. Subsurface irrigation is best adapted to peat, muck, and sandy soils, whereas overhead irrigation is adaptable to a wide variety of areas. It is especially well adapted for use in most nurseries. Water can be applied fairly uniformly over uneven topography, and the system is highly adaptable to the many variable situations found in nurseries.

In a permanent installation, the pump, the power source, the main lines and laterals, and in some cases the sprinkler heads are in fixed positions. The pump and power source are enclosed in a building. The pipes used in the permanent system may be reinforced concrete, asbestos cement, or poly(vinyl chloride) (PVC). All are satisfactory and will withstand the operating pressure of the system if the proper pressure-rated pipe has been selected. The lines should be of a diameter large enough to permit delivery of water without excessive friction loss. Since most of the pipes in a stationary system are below ground, they must be set deep enough to permit cultivation, and in cold climates deep enough to prevent freezing or be installed on a slight gradient to permit draining prior to the onset of freezing temperatures. The permanent system, although relatively more expensive, requires less labor to operate. They are used primarily in high-value, intensive-production areas: (e.g., propagation, seed beds, liner, and container production).

In a semiportable system, the pump, power source, and main distribution lines are permanent, but the lateral lines and application equipment are portable. In a fully portable system, everything can be moved from place to place. The pipe used in portable systems is mostly manufactured from either lightweight aluminum or PVC and is equipped with various types of quick-coupling devices. For efficiency it is suggested that all irrigation pipe and couplers in a system be of the same brand. The portable system, although the least expensive to install, requires considerable labor to operate. It is used most commonly in field production areas.

Sprinkler heads are available in a wide selection of types. Nurserymen should select the type best adapted to their needs and to the soil's ability to absorb water. Water should be applied at a rate equal to but no faster than the soil's absorptive capacity or water is lost to evaporation and soil erosion occurs, expecially on hilly terrain. Rotating sprinklers used in nurseries are commonly spaced 50-60 ft apart, operate at a pressure of 50-60 psi, and deliver 5-20 GPM. The spacing between heads and lateral lines, on an average, should not exceed 65-70% of the diameter of the spray pattern of the sprinkler head.

Some nurserymen use traveling, gun-type sprinklers (Fig. 10-1) that discharge about 500 GPM at 80-90 psi pressure. They cover large areas and save labor but require more power to operate and may deliver water too fast for the soil's absorptive capacity.

Figure 10-1 Traveling, gun-type irrigation sprinkler in a field production nursery.

WATERING FIELD-GROWN CROPS

Since field-grown nursery crops are watered to increase survival rate following transplanting or to increase growth, and since they may be produced on either close or wide spacing, depending upon the type of plant material and the market objective, it is desirable to discuss irrigation of these crops accordingly.

To Increase Survival Rates

Following transplanting, the plants must be watered immediately following planting. This can be accomplished with some type of irrigation system or with the aid of a water wagon. In intensive areas, a permanent overhead system may be most appropriate, but as the spacing is increased, a semiportable system may be the most economical approach. In areas where the density of plants per unit area is low, the most economical approach may be the use of a water wagon. However, in situations where the crop is of high value (e.g., large-caliper shade trees), it may be more desirable to use trickle irrigation.

To Increase Growth

Most field production nurseries are located in areas where the natural rainfall throughout the growing season is sufficient, at least in most years, to supply the water necessary for growth. Therefore, they seldom install irrigation systems to increase growth. However, production nurseries located in drier climates and nurseries that produce high-value crops find it financially advantageous to invest in some form of supplemental irrigation to increase growth rates. In some situations, the system may be used only once every 5-6 years, whereas in other situations it may be used yearly. In nurseries where the stock is grown fairly intensively, a semiportable system can be most effective and efficient. But in nurseries where the plants are grown on fairly wide spacing, the use of trickle irrigation may be more efficient.

Trickle irrigation, a relatively new concept of applying water to orchard trees, is gaining in acceptance by nurserymen for the production of large shade trees (Fig. 10-2). It is based on the concept that best plant performance is obtained by maintaining a favorable soil moisture condition in the root zone. With trickle irrigation it is possible to produce a salable tree more rapidly and with a more compact root system. Water is applied under low pressure (less than 15 psi) and at a slow rate (1-2 GPH) for a time period sufficient to maintain the soil in which the roots are developing at or close to field capacity. Since only a portion of the soil area (10-20%) is irrigated less water is used (Fig. 10-3). A time clock and solenoid valve can be installed into the line to activate the system for a predetermined time period each day when in use.

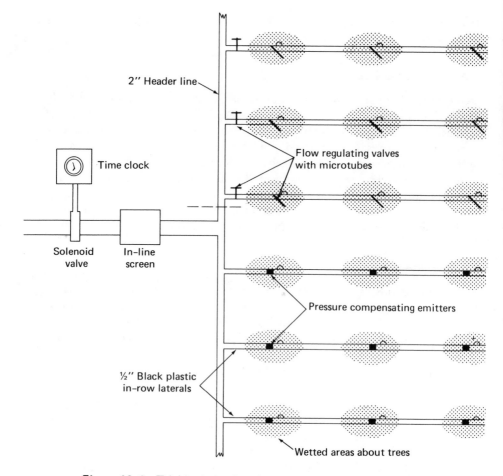

Figure 10-2 Trickle irrigation in a nursery. Upper half of the diagram illustrates the use of flow regulating valves and microtubes; lower half of the diagram illustrates use of pressure compensating emitters.

Water is delivered to each tree by means of either a microtube or a pressure-compensating emitter. When microtubes are used, it is necessary to control the water delivery rate. This is best accomplished by inserting a flow regulating valve in each lateral and adjusting the number and size or length of the microtubes so that the system is balanced. For example, using a 1.0-GPM flow valve will require using either 30 microtubes at 2.0 GPH, or 60 microtubes at 1.0 GPH, or 120 microtubes at 0.5 GPH. The use of pressure-compensating emitters, although more expensive, negates the needs for balancing of

Figure 10-3 Trickle irrigation.

the system. Emitters are available in various flow rates, permitting flexibility in designing a system to meet the production plan of the nursery.

Estimating Water Requirements

Irrigating field-grown nursery crops is based primarily upon experience, but it does vary with the size of the area to be irrigated, the size of the plant material, and the level of moisture in the soil. Since acreages vary, it is desirable to discuss water requirements on an acre basis and adjust total requirements accordingly. To apply 1 acre-in. of water requires 27,154 gal of water. It is a common practice in many nurseries to apply ½ in., 1 in., or 2 in. of water at a time. This would require between 13,600 and 54,300 gal of water, whereas in other nurseries water for growth is applied when the soil moisture drops to some predetermined level. For example, a soil with a 30% moisture-holding capacity is to be irrigated when the soil moisture in the upper 9 in. has dropped to 50% of field capacity. Since only 30% of the 9-in. depth is moisture, it may be estimated that this equals 2.7 in. of water. Fifty percent of this value equals 1.35 in. or a requirement of 37,000 gal of water to restore the soil to field capacity. If the irrigation system is 75% effective (allowing for evaporation and drift), it would require approximately 50,000 gal of water or 1.85 acre-in.

The water should be applied at a rate not to exceed the infiltration and percolation rates of the soil, and under some conditions the rate of application may be further limited by work schedules. At a percolation rate of $\frac{1}{2}$ acre-in./hr, it would take 3 hr and 40 min to apply the needed water, in the previous example. If applied at a faster rate, the net result would be either a puddling of the soil or erosion of the soil, plus the extra expense of pumping more water than necessary.

A source of supply and a pump with a capacity of 13,600 gal/hr (230 gal/min) per acre would be needed. Nurserymen can, by making similar calculations, estimate their water needs on a per acre basis and then with a knowledge of water availability, work schedules, and costs involved, estimate the size of the irrigation system that will be required for a specific situation.

WATERING CONTAINER-GROWN PLANTS

Container-grown plants are watered with the aid of an irrigation system modified to meet the needs of the situation. In parts of the country where water is costly or availability is limited, the system should be both effective and efficient. In areas where water is inexpensive, readily available, and where runoff is not a problem, the system need only be effective. To be effective, water must be applied to the containers when it is needed and in an amount necessary to maintain quality growth. To be efficient, the water must be applied to the interior of the containers.

Enough water must be applied to each container to replace that which is lost by evapotranspiration, to provide for growth, and to assure control of salinity within the medium. The daily loss due to evapotranspiration is a function of environment (temperature, humidity, wind, etc.) and the size and species of the plants. Experienced plantsmen estimate this loss on a daily basis by the appearance of their plants. Also, a correlation can be developed with the loss of water, by evaporation, from a pan of water located in close proximity to the plants.

Salinity control in container-grown plants requires that the entire soil mass become wetted and that some water leach through the container and drain away from the root zone. In some studies, as little as 0.14 quart of water per day were needed to irrigate plants growing in 1-gal containers, whereas 2 gal water/day were needed to water larger plants growing in 15-gal containers. The actual water regimen for a nursery growing container-grown plants will have to be developed by experience. There are a number of systems available to supply water to container-grown plants; each has its advantages and limitations. A system or systems that will accomplish the job most effectively with minimum degradation of the environment should be employed.

Overhead sprinkler irrigation is the most common system used to water small container-grown plants. It applies the water over the tops of the plants at a fairly rapid rate. It is relatively inexpensive to install and operate. But it can be relatively inefficient in the use of water, depending upon placement and size of containers; as much as 80% of the water can be lost between the containers. It is most efficient when watering 1- to 5-gal containers, spaced close together. It is least efficient when watering containers on wide spacing. However, where water is inexpensive and where no damage results to the environment, it may be the most economical system to use.

The actual design of a permanent system for a large container nursery will vary with the size of the area and the capacity of the pump. But the input and output should be in balance, and the design must provide for overlap of distribution patterns to assure fairly even distribution of water. A modular design adapted to meet the needs of various situations is effective for many container production areas. The output of water is balanced with the input and the area modified accordingly. For example, using a pump that delivers 1600 gallons per minute (GPM) would permit the use of 100 sprinkler heads with a discharge of 16 GPM or the use of 200 heads with discharge of 8 GPM. Since it is desirable to have as even a water distribution pattern as possible, it is more advantageous to use the larger number of heads at low GPM but at the higher suggested operating pressure.

If a container area is designed as shown in Fig. 10-4, it is possible to develop a modular design for the irrigation system. One approach would be to arrange the water distribution by beds, using full-circle (360°) sprinkler heads in the center, half-circle (180°) heads on the sides, and quarter-circle (90°) heads on the corners. If the beds are designed to be 100 ft wide and the sprinkler heads were distributed on a GPM equivalent basis over eight beds, it would require 11 full-circle heads at 8.35 GPM with a radius of 41 ft, 24 half-circle heads at 4.40 GPM with a radius of 40 ft, and 4 quarter-circles at 2.86 GPM with a radius of 35 ft per bed, and the beds would be 600 ft long. The eight beds, totaling 480,000 ft^2, a little over 11 acres, would require approximately 3 hr to irrigate with 1 in. of water. This would amount to approximately 0.7 in. of water falling on the container-

Figure 10-4 Container production area overhead irrigation system.

bed area if 30% was lost to evaporation and drift. Total water efficiency would depend upon spacing of the containers. When spaced pot to pot in the equilateral triangle design, the water efficiency would be close to 63%.

Small to medium-sized areas can be watered effectively by using self-propelled rotating sprinklers. Each container, within the radius of discharge, receives an equal volume of water as the sprinklers propel themselves forward. The advantages of this system are: (1) uniform water distribution, (2) highly portable, and (3) relatively inexpensive. However, it does require more labor to operate.

Subsurface irrigation, also known as capillary irrigation, is used to water plants in greenhouses and by nurserymen in Europe, but it has not been widely used by nurserymen in the United States. It requires a level area for construction of a capillary reservoir and soils with good capillary conductivity. It works best for small containers placed close together. The water level in the bed can be controlled effectively with a float valve and a microswitch (Fig. 10-5).

Surface irrigation applies water to the surface of the medium within the container and is a most efficient means for watering large containers. It requires an extensive system of pipes and tubes, which gives rise to its more commonly used name, "spaghetti" system. This system must be designed to meet the water requirements of the plants and the cultural operations of the nursery. In general, the system utilizes 1-in. plastic pipe as a secondary supply line to which are attached a number of 3- to 5-ft distribution tubes to which are attached a number of small diameter tubes to carry the water to each container (Fig. 10-6). Depending upon the texture of the soil and the size of the container, it may be necessary to spread the water in some way so that the entire surface is wetted rather than just a small area beneath the emitter.

A few problem areas that have been encountered with the use of plastic tubing are: (1) plugging with dirt and mineral deposits; (2) displacement of the tubes by workers or animals; (3) rodents biting the tubes, causing them to leak, (4) algae developing in clear tubing; and (5) water freezing in the tubes, causing splitting. The rodent problem can be minimized by the use of rodenticides, and the algae problem can be minimized by using black tubing. To avoid having water freeze in the tubes, the system is drained or blown out prior to freezing temperatures. Blowing out the system with an air compressor is the most effective way to assure that it is free of water.

Poly(vinyl chloride) (PVC) pipes can be used to overcome many of the problems associated with the more flexible tubing. By using nozzles of the same material and with the aid of solvents, it is possible to put together a system that is extremely functional. The main lines and laterals can be buried below ground, eliminating the problem of exposed laterals; and not being exposed to the sun also increases the useful life of the system. Many types of nozzles, emitters, and spitters are available to apply water directly to the containers at controlled flow rates which increase the effective and economic use of water and soluble fertilizers. Sand traps or filters should be installed to prevent plugging of the nozzles. Also, with the addition of electronic control units it is possible to regulate irrigation periods for time intervals of a few seconds to many minutes. Electronic controls provide a high degree of flexibility to the system. It

Micro switch

Water line

Float valve

Flow valve

Water level

Solenoid

Capillary water movement

Sand

Figure 10-5 Capillary irrigation bed.

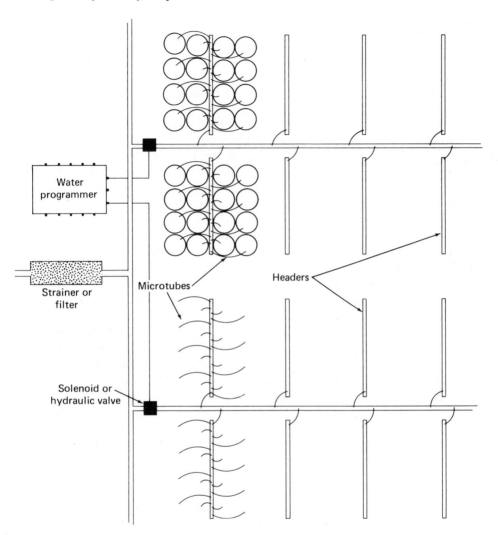

Figure 10-6 Container irrigation automated microtube system.

can be expanded very easily by the simple addition of a few extra subunit controls and low-voltage solenoid valves.

Estimating Water Requirements for Container-Grown Plants

The amount of water required to water container-grown plants varies with a number of factors, including the type and size of the plant material, the container capacity for holding water, climatic conditions (temperature, humidity, wind), and the type of irrigation system. Some species of plants transpire moisture at a faster rate than do others. Also, large plants, contained in a pot of similar size and conformation, use water at a more rapid rate than do smaller plants of the same species.

The *capacity of the containers* to hold moisture varies with each type of medium and with the depth and conformation of the container. Materials such as peat moss and composted bark have a much higher moisture-holding capacity than does material such as sand or milled bark. Therefore, plants growing in a medium with a low container capacity for moisture must be watered more frequently than those growing in a medium with a high container capacity. However, this varies with the volume of the medium in the container and with the height/diameter ratio of the container. Plants growing in wide, shallow or tall, narrow containers require watering more frequently than do plants growing in containers that have a height/diameter ratio that is close to 1.0. Wide, shallow containers lose substantial amounts of water by evaporation; whereas tall, narrow containers do not hold as much available water, owing to the downward force of the longer water column.

Climatic conditions strongly influence the need for water. Transpiration rates are rapid during periods of warm temperature and low relative humidity, as are evaporation rates from soil surfaces, requiring more frequent watering of container-grown plants. Transpiration loss is greatest during periods of bright sunshine, when leaf temperatures can be 20–30°F higher than air temperature. During such periods a high vapor-pressure deficit develops between the plant and the ambient air (see Chapter 13), resulting in a rapid loss of moisture from the plants.

The water requirement of container-grown plants is influenced by each of these factors and must be considered when planning the irrigation program. When small containers are placed close together in beds, the most effective way to water the plants is by overhead irrigation, even though some of the water will fall between the containers and upon paths and roadways. The actual amount will vary with the size of the container and the watering practice of the nursery. However, 1-gal containers, which have an actual volume of close to 100 fluid ounces (3 liters) would have a water requirement of 7.6 fluid ounces when the upper half of the medium reached 50% water-holding capacity (assuming that the medium has a moisture-holding capacity of 30%). This would require 0.7 acre-in. of water or approximately 20,000 gal/acre per irrigation. It is fairly common practice to apply $\frac{1}{2}$–1 in. of water at each irrigation and to vary the frequency of application as influenced by the need for water. During periods of cool, cloudy weather the plants may need to be irrigated only once in 3–6 days, whereas during hot, dry periods they may require water every day and for some species even twice a day. Overhead irrigation is best accomplished in the late afternoon or early evening, to minimize loss of moisture due to evaporation. However, for plants that are subject to diseases (e.g., botrytis and mildew) it is best to apply the water early in the morning or to use surface irrigation.

When using overhead or surface irrigation, the plants should be grouped according to the size of the container and a large enough volume of water should be applied so that some flows out the drainage holes. The actual water requirement will vary with the factors previously discussed, but about 2 gal of water is needed per irrigation for containers described as the 15-gal size.

Excess Water

In some parts of the country disposing of the excess water following the irrigation of container-grown plants can be a problem. Prior to 1975, excess water that did not percolate into the soil was channeled into drainage ditches and discharged either into county drainage systems or municipal storm sewers. Since the early 1970s, many municipalities have enacted laws prohibiting the discharge of water high in soluble salts into storm sewers. Therefore, this excess water must be disposed of by other means.

One step in solving the problem is to use irrigation water more efficiently, reducing the volume of wastewater that is generated by container production. The wastewater can be disposed of in some manner or it can be impounded and reused for irrigation. If the site conditions and local laws permit, the wastewater can be disposed of through a leach-field system. The runoff from the beds can be channeled into a series of settling tanks (e.g., 30-in. cement culverts placed on end), where the particulate matter is allowed to settle out before the water flows into the leach field. The county drain commissioner or appropriate water management authority should be consulted prior to constructing the system. A permit may be required, and the authority may be in a position to offer constructive suggestions relative to the construction and operation of the system. If the wastewater cannot be disposed of via a leach field or if it is desired to reuse the water, it will be necessary to construct a collecting pond. Information pertaining to the construction of collecting ponds can be obtained from the U.S. Soil Conservation Service.

Waste irrigation water impounded in a collecting pond is generally high in soluble salts (see page 239) and could be polluted with herbicides or disease organisms. Therefore, it should not be reused for watering of nursery stock without proper testing. If the water is free of pollutants and the soluble salt level is low, it can be used to irrigate container-grown plants. Where the level of soluble salts is too high for use on nursery stock, it might be possible to use the water to irrigate a salt-tolerant agricultural crop. If this is not a feasible option, the wastewater will either have to be desalted to remove part or all of the soluble salts prior to reuse or be diluted with water low in soluble salts. This can be accomplished with the aid of a proportioner. The resulting mixture has a salt concentration acceptable for irrigating container-grown plants.

By developing a fully integrated system of production that (1) makes use of slow-release fertilizers to maintain optimum nutrient levels, especially for nitrogen and potassium; (2) minimizes the use of soluble fertilizers; and (3) maximizes efficient use of water, it is possible to solve the excess water problem in a manner that it becomes an asset rather than a liability to the nursery.

Fertilizing by Means of an Irrigation System

Sprinkler irrigation can be used to apply fertilizers. Most water-soluble fertilizers can be applied through the irrigation system, but because of economic considerations and various chemical and biological reactions that take place within the soil, it is generally not practical to apply all these materials through the irrigation system. Application should be restricted to those that can be economically applied through the irrigation system and which do not form complex chemical compounds in the soil that render them unavailable for plant growth.

Fertilizing through the irrigation system saves labor and permits greater control over levels of nutrition. Many growers apply small quantities of fertilizer (especially nitrogen) at each watering. When a constant fertilizer program is employed, it is necessary to soil-test on a regular basis, keep accurate, meaningful records, and adjust the fertilizer program to the condition of the crop and the environment. Various agencies, including the Cooperative Extension Service, fertilizer companies, and private horticultural consulting firms, are available to develop fertilizer programs for the crops to be grown in a given environment. Some agencies also publish bulletins that are helpful in developing and understanding fertilizer programs for crop production.

Nitrogen. Most forms of nitrogen, except those that contain free ammonia, can be applied successfully through the irrigation system. Sources containing free ammonia can damage the leaves of plants, and much of the ammonia would be lost by volatilization. Three common nitrogen salts—ammonium nitrate, ammonium sulfate, and potassium nitrate—can be used when applied at recommended rates.

Potassium. The common potassium salts—potassium chloride, potassium sulfate, potassium nitrate, and potassium carbonate—are all soluble in water and can be applied through the irrigation system if necessary, particularly with container-grown plants.

Phosphorus. Most of the common fertilizer salts of phosphorus are relatively insoluble and if introduced into the irrigation system may clog the smaller sprinkler heads. The soluble form may be economically used for container production, but it is not suggested for field culture because of its high cost.

Other nutrient elements. Most of the other nutrient elements can be applied through the irrigation system if necessary. However, most agricultural soils have a sufficient supply for field-grown nursery stock, and for container-grown plants they should be added to the medium at the time of soil preparation.

Fertilizer amendments can be easily introduced into the irrigation system by a number of means. One simple method is to pour the dissolved fertilizer into the water source and to allow the pump to draw the solution into the system. However, this is not a very accurate method. More accurate and dependable methods require that the nutrient solutions be injected or proportioned into the distribution system.

For centrifugal pumping systems, the suction pipe can be tapped close to the pump and fitted with the necessary pipe or hoses to connect the nutrient supply to the irrigation system. The pump will draw the solution into the system when the valve is opened. With turbine pumps the nutrient solution must be injected into the system under a pressure greater than that of the irrigation system.

Soluble fertilizers can be injected into the irrigation system by means of various types of proportioners or injectors. These mechanical devices are designed and constructed to combine specific amounts of concentrated stock solution and water in various predetermined ratios. When 1 unit of stock solution is combined with 99 units of water, forming a total of 100 units, the proportioner is listed as having a dilution ratio of 1 : 100, whereas when the combination is 1 unit to 11 units, making a total of 12, the proportion is listed as 1:12.

Proportioners, currently available, utilize either Bernoulli's principle or positive displacement. In the first type, a venturi is constructed in the water main, and the line supplying the liquid concentrate is connected at the low pressure point in the venturi. This system is subject to variation in dilution ratios as a result of differences in flow rate or in line pressure. However, these limitations can be modified with the aid of pressure regulators and adjustable valves.

Positive displacement units inject a measured quantity of stock solution into a measured volume of water with the aid of pistons of varied stroke length and cylinders of known diameters and lengths. Such units are designed to give relatively consistent dilution ratios over rather wide variations in water pressure. When selecting a proportioner (injector) for a container production nursery, consideration should be given to the capacity of the system, the dilution ratios available, desired mobility, and maintenance of the unit.

The major advantages to be gained by nurserymen utilizing proportioners are: (1) fertilizer can be applied uniformly at a known concentration, (2) the fertilizer may be applied at the optimum concentration for the species and for the prevailing climatic condition, (3) the fertilizer is applied at the same time that the plants are watered thus saving labor, and (4) the loss of plants due to excess soluble salts is minimized.

Fertilizer concentration may be stated by any one of a number of methods, but one of the best for constant feeding is to state the concentration in parts per million (ppm). The most common concentrations used for fertilizing container-grown plants are 50, 100, or 200 ppm. To obtain a specific concentration with the aid of a proportioner, it is necessary to formulate a concentrated stock solution of known concentration. To accomplish this, it is necessary to know the dilution ratio of the proportioner and the percentage availability of the nutrient element to be applied. If, for example, it is desired to apply nitrogen at a concentration of 100 ppm with the aid of a 1 : 100 proportioner and the fertilizer analysis is 33-0-0, the stock solution should contain 4.05 oz/gal.

$$\text{wt/gal} = [\text{PPM} \times \text{weight of water} \times \text{proportioner ratio}]$$

$$\div \text{ \% nutrient in fertilizer}$$

$$= \left[\frac{100}{1,000,000} \times 8.34 \text{ lb/gal} \times 16 \text{ oz/lb} \times 100 \right]$$

$$\div\ 0.33 = 4.05\ \text{oz/gal}$$

This information for various types of proportioners and fertilizers is tabulated in tables available from many suppliers of water-soluble fertilizers, or it can be readily estimated from the fertilizer proportioner nomograph (Appendix G).

Hydraulic displacement of fertilizer solutions from a tank is an efficient, inexpensive, nonelectrical injection system adaptable to trickle irrigation systems. The tank(s) must be air- and watertight. The flow through the tank can be controlled by placing a pressure regulator in the line.

The prevailing climatic condition will influence the metabolism of plants and their need for moisture and fertilizer. During periods of high temperature and high light intensities, most plants grow faster requiring more water and nutrients. During periods of low temperature and low light intensities, plants grow at a slower rate and utilize less water and nutrients. Constant feeding automatically adjusts to these conditions, since fertilizer is applied simultaneously.

Acidifying Water

At times it may be advantageous to acidify irrigation water. This is particularly true for nurseries that grow their crops in containers or benches and use water that has an alkaline reaction. Water used to irrigate nursery and greenhouse crops nearly always contains calcium and magnesium carbonate. The concentrations will vary with geographic areas and the depth of water supply, but carbonates cause the water to have an alkaline reaction. The constant use of alkaline water tends to increase the alkalinity of the soil. Since many species of plants do not grow well in alkaline soils, it is desirable, in some situations, to acidify the water. This can be accomplished by neutralizing the alkalinity of the water with the aid of acid.

A high grade of phosphoric acid has been used to neutralize the alkalinity of greenhouse water for many years, and more recently the process has been used in the production of container-grown plants in nurseries. The advantages of acidification are:

1. Avoids a gradual increase in the soil reaction (pH) from carbonate accumulation.
2. Permits injection of one or more of the anions essential for plant growth with minimum modification of salt concentration.
3. Minimizes plugging of small-diameter irrigation equipment.

4. Reduces sodium uptake by foliage in areas where sodium is a problem salt.

When acid is mixed with concentrated fertilizer solutions, the resulting mixture will contain acids of the salts present in the fertilizer. These mixtures have a high corrosive potential to the irrigation equipment that is exposed to the concentrated solutions prior to dilution. Thus, separate injectors are advisable when employing both acid treatment of irrigation water and concentrated fertilizer solutions.

Acidified water used in irrigation of nursery stock should have a pH between 5.8 to 6.5, which is considered optimum for use on most plants. To estimate the quantity of acid required, determine the milliequivalents per liter of carbonates in the water and multiply by the acid factor (Table 10-3). For example, water analysis reports 2.5 mEq/liter of carbonates. The acid injector has a ratio of 1 : 200 and a 50-gal acid stock solution tank is available. Two hundred × 50 equals 10,000 gal of water to be neutralized (ten 1000-gal units). To neutralize with 75% phosphoric acid requires 175 fluid ounces (10 × 7.0 × 2.5) be mixed with the 50 gal of water for acid injection. The treated water as it is delivered from the nozzle should be tested and the acid solution adjusted accordingly to obtain the desired pH. The solution should be monitored on a regular basis to assure uniformity of water quality.

Table 10-3   Percent grade or degree Baumé, acid factor, and comments on three acids used to acidify irrigation water in nurseries and greenhouses

Acid	Percent grade or degree Baumé	Acid factor (oz/1000 gal)	Notes
Phosphoric	75%	7.0	Most commonly used. Contains 52% P_2O_5. Use food grade. Avoid by-product acids—contain harmful heavy metals.
Sulfuric	66°Be (98%)	3.2	Dangerous to handle. An explosion can occur if water is added to the acid.
Nitric	42°Be (67%)	10.5	Contains 15% N. Avoid mixing with organic materials. Dangerous to handle.

SOURCE: Adapted from Matkin and Petersen, 1971.

Acids can be very dangerous materials and should be used with great caution. They are available in various strengths and degrees of purity. Sulfuric acid is commonly available at 66° Baumé grade, which is highly concentrated. When added to water, considerable heat is generated. Therefore, it should be added slowly in small quantities, preferably with rapid stirring. Water should not be added to the acid, as an explosion can occur.

Frost Protection

Sprinkler irrigation can also be used to protect certain nursery crops against cold injury due to radiation frosts in late spring. It is common in some areas of the country to experience seasons when nursery crops, particularly certain *Taxus* clones, are in their first flush of growth, and if they are subjected to early morning freezing temperatures, the new growth will be destroyed and the plants made unsalable for that year. Such plants, if continuously sprayed with water during the danger period, can be protected against this form of injury. This is due to the liberation of latent heat upon the freezing of water. Part of the liberated heat is absorbed by the plants, which is enough to protect them from freeze injury down to a temperature approaching 10°F, depending upon the volume of water applied. But to accomplish this, water must be applied continuously or in frequent repeat intervals if applied with the aid of rotating sprinklers. This amounts to approximately $\frac{1}{8}$ in. of water/hr, which is equivalent to 60 GPM/acre. Sprinklers should rotate at least once every 20–30 sec to provide frost protection. To assure protection, the irrigation system must be in good working condition and be activated when the temperature approaches 34°F and continue until the temperature warms to above 32°F and the ice has melted from the plants. A reliable temperature alarm system should be installed at plant level in the area to be protected to warn that the frost protection system should be activated. Close communication with the local weather station is desirable during frost-sensitive periods.

Certain types of plants, unfortunately, are much too brittle to withstand the ice load that builds up during such a situation and should not be treated, as the damage due to breakage could be far greater than the protection offered against a radiation frost. Freezing of water to liberate the latent heat is not too effective in protecting plants against windborne freezes, since the wind removes the liberated heat too rapidly to be effective. This also creates an evaporative cooling situation, which reduces plant temperatures below air temperature.

Excess Soil Moisture

Although plants require water for growth, too much water about their roots for too long a period of time can cause problems. The problem results from oxygen restriction to the growing roots. The roots have a continual need for oxygen to carry on the process of respiration, which in turn produces energy needed for growth. When plants suffer from excess moisture, they often exhibit one or more of the following symptoms: wilting of the foliage and succulent shoots, chlorosis of the foliage, reduced vigor, necrosis of the foliage and tender shoots, and death. The degree of expression of the symptoms is dependent upon the plant species and the duration of the flooded condition.

Plants that have been growing well, as a result of good culture, will often exhibit a sudden wilting of new leaves and shoots when their roots are inundated with water, especially if the water remains for more than a few hours. Plants that have been exposed to flood conditions for a number of days may completely dehydrate some weeks after the flood. This is due to injury that was done to the roots during the flood period. Plants that are classified as drought-tolerant have a greater tendency to exhibit this type of injury. However, most plants will dehydrate if the excess water remains in the soil long enough to damage their root hairs.

Excess moisture in a propagation bench or liner bed will often result in wilting and death of new shoots. Examination of the cuttings will reveal dead bark on the basal portion of the cutting and a discoloration of the pith. In advanced stages the basal area of the cutting will exhibit rot. However, similar symptoms can be produced by an application of a root-inducing hormone at too high a concentration.

Trees and shrubs planted into areas with poor drainage will soon exhibit chlorosis of the foliage and lack of vigor. Where the poor drainage situation is compounded by excessive water, the plants may fail to leaf out in the spring and will die.

The reasons for excess water in the root zone of plants are many and varied. However, they can be reduced to two primary causes: poor drainage and excessive or too frequent applications of water. Poor drainage may be due to soils of medium to low porosity or to artificially created situations that impede drainage. If plants must be planted in poorly drained sites, some thought should be given to selecting species that are adapted to such a site, or to artificially draining the areas.

When planting in pots, containers, benches, or in disturbed-soil areas, attention must be given to providing for adequate drainage. All too often pots and containers have no drainage holes or the holes have become plugged, and disturbed sites have had the soil structure destroyed so that the planting site functions as a sealed basin. The practice of mulching to reduce weed growth and evaporation from the soil surface can sometimes accentuate an excess-moisture problem in the soil. This is particularly true on clay sites during periods of abundant rainfall.

For a plant to grow it must have water, but too much water can be detrimental. Good drainage is one of the cardinal points in growing healthy plants. Never plant into containers without drainage holes, and check the percolation rate of clay and disturbed soils prior to planting. If it is found to be lacking, some type of artificial drainage should be installed prior to planting.

SUMMARY

Water is a biochemical reagent for photosynthesis and as such is a major modifier of plant growth. It is used as a carrier or a distribution agent for water-soluble fertilizers and for various pesticides and growth regulations. It can also be used to protect tender nursery crops from damage due to late spring frosts and to moisten the soil to aid digging and transplanting operations. Various types of irrigation systems are available for use in a nursery. The specific type should be selected based upon objectives and economic considerations. Intensive production areas such as container production and propagation facilities warrent an investment in a permanent, labor-efficient system, whereas extensive field production areas may warrant only an investment in a semiportable system or a trickle-irrigation system for shade trees.

Other considerations in selecting and developing an irrigation system for a nursery are daily water needs, availability of quality water, power for operation of the equipment, and the disposition of excess waste water from container production areas, at least in some states. The effective and efficient use of an irrigation system can increase the productive potential of many nurseries and improve their profitability where this is a major management objective.

REFERENCES

BOODLEY, J. W., C. F. GORTZIG, R. W. LANGHANS, and J. W. LAYER. 1966. Fertilizer proportioners for floriculture and nursery crop production management. N. Y. State Coll. Agric. Cornell Ext. Bull. 1175.

BOOKER, L. J. 1967. Irrigating container-plants. Am. Nurseryman 126(7):71.

_____., and N. W. STICE. 1964. Mechanized irrigation for nurseries. Proc. Int. Plant Propag. Soc. 14:336.

BOSLEY, R. W. 1966. A fertilizer injection system. Proc. Int. Plant Propag. Soc. 16:311-314.

BOUYOUCUS, G. J. 1937. Evaporating the water with burning alcohol as a rapid means of determining moisture content of soils. Soil Sci. 44:337-383.

_____. 1950. A practical soil moisture meter as a scientific guide to irrigation practices. Agron. J. 42:104-107.

COSTELLO, L., and J. L. PAUL. 1975. Moisture relations in transplanted container-plants. HortScience 10(4):371-372.

DAVIS, J. R., and R. L. COOK. 1954. Fertilizing through irrigation water. Mich. State Univ. Ext. Bull. 324.

_____, and R. L. COOK. 1955. Frost protection with sprinkler irrigation. Mich. State Univ. Ext. Bull. 327.

FURUTA, T. 1973. Studies of plant subsystems in container production. Am. Nurseryman 138(12):8.

_____. 1974 Irrigation of ornamentals. Proc. Int. Plant Propag. Soc. 24:99-104.

KENWORTHY, A. L. 1974. Trickle irrigation, simplified guidelines for orchard installation and use. Farm Sci. Mich. State Univ. Agric. Exp. Sta. Res Rep. 248.

KIDDER, E. H., and R. Z. WHEATON. 1958. Supplemental Irrigation. Mich. State Univ. Ext. Bull.309.

MATKIN, O. A., and F. H. PETERSEN. 1971. Why and how to acidify irrigation water. Am. Nurseryman 133(12):14.

MONK, R. 1962. Tolerance of some trees and shrubs to saline conditions. Proc. Am. Soc. Hort. Sci. 81:556-561.

OKI, G. 1964. B-1-F fertilizer metering system proceedings. Proc. Int. Plant Propag. Soc. 14:335.

PATEL, S. I., and H. H. TINGA. 1973. Growth of subirrigated Japanese holly as affected by soil type and depth. HortScience 8(1):27-28.

PONDER, H. G., and A. L. KENWORTHY. 1975. Hydraulic displacement of tank fertilizer solution(s) into a trickle irrigation system. HortScience 10(3):261-262.

_____, and A. L. KENWORTHY. 1976. Trickle irrigation of shade trees growing in the nursery: I. Influence on growth. J. Am. Soc. Hort. Sci. 101(2):100-103.

RICHARDS, L. A. 1954. Saline and alkali soils. USDA Agricultural Handbook 60.

ROBERTS, B. 1972. The role of water in shade tree growth. Am. Nurseryman 135(3):12.

ROHWER, C., and M. R. LEWIS. 1940. Small irrigation pumping plants. USDA Farmer's Bull.1857.

SACHS, R. M., T. KRETCHUM, and T. MOCH. 1975. Minimum irrigation requirements for landscape plants. J. Am. Soc. Hort. Sci. 100(5):499-502.

SPURWAY, C. H., and C. E. WILDON. 1938. Water conditioning for greenhouses. Mich. Agric. Exp. Sta. Circ. Bull. 166:3-10.

STAEBNER, F. E. 1940. Supplemental irrigation. USDA Farmer's Bull. 1846.

STOECKELER, J. H., and E. AAMODT. 1940. Use of tensiometers in regulating watering in forest nurseries. Plant Physiol. 15:589-607.

TOMLINSON, W. M. 1964. Automatic one-gallon container irrigation. Proc. Int. Plant Propag. Soc. 14:308-312.

WALLIS, M. T. 1971. Capillary watering. Proceedings of the Refresher Course for Nurserymen, Pershore College of Horticulture, Pershore, England, pp. 32-33.

WHITE, R. G., and E. H. KIDDER. Tractor power take-off driver pumps. Mich. State Univ. Coop. Ext. Serv. Misc. Ser. Circ. E-23.

WILCOX, L. V. 1955. Classification and use of irrigation waters. USDA Circ. 969.

SUGGESTED READING

JOHNSON, M. 1972. Irrigation, nursery container production. Coop. Ext. Serv. Univ. Mass. Publ. 73, pp. 23-25.

McDONALD, S. E. and S. W. RUNNING. 1979. Monitoring Irrigation in Western Forest Tree Nurseries. USDA, Forest Service, Rocky Mtn. Forest and Range Exp. Sta., Gen Tech. Rpt. Rm-61.

PAIN, C. H., W. W. HINZ, C. RIED, and K. R. FROST. 1975. Sprinkler irrigation. Sprinkler Irrigation Association, Silver Springs, Md. 20906.

RUBEY, H. 1954. Supplemental irrigation for eastern United States. Interstate Printers and Publishers, Inc., Danville, Ill. 209 pp.

Chapter 11

Modifying Plant Growth and Development in the Nursery

Plants, like any other biological organism, are the product of heredity and environment. Trees growing in a natural environment develop a form and structure related to the multiplicity of stresses to which they are exposed over a period of time. A tree that developes in a dense stand within a forest will have a narrow crown and a tall, lean stem due to crowding and limited light within the stand, whereas a tree that develops in an open area will have a broader, fuller crown with a stem of greater caliper and more taper. Trees growing in a nursery also develop a form and structure related to the stresses imposed upon them by nature and by the nurserymen who produce them. In addition to the major environmental modifiers—climate, moisture, soil, nutrients and light—plants in a nursery can also be modified in their development by various cultural modifiers, such as spacing, staking, pruning, spraying of chemicals, planting, digging, and by a host of biological modifiers, such as diseases, insects, vertebrates, weeds, and human beings (Table 11-1). Unfortunately, too

Table 11-1 Summary of primary and cultural modifiers of various plant characteristics or plant qualities

Plant part	Quality or characteristic	Primary modifiers	Cultural modifiers
Stem (trunk)	Diameter (caliper)	Site, moisture, light, wind	Spacing, shoot pruning, fertilizing, spacing, shoot pruning, staking
	Taper	Same as for diameter	
	Height	Light, moisture	Fertilizing, pruning, space, day length, root pruning, cultivation, chemicals
Branches	Length and compactness	Species selection, moisture, light	Same as for stem height
	Branch angle	Species or cultivar selection	Pruning, branch spreading, cytokinin
Foliage	Color and size	Light, moisture, species selection	Fertilizing, root pruning, irrigation
	Sheen of needles	Cultivar selection	Dormant oil on some species
	Defoliation	Cold temperature, short days.	Chemical defoliants, root pruning
Roots	Depth	Site, species selection, soil aeration	Root pruning, copper screening
	Branching	Species or cultivar selection	Root pruning
	Compactness	Drainage	Trickle irrigation, fertilizer placement, organic matter
	Malformation (curl and kink) (J or bilateral)	Container	Improper planting
Method of planting
Flowers	Induction	Maturity	Photoperiod, chemicals, C/N ratio, pruning, root pruning, ringing, bending
	Inhibition	Juvenility	Chemicals, C/N ratio, pruning
Fruit	Set	Pistillate (female) flowers	Pollinizers, hormone sprays, fertilizer (N)
	Prevention	Male plants of dioecious species, double-flowered forms	Hormone sprays, removing flower buds
Plant	Cold acclimation	Low-temperature, short-photoperiods, ecotype	Root pruning, withholding water

little attention has been given to the effects of the various cultural modifiers (practices) on the development of plants in nurseries, whereas considerable information is available on the major environmental and biological modifiers.

SHOOT MODIFICATION

Spacing was discussed in Chapter 5 from the point of view of organization of the nursery for land utilization and various management practices. However, spacing also has an effect upon the growth and development of plants in the nursery. Plants, either in the field or in containers, that are to be sold as specimens must be spaced far enough apart so that they can grow in an unrestricted manner. If they are spaced too closely, or allowed to remain too long in high-density plantings, their branches touch, they become malformed, and their sales appeal decreases. With sapling trees, whether grown in the field or in containers, there is a tendency to overlook the importance of spacing and to grow them too close. At close spacing, saplings tend to grow taller, but the lower foliage is shaded and tends to drop off. At wider spacing, which allows a greater volume of space per plant, they develop more caliper, better taper, and better appearance. Where possible, nursery rows for saplings should be oriented in a north-south direction to maximize exposure of the lower branches of young trees to sunlight.

The density of seeding also affects the growth and development of seedlings. Most buyers prefer seedlings of good caliper ($\frac{3}{16}$ – $\frac{1}{4}$ in. or $\frac{1}{4}$ in. and up) with appropriate height and appearance, plus a well-developed root system. However, too low a density in the seedbed results in fewer seedlings that are too large for profitable management. The optimum density should be determined for each species to be grown. Information on seeds and seedling culture is contained in USDA Agricultural Handbook 450, *Seeds of Woody Plants in the United States,* and in *Plant Propagation Principles and Practices* (see Appendix A).

Staking and Pruning

Staking and pruning are strong modifiers of plant form and structure. Since they are closely related and interact with wind, they will be discussed together. Pruning the stem (trunk, bole) of young trees induces a preferential distribution of the photosynthates toward the upper portion of the stems, whereas the action of wind induces a preferential distribution of the photosynthates toward the lower portion of the stem. Staking young trees has a tendency to promote growth of the upper portion of the stem to the detriment of the basal portion. In experiments where the stems of young trees were staked for a number of years, it was found that the stems became unstable and could not support their crowns when the stakes were removed and subjected to the stress of crown weight and wind action. Unstaked trees exposed to the stress of moderate, multidirectional wind produced stems that supported their crowns under the stress of normal wind conditions. Staked trees grew taller but produced stems of less caliper and less taper. Unstaked trees, exposed to moderate multidirectional winds, produced stem growth that was uniformly distributed around the circumference of the stem and was of normal cell structure, whereas trees exposed to a unilateral wind force tended to increase the growth of the stem in the area of maximum stress. This can be seen on trees along an ocean front and on trees improperly staked. Removing the lower branches from the stem contributed to a decrease in caliper and taper of some but not all species of trees.

The development of stems of trees is related to the amount of photosynthate available and its distribution within the tree. There is a strong tendency for the photosynthate (carbohydrates) to accumulate and be utilized in growth processes in the upper portions of a tree. But, owing to physical stresses that are produced in free-swaying stems, there may be an increase in the level of auxin which causes the food materials to be distributed to the stress areas, resulting in greater caliper and improved taper of the stem.

Taper is the gradual decrease in diameter of the trunk in an apical direction. Taper can be calculated between two points on the stem by dividing the diameter difference between the two points by the diameter of the basal point (Fig. 11-1). Since diameter of the apical measurement is usually smaller, the taper value is negative. It has been determined experimentally that the taper parameter for sapling trees, where the wind load occurs at a point about 0.6 of the height of the tree, should be close to -0.60. A taper of this magnitude produces a tree in which stress is distributed uniformly in the region of the trunk where wood development is most advanced and decreases rapidly in the region toward the top, where the wood is least developed.

One objective in producing shade trees in a nursery is to develop a straight, strong leader. For most species, this can be accomplished by allowing the saplings to sway in the wind. But with some species and with budded clones, especially when growing on sites where the

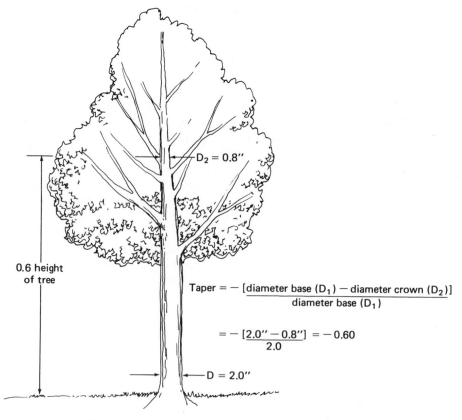

$$D_2 = 0.8''$$

0.6 height
of tree

$$\text{Taper} = - \frac{[\text{diameter base } (D_1) - \text{diameter crown } (D_2)]}{\text{diameter base } (D_1)}$$

$$= - \frac{[2.0'' - 0.8'']}{2.0} = -0.60$$

$$D = 2.0''$$

Figure 11-1 Determination of taper for a young tree.

wind is strong or primarily from one direction, it may be necessary to support the sapling temporarily by staking. If staking is done, it should be confined to the lower portion of the stem, allowing the upper portion to sway in the wind. The support should be removed as soon as the tree has developed sufficient caliper to support the crown.

Pruning practices vary with cultivar, market objective, and the personal preference of nurserymen. All pruning in the nursery should be done to enhance the natural form and beauty of the plants. The market objective will also influence the type and amount of pruning that can be done. A market objective that calls for small plants at low price does not permit much pruning, whereas a market objective that is to supply specimen shade trees requires considerable pruning.

A good nursery pruning program commences with the planting of the liners. Spreading evergreens and some shrubs should be cut back to induce branching and compactness of growth. Trees that normally grow with a central leader should have multiple leaders reduced to one—the straightest. Trunk pruning of shade trees may or may not be done, depending upon the market objective and preference of the nurseryman. Some nurserymen prefer to retain lateral branches and branchlets as long as possible to aid in the development of the trunk, whereas others prefer to strip the buds and branchlets from the trunk to aid in developing smooth bark. Small branchlets can easily be removed by running a gloved hand along the trunk. If branchlets are left on, they can be headed back to permit cultural operations within the blocks. When the desired caliper and taper are established, the lower laterals can be removed to produce a tree with the desired form.

In addition to developing good stem structure for trees, pruning young plants in the nursery is done to improve the crown structure. Thinning the crown will reduce the weight and wind resistance during the early life of young trees, thus aiding in stem development. Excurrent tree species should be limited to a single leader. Double or multiple leaders often are subtended by narrow branch angles which are generally weak and tend to break during storms in later life. Also, branches that join the stem at acute angles should be removed if they are not absolutely necessary for the overall form of the tree. They, too, are weak structurally and can be easily damaged as they grow larger. Branches selected for the main scaffolds should form wide angles (30-60°) to assure that they will withstand stress when they are older. As the tree grows and matures in the nursery, branches that grow inward or that cross and rub other more desirable branches should be removed. In more vigorous species, it may be necessary to headback branches that grow more rapidly than others to keep the crown in balance. Should it become necessary to headback a leader, owing to excessive growth, the cut should be made directly above a bud. If the tree has two or more buds per node, a desirable practice is to remove all but one of these buds. This encourages the development of a single leader and avoids the problem of multiple leaders. To minimize the development of a crook at the point where the new leader develops, support the bud with a small piece of masking tape wrapped about the bud's stem. This practice aids in the development of straight, upright growth of the new developing leader.

Evergreens are pruned or sheared either to enhance their natural form or to correct malformations in growth. Most large evergreens require little pruning; a double or multiple leader may need to be removed periodically. Rapidly growing pines are best pruned during a flush of growth (candle stage) to ensure the development of terminal buds; to delay until the flush of growth has terminated results in poorly shaped trees. Evergreen shrubs (e.g., junipers and yews) will often benefit by two shearings during the growing season, developing into dense plants.

Clean tools must be used when pruning in the nursery. It is a good practice to clean and sterilize pruning equipment at the end of each row and especially after pruning a tree or shrub that was or is suspected of being infected with a disease. All open wounds are potential sites for disease infection. Closure of pruning wounds can be hastened by keeping the plants in a healthy, vigorous condition by maintaining adequate levels of moisture and nutrition. The application of tree paint to wounds is of minimal value and is seldom used in nurseries.

Water Modifiers

The growth of plants in the nursery is greatly influenced by the availability of water. Trees suffering from moisture stress produce significantly less growth than trees growing under optimum levels of soil moisture. Trickle-irrigated trees growing in nursery rows exhibited greater trunk diameter increase than do nonirrigated trees. Plants growing in containers can also be modified by availability of water. Maximum growth of forsythia plants was achieved when the media were irrigated after 0.1 atm but before 1.0 atm of moisture stress was attained (Table 11-2). Significant growth reduction resulted when soils were allowed to dry to a point where 5 or more

Table 11-2 Influence of five moisture regimes on growth of *Forsythia intermedia* grown in containers

	Grams of oven dry weight	
Moisture regime	*Mean shoot growth*	*Mean root growth*
1. Irregular below 0.1-atm stress	3.69	5.06
2. Irregular at 0.1-atm stress	5.28	6.65
3. Irregular at 1-atm stress	5.26	5.81
4. Irregular at 5-atm stress	3.99	4.81
5. Irregular at 15-atm stress	2.19	3.26
L.S.D.		
0.05	1.37	0.31
0.01	1.86	0.42

SOURCE: Wikle, Davidson, and Erickson, 1961.

atmospheres of moisture stress had developed. Maintaining medium soil moisture at high levels is unnecessary after growth has stopped due to limitations by other climatic modifiers, such as low temperature or short day lengths.

Chemical Modifiers

Shoot growth of some species can be modified by chemical means. Various chemicals are effective in reducing growth of shoots, while others are effective in accelerating shoot growth. Still other materials can be used as chemical pruning agents and for control of sprouting.

Maleic hydrazide (MH–40), succinic acid (commonly known as aminozide), abscissic acid (ABA), ancymidol, and other chemical growth regulators have been used to restrict the growth of woody plants. Gibberellic acid accelerates the growth of some species of woody plants. Selected fatty acids (e.g. Off-Shoot-O) can be used as chemical pruning agents, whereas the ethyl ester of naphthaleneacetic acid has been used to inhibit sprouting following pruning, and from the base of some grafted or budded plants (e.g., crabapples). However, most of the chemical modifiers are still in the developmental stage and should be used with caution. Only products that are registered for a specific use should be used, and they should be applied according to the product label.

The effectiveness of chemical growth regulators varies with species, stage of growth, climatic conditions, and method of application. As a general rule, plants that have hairy leaves and distinct internodes respond better to foliar sprays than do plants that have waxy leaves or enclosed growing points. Also, plants in the early stages of vegetative growth respond better than those that are dormant, in flower, or in a late stage of growth. Foliar applications should be made when the temperature is between 60 and 80° F and the relative humidity is high (50% or greater). At low temperatures the chemical fails to penetrate, and at high temperature with low relative humidities the materials evaporate prior to penetration. The chemicals should remain on the foliage for at least 1 hr to assure effective penetration. The effectiveness of treatment is also influenced by formulation of the chemical. Some materials are emulsions and must be carefully mixed with water to produce a stable mixture. Emulsions should be applied as a fine mist uniformly over the entire plant. Excessive applications should be avoided, since large accumulations of the emulsion can girdle stems of tender plants. Chemical pruning agents selectively kill the meristematic growing point of a shoot without affecting the subsequent growth of lateral buds; therefore, timing and method of application are extremely important. The best response on woody species has been when the chemical was applied as a fine mist when the plants were in the early stages of a flush of growth and the new shoots were 2–4 in. in length. Sprays applied prior to bud break, in the spring, have not been effective, and later applications have resulted in phytotoxicity.

Sprouting, which commonly develops at the base of grafts, can be successfully inhibited in nursery stock by a single spray application of naphthaleneacetic acid ethyl ester (NAA-ethyl ester), when applied at a concentration of either 0.25 or 0.50% to the base of the trees just prior to bud swell in the spring.

Chemical growth regulators have also been used to modify the angle of branching on young trees. Although the technique has not been tested extensively, applying cytokinins at a concentration of 0.02% on the lateral buds of young apple trees resulted in crotch angles of 60° versus 36° for nontreated buds.

Modification by Light

The growth of stems can be influenced by light. The juvenile growth and development of seedlings of many woody species can be modified by light intensity and photoperiod. Long photoperiods, produced by extending the natural day length to approximately 16 hr by supplementary low-intensity light [100 foot-candles (ft-c)] or by breaking the night period with a short period of light (Fig. 11–2), will cause many species of plants to remain vegetative (Table 11–3). Species such as rhododendron and white oak grow in flushes. By control of light intensity or photoperiod where possible, growth of many species of plants can be accelerated. However, all other modifiers (temperature, moisture, nutrition) must be maintained at optimal levels. The plants must also be conditioned for low-temperature survival prior to planting outdoors if the plants are to be grown in areas exposed to low temperature.

Blue spruce seedlings grown in a greenhouse for 20 weeks under continuous light at 900 ft-c made six times the growth of similar seedlings grown under short days. They also made twice the growth of seedlings grown under a light regime that provided 12 hr of light at 900 ft-c or a 2-hr light break (50 ft-c) in the middle of the dark period. Seedlings of hardwood species responded in a similar manner.

In another experiment, 1-year-old nursery-grown seedlings of 20 hardwood species were grown for 20 weeks with supplemental light at night. VHO fluorescent lamps supplied 700–800 ft-c of light to the seedlings. Control plants were grown both in a greenhouse with-

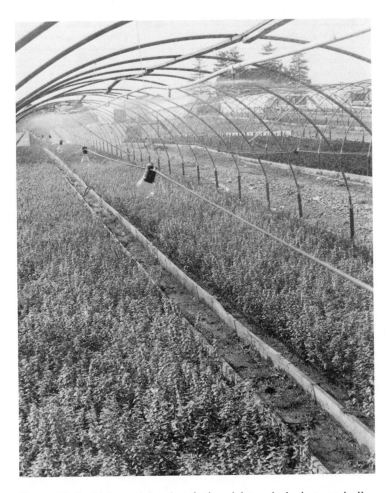

Figure 11-2 Lights used to break the night period; photoperiodic responsive plants remain vegetative. (Courtesy Conard-Pyle Co.)

out light and in a nursery adjacent to the greenhouse. At the end of the experiment, 18 of the 20 species had responded to supplemental light by increased height growth. Smoke trees under supplemental light made nine times more growth than similar seedlings grown in the nursery. Most hardwood species doubled or quadrupled their growth rates when given supplemental light at night. It is highly probable that most species of woody plants, in their juvenile state, are amenable to increased growth by the use of extended photoperiods.

It is also possible to increase growth of some species by shading. For example, it is reported that of Red-Osier dogwood made their

Table 11-3 Partial list of woody species vegetatively responsive to long days

Botanical name	Common name
Acer negundo	Boxelder
Acer palmatum	Japanese maple
Acer rubrum	Red maple
Acer saccharum[a]	Sugar maple
Aesculus hippocastanum[a]	Common horsechestnut
Betula platyphylla	Asian white birch
Betula pendula	European white birch
Catalpa bigononiodies	Common catalpa
Catalpa speciosa	Western catalpa
Cercis canadensis	American redbud
Cornus florida	Flowering dogwood
Cornus kousa	Japanese dogwood
Cornus nutallii	Mountain dogwood
Fagus grandifolia	American beech
Fagus sylvatica[a]	European beech
Hibiscus syricus	Rose-of-sharon
Juniperus horizontalis	Creeping juniper
Kolkwitzia amabilis	Beautybush
Larix decidua	European larch
Larix sibirica	Siberian larch
Liquidambar styraciflua[a]	American sweet gum
Liriodendron tulipifera[a]	Tulip tree
Magnolia soulageana	Saucer magnolia
Paulownia tomentosa[a]	Princess tree
Phellodendrom amurense	Cork tree
Picea abies[a]	Norway spruce
Pinus banksiana[a]	Jack pine
Pinus caribaea	Cuban pine
Pinus echinata	Shortleaf pine
Pinus resinosa	Red pine
Pinus sylvestris	Scots pine
Pinus taeda	Loblolly pine
Platanus occidentalis	Eastern sycamore
Populus alba	White poplar
Populus deltoides	Eastern cottonwood
Populus balsamifera	Balsam poplar
Quercus alba[a]	White oak
Quercus rubra[a]	Red oak
Quercus robur	English oak
Rhododendron catawbiense[a]	Mountain rosebay
Robina pseudoacacia	Black locust
Salix babylonica	Weeping willow
Tsuga canadensis	Canada hemlock
Ulmus americana	American elm
Viburnum carlesii	Korean spice viburnum
Viburnum opulus	Cranberry bush
Weigela florida	European flowering weigela

[a]Growth in flushes.

best growth when grown under 75% natural light. Similar findings have been observed for other species. Apparently, light saturation for some species is less than full natural light; growing these species in partial shade results in improved growth. The majority of species responding to shade are those found naturally growing as understory plants in forests.

ROOT MODIFICATION

Root pruning as practiced in nurseries is done to reduce vegetative growth, develop more compact root systems, aid in the hardening of plants for digging prior to placing them in storage or shipping to market, modify the root system to fit a given container, and encourage a radial root distribution. Root modification in the nursery is generally accomplished by various methods of root pruning. But roots can also be modified by planting method, fertilizer placement, trickle irrigation, the use of toxic barriers such as copper, and with container-grown plants by the container.

Plants that are becoming too large for the space available in a field nursery or are growing too rapidly can be modified in growth by root pruning, which will reduce the rate of vegetative growth and help control size. To ensure greater success in transplanting, nurserymen root prune plants that develop sparse root systems or taproots (e.g., *Sophora japonica, Pinus sylvestris*). Root pruning for these purposes is best done when the plants are young, either before planting in the field or 1–2 years after planting. Root pruning in the field should be done after the plants have completed a flush of growth and when there is an adequate supply of soil moisture. Root pruning should not be done during a flush of growth, during drought periods, or just prior to an anticipated drought. Immediately following root pruning, the area should be watered to settle the soil about the roots, to establish soil to root contact, and to assure a supply of water for the plants' metabolic requirements. If no irrigation is available, delay root pruning until there is a high probability of rain.

Root pruning in the field is generally accomplished with a "U-blade." The blade is attached to a high-powered tractor (Fig. 1–3) and either pushed or pulled at the appropriate soil depth to prune the roots.

The method of planting can materially modify the root system of nursery-grown trees. At the time of planting, it is essential that the roots of bare root plants be carefully positioned to assure uniform, radial distribution. When bare root trees and shrubs are hand-planted, the roots are generally distributed. But with mechanical planters there is a great chance of roots being poorly distributed. Some machines open a narrrow trench into which the roots are inserted. This often results in a bilateral root system, especially in heavy soils. In other situations, if the roots are dragged in planting, the plants develop a unilateral root system (Fig. 11-3). Plants with either a uni- or bilateral root system do not develop good anchorage in the soil and blow over fairly easily in wind storms. They are restricted to a limited moisture supply and are prone to dehydrate more rapidly during periods of drought than plants with well-distributed, radial root systems.

Figure 11-3 Unilateral root system, the results of roots that were dragged when planted as a liner.

Aeration

Root systems can be modified by aeration and the addition of various soil amendments. Aerating compacted soils will often result in improved root growth. Incorporating organic matter and slow-release fertilizers into the soil about the roots can greatly influence their development. This technique can be used when preparing large trees for transplanting. A trench is dug around the tree in the area where maximum root growth is desired. It is then backfilled with a loam soil enriched with organic matter and a slow-release form of fertilizer. In a few months the trench will be filled with a mass of fibrous roots that aid in successful transplanting.

Trickle irrigation is effective in modifying the root system of plants growing in field production nurseries. An examination of the roots of a number of species of trees grown under trickle irrigation showed that sugar maples produced more fibrous roots, whereas honey locust produced larger roots than did nonirrigated trees. Pin oaks produced both more fibrous roots and larger roots. Trickle irrigation did not affect the depth of root penetration but did increase the mass of the root system contained within the root ball.

Container Effects

Root systems of container-grown plants can be modified by the size, depth, and shape of the container, as well as by various root pruning techniques. Root development of container-grown plants is proportional to the volume of medium in the container in which the plant is growing, which in turn is a function of the diameter and the depth of the container. The shape of the container is also a significant root modifier. In round containers with smooth interior surfaces, plants that remain for too long a period of time develop root curl, whereas in square containers or in round containers with vertical ridges on the sides, the roots have a tendency to grow to the corner or to the ridge and then grow down rather than develop in a circular manner. The roots of container-grown plants can also be effectively root-pruned by growing the plants either on a wire bench or on a copper screen. When grown on the wire bench, the roots are air-pruned, whereas when grown on a copper screen, they are pruned by the toxic effect of the copper.

Temperature Response

The temperature of the root medium can also modify the growth of roots. For most plants, the optimum temperature range for root growth is 60–80°F. Both low and high temperatures can result in injury to or death of roots. Plants growing in metal or high-density polyethylene containers exposed to direct solar radiation will often have media temperatures in the range of 100–120°F. These high-temperature effects can be reduced by shading the sides of exposed containers or by using fiber or papier-mâché-type containers, which are poor conductors of heat. The use of light-colored containers (white, yellow, or silver), which reflect the sun's heat, will significantly reduce medium temperature as compared to the use of black or dark green containers, which absorb more of the heat and transfer it to the soil medium. (See page 329 for low-temperature effects.)

FLOWERING AND FRUITING

Modifying flowering and fruiting varies with the objective of nurserymen. Nurserymen often want plants to produce flowers or fruits, because they are more marketable. At other times they may want to prevent flowering or fruiting, since fruiting usually causes a reduction in growth.

They may also desire to keep plants in a juvenile condition, since cuttings from juvenile plants initiate roots more readily than do cuttings from mature plants. Flowering plants that are heavily set with flower buds or are in flower will not only sell much more readily than similar-sized plants without buds or flowers, but the plants will command a higher price in the market place. There is also a sales advantage to having fruit on plants such as English and American holly, fire thorn, mountain ash, and others, since this is what the customers desire.

The physiology of flowering and fruiting is very complex and is thoroughly discussed in other books and scientific reviews (see Suggested Reading). But the basic information developed by plant scientists can be used by nurserymen to modify the flowering and fruiting of plants in the nursery. For years nurserymen have attempted to induce plants to flower by stem pruning, root pruning, ringing of stems, bending of branches, bark inversion, and withholding water and nitrogen. They have maintained plants in a juvenile condition by heavy pruning and by applying high levels of nitrogen. Since the mid-1950s, plant scientists have learned to control the growth and flowering of a number of woody plants by modifying the photoperiod, and since the 1960s they have been able to modify, to a certain degree, the flowering response of woody species with the aid of chemical growth regulators.

Early spring pruning of young vigorous apple trees helps to stimulate growth but discourages the formation of flower buds, whereas pruning similar trees at the time of flower bud differentiation can stimulate flower bud formation but retard vegetative growth. The same response has been reported for the application of nitrogen fertilizer to young apple trees. For many years it was thought that applying nitrogen to plants would keep them in a vegetative condition, while withholding nitrogen would cause them to differentiate flower buds. It has been demonstrated, on young apple trees, that applying nitrogen in the late fall or early spring prior to growth will, in fact, induce more vegetative growth. But once extension growth has ceased, an application of nitrogen can stimulate floral differentiation in those buds still undifferentiated. Timing is the important factor.

Root pruning or digging plants such as flowering dogwood a year in advance of sale is done by some nurserymen to stimulate the initiation and development of floral primordia. Root pruning is basically a growth-retarding process, but if performed at the right time in the growth cycle it can be effective in stimulating flower bud development on some species (e.g., wisteria). The pruning should be done when the foliage is fully developed and just prior to bud initiation for the species.

The *practice of ringing* (girdling) or scoring and bark inversion are used by orchardists to induce a "tardy" fruit tree into bearing, and it has been and is used, to a limited degree, to promote flowering. Ringing is the practice of removing a strip of bark from a branch or the trunk of a tree, whereas scoring is cutting through the bark of a tree into the wood without removing any bark. Bark inversion involves removing a ring of bark from the trunk of the tree and replacing it in an inverted position. The operation is best performed in the spring of the year when the bark is slipping; this will leave the cambium in place to heal the wound. It is recommended that the exposed area be protected from the sun to prevent drying. The injury disrupts the downward movement of elaborated carbohydrates and organic substances, thus reducing root growth. The net effect is to decrease vegetative growth and to induce flower bud initiation. Ringing should not be practiced on stone fruits, since it usually results in death of the tree.

The *effect of photoperiod* on the flowering of plants has been known since 1920 when the length of the day was found to be the controlling factor in the flowering of tobacco. Since that time photoperiodism has been thoroughly researched and is known to control many other responses in plants, including germination of some seeds, shoot elongation, rhizome formation, sex expression, winter hardening, and others. Commercial flower growers soon took advantage of the knowledge that chrysanthemums and poinsettias could be induced to flower by short days. They used long days to keep plants vegetative and induced them into bloom by putting them under short days. This is commonly done by pulling black cloth over the plants in the late afternoon or by interrupting the night period by a half-hour of low-intensity light. Unfortunately, there are only a few reports relating the influence of photoperiod to flower initiation and expression in woody plants (Table 11–4).

Flower bud formation in *Rhododendron catawbiense* is enhanced by growing the plants on long days (16 hours) until the flush of growth is about one-half complete (10–14 days), at which time they should be transferred to short days. Maintaining the plants under long days results in malformed flower buds with leaflike bracts and petal-like stamens.

Flower development and expression in *Abelia grandiflora* and *Hibiscus syriacus* occur under long days on the current season's growth. However, flowering in weigela is more typical of other woody species in which initiation of flower buds occurs one season

Table 11–4 Classification of woody species with respect to day-length requirement for flowering

Botanical name	Common name
Long-day species	
Abelia grandiflora	Glossy abelia
Caryopteris incana	Blue spiraea
Hibiscus syriacus	Rose-of-sharon
Ribes rubrum	Red currant
Short-day species	
Bougainvillea glabra	Paper flower
Coffea arabica	Coffee
Long-day/short-day species	
Cestrum nocturnum	Night jessamine
Rhododendron catawbiense	Mountain rosebay
Day-neutral species	
Buddleia davidii	Summer lilac
Calluna vulgaris	Scotch heather
Cornus florida	Flowering dogwood
Hydrangea macrophylla	French hydrangea
Malvaviscus arboreus mexicanus	Turk's cap
Pinus sp.	Pine
Salix repens	Creeping willow
Syringa vulgaris	Common lilac
Viburnum sp.	Viburnum

SOURCE: Davidson and Hamner, 1957.

and flowering the next season after certain physiological requirements are satisfied. Weigela can be induced to flower the same season by growing the plants on long days for a period of 6-8 weeks, exposing the plants to short days for 6-8 weeks, followed by defoliation and a return to long days. Within 7-8 weeks following return to long days, the plants will be in full bloom. There are some cultivars of weigela that produce flower buds and bloom on current season's wood when exposed to long days. Weigela fails to bloom when exposed to short days.

Chemical growth regulators can also be used to modify the flowering response in some woody ornamental plants. In weigela, spraying plants growing under long days with maleic hydrazide (MH) 2500 ppm is as effective as subjecting the plants to short days for 6-8 weeks. Plants sprayed with MH will bloom about 7-8 weeks following treatment.

Flower bud development in rhododendron can be enhanced by soil or foliage application of growth regulators. Soil applications of Phosfon (2,4-dichlorobenzyltributal phosphonium chloride) 0.4 g/gal container or foliar applications of succinic acid (0.25-1.0%) enhanced the development of flower buds on young plants. Azalea plants can also be induced by short days or by the use of growth retardants. The growth regulator should be applied to elongating shoots at the time that shoot elongation is about one-third to one-half complete, since this is the time that the meristem is most precocious. Flowering and fruiting of holly can be enhanced by the use of growth retardants. Phosfon applied as a soil drench to young holly plants in a vegetative condition resulted in flowering and an abundance of fruit.

Fruiting of trees for use in orchard plantings is an essential requirement and is generally considered to be a desirable attribute in most ornamental trees, but not in all. Under some situations the development of fruit on plants can be less than desirable. Most people like to see fruit on holly, yews, mountain ash, and crabapples, but wish to avoid fruit set on ginkgo, mulberry, maple, and elm. Others would like to prevent the fruiting of crabapples, apples, cherries, and so on. Thus, nurserymen must be able to meet the demands of all groups relative to fruiting. To assure fruiting, it is necessary to plant those that have the ability to produce fruit, that is, plant species that have perfect or monoecious flowers or female plants of dioecious species.

Perfect flowers are those that have both anthers and pistils in the same flower. In most species they will produce fruit by self-pollination, but other species may require cross pollination to set fruit. It is important to know if cross pollination is required for fruit production in fruit tree species. Most of the following fruit trees are self-fruitful: apricots, citrus, European-type plums (fruitfulness aided by planting two varieties), figs (except Smyrna types), peaches (except 'J. H. Hale' and a few other varieties), quince, and sour cherries. A number of apples, pears, sweet cherries, and American-Japanese-type plums are self-unfruitful. To ensure fruit set, plant at least two and sometimes three varieties near each other. Some fruit tree varieties produce little or no pollen, or their pollen fails to fertilize the ovules. Therefore, at least two varieties should be planted in the same vicinity: *apples:* 'Baldwin', 'Gravenstein', 'Turley', 'Rhode Island Greening', 'Stamen', and 'Winesap'; *pears:* 'Bartlett' and 'Seckel'; *sweet cherry:* 'Bing', 'Lambert', 'Napoleon'. When planning an orchard, it is advisable to check the planting plan with a fruit specialist to assure proper plant selections and fruitfulness of all trees.

In *monoecious species* the reproductive structures are in separate flowers but on the same plant (e.g., pine, spruce), but only the female flowers or strobile produces fruit. In dioecious species the reproductive structures are on separate plants. The word "dioecious" is derived from the Greek words *di* (two) and *oikos* (house): thus, two households. The fruit is borne by the female plants, but a pollinizer (a male plant) must be located in the vicinity to ensure fertilization. A number of valuable fruit and ornamental plants are dioecious (Table 11-5).

Over the years plants have been selected and grown either for their outstanding fruiting characteristics (e.g., holly, pyracantha, yew) or for the lack of fruiting (e.g., ginkgo, mulberry, yew). When propagated by vegetative means, these selections become established as either male or female clones. For example, in *Taxus* the clones 'Densiformis', 'Nigra', and 'Wellesley' are male, whereas 'Kelsey', 'Vermeulen', and 'Jeffrey' are female. But 'Brown', 'Hatfield', and 'Hicks' have both male and female plants being sold within the clone. In the case of 'Hicks', there were apparently two selections made, one male and the other female. They should have separate clonal names. Brown was introduced as a male clone, but at some point there was a mixup in propagation, or sex reversion took place and went unnoticed. In order to conform to standards of nomenclature, a clone must maintain the characteristics for which it was selected. Thus, considerable care must be exercised in propagation and production to assure trueness to name.

Fruiting can be avoided, at least in some species, by planting either the male form of dioecious species or by planting double-flowered forms (e.g., horsechestnut, cherries, Paul's scarlet haw-

Table 11-5 Partial list of genera with one or more dioecious species

Genera	Common name
Acer	Maple
Actinidia	Actinidia
Ailanthus	Tree of heaven
Aucuba	Aucuba
Baccharis	Saltbush
Celastrus	Bittersweet
Cephalotaxus	Plum-yew
Chionanthus	Fringe tree
Cotinus	Smoke tree
Diospyros	Persimmon
Fraxinus	Ash
Ginkgo	Maidenhair tree
Glymnocladus	Kentucky coffee tree
Helwingia	Helwingia
Hippophae	Sea buckthorn
Ilex	Holly
Juniperus	Juniper
Lindera	Spice bush
Maclura	Osage orange
Morus	Mulberry
Myrica	Bog myrtle
Nemopanthus	Mountain holly
Orixa	Orixa
Phellodendron	Cork tree
Populus	Poplar
Rhus	Sumac
Ribes	Currant
Salix	Willow
Schisandra	Magnolia vine
Shepherdia	Buffalo berry
Skimmia	Skimmia
Smilax	Greenbrier
Taxus	Yew
Vitis	Grape
Zanthoxylum	Prickly ash

thorn). Many of the double-flowering forms are unfruitful because of the morphology of their floral structures.

Fruit set can be influenced by temperature and to some degree by day length. Fruit set in Burford holly, for example, was enhanced by growing the plants under short days (9-hr day length) and low-temperature regimes (18°/14°C day/night temperature). Plants grown under long days and higher day/night temperature made more vegetative growth but set less fruit.

Fruiting can also be prevented, at least in some species, by the use of chemical sprays [e.g., naphthyleneacetic acid (NAA), maleic hydrazide (MH-30), caustic agents, and emulsifiable polyethylene films]. Various caustic agents such as dinitro compounds can be used to prevent fruiting, but some foliage burn can be expected. Sprays of emulsifiable polyethylene applied to *Thuja* at full bloom completely prevented cone formation, but the material was of little value in preventing fruiting on other species. NAA has been the most versatile hormone spray for preventing fruiting of trees.

Before applying chemical sprays to prevent fruit set or to remove unwanted fruit, nurserymen should be familiar with a number of limitations in their use.

1. All chemicals have registered uses. By law, a chemical must be registered with the Environmental Protection Agency (EPA) before it can be used. Unfortunately, many of the chemicals have been cleared for use only on fruit crops.

2. Concentration is critical. At low concentration, hormone sprays cause the set of fruit; at high concentrations they can cause phytotoxic effects on the flowers and growing shoots.

3. The time of application and weather conditions can modify the response. If applied at the wrong stage of flower or fruit development, the response can be different from that which was anticipated. If applied prior to a rain or a cold period, the results may be negative. If hormone sprays are to be used to prevent the development of fruit, they should be applied at the proper time for a given species and at the recommended concentration. If a dinitro is used, it should be applied in such a manner as to avoid contact with the foliage of evergreens, since it may cause them to drop their needles.

WINTER SURVIVAL

The winter survival of plants is important to nurserymen everywhere, but especially to those located in the colder climates. Nurserymen have a sizable investment in plant material, which if injured, could result in a serious economic loss. They are, therefore, concerned with the causes of winter injury and measures that can be taken to prevent or minimize the extent of damage. Winter injury to plants can be caused by desiccation, low temperature, or by various physical and biological agents.

Winter desiccation injury is most commonly associated with evergreens, both narrow- and broadleaved, and semievergreens. During the late winter months when the soil in the root zone is frozen and the foliage is exposed to radiation from the sun, the leaves lose moisture which the plant cannot replace. This results in desiccation of the leaves and sometimes of the stems of sensitive species. The response varies with species and even with cultivars within the species. For example, *Pinus strobus* is more sensitive to windburn injury than is *Pinus nigra*. This is also true for *Taxus baccata* compared to *Taxus cuspidata* or *Taxus media*. Within *T. cuspidata* the cultivars most sensitive to desiccation in the Midwest are 'Aurescens' and 'Thayerae'. In the *T. media* group the most sensitive are 'Brownii' and 'Green Mountain'. This may be due to the degree of water deficiency that the plants can endure. It can be prevented by shielding tender species from the direct rays of the sun and from wind during the winter months. The application of antidesiccants (transpiration inhibitors) to minimize desiccation injury has not been fully successful. Some success has been reported when the antidesiccant is applied in two applications during the winter, especially covering the lower surface of the leaves.

Low-temperature injury can be classified into three areas: (1) early fall or late spring frosts, (2) extremely cold temperature, and (3) rapid change from warm to cold. Early fall or late spring frosts, at temperatures slightly below freezing, will often injure plants that would normally withstand temperatures some 30-40° lower if the plants had been fully acclimated for winter. These frosts are the unseasonably low temperatures that occur once every 5-10 years. When it occurs in the fall of the year, the injury is manifested by the splitting of stems in plants like azaleas, holly, and rhododendrons. The same type of injury can take place in the late winter if there is a period (3-5 days) of warm temperature (40-50°F) followed by a rapid drop in temperature across the freezing point. A condition like this occurred in the Midwest in 1973, causing extensive injury to young evergreen transplants. However, when the frost takes place in late spring, the drop in temperature may not be as great, and the injury is primarily the freezing of the tender new shoots. Although the injury may appear to be rather extensive, the plant will soon recover and in 3 months to a year the aesthetic damage will be remedied, but the nursery may have sustained an economic loss. Extremely low temperatures, which normally occur in midwinter, can result in injury to flower buds, roots, shoot buds, branches, or stems, and at times if the temperature is low enough in death of the plant.

Plants that survive cold periods have the unique ability to acclimate themselves prior to the onset of cold temperatures. The actual mechanism of cold acclimation is not fully understood.* But it appears that decreasing day length and/or gradually decreasing temperatures in the fall of the year aids in increasing cold acclimation of woody plants in northern latitudes. Exposing weigela, rhododendron, and hibiscus to short days prior to the onset of low temperatures was effective in inducing cold hardiness, whereas exposing the plants to long days prior to the onset of low temperature resulted in considerable winter injury.

Exposure to short days and low temperatures prior to the onset of freezing temperatures aided in developing cold hardiness in yews and Red-Osier dogwood, whereas only declining air temperature was associated with increased cold acclimation of 'Hetzi' juniper and other conifers. Woody plants respond to the short days and/or low temperature by a significant reduction in the water content of their stems. In Red-Osier dogwood, it was noted that there was a decrease in water permeability of root cells which acted as a barrier to water uptake. Thus, it appears that cold acclimation is related in part to moisture relationships and tenderness of growth. High soil moisture and high levels of fertility do not appear to bear a direct relationship on winter hardiness. However, species that do not harden in response to short days may be predisposed to low-temperature injury by maintaining high levels of moisture and nutrition during a warm fall.

To aid in hardening plant material for winter, avoid cultural practices that predispose the plants to injury.

1. Do not expose plants to long days or high temperatures prior to the onset of winter. Plants that were growing under lights or in warm places (greenhouse) should be gradually conditioned for winter either by 2–3 weeks' exposure to low temperature or short days.

2. Avoid late (time varies with area of the country) pruning, cultivating, fertilizing, and field irrigation of plants susceptible to winter injury.

*Readers wishing to study this area in detail are referred to the articles listed under Suggested Reading.

3. Dig tender plants (e.g., althea, buddleia, deutzia) prior to onset of low temperature and place them into winter storage, where temperature control is possible.

4. Avoid growing plants that are not cold-hardy.

Various physical and biological agents, including frost, ice and snow, snowmobiles, rabbits, mice, and deer, can also be the cause of winter injury to plants in the nursery. Frost heaving is primarily associated with young plants transplanted into clay or clay loam soils in the fall. As the ground freezes and thaws, the young plants which have not established firm root contact with the soil are heaved out of the ground and eventually dehydrate and die unless they are replanted prior to dehydration. This type of injury can be avoided by planting fall transplants into well-drained sites or by delaying the planting onto clay sites until spring.

Damage due to ice and snow is a physical injury sustained by plants due to the weight of the materials. In most cases the injury is immediately visible, but with some plants (e.g., boxwood) the injury may not be apparent for a year or two following the ice or snow storm. The plant appears to recover from the physical crushing of the snow or ice, grows well the following summer, but begins to die the following year. The delayed appearance of damage is because only the lower bark was injured. The plant is able to obtain water and nutrients from the soil for about a year, but eventually the roots die as a result of the injury to the bark, which in effect girdled the stem. This type of injury can be avoided by providing support to the plants prior to the onset of winter. This may be a wire or wire fencing stretched along both sides of a row of boxwood or similar plants.

With the advent of the recreational use of snowmobiles, some nurserymen, in northern areas of the country, have experienced injury to plants due to snowmobiles. This injury has been confined mostly to the loss of leaders from young evergreens, such as pine, spruce, and fir. The leaders are broken by the vehicle as the driver speeds across the snow-covered landscape unaware of the damage being done to the plants below. The only protection from this type of injury is to fence or post the property against trespass, which may or may not be effective.

Rabbits, mice, and deer can do considerable damage to nursery stock during the winter months. Rabbits will either chew the bark off the stems and larger branches of deciduous trees or they will bite off the tops and side branches of smaller transplants. All types of young fruit trees, crabapples, flowering dogwood, and sweetgum are subject

Figure 11-4 Girdling of trees by mice in a nursery.

to their depredation. Rabbits can be kept out of limited areas of the nursery by various types of exclosures. But the most satisfactory method in extensive plantings is to reduce their population by shooting (permit may be necessary). The use of repellents to keep them away from valuable plants is of limited value.

Mice depredate nursery stock mostly by girdling plants at the ground line (Fig. 11-4). Occasionally, when the snow level is high, their activity is extended up onto the trunk and lateral branches. Mice have a special fondness for crabapples, arborvitae, junipers, and yews but will also work on pines and deciduous trees, if their preferred food source is not available, although they seldom chew on any trees within the stone fruit classification (e.g., peach, cherry). Removal of their natural shelter, such as weeds and sod, will aid in minimizing their depredations, but it is not a guarantee. Various types of poison baits can be used to reduce mice populations, but nurserymen must be cautious in their use, since they are toxic to fish, birds, and warm-blooded animals. Where possible, encouraging or stocking an area with natural predators may be one of the best methods of reducing rodent populations in nurseries located in rural areas.

Deer can cause extensive damage to nursery stock by chewing buds and tender branches (arborvitae, birch, yew), rubbing the trunks of young trees when developing their antlers, and trampling small plants when they are in large herds. Winter injury due to deer activity can be minimized by the use of repellents, but shooting (by permit) may be necessary if the herd is large and known to have its winter feeding area in the vicinity of the nursery.

Nurserymen must take steps to minimize the depredations of deer and rodents in the fall of the year. Baits should be in place before snow covers the ground, and repellents must be applied while it is still warm. Inspection of the nursery should be made weekly during the winter months to check for deer or rodent activity. If deer or rodents are found to be active, appropriate action can be taken to reduce their population and minimize damage to valuable plants. Table 11-6 is a partial list of animal repellents. They should be used according to label instructions. Tabasco sauce (also Louisiana hot sauce) 1 tablespoonful/gal has been used fairly successfully as a repellent to protect plants from injury due to the activities of deer, mice, and rabbits. Plants to be protected should be sprayed biweekly. A small amount of a spreader-sticker (1 tablespoonful/gal) added to

Table 11-6   Partial list of animal repellents

Material	*Repellent for:*
Alkylpyridines	Dogs
Aluminum powder	Seed deterrent for birds
Bloodmeal	Rabbits
Bone tar oils	Deer, dogs, and rabbits
Copper naphthenate	Porcupine and squirrels
Lemon grass, oil of	Dogs
Mustard, oil of	Dogs, rats, and raccoons
Nicotine sulfate	Many animals
Rosin	Deer and rabbits
Sodium pentachlorophonate	Mice and rats
Sulfur	Rodents
Tabasco sauce	Deer and rabbits
Thiram (tetramethylthiuramdisulfide)	Animals and birds
TNB-A (trinitrobenzene-aniline complex)	Rabbits
ZAC (zinc dimethyldithiocarbamatecyclohexylamine)	Deer and rodents

the mixture will improve its effectiveness. Additional information on repellents and bait for the control of birds, deer, mice, and rabbits in the nursery may be obtained from the local county agricultural agent or the U.S. Fisheries and Wildlife Service. In many states it is unlawful to gas, poison, shoot, trap, or otherwise harm wild animals or wild birds without special permits. Nurserymen should check with the law enforcement division of their Department of Natural Resources and obtain the necessary permits prior to instituting a vertebrate control program that involves harming wildlife.

DISEASES, INSECTS, WEEDS, AND OTHER PESTS

Diseases, insects, and weeds are the three most noxious, negative modifiers of plant growth in nurseries. They are common to all nurseries and cause a significant loss in either quantity of production or in plant quality, which, in turn, can result in a significant economic loss to a nursery. The negative aspects of these and other pests can best be minimized by an integrated crop production program that is directed toward quality plant production, which is the overall objective of the nursery. The program should be oriented primarily toward preventing pest problems from developing in the nursery. When they do develop, the program should be oriented to rapid eradication of the pest to minimize damage to valuable plants.

Pest problems can best be prevented by following cultural practices designed to produce healthy, vigorous plants. Plants that are properly spaced, pruned, fertilized, and watered are much less prone to pest problems than are plants that are exposed to undesirable environmental conditions. Improper irrigation management, especially overwatering in the propagation or container production areas, predisposes plants to infection by disease organisms that are either spread by water or require warm, humid environments in which to develop.

Other practices that can be used effectively in a nursery to prevent some pest problems from developing and to eradicate others are:

1. Selecting and growing cultivars that are known to be free of a specific pest (e.g., virus-free strawberries).

2. Avoid growing species that are known to have a major pest problem that is difficult to control (e.g., white birch/bronze birch borer).

3. Avoid growing in adjacent plantings any combination of species where one serves as the alternate host for a serious disease problem for another species (e.g., cedar–apple rust, Cooley spruce gall–Douglas fir/blue spruce).

4. Sterilizing, pasteurizing, or composting of media prior to use can be used to effectively reduce the incidence of many disease, insect, and weed problems within the nursery.

5. Timely cultivating and mowing can effectively reduce weed populations.

6. Constructing various types of exclosures to keep certain pests out of specific parts of the nursery. Screens can be used to protect propagation structures from some types of insects. Fences can be used to exclude rabbits.

7. By the careful use of predators, repellents, and baits, it is possible to reduce the depredations of insects, rodents, deer, and slugs.

8. Trapping and shooting can be used to reduce populations of various types of pests.

9. Applying target pesticides to control various insects, diseases, and weeds. Since pesticide recommendations are fairly specific and their use regulated by law, it is suggested that nurserymen obtain current pesticide recommendations from their local county agricultural agent or from the state pesticide specialist, generally located at the various land grant universities.

SUMMARY

Plants growing in a nursery can be modified in their growth by various environmental, cultural, and biological modifiers. These modifiers may have either a positive or a negative effect upon the plants. By good ecological management, it is possible for nurserymen to produce high-quality plants while reducing the negative effects of pests.

REFERENCES

ADAMS, D. G., and A. N. ROBERTS. 1968. Time of flower initiation in *Rhododendron* 'Roseum Elegans' as related to shoot and leaf elongation. HortScience 3(4)278–279.

BEATTIE, D. J., and H. L. FLINT. 1973. Effect of K level on frost hardiness of stems of *Forsythia intermedia* Zab. 'Lynwood'. J. Am. Soc. Hort. Sci. 98(6):539-541.

CATHEY, H. M. 1965. Initiation and flowering of rhododendron on following regulation by light and growth retardants. Proc. Am. Soc. Hort. Sci. 86: 753-760.

_____. 1968. Response of some ornamental plants to synthetic abscissic acid. Proc. Am. Soc. Hort. Sci. 93:693-698.

_____. 1970. Chemical pruning of plants. Am. Nurseryman 131(9):8.

CHADWICK, L. C. 1962. Use of growth regulators to prevent fruiting. Am. Nurseryman 115(6):96.

CHEN, P., P. H. LI, and C. J. WEISER. 1975. Induction of frost hardiness in red-osier dogwood stems by water stress. HortScience 10(4):372-374.

COLLINS, W. C. 1962. Hardening plant materials for winter. Proc. Int. Plant Propag. Soc. 12:86-88.

CRILEY, R. A. 1969. Effect of short photoperiods, cycocel and gibberellic acid upon flower bud initiation and development in azalea 'Hexe'. J. Am. Soc. Hort. Sci. 94(4):392-396.

DAVIDSON, H., M. J. BUKOVAC, and D. C. MACLEAN. 1963. Photoperiodic and chemical control of vegetative growth and flowering in weigela. Proc. Am. Soc. Hort. Sci. 82:589-595.

_____, and C. L. HAMNER. 1957. Photoperiodic responses of selected woody ornamental shrubs. Quart. Bull. Mich. Agric. Exp. Sta. Mich. State Univ. 40(2):327-343.

_____, and A. OLNEY. 1964. Clonal and sexual differences in the propagation of Taxus. Proc. Int. Plant Propag. Soc. 17:156-161.

_____, and D. P. WATSON. 1959. Teratological effects of photoperiod on *Rhododendron catawbiense* Michx. Proc. Am. Soc. Hort. Sci. 73:490-494.

DAVIS, R. E., and C. E. WHITCOMB. 1977. Effects of propagation container size on development of high quality seedlings. Proc. Int. Plant Propag. Soc. 25:448-453.

DE WILDE, R. 1962. Hardening of plant materials for winter. Proc. Int. Plant Propag. Soc. 12:84-85.

DRINKARD, A. W., JR. 1915. Some effects of pruning, rootpruning, ringing and stripping on the formation of fruit buds on dwarf apple trees. Va. Agric. Exp. Sta. Tech. Bull. 5:96-120.

FRETZ, T. A. 1973. Soil temperature influences. Am. Nurseryman 137(1):16.

FUCHIGAMI, L. H., C. J. WEISER, and D. R. RICHARDSON. 1973. The influence of sugars on growth and cold acclimation of excised stems of red-osier dogwood. J. Am. Soc. Hort. Sci. 98(5):444-447.

FURUTA, T., W. C. STONE, W. HUMPHREY, and T. MOCK. 1973. Chemical control of root growth in containers. Am. Nurseryman 137(8):9.

GARNER, W. W., and H. A. ALLARD. 1920. Effect of the relative length of day and night and other factors of the environment on growth and reproduction in plants. J. Agric. Res. 18:553–606.

GOUIN, F. R. 1977. Hot news for rodents and deer. HortScience 12(1):10.

GOURLEY, J. H., and F. S. HOWLETT. 1927. Ringing applied to the commercial orchard. Ohio Agric. Exp. Sta. Bull. 410.

HANOVER, J. W., and D. A. REICOSKY. 1972. Accelerated growth for early testing of spruce seedlings. For. Sci. 18(1):92–94.

_____, E. YOUNG, W. A. LEMMIEN, and M. VAN SLOOTEN. 1976. Accelerated-optimal-growth: a new concept in tree production. Mich. State Univ., Agric. Exp. Sta. Res. Rep. 317.

HARRIS, R. W. 1969. Staking and pruning young *Myoporum laetum* trees. J. Am. Soc. Hort. Sci. 94(1):359–361.

_____, W. B. DAVIS, N. W. STICE, and D. LONG. 1971. Root pruning improves nursery tree quality. J. Am. Soc. Hort. Sci. 96(1):105–108.

_____, W. B. DAVIS, N. W. STICE, and D. LONG. 1971. Influence of transplanting time in nursery production. J. Am. Soc. Hort. Sci. 96(1):109–111.

_____, et al. 1972. Spacing of container-grown trees in the nursery. J. Am. Soc. Hort. Sci. 97(4):503–506.

HASKELL, T. 1953. Practical blossom control for the arborist. Proc. Nut Shade Tree Conf., 29:4–17.

HAVIS, J. R. 1964. Freezing of rhododendron leaves. Proc. Am. Soc. Hort. Sci. 84:570–574.

_____. 1965. Desiccation as a factor in winter injury of rhododendron. Proc. Am. Soc. Hort. Sci. 86:764–769.

_____. 1973. High summer temperatures of containers in New England. Am. Nurseryman 137(2):7.

_____, R. D. FITZGERALD, and D. N. MAYNARD. 1972. Cold-hardness response of *Ilex crenata* Thumb. 'Hetzi' roots to nitrogen source and potassium. HortScience 7(2):195–196.

HENINGER, R. L., and D. P. WHITE. 1974. Tree seedling growth at different soil temperatures. For. Sci. 20:363–367.

HOWE, G. H. 1914. Ringing fruit trees. N.Y. (Geneva) Agric. Exp. Sta. Bull. 391.

KELLEY, J. D. 1972. Nitrogen and potassium rate effect on growth, leaf nitrogen and winter hardiness of *Pyracantha coccinea* 'Lalandi' and *Ilex crenata* 'Rotundifolia'. J. Am. Soc. Hort. Sci. 97(4):446–448.

KOZEL, P. C., and K. W. Reisch. 1972. Guidelines for chemical pruning. Am. Nurseryman 135(2):13.

KRIZEK, D. T., and R. H. ZIMMERMAN. 1973. Comparative growth of birch seedlings grown in the greenhouse and growth chambers. J. Am. Soc. Hort. Sci. 98(4):370–373.

KUHNS, L. J., and T. D. SNYDER. 1975. Phytotoxicity of copper-treated burlap on balled and burlapped *Cotoneaster divaricata*. HortScience 10(6): 613–614.

LARSON, P. R. 1965. Stem form of young *Larix* as influenced by wind and pruning. For. Sci. 11(4):412–424.

LEISER, A. T., and J. D. KEMPER. 1968. A theoretical analysis of a critical height of staking landscape trees. Proc. Am. Soc. Hort. Sci. 92:713–720.

____, and J. D. KEMPER. 1973. Analysis of stress distribution in the sapling tree trunk. J. Am. Soc. Hort. Sci. 98(2):164–170.

____, et al. 1972. Staking and pruning influence trunk development of young trees. J. Am. Soc. Hort. Sci. 97(4):498–502.

LUMIS, G. P., and H. DAVIDSON. 1967. Preventing fruit formation on landscape trees. HortScience 2(2):61–62.

____, R. A. MECKLENBURG, and K. C. SINK. 1972. Factors influencing winter hardiness of flower buds and stems of evergreen azaleas. J. Am. Soc. Hort. Sci. 97(1):124–127.

MC GUIRE, J. J., and H. L. FLINT. 1962. Effects of temperature and light on frost hardiness of conifers. Proc. Am. Soc. Hort. Sci. 80:630–635.

____, J. T. KITCHIN, and R. DAVIDSON. 1965. The effect of different growth retardants on growth and flowering of *Rhododendron obtusum* 'Hinodegeri'. Proc. Am. Soc. Hort. Sci. 86:761–763.

MC KENZIE, J. S., and C. J. WEISER, and P. H. LI. 1974. Changes in water relations of *Cornus stolonifera* during cold acclimation. J. Am. Soc. Hort. Sci. 99(3):223–228.

MARTH, P. C. 1963. Effect of growth retardants on flowering fruiting and vegetative growth of holly (*Ilex*). Proc. Am. Soc. Hort. Sci. 83:777–781.

MEIER, K. 1972. Pruning: the key to salable plants. Am. Nurseryman 136(6): 112.

MITYGA, H. G., and F. O. LANPHEAR. 1971. Factors influencing the cold hardiness of *Taxus cuspidata* roots. J. Am. Soc. Hort. Sci. 96(1):83–86.

MYERS, S. P., and P. C. KOZEL. 1972. Practical procedures for increasing flower bud initiation of rhododendron. Am. Nurseryman 135(3):13.

PELLETT, N. E. 1973. Influence of nitrogen and phosphorus fertility on cold acclimation of roots and stems of two container-grown woody plant species. J. Am. Soc. Hort. Sci. 98(1):82-86.

____, and D. WHITE. 1969. Soil–air temperature relationships and cold acclimation of container-grown *Juniperus chinensis* "Hetzi." J. Am. Soc. Hort. Sci. 94(5):453-456.

____, and D. WHITE. 1969. Effect of soil nitrogen and soil moisture levels on the cold acclimation of container-grown *Juniperus chinensis* "Hetzi." J. Am. Soc. Hort. Sci. 94(5):457-459.

____, and D. WHITE. 1969. Relationship of seasonal tissue changes to cold acclimation of container-grown *Juniperus chinensis* "Hetzi." J. Am. Soc. Hort. Sci. 94(5):460-462.

PONDER, H. G., and A. L. KENWORTHY. 1976. Trickle irrigation of shade trees growing in the nursery: I Influence on growth. J. Am. Soc. Hort. Sci. 101(2):100-103.

____, and A. L. KENWORTHY. 1976. Trickle irrigation of shade trees growing in the nursery: II. Influence on root distribution. J. Am. Soc. Hort. Sci. 101 (2):104-107.

ROSE, G. 1962. Hardening plant material for winter. Proc. Int. Plant Propag. Soc. 12:88-90.

RYAN, G. F. 1970. Effects of succinic acid 2,2–demethyl hydrazide and phosphorous treatments on rhododendron flowering and growth. J. Am. Soc. Hort. Sci. 95(5):624-626.

SACHS, R. M., and R. G. MAIRE. 1967. Chemical control of growth and flowering of woody ornamental plants in the landscape and nurseries: tests with maleic hydrazide and alar. Proc. Am. Soc. Hort. Sci. 91:728-734.

SANDERSON, K. C. 1973. Screening chemicals for controlling growth and flowering of *Forsythia intermedia* Zabel. HortScience 8(6):477-479.

SHUGERT, R. 1962. Rootpruning, mudding and fertilization. Proc. Int. Plant Propag. Soc. 12:82-84.

SMITH, E. M., L. C. CHADWICK, and K. W. REISCH. 1966. The use of antidesiccants in reducing transpiration and protecting ornamental plants against winter injury. Proc. Am. Soc. Hort. Sci. 88:703-707.

STAHLY, E. A., and M. W. WILLIAMS. 1967. Size control of nursery trees with *N*-dimethylamenosuccinamic acid. Proc. Am. Soc. Hort. Sci. 91:792-794.

STUART, N. W. 1961. Initiation of flower buds in rhododendron (azalea) after application of growth retardants. Science 134:50-52.

TICKNOR, R. L., and C. A. NANA. 1968. Chemical control of rhododendron growth and flowering. Quart. Bull. Am. Rhodo. Soc. 22:90-95.

VAARTAJA, O. 1954. Photoperiodic ecotype of trees. Can. J. Bot. 32:392–399.

WEIGLE, J. L., and A. R. Beck. 1971. Flowering characteristics of weigela and their relationship to progeny age at first bloom. J. Am. Soc. Hort. Sci. 96:685–686.

WHITE, W. C., and C. J. WEISER. 1964. The relations of tissue desiccation, extreme cold and rapid temperature fluctuations to winter injury of American arborvitae. Proc. Am. Soc. Hort. Sci. 85:554–563.

WIKLE, J. S., H. DAVIDSON, and E. A. ERICKSON. 1961. Soil moisture studies with container-grown plants. Quart. Bull. Mich. Agric. Exp. Sta., Mich. State Univ. 44(1):125–128.

WILLIAMS, D. J., and B. C. MOSER. 1974. Response of woody ornamentals to a fatty acid pinching agent. HortScience 9(4):349–350.

WILLIAMS, M. W., and H. D. BILLINGSLEY. 1970. Increasing the number and crotch angles of primary branches of apple trees with cytokinins and gibberellic acid. J. Am. Soc. Hort. Sci. 95(5):649–651.

WILLIAMS, R. R., and R. W. RENNISON. 1963. Summer nitrogen: a new method of bringing apple trees into bearing. Exp. Hort. 9:34–38.

WONG, T. L., R. W. HARRIS, and R. E. FISSELL. 1971. Influence of high soil temperatures on fine woody plant species. J. Am. Soc. Hort. Sci. 96(1): 80–82.

WRIGHT, R. D. 1976. Influorescence development and fruit set in *Ilex cornuta* Lindl. et Paxt. cv. "Burfordii" as influenced by temperature and photoperiod. J. Am. Soc. Hort. Sci. 101(2):182–184.

ZEHNDER, L. R., and F. O. LANPHEAR. 1966. The influence of temperature and light on the cold hardiness of *Taxus cuspidata*. Proc. Am. Soc. Hort. Sci. 89:706–713.

SUGGESTED READING

CATHEY, H. M. 1975. Comparative plant growth retarding activities of ancymidal with ACPC, Phosfan, Chlormequat and SADH on ornamental plant species. HortScience 10(3):204–216.

LEVITT, J. 1956. The hardiness of plants. Amer. Soc. of Agronomy, Academic Press, 111 Fifth Ave. N.Y., N.Y. 10003.

SACHS, R. M., and W. P. HACKET. 1972. Chemical inhibition of plant height. HortScience 7(5):440–447.

WEISER, C. J. 1970. Cold resistance and acclimation in woody plants. Hort-Science 5(5):403–410.

____. 1970. Cold resistance and injury in woody plants. Science 169:1269–1278.

ZIMMERMAN, R. H. 1972. Juvenility and flowering in woody plants. Hort-Science 7(5):447–455.

Chapter 12

Nursery Inventory Control

An inventory or stock control system is needed in all phases of nursery production and merchandising in order to maintain control of plant materials, equipment, tools, and supplies. Numerous systems are available, from the very simple to the complex. The following systems can be used effectively to maintain control of materials within nurseries.

PLANT MATERIAL INVENTORY

A plant inventory system is designed to provide management with data that can be used for making management decisions. An inventory of plants is needed to plan a sales campaign and project future trends. By maintaining an up-to-date sales inventory, management can minimize overselling or leaving plants unsold, thus assuring a higher percentage of satisfied customers. A knowledge of the plant inventory can be the basis of planning work schedules, labor needs, storage requirements, and land use. Inventory data are needed when planning production programs, calculating production costs, and making pricing decisions. Plant inventory systems can also provide information to evaluate cultural practices. To accomplish these ends a nurseryman must know how many plants of each variety (cultivar) are available, in each size, within the nursery. The actual system of plant inventory control will vary with the size and type of nursery and with the degree of sophistication desired by the nurseryman. Plant inventory systems vary from a daily update available from a computer to little, if any, control. For a small nursery or a large nursery specializing in one genera, such as rhododendrons, or one type of plant material, such as selected shade trees, the system can be relatively simple. But for a large, general nursery growing a wide selection of plants, the system can be rather complex. A common technique is to inventory and obtain cost of production data by plant groups (Table 12-1).

Taking of the physical inventory is facilitated by an integrated layout of the nursery using planting blocks and standard labeling of rows (see Chapter 5). The count is made by trained individuals using calipers and measuring sticks (Fig. 12-1) to obtain diameters of trees and heights or spread of shrubs. Tree diameters can be done simply, quickly, and accurately with the aid of a Hillier electronic tree grader, powered by long-life batteries. Another handy device is a template tree grader, designed to caliper trees up to 3 in., by sizes, as recommended by American Standards for Nursery Stock. An aid in measuring height and spread of shrubs is a stick marked in size classes. For tabulating the actual count in the field, a clipboard equipped with a series of mechanical counters is most commonly used.

Nurserymen generally count and measure all trees and specimen plants, whereas representative samples—portions of rows, or small plots—are used to estimate the inventory of seedlings, small ever-

Table 12-1 Grouping of plants for inventory and production cost analysis

1. Shade trees	6. Fruit trees
2. Small or flowering trees	7. Small fruits
3. Large evergreens	8. Container stock
4. Small evergreens	9. Bed material
5. Deciduous shrubs	10. Propagation

Figure 12-1 Equipment used for grading trees and shrubs in nurseries. (a) Template-type tree grader; (b) Hillier electronic tree grader; and (c) measuring stick shrub grader.

greens, deciduous shrubs, roses, and so on. A complete inventory is taken in most field production nurseries at the end of the growing season and periodic inventories are made as needed. In large container production nurseries the inventory is updated daily, weekly, or monthly. The data are recorded onto the *field inventory data collection form* (Fig. 12-2). In some nurseries this may be the extent of the plant inventory, but in others these field data are processed into more meaningful information for use by management.

Block _17_

Rows or parts of rows	Species	Size	Date 11/17/80		Date_____		Date_____	
			REG	PG	REG	PG	REG	PG
30-31 ↑ N	Acer rubrum 'Red Sunset'	NS	2	1				
		2-2½	54	0				
		2½-3	107	5				
		3-3½	16	1				
		3½-4	3	1				
		4-4½	1	0				
		4½-5	—	—				
31-32	Acer rubrum 'October Glory'	NS	14	1				
		1¾-2	73	—				
		2-2½	115	3				
		2½-3	76	—				
		3-3½	14	1				

REG = Regular Grade   Initials: _____ _____ _____
PG = Park Grade (less than standard quality)
NS = Not Saleable

Figure 12-2 Example of a field inventory data collection form.

Acer rubrum 'Red Sunset'

Var. Year / Pg.		N				N+1				N+2				N+3			
		Units sold	End inv.	Est. unit sales	Est. end inv.		Units sold	End inv.	Est. unit sales	Est. end inv.		Units sold	End inv.	Est. unit sales	Est. end inv.		Units sold	End inv.	Est. unit sales	Est. end inv.
N	Planting year NP		(100)			NP					NP					NP				
	NS		100			NS		97			NS		19			NS				
	1¼" or 4"					1¼" or 4"					1¼" or 4"					1¼" or 4"				
	1½"					1½"					1½"		45			1½"		15		
	1¾"					1¾"					1¾"		29			1¾"		38		
	2"					2"					2"					2"		25		
	2½"					2½"					2½"					2½"	10	5	30	
	3"					3"					3"					3"				
	3½"					3½"					3½"					3½"				
	Total		100			Total		97			Total		93			Total	10	83		
	Loss	U	%	%B		U	3 %	3 %B			U	4 %	4 %B 7			U	0 %	0 %B 7		

Var. / Pg.		N				N+1				N+2				N+3			
		Units sold	End inv.	Est. unit sales	Est. end inv.		Units sold	End inv.	Est. unit sales	Est. end inv.		Units sold	End inv.	Est. unit sales	Est. end inv.		Units sold	End inv.	Est. unit sales	Est. end inv.
N+1	Planting year NP					NP		(60)			NP					NP				
	NS					NS		60			NS		45			NS		16		
	1¼" or 4"					1¼" or 4"					1¼" or 4"					1¼" or 4"				
	1½"					1½"					1½"		13			1½"		20		
	1¾"					1¾"					1¾"					1¾"		13		
	2"					2"					2"					2"		9		
	2½"					2½"					2½"					2½"				
	3"					3"					3"					3"				
	3½"					3½"					3½"					3½"				
	Total					Total		60			Total		58			Total		58		
	Loss	U	%	%B		U	0 %	0 %B			U	2 % 3.3	3.3 %B			U	0 %	0 %B 3.3		

Var. / Pg.		N				N+1				N+2				N+3			
		Units sold	End inv.	Est. unit sales	Est. end inv.		Units sold	End inv.	Est. unit sales	Est. end inv.		Units sold	End inv.	Est. unit sales	Est. end inv.		Units sold	End inv.	Est. unit sales	Est. end inv.
N+2	Planting year NP					NP					NP		(100)			NP				
	NS					NS					NS		100			NS		36		
	1¼" or 4"					1¼" or 4"					1¼" or 4"					1¼" or 4"				
	1½"					1½"					1½"					1½"		58		
	1¾"					1¾"					1¾"					1¾"				
	2"					2"					2"					2"				
	2½"					2½"					2½"					2½"				
	3"					3"					3"					3"				
	3½"					3½"					3½"					3½"				
	Total					Total					Total		94			Total		94		
	Loss	U	%		U	%	%B			U	4 % 4	4 %B			U	2 % 2	6 %B		

Page totals		N				N+1				N+2				N+3			
Page totals	Sub total	100				Sub total	157				Sub total	247				Sub total	235			
Sub total loss	U	%	%B		U	3 %	%B		U	%	10 %B		U	%	%B		2 U	%	%B
	Total				Total				Total				Total			
Total loss	U	%	%B		U	%	%B		U	%	%B		U	%	%B	

Use for 2 or more pages

ABBREVIATIONS

NP = number planted
NS = not saleable
U = units
%B = percent of base planted

NOTES

Units sold: obtain from sales records
End inventory: obtain from field inventory
Est. unit sales: manager's best estimate
Est. end. inventory: estimated end inventory

Figure 12-3 Growing inventory flow sheet. (Courtesy Studebaker Nurseries, Inc.)

In some larger nurseries the field inventory data are posted to an *inventory flow sheet* (Fig. 12-3) together with new planting and sales data. By proper posting of the flow sheets, it is possible to determine fairly accurately the status of the plant material within the nursery by type and location. If accurate data are collected, it is possible to determine plant losses and to estimate growth rates. This information can also be used to pinpoint problem areas and to check on cultural practices. The inventory flow sheets should be designed to fit the needs of the nursery manager. Figure 12-3 is an example of a form designed for a nursery specializing in the production of shade trees. The columns headed "Est. Unit Sales" and "Est. End. Inv." are for the manager's best estimate of sales and final inventory. If they are not needed by management, they can be omitted from the form.

Data from the flow sheets or from the field inventory forms are used to post the *sales inventory*. This is generally done at the end of the growing season but prior to the sales period for field production nurseries. However, for container production nurseries the sales inventory is posted with new data (plants for sale) on a daily, weekly, or monthly basis. The sales inventory, maintained by the sales department, can be posted either to a *sales inventory card* (Figs. 12-4

Species: Acer rubrum		Cultivar: 'Red Sunset'												
Sales inventory card	Size	2"			165/350					2½"			550*	
	Blocks	10	17	96	10**	17	≤						≤	
'80 Date Buyer	No	4	20	5	1	1	31							
1/10 Cot Gard	10	10/10					21							
3/11 D&L Land	15	10/10	5/0				6							
3/16 Lan. P.D.	2				1/0	1/0	4							

*Price code: Last digit is number of dimes; previous digits are dollars: e.g. 165 = $16.50, 550 = $55.00.
**Underlined numbers are park grade classification.

Figure 12-4 Example of a sales inventory card.

and 12–5) or it can be entered into the inventory file of a computer. Sales data must be posted promptly if the system is to be effective. Notation is made of the buyer and the sales posted by use of the sales inventory fraction, the numerator being the number of trees removed from inventory and the denominator the number of plants remaining. The summary column provides quick reference as to the total balance remaining within the size class. At the time of posting the sales inventory cards, the block number where the plants are to be dug can also be noted. The production manager can precode the cards if he or she desires that the blocks be cleared on a priority basis. The data are filed alphabetically either by botanical names or by common names within plant groups (Table 12–1). The sales inventory can also be posted with current price information as an aid in quoting prices to customers during the selling season.

Species: *Ilex crenata* 'Green Thumb'

Size	1 Gallon			5 Gallon			___ Gallon		
Stage	I	II	III	I	II	III	I	II	III
Date									
1/4	77/001 A-1 1000	76/391 A-1 500	76/411 A-2 755			75/531 B-3 355			
1/10						B-3 255			
2/7	77/215 500								
2/12		A-1 955	A-2 1255			B-3 200			
2/20			A-2 1055						
2/25			A-2 705						
3/7			A-2 205	B-1 500					
3/15						B-3 100			
3/20					B-1 500				

— Accession number
— Quantity
Location

Stage I: Newly planted
II: Actively growing
III: Saleable plants

Figure 12-5 Example of an inventory form for a small- to medium-sized container production nursery.

Figure 12-6 Computer used for inventory control and for other business records. (Courtesy Monrovia Nursery Co.)

Each nursery manager must adjust the plant inventory system to the situation and develop it to provide the control and information necessary to make sound management decisions. Electronic computers (Fig. 12-6), particularly those equipped with video readout screens, are ideal for the rapid and efficient processing of sales data within large nurseries. They can be used to provide an immediate update of sales inventory. They can be programmed to provide an analysis of sales, by variety, customer, geographic area, and by salesperson. In addition, the computer can be used to update sales books, prepare price schedules, and with the input of field inventory data, can be programmed to estimate potential sales inventory.

EQUIPMENT INVENTORY

A considerable financial investment is made in equipping and maintaining a production nursery. Equipment needed for the many and varied operations within a modern nursery includes cars, trucks, tractors, and wagons; tillage, planting, and potting machines; fertilizer spreaders; pumps; injectors and irrigation equipment; sprayers; digging machines; and storage equipment. Besides the large equipment, many types of hand tools, such as axes, digging spades, shovels, pruning equipment, knives, sharpening stones, towing chains, drafting equipment, and so on, are also needed. Some form of management control must be maintained over the equipment if the organization is to function efficiently. The primary means of gaining control of equipment is to maintain a physical inventory of all equipment and to develop plans for security, proper use, and maintenance.

When major pieces of equipment are purchased by the nursery, they should be given an inventory number. A code number combining year of purchase, functional unit, and purchase can be used. For example, if the 34th purchase of the year was a tractor purchased in 1980 for use primarily by the production division (Division A), it would be identified as 80A34. This number should be painted or stamped onto the equipment and then entered into the inventory and maintenance records. The equipment inventory, either a card file or a computer file, is kept in the business office as a record of purchase with name of supplier, purchase price, depreciation schedule, and other related information. The maintenance card, with proper identification number, name, year, and model, is sent to the mechanic to record all maintenance and repair data. Equipment purchases should be limited to as few manufacturers as is feasible to reduce the inventory of parts that need to be maintained by the mechanic. Knowing which parts are stocked by a local supplier can reduce the nursery's spare parts inventory.

Some nurseries find it desirable to maintain a "use log" on some equipment (tractors, trucks, diggers, etc.) to determine the efficiency of the equipment. For efficient use and security, all equipment should be assigned to responsible individuals and the individuals properly instructed in its use and maintenance. Company policy pertaining to use and maintenance of equipment should also be clearly stated in a policy manual of the nursery. Painting equipment, especially small items and hand tools, in a distinctive color can aid immeasurably in preventing loss. The use of distinctive markings can also minimize the mixup of equipment among divisions of a nursery or among crews in a landscape company.

Valuable equipment should be stored in a locked facility that also provides protection from the weather. Company policy should provide the necessary guidelines for the cleaning and storing of equipment. By establishing and maintaining a good equipment inventory and management system, it is possible to gain a high degree of control over the equipment, and at the same time assure its effective and efficient use.

SUPPLIES

Nurseries also have large financial investments in supplies. Management can gain control over the use and expenditure of supplies by maintaining an inventory control system, providing appropriate areas for storage, and by establishing security methods. Table 12-2 is an example of a supply inventory system for a production nursery. The items are classified by phases of production (propagation, planting, harvesting), equipment maintenance, and physical-plant supplies. Each stocked item is described along with the common unit of purchase. In addition, it is desirable to list sources of supply, price per unit, and pertinent comments. These data, commonly kept on file cards, can also be put into a computer for rapid video display of supply information as well as an electronic means of supply inventory control.

Supplies for the divisions of the nursery should be purchased primarily by the business office. But provision should be made for a responsible employee to make purchases for the nursery in an emergency or in the best interests of the business. Supplies should be stored in proper facilities and when appropriate under proper security. Packaged supplies such as fertilizer and peat moss should be stored in covered sheds to minimize destruction by wind and rain, whereas inorganic materials such as brick or stone may be left exposed. All chemicals should be stored in their original containers and marked with the year of purchase and used in order of purchase date. Poisonous chemicals should be stored in a specially marked storage cabinet and flammable materials kept in fire-resistant containers. Only usable quantities of supplies should be kept in work areas with the balance in a locked supply-storage facility.

A periodic inventory (monthly, quarterly) of supplies should be taken to determine use rates and to prepare orders for bidding. In

Table 12-2 Inventory of supplies for a production nursery (example of selected items, not a complete list)

Class	Item	Units
Propagation		
1. Budding and grafting	Strips, 0.016 gauge,	
	¼ × 5 in., 1200/lb	lb
	Ties, no. 4 fruit	M
	Tape, ½ in. wide	roll
	Wax	lb
2. Containers	Pots, clay	
	2½ in.	ea.
	3 in.	
	4 in.	
3. Labels	Pot, wooden, painted	
	3½ × ⅝ in.	M
	10 × ⅝ in.	M
	Plant, plastic	
	5½ × ½ in.	M
4. Media	Sand	yd^3
	Peat moss	bale
	Perlite, 50 lb	bag
5. Rooting	Hormone, IBA, 0.2%	lb
Planting and Maintenance		
1. Containers	Fiber, 6 × 6	ea.
	Poly, 2 qt, 600 per	case
	Zarn	
	6 qt, 160 per	case
	3 gal, 100 per	case
2. Fertilizers	18-9-9, 50 lb per	bag
	10-6-4, 40 lb per	bag
	0-20-0, 50 lb per	bag
3. Fungicides	Captan, 50 wp, 5 lb per	bag
	Karathane, 25 wp, 3 lb per	bag
	Truban, 25 EC	qt
4. Herbicides	Casoron, 4 G, 5 lb per	bag
	Princep, 80 wp, 5 lb per	bag
	Roundup, 5 gal per	cont.
5. Insecticides	Chlordane, 10 G, 50 lb per	bag
	Guthione, 50 wp, 2½ lb per	bag
	Sevin, 5 dust, 50 lb per	bag
6. Media	Sand	yd^3
	Bark, hardwood	yd^3

Table 12-2 (continued)

Class	Item	Units
7. Polyethylene film	Std.	
	Clear 4 ml, 40 × 100	roll
	White, 4 ml	1000 ft^2
8. Shade cloth	Saran, 63% shade	1000 ft^2
9. Soil fumigants	Dowfume, six 1½-lb cans per	carton
Harvesting		
1. Baskets	Wire	
	24 × 20 in., 100 per	ea.
	30 × 24 in., 100 per	ea.
2. Burlap	Untreated, 36 × 36 in., 500 per	bale
	Treated, 36 × 36 in., 500 per	bale
3. Containers	Fiber, 10 × 10 in.	ea.
4. Nails	Pinning	
	6D oval head	
	350 per lb, 45 lb per	carton
5. Tape	Plastic tagging, ⅝ in., 12 rolls per	box
6. Tree wrap	4-in width, 50 yd/roll, 12 rolls per	carton
7. Twine	Sisal, 3-ply, 6 balls per	bale
	Jute, 4-ply, 10 lb per	ball
Storage and Shipping		
1. Containers	Shipping, cardboard	ea.
2. Media, packing	Peat moss	bale
	Shingletoe	bale
3. Tarps	Shade, poly, 15 × 20 ft	ea.
Equipment Maintenance		
1. Antifreeze	Prestone	gal
2. Fuels	Gas	
	Leaded	gal
	Unleaded	gal
3. Lubricants	Slip grease	lb
4. Oils	10-W-40, 9 qt per	case
Physical Plant		
1. Heating	Oil	gal
2. Paper	Stationery, 500 sheets per	box
	Hand towel, 16 rolls per	box
	Toilet, 100 rolls per	box

some nurseries, considerable quantities of material (gas, oil, containers, plastic, soil, peat, etc.) are used, and competitive bids from three or more suppliers are worthy of consideration. If the use rate exceeds the normal rate as determined by past history or by logical estimates of use, the manager should review the situation with his key supervisors and determine if corrective measures are needed.

SUMMARY

Inventory data on plants, equipment, and supplies must be collected and processed in a meaningful manner if the nursery is to attain its objective. However, it should be remembered that few people like to collect data and to keep records. All forms should be as simple as possible, and methods of recording data should be carefully worked out to make certain that it can be done expeditiously and correctly. Steps should be taken to explain the need for record keeping to everyone involved and to make the process as painless as possible. Recording, filing, and analyzing data requires time and is expensive. Do not record too many data; this can be as bad as recording too few; record only what can and will be used. A well-planned and carefully monitored system of inventory control can provide management with an effective tool for maintaining control over materials.

Chapter 13

Nursery
Storage Facilities

Storage facilities are employed by nurserymen for many reasons, including temporary and winter storage of plants, seeds, equipment, and supplies. The greatest need is for the storage of plants.

The oldest and most basic reason for the storage of plants in controlled environments is to maintain viability and quality during the period after removal from their production sites until they are replanted either in the nursery or in the landscape. Once plants are dug in the field or taken from the container-growing area, they are removed from their primary source of water. If they are not properly cared for, they will dehydrate and die.

Controlled environment storage is also used for the protection of tender or semitender plants that would be injured or killed if left exposed to the rigors of the winter climate. This is especially true for container-grown plants, which may be vulnerable to root injury if the temperature falls below the critical minimum for the species. Also, when the soil is frozen, many species are very vulnerable to desiccation, particularly during periods of high sunlight, wind, or both.

Storage facilities can also be used to precondition plants for flowering and transplanting. Many bulbs and plants, such as azaleas and hydrangeas, that are forced for special holidays, require a period of exposure to cold temperature before they will bloom; this can best be accomplished in controlled-temperature rooms. Cool temperatures obtained in storage buildings can be used to delay bud break and to hold back the growth of plants in early spring so that the spring planting season can be extended. Also, they can be used to condition the tender growth on landscape plants that are dug in full leaf during the growing season, assuring a greater success following transplanting. In addition to modifying the environment to affect a plant response, storage facilities are used to aid in the processing and marketing of plants. In many parts of the nation the spring digging season starts late, because of climatic conditions. It is often much too short to allow sufficient time to dig, process, and deliver plant material for spring sales. On the other hand, the fall season is generally mild, and there is sufficient time to dig and store plants. Many nurseries have constructed plant storage facilities so that plants can be dug in the fall; placed into winter storage, where they are processed (graded, packaged into wholesale units, and labeled) and maintained in good condition for many months until they are shipped in later winter or early spring.

Plant propagators use cold-temperature storage facilities to store seeds, cuttings, budwood, and scions. Since seed production is affected by a multitude of environmental, biological, and physiological factors, it is necessary to collect seed when it is available and to store it for use in years when there is little or no seed produced. For example, shortleaf pine (*Pinus echinata*), which is an important conifer for reforestation in the south, produces a good crop of seed about once in 10 years. Therefore, it is necessary to collect and store the seed for a decade or longer to ensure an adequate annual supply. Fortunately, seeds from most woody plants can be stored successfully for long periods of time. This topic is thoroughly discussed in USDA Agriculture Handbook 450, *Seeds of Woody Plants in the United States* (see Appendix A). Storing rooted cuttings in polyethylene bags under controlled low temperature allows the propagator to use high-cost greenhouse space more efficiently. It is possible to obtain two or three crops of cuttings from the same bench space that would normally be used to propagate and hold one batch of cuttings until the time of planting.

Plant storage is another tool by which the nursery manager can gain a degree of control over both the plants and various marketing problems. There are a number of different types of facilities in which plants can be stored; each has its advantages and disadvantages. The nurseryman should consider these carefully and then construct those that best fit his or her and the plants' needs.

STORAGE FACILITIES

Use of *heeling-in grounds* is the oldest and simplest method of plant storage. It was used in ancient times and is still used extensively today. It is a method of temporary storage, providing minimal control of the environment, although sometimes plants are stored for many months. The plants are placed either on top of the ground or into a trench and the roots or rootballs are covered with a loose, damp medium. A mixture of peat and sawdust is often used to protect the roots of bare-root plants, since it is lightweight, retains moisture, and is easily worked about the roots. Year-old wood chips are used also for temporary storage of B&B plants where they are available. This method is used fairly extensively in nurseries, garden centers, and at landscape sites prior to planting (Fig. 13-1).

Dormant, bare-root, deciduous plants should be heeled-in with their stems oriented parallel to the noontime rays of the sun. This helps to minimize desiccation of the stems during storage. When plants are received in a dehydrated state, they will benefit by soaking in water for 2–3 hr prior to heeling-in or planting. The roots of plants should not be exposed to long periods of freezing temperatures, especially below 25°F, since roots are very vulnerable to low-temperature injury (Table 13-1). They should be mulched prior to the onset of freezing temperatures. Balled and burlapped (B&B) or containerized plants that are mulched after the soil balls have frozen are very prone to desiccation injury.

Cold frames, of all types of construction, have been used for hundreds of years to modify the environment about young tender plants. In addition to their use as propagation structures, they can be used to overwinter plants. Although both shallow and deep-pit frames can be used as an overwintering structure, the deep pit provides the best protection. The environment is modified by the warmth of the soil and by the shadow cast by the south wall of the pit during the winter storage period. Therefore, the best orientation of the cold frames used for winter storage is in an east-west direction.

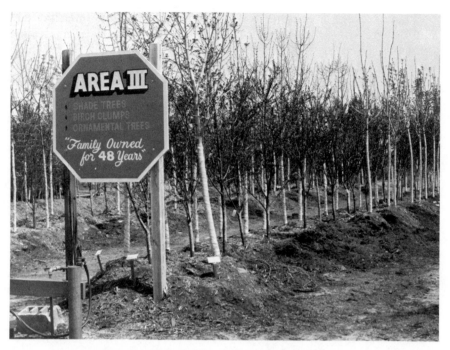

Figure 13-1 Nursery stock in temporary heeling-in storage. (Courtesy Kluck Nursery.)

To ensure successful storage, the plants must be fully dormant prior to sealing of the frame for the winter storage period. To ensure maintaining low storage temperature conditions within the cold frame, the sash may need to be shaded, and the structure or the plants within may need to be insulated. Bales of straw, a straw mulch, microfoam, or other appropriate materials can be used for this purpose.

The *shade house,* more commonly known as the lathhouse when lath construction is employed, modifies temperature, light intensity, and relative humidity. These, in turn, reduce the amount of transpiration that takes place from the plants stored within. Large groves of trees can serve the same purpose. The shade house is commonly utilized for the temporary storage of plant material during the shipping season and is often used in conjunction with the heeling-in grounds. Some nurseries utilize the shade house in the production of shade-tolerant species such as *Pachysandra* and *Vinca* and in the production of young evergreen transplants (e.g., *Taxus*).

When building lathhouses or constructing seed or transplant beds that will be protected with lath covers, it is best to construct them

Table 13-1 Average killing temperatures[a] for roots of selected species of woody ornamental plants

| Botanical name | Common name | Killing temperature | |
		°C	°F
Magnolia soulangiana	Saucer magnolia	–5.0	23
Magnolia stellata	Star magnolia	–5.0	23
Cornus florida	Flowering dogwood	–6.7	20
Daphne cneorum	Garland flower	–6.7	20
Ilex crenata 'Convexa'	Convex Japanese holly	–6.7	20
Ilex crenata 'Hetzi'	Hetz Japanese holly	–6.7	20
Ilex opaca	American holly	–6.7	20
Ilex crenata 'Stokesii'	Stokes Japanese holly	–6.7	20
Pyracantha coccinea	Fire thorn	–7.8	18
Cryptomeria japonica	Japanese cedar	–8.9	16
Cotoneaster horizontalis	Rock cotoneaster	–9.4	15
Viburnum carlesii	Korean spice viburnum	–9.4	15
Cytisus praecox	Warminster broom	–9.4	15
Buxus sempervirens	Common boxwood	–9.4	15
Ilex glabra	Inkberry	–9.4	15
Euonymus fortunei 'Carrierei'	Carrier euonymus	–9.4	15
Euonymus fortunei 'Argenteo-marginata'	Variegated euonymus	–9.4	15
Hederia helix 'Baltica'	Baltic ivy	–9.4	15
Pachysandra terminalis	Japanese pachysandra	–9.4	15
Vinca minor	Common periwinkle	–9.4	15
Pieris japonica 'Compacta'	Compact lily-of-the-valley bush	–9.4	15
Acer palmatum 'Atropurpureum'	Bloodleaf Japanese maple	–10.0	14
Cotoneaster adpressa praecox	Nan-Shan cotoneaster	–12.2	10
Taxus media 'Nigra'	Black Anglojap yew	–12.2	10
Rhododendron 'Gibraltar'	Gibraltar azalea	–12.2	10
Rhododendron 'Hinodegiri'	Azalea hybrid	–12.2	10
Pieris japonica	Lily-of-the-valley bush	–12.2	10
Leucothoe fontanesiana	Drooping leucothoe	–15.0	5.0
Pieris floribunda	Fetterbush	–15.0	5.0
Euonymus fortunei 'Colorata'	Purple leaf wintercreeper	–15.0	5.0
Juniperus horizontalis	Creeping juniper	–17.8	0.0
Juniperus horizontalis 'Douglasii'	Waukegan juniper	–17.8	0.0
Rhododendron carolinianum	Carolina rhododendron	–17.8	0.0
Rhododendron catawbiense	Mountain rosebay	–17.8	0.0
Rhododendron P. J. M. hybrids	P.J.M. rhododendron	–23.3	–10
Potentilla fruticosa	Shrubby cinquefoil	–23.3	–10
Picea glauca	White spruce	–23.3	–10
Picea omorika	Serbian spruce	–23.3	–10

[a]Highest temperature that killed more than 50% of root system and reduced top growth.

SOURCE: Adapted from Havis, 1964.

so that the lath strips are oriented in a vertical position on the south and west sides and in a north-south direction on the top. This orientation of the lath provides for a moving sun–shade pattern on a daily basis. During hot, dry periods this small difference can be critical, especially for young seedlings or recently transplanted plants. Structure orientation is less important when it is covered with shade cloth rather than with lath.

Plastic houses, although originally designed as a temporary structure for growing plants, are now used extensively for the winter storage of plants, especially for evergreens in northern areas. The houses are primarily of a quonset-type construction (Fig. 13–2) and covered with one or two layers of polyethylene. The double-layer, air-separated structure provides greater insulation due to the dead air space between the two layers of polyethylene. A small electric air blower positioned to blow air between the layers provides enough air pressure to keep the plastic layers separated, even on very large structures. The film used as the cover for plastic houses should be 4- to 6-mil polyethylene, to withstand the stress caused by winter storms. The film may be either clear or milky, depending upon the storage objective. The house should be constructed and the plastic installed in such a way as to form a relatively vaportight chamber to aid in maintaining a high relative humidity within the structure. Where clear plastic is utilized or where there is not a vapor seal, it will be necessary to shade or irrigate the plants occasionally in the late winter or early spring. It may also be necessary to ventilate to keep the temperature low to avoid rapid dehydration of plant tissue and prevent early breaking of dormancy. However, when houses are vented, they must be irrigated more frequently to replace the moisture lost during venting.

Polyhouses, constructed primarily for overwintering of evergreens in the most northern regions of the country, are best when they are designed with a low profile to reduce the heat-transfer area and to aid in retaining snow for insulation; oriented in a north-south direction to reduce solar heating; and covered with milky plastic to minimize penetration of the sun's rays. The combination of low profile, north-south orientation, and milky plastic aids in maintaining the desired environment for keeping stored evergreens in good condition through the winter period. However, plants stored in plastic houses can be induced into early growth by constructing them with a higher profile, orientating in an east-west direction, and covering with clear plastic. The plants must be irrigated periodically, since they will transpire more moisture under the warmer, low-humidity conditions. It will be necessary to ventilate the house on sunny days

Figure 13-2 Plastic storage house for overwintering evergreens.
(Courtesy Conard-Pyle Co.)

to minimize high interior temperatures, but venting should be avoided when soil balls are frozen.

The *common storage* is a building designed to take advantage of changes in air density and the insulating properties of soil. When air cools, it becomes heavy and flows like a fluid into areas of lower elevation forcing the lighter, warmer air up into the higher elevations. Early common storage buildings were constructed either below ground or in hillsides to gain these advantages. However, since the development of high-quality insulation materials, most common storage facilities are constructed totally above ground. By timely control of vents in the lower part of the walls and in the roof of the buildings, or by opening the drive-through doors at both ends of the building in the evening when the outside air temperature is lower than the interior temperature and closing them at sun-up, low temperatures can be maintained fairly successfully within the building during winter and early spring. However, common storage is not too effective in maintaining dormancy of plants in the late spring because of loss of cold-temperature control.

Refrigerated storage is an advanced model of insulated common storage. It is used to gain a greater degree of control over temperature and humidity to extend the storage period. The construction of a refrigerated storage is similar to that of an insulated common storage except that (1) the insulation is generally thicker, (2) the floor is of concrete and may be insulated, (3) refrigeration equipment is installed to control the temperature, and (4) humidification devices are used to control humidity.

There are many types of excellent insulating materials available, and since most of them have relatively low thermal conductivity, the choice of an insulator to use in the construction of a refrigerated storage will depend more on the total cost of construction and the cost of upkeep. The semirigid plastic or polystyrene foam types are easy to install and are relatively inexpensive. The thickness of insulation that is needed varies with the temperature differential between the outside and the interior of the storage and the relative cost of insulation versus the cost of refrigeration equipmentand operating energy. For most nurseries in the northern part of the United States, the insulation equivalent of 4 in. of corkboard on the walls and 6 in. on the ceiling appears to be adequate. This is equal to a total resistance (R_t) value* of 20 for vermiculite-filled cinderblock walls and about 23 for the ceiling.

Whenever there are temperature differences on two sides of a wall, such as the walls of a storage facility, there will be movement of water vapor from the warm side to the cold side. When this takes place, the insulation becomes damp, thus reducing its effectiveness. A vapor barrier of material such as aluminum foil, polyethylene film, or asphalt-covered or impregnated materials should be installed to impede the flow of moisture into the insulation.

It is not advisable to place a vapor barrier on both sides of the insulation, since the moisture can become trapped within the insulation. The cool side should always remain unsealed to allow the insulation an opportunity to dry if it should become damp. The barrier should be placed on the high-vapor-pressure side, which is the interior side of the insulation for most nursery storage buildings during the winter months. Nursery storage buildings can be insulated with a moisture-resistant, rodent-proof insulation material that can be sprayed onto the interior walls and ceiling, thus avoiding the need to install a vapor barrier. A polyurethane, low-flame foam can be used for insulation, but it is flammable and when burned produces a gas

---

*Calculated from values obtained from Heating, Ventilating, and Air Conditioning Guide, Amer. Assoc. Heat., Ref., and Air Conditioning Eng., N.Y., 1959.

that is very toxic to human beings and animals. It should be used only when suitable thermal barriers are provided.

Details on the construction and operation of nursery storages are contained in *Storage of Nursery Stock,* available from the American Association of Nurserymen, and USDA Agricultural Handbook 66, *The Commercial Storage of Fruits, Vegetables and Florist and Nursery Stocks.*

ADDITIONAL FACILITIES

In addition to the previously discussed facilities used for the storage of plant material, the following facilities are used to prolong the storage life of various high-value horticultural products. They may at some time in the future be used more extensively for the storage of high-value nursery products. Therefore, a brief description of each is warranted.

The *jacketed system* of storage, originally designed for the storage of frozen foods, has been adapted for the storage of fresh fruit, vegetables, and nursery products. It is used fairly extensively by European nurserymen to provide better storage conditions and control pathogens such as botrytis. Bare-root nursery stock has been stored successfully up to 8 months with a good rate of survival following planting in the field. The system is designed to maintain a suitable low temperature (0°C/32°F), high relative humidity (95–98%), with a minimum amount of air movement. The jacket-cooled storage is a standard insulated refrigerated storage room with a built-in inner storage chamber constructed of asbestos plates which have high heat transmission. The inner storage room air is cooled by circulating cold air in the air space between the inner storage chamber (called the jacket) and the outer insulated storage room. This system prevents the plant material from being in direct contact with the cold, dry air from the evaporator. Also, the relative humidity within the storage room is not directly affected by the refrigeration equipment. The jacketed system prevents the condensation of water vapor in the insulation of the room and reduces frost formation on the refrigeration coils.

To assure high relative humidity within the jacketed chamber, the floor is wetted prior to loading, damp sphagnum moss is used on the roots of the plants, and the floor is dampened periodically, as needed, during the storage period.

Since the inner jacketed storage room temperature is dependent upon the air flowing outside the jacket, it is important that a high degree of control be obtained over air distribution patterns, volume of flow, and temperature. The temperature within the jacketed chamber can be controlled to within a half degree of the desired temperature with the aid of electronic thermostats. It is desirable that a number of sensors be employed and that they be aspirated.

A design that has proven practical and maintains a uniform temperature throughout the jacketed storage is one in which the rate of cool air flow in the side wall spaces between the jacket and outer storage wall is uniform all around the room. The air is blown into the ceiling space with fans and then flows by gravity down through the wall spaces and returns under the floor to the cooling coils. The volume of air flowing over the jacket should be sufficient to limit the temperature differential to $3°F$ ($1.5°C$) between the air entering and that leaving the jacket wall spaces. A vapor barrier is required to prevent the movement of moisture from the storage chamber into the jacket atmosphere. Details of design to meet the individual requirements can be obtained from the extension specialist in post-harvest physiology, located at a land grant university, or from engineering firms familiar with the construction and operation of storage facilities.

The *filacell* is another method for maintaining a high relative humidity within a storage chamber at low temperature. A filacell is an efficient air washer that provides a high humidity at low temperatures with a high rate of air circulation. The filacell provides a massive wet-surface area within a small volume (2000 linear feet of nonfilament polypropylene per cubic foot of cell). It functions by chilled water moving down through the cell after being evenly sprayed, at low pressure (3–5 psi), over the upper surface as air moves upward through the cell. The temperature of the water controls the air temperature to within a variation of $\frac{1}{2}°C$.

In practice, a bank of filacell units is supported over a large tank of water. The water temperature in the tank is controlled with refrigeration or heating units. The water is pumped to a spray nozzle located above the filacell. As the water moves downward in the cells, air is forced upward at a high velocity ($600 \ ft^3/min$) producing a moisture-ladened air that both cools and humidifies the storage.

Controlled atmosphere (CA) *storage,* designed for the long-term storage of apples and pears, is not used for the storage of nursery stock, since the economic gain does not, at present, justify the investment in the construction of a gastight building. It decreases the rate of respiration, which is accomplished by increasing the level of carbon dioxide while decreasing the level of oxygen in the atmosphere. High concentrations of CO_2, 40% and greater, have been used to retard bud break and growth of dormant rose plants and herbaceous perennials. Use of this technique has been limited to small size containers. But it could be a useful technique to control bud break of dormant nursery stock.

Hypobaric storage or low-pressure storage (LPS) is a relatively new concept for the storage of perishable commodities. The idea originated in the late 1960s with Dr. S. P. Burg of Miami, Florida. The commodity to be stored is maintained in a refrigerated, vacuum chamber at a constant subatmospheric pressure. The chamber is ventilated with fresh, humid air by continuously evacuating the storage chamber with a vacuum pump. The optimum temperature, absolute pressure, and rate of air change vary with the commodity. LPS has been used successfully for the storage of a number of high-value flowers, fruits, and vegetables. Its economic feasibility for the storage of nursery products depends on the cost versus gain considerations compared to standard storage methods.

The selection and development of a plant storage facility must be related to the storage requirements and value of the plants to be stored, but must also meet the needs of management in attaining production and market objectives. It must be adjusted to the climate of the area where it is to be built and operated. Because construction of storage facilities represents a large capital investment, they should be carefully planned, constructed, and maintained. If properly managed, they are another tool that management can use to gain control over the environment, to provide quality plant material at the time the customer desires delivery, and to better program utilization of the labor force.

FACTORS INVOLVED IN STORAGE OF NURSERY CROPS

Four important factors for the successful winter storage of nursery crops are physiological condition of the plants placed into storage, effective control of storage temperature, maintenance of a high relative humidity, and air quality.

Physiological Condition of Plants

Nursery stock intended for winter storage should be fully mature and dormant, free of insects, diseases, and mechanical injury. Deciduous species should be defoliated. Changing climatic conditions in the fall of the year, including short days and cold temperatures, aid in the maturation of plant tissue to withstand the rigors of winter. These same conditions also aid in conditioning plants for winter storage.

Mature plant tissue is less prone to injury due to cold temperature and desiccation than is immature tissue. Determinate species and plants that respond to short days appear to develop cold-temperature hardiness sooner than indeterminate species or plants that are not responsive to day length. Shoots and vegetative buds develop a greater tolerance to cold temperature than do roots or flower buds. Some species stored above ground in containers are more subject to root injury than are their shoots. Flower buds are often killed by exposure to specific low temperature, while the shoot buds remain fully viable.

Bare-root conifers, to be lifted in the fall for overwinter storage, should have completed their growth phase. The end of the root-growth period coincides with the time that soil temperature in the root zone declines to $50°F$ $(10°C)$ and the white root tips are $\frac{1}{2}$ in. or less in length. An examination of the root system can be a subjective guide to time of digging. Root systems of Norway spruce seedlings become inactive early in the fall and are sequentially followed by balsam fir, Douglas fir, white pine, and then red, Scots, and Austrian pine.

Dormant, mature plants should be placed in storage prior to onset of the adverse environmental conditions that prevail during winter. Nurserymen can speed up the process of maturation so that plant material programmed for winter storage can be begun earlier and the workload spread out over a longer time period. This can be accomplished to some degree by (1) withholding water in late summer, (2) withholding ammonium-nitrogen fertilizers in late summer, (3) root pruning in early fall, and (4) avoidance of top pruning after midsummer. Although it is not possible to control natural rainfall, irrigation practices can be terminated to aid in maturing plants. Plants in a healthy, vigorous condition will store better than unhealthy plants in a weaker condition. Therefore, plants should be maintained on a fertilizer program that results in good vigor. However, some plants appear to be less hardy when fertilized late in the growing season, with ammonium-nitrogen fertilizer.

Deciduous plants that fail to defoliate naturally, prior to digging for storage, can be aided in the process by employing one or more of the following practices: (1) hand stripping, (2) use of rubber-fingered mechanical beaters, (3) grazing activities of sheep, (4) sweating, and (5) by the use of chemical defoliants. Hand stripping, although used, is too expensive to employ when labor costs are high. Mechanical beaters or sheep can do considerable damage to the plants and should be used with care. However, all three methods have been or are used to defoliate nursery stock. The process of sweating is still used to remove remaining leaves prior to storing deciduous plants. It is time-consuming and, if not carefully done, can cause considerable injury to plants due to overheating.

Chemically induced defoliation, prior to digging for storage, is a potentially promising method of defoliation. Unfortunately, no single chemical has been found to be effective on a wide variety of plants. Research has demonstrated certain chemicals to be effective defoliants on some crops. Potassium iodide at a concentration of 0.2–0.3% was effective in causing defoliation (75–100%) in most cultivars of apple, cherry, peach, and apricots, although seedling tree fruits responded poorly. Bromodine was effective on a number of species. When applied at a concentration of 0.25% (200–300 gal/acre-in.), in two or three applications, at weekly intervals, leaf abscission (90–100%) was effected in cherry, pear, and peach. A 0.50% concentration was needed for similar results on apple and prune, and a 1% spray has effectively defoliated roses. Nacconol NR (0.5–4.0%) has been used to defoliate nursery stock in some nurseries. Ethrel (2-chloroethylphosphonic acid) applied at 2000 ppm in two to three weekly applications was effective in defoliating apples and Italian prune, whereas only 500–1000 ppm was needed to defoliate Mazzard cherry and Bartlett pear. However, a combination of ethephon (200–400 ppm) with a surfactant has caused injury to shoots of some cultivars of apple when used as a defoliant.

Nurserymen planning to use chemical defoliants should test the chemicals on a limited basis prior to extensive field application, since plant response is variable with species, cultivar, environment, and condition of the plant at time of treatment. Best response has been in late season, to hasten the natural abscission process. Legally, only chemicals registered as a chemical defoliant for nursery stock may be used.

After the plants have been dug, they must be transported to the storage building, graded, and placed into storage. Some plants, for example, roses, may be graded and bundled in the field and then transported to storage. However, most plants are dug and transported to a temporary storage until most of the digging has been completed. Following the rush of the digging season, the material is graded, pruned, tagged, bound, or packaged into wholesale units and placed in storage.

In most common storages, the plants are placed into ricks, whereas in refrigerated storages the practice is to use bins, pallets, or polylined boxes and stack them with the aid of forklift trucks. Snap-on frames, made of tubular steel, can be attached to pallets for storing container-sized material or B&B plants. Portable metal racks are used by some nurseries to good advantage. These free-standing, portable storage racks are available in a number of sizes and allow the storage manager greater flexibility in the utilization of the storage area than is permitted with stationary wooden structures. Also, the metal construction has a longer functional life than does wood. When possible, species that respond in a similar fashion should be stored together. Experience and good plant sense can be used as a guide in choosing the species that store well together. Superior storage life of nursery plants requires that only mature, quality plants be placed in storage.

Temperature Control

Temperature has been defined as the degree of hotness or coldness measured on a definite scale and its degree determines the flow of heat. When a warm object is brought in contact with a cold object, the former is cooled while the latter is warmed. Thus, heat flows from the warm object to the cool object. If a layer of felt, rockwool, styrofoam, or a vacuum is placed between the two objects, the rate of change in temperature is much slower. It is this principle which is employed in the construction and operation of common and refrigerated storages.

Temperature plays an important part in all metabolic functions of plants. At high temperatures, photosynthesis, respiration, transpiration, and so on, go on at a rapid rate, whereas at a lower temperature the rate is much slower. The storage life of plants is prolonged by reducing respiration and transpiration to a low level by maintaining the plants at as low a temperature as possible without injury to the plants. Low ambient temperatures also reduce the incidence of infection by fungi.

In general, most deciduous, bare-root, plant material, when maintained at a temperature of 32-35°F, will remain dormant and free of mold. However, some will not and must be maintained at a colder temperature. It has been found, for example, that cherries, peaches, and lilac do best if maintained at a temperature of 33-35°F, whereas roses, herbaceous perennials, strawberry plants, and conifer seedlings do best if kept at a temperature below freezing in the vicinity of 28-30°F. Rooted cuttings store successfully at temperatures between 33 and 39°F.

Plant material in containers and B&B plants overwintered in plastic houses, which afford minimum control of temperature, are very subject to root injury at temperatures below 24°F (Table 13-1). Therefore, measures must be taken to protect the roots of sensitive species from cold-temperature injury; this normally involves mulching.

The actual killing temperature will vary with the degree of plant dormancy at the time of exposure to the low-temperature stress. When plants are preconditioned for low-temperature storage and the temperature remains uniformly low prior to exposure to cold-temperature stress, the roots will generally survive provided that the temperature does not go below the average killing temperature for the species. However, if the low-temperature stress follows a period of fluctuating temperatures, especially temperatures that are conducive to growth, the roots could be injured at temperatures significantly higher than the average killing temperature. Also, the roots of newly rooted cuttings have a tendency to be less tolerant of cold-temperature stress than plants with a year or more of growth. To minimize root injury, plants should be stored at a temperature at least 3–5°F above the average killing temperature.

Best results in the storage of bare-root nursery stock are obtained if the temperature of the storage room is held fairly constant. Fluctuations of more than 3°F above or below the desired temperature are undesirable. An increase in temperature can result in decreasing storage life of the nursery stock, development of sprouts, and increased incidence of decay. A decrease in temperature by a few degrees can result in the formation of dew, and a large drop in temperature, below the critical temperature minimum, can result in freezing injury to the roots.

Large variations in storage room temperature can be avoided if the building is properly constructed, insulated, and provided with sufficient refrigeration equipment. Under these conditions, the temperature difference between the refrigerant and the ambient air of the storage room is kept relatively small (2–3°F). Temperature control is generally maintained better in large rooms than in small ones when both are filled to capacity. This is because the larger mass functions as a cold temperature "sink," moderating temperature changes.

Good-quality thermometers should be used to check temperatures of the storage room on a regular basis and to obtain data for the maintenance of continuous-temperature records. In many nursery storage rooms, thermometers are placed on a pole near a door at a height of 5½ ft as a matter of convenience. Temperatures should be taken at the floor, ceiling, and halfway levels, plus within bundles of nursery stock to determine if a uniform ambient temperature prevails throughout the room. By proper use of thermometers, it is possible to gain a high degree of temperature control, which in turn will increase the storage life and maintain the quality of the stored plants.

When placing the plant material into cold-temperature storage, it is desirable to remove the field heat of the plants and to obtain equilibrium between the product temperature and the ambient air of the storage as quickly as possible. This will reduce moisture loss, increase storage life, and maintain the quality of the product. Under most situations, plant material being placed into cold-temperature storage will be 20–40°F warmer than the air in the storage chamber. Under these conditions, the plant material loses moisture, which could result in desiccation of the plants. Plant material that is more than 10°F warmer than the storage air into which it will be placed should be precooled. This can be accomplished either by placing the plant material in a precooling room and circulating cold air (35–40°F), or by holding the material out of doors overnight (provided that the temperature does not go below the dew point or that which would injure the roots). Also, there should be a low probability of rain if the plant material is to be left out overnight. Wet plant material placed into storage increases the possibility of disease infection. Plant material harvested during periods when cold temperatures prevail can be placed directly into storage without precooling. Storage rooms should also be precooled to the desired temperature prior to loading with plant material. In some situations, particularly with common storage facilities, the storage room air can be cooled by opening the vents during cool night or evening periods and closing the vents during warm daytime periods.

A simple practice that can aid in reducing energy requirements in the operation of nursery storages is the planting of evergreen trees on the south and west sides of the structures to shield the walls from the direct rays of the sun. For small structures a hedge planting of arborvitae or a similar type of evergreen is satisfactory. For larger structures, a planting of pine or spruce trees is more appropriate.

Humidity Control

Maintaining proper water-vapor levels within nursery storage facilities is an important factor in the successful storage of plant material. The moisture condition in the air of nursery storage rooms is generally described by relative humidity (RH). This is a ratio of the water vapor actually contained in the air to the amount that it would contain if the air were saturated at the observed temperature. Water vapor functions as a gas and exerts a pressure proportional to the amount present. For physiological purposes, the vapor pressure (VP) is expressed in millimeters of mercury (mm Hg). The moisture diffusion rate, all other factors being equal, is a function of the difference between the VP within the plant and the VP of the ambient atmosphere. This difference is known as vapor pressure deficit (VPD). The smaller the VPD, the slower the rate of moisture loss. For example, plant material in cold storage at 32°F with its intercellular spaces fully saturated has a VP of 4.5 mm Hg, whereas the storage atmosphere at a RH of 90% has a VP of 4.0 mm Hg, producing a VPD of 0.5 mm Hg (which is a small difference). With an increase in temperature to 41°F the VP of the plants (100% saturated) becomes a 6.5 mm Hg and the VP of the storage at 80% RH becomes 5.4 mm Hg, producing a VPD of 1.1 mm Hg, which is two times greater than the previous combination, resulting in a more rapid loss of moisture from the plant material.

Plants stored in plastic structures are subject to considerable variation in VP. If they are exposed to conditions that create a high VPD within the structure, they will desiccate. As previously stated, the orientation of the structure and the type of covering can seriously affect the VP conditions within the structure. When the sun's rays strike the structure in such a manner that they penetrate, they will warm the interior atmosphere, and if they strike the leaves the leaf temperature will be increased substantially. Under such conditions, a high VPD is produced, causing a rapid loss of moisture from the leaves. If the soil is frozen or if the plants are not watered, they will soon desiccate.

It is not uncommon for temperatures in clear plastic houses, oriented in an east-west direction, to reach 60-70°F, and leaf temperatures to attain levels of 100°F or more on clear, sunny days in winter when the outside air temperature may be in the low 30s (Fig. 13-3). If the inside air temperature were 68°F with a RH of 40% and the leaf temperature reached 104°F, the VPD would be 48.5.

	Temp. (°F)	RH	VP
Leaf	104	100	55.5
Air	68	40	7.0
VPD			48.5

Plants stored in clear polyethylene houses and oriented in an east-west direction are most prone to this type of injury, whereas plants stored in a house oriented in a north-south direction and

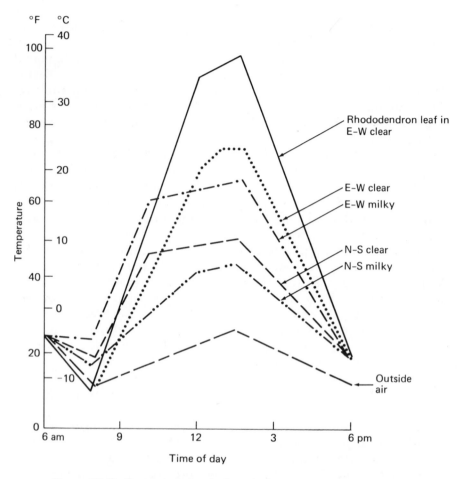

°F   °C

Figure 13-3 Representative leaf and air temperatures occurring on a clear day in winter within plastic structures as affected by structure orientation and type of plastic covering. (Source: Davidson and Mecklenburg, 1974.)

covered with milky polyethylene will be exposed to a much lower VPD and generally will survive rather long periods of winter storage. The relationship between temperatures, RH, VP, and VPD is summarized in Appendix L.

Water vapor can be added to the storage atmosphere by various means. In refrigerated structures it is commonly added with the aid of humidifiers or by flooding the floor in concrete structures at periodic intervals. In common storages with dirt floors, it is maintained by placing damp shingletow* about the roots of the plants and wetting the floor periodically during the storage period. In plastic structures, it can be maintained at fairly high levels by using milky plastic as the outside cover, by spraying a latex paint onto clear plastic, by the use of shade cloth, or by adding water vapor to the enclosed atmosphere. Maintenance of a high RH in storage structures is directly related to maintaining the storage life and plant quality. Therefore, it should be checked periodically. This can be accomplished with the aid of a sling psychrometer, a hygrometer, or with electrical sensors. Instructions for use and calculation of RH are furnished with the psychrometer. The hygrometer and electrical sensors have direct readout of RH.

Air Quality and Movement

Air quality and circulation are also important factors in maintaining the quality of plants in storage. The air must be fresh and free of pollutants that might cause problems to stored plants. The unsaturated hydrocarbons, ethylene and carbon monoxide, have been reported to adversely affect nursery plants in storage. Since fruit, particularly ripe or decaying fruit, generates ethylene, it should not be placed in the same storage with nursery plants.

Loading equipment operated within the storages should be powered either by batteries or propane, to avoid contamination of the air with carbon monoxide and ethylene. Gasoline-powered equipment should be used only in well-ventilated structures, although they can be equipped with a catalytic burner for use in closed structures. The burners are effective only on equipment that operates many hours at a time because they must be hot in order to function efficiently. They are of little value for equipment that is used for only a few minutes at a time.

Air in the storage area must circulate to maintain an even temperature throughout the structure. Good stacking and spatial arrangements within the storage are needed (Fig. 13–4). There should be air passages between the plant material and the walls and ceiling, as well as between stacks, ricks, boxes, bins, or pallets. To assure even air distribution throughout the storage, a horizontal circulator fan should be installed in the ceiling of refrigerated storages and vertical circulator fans on the floor of common storage facilities. The air movement within the storage area should not be too rapid; a rate of approximately 50 linear feet per minute is usually sufficient.

*Fine, shred-like shavings produced as a by-product in the manufacture of cedar shingles.

Figure 13-4 Bare-root plants in refrigerated storage. (Courtesy Bailey Nursery.)

PROBLEM AREAS

Five fairly common problems encountered in nursery storages are air pollution, desiccation, freezing, fungi, and rodents.

The *air pollutant* that has caused the most problems in nursery stock is ethylene. It is produced primarily by stored fruits and vegetables, but it is also produced by decaying plant material and certain woody plants, particularly arborvitae. Woody deciduous plants exposed to 1 ppm ethylene during storage may develop lesions on the stem, abscission, or death of buds and exhibit delayed bud break in the spring following planting. Broadleaved evergreens may exhibit wilting or dropping of the leaves. Rose plants exposed to 10 ppm ethylene during storage are slow to initiate new growth following planting; flowering is delayed and total growth can be reduced. The ethylene problem can be avoided by storing only fully hardened, disease-free plants within the closed storage facility. Avoid storing fruit and plants in the same closed room. The room should also be maintained in a sanitary condition to avoid sources of ethylene production.

Ammonia gas, which can cause necrosis of foliage, is a potential problem for container plants stored in polyethylene structures. Therefore, ammonium-nitrogen fertilizers should not be used while the plants are enclosed in airtight structures.

Desiccation of plants in storage can be minimized by maintaining a low temperature and a high relative humidity. Another method used to minimize the loss of moisture from dormant nursery stock, particularly rose plants, is to coat the canes with paraffin wax. The dormant tops are dipped in large baths containing paraffin wax at temperatures between 170 and 175°F. The solidified wax acts as a physical barrier, reducing both the loss of moisture and the rate of respiration. The net effect is the maintenance of quality plants that have a greater chance for survival after planting. Waxing is commonly done at the time of packaging, just prior to shipping to market. Root-wrapped plants displayed for sale are especially vulnerable to desiccation, owing to the high temperatures and relatively low humidities that commonly prevail in retail sales areas. Wax emulsions containing bentonite have been used successfully to spray wax onto dormant ornamental deciduous and evergreen trees and shrubs to protect them from desiccation. A solution should contain 13.8% solids, and the spray must be applied at temperatures above freezing, preferably above 60°F.

To reduce the loss of moisture from herbaceous plants or evergreen seedlings stored at temperatures close to or below freezing, the crates are lined with polyethylene, which functions as a vapor barrier and provides a confined atmosphere with a high RH. This method can also be used to protect small evergreens, especially broadleaved evergreens, when stored in plastic houses. A thin sheet of plastic laid over the plants and sealed along the edges acts as an excellent vapor barrier, maintaining a high humidity about the plants. It should be used only during the midwinter storage period. The plants should be thoroughly watered prior to covering and checked periodically for dryness, fungi, and for the activities of rodents.

Freezing of roots is the most common form of cold-temperature injury to woody nursery stock during storage. Container-grown and B&B plants left unprotected above ground in cold climates will often sustain root injury due to freezing. Roots are much more sensitive to low-temperature injury than the crowns and should be properly protected. Plants in large containers or with large root balls may not have their roots completely killed, because of the insulation value of the soil. Plants that have suffered root injury normally appear healthy as long as they remain in a cool, humid environment. But when exposed to warmer, dryer conditions they express stress symptoms: evergreens fail to grow and soon desiccate; deciduous species may start to grow but new shoots wilt and the plant dies. Plants that sustain only partial root injury commonly display less vigor than plants without damaged roots.

In places where temperatures below 25°F. (-4°C) are expected, it is necessary to protect the roots of sensitive species (Table 13-1) with a mulch such as wood chips, sawdust, or shredded expanded polystyrene. Another practice is to tip small-sized, container-grown plants on their sides, following a thorough watering, and cover the closely packed plants with a thermal blanket, (e.g., microfoam). Microfoam is an excellent, lightweight, flexible insulator. Holly, boxwood, fire thorn, and other ornamental plants have been successfully overwintered under a blanket of microfoam. The microfoam should be protected with a covering of polyethylene so that it does not become impregnated with water, which would reduce its thermal properties. The blanket must be removed when ambient air temperature raises to 30°F (-1°C).

Freezing injury to the crowns of woody plants is not too common in well-operated storage facilities. Occasionally, plants stored in the vicinity of the evaporator in refrigerated storages may be frozen. Also, broadleaved evergreens (e.g., rhododendron, euonymus, and boxwood) may be frozen while in winter storage in plastic houses. However, if the cold-temperature killing points were not reached, the plants would recover if left to thaw out gradually at temperatures slightly above freezing.

Fungi can be a serious problem in common and refrigerated storage if the room is not thoroughly cleaned prior to loading or if the plant material is not in a mature condition. Good sanitation must be practiced during the loading procedure and throughout the time the storage is in operation. Prior to loading the storage should be thoroughly cleaned. All sources of mold and disease infection should be removed and the walls, ceiling, floor, and storage bins disinfected. A solution of copper sulfate ($1\frac{1}{2}$–2 lb/100 gal water) is an effective and economical disinfectant for this purpose, although various commercial products can also be used. A good practice is to dust all plants with a fungicide just prior to ricking at the time the plants are graded, bundled, and labeled.

Rodents can cause considerable damage to plants in storage if proper precautions are not taken to exclude their entry or to kill or trap them if they gain entry or are accidentally enclosed within the structure. Mice cause the greatest damage by chewing the bark off plants. Rabbits and other rodents damage plants by cutting off branches and chewing the bark and foliage. The losses caused by rodents can be minimized by screening all vents and doors that must be open periodically for air exchange. Rodenticides and traps can be placed within the storage buildings. If rodenticides are used they should be put into specially marked safety containers.

Methylbromide, $\frac{1}{4}$ lb/1000 ft^3, is effective in killing mice that infest cold storage buildings. Carbon monoxide, 0.07% or more, for 3 hr at 32°F is also effective but should only be used when no plants are in the storage. Considerable caution must be exercised when using chemicals to avoid injury to human beings, domesticated animals, and wildlife.

STORAGE OF CHEMICALS

Chemicals of all types, including fertilizers, insecticides, fungicides, herbicides, rodenticides, and growth regulators, should be stored with care. The materials are not only expensive and need to be protected from the elements to minimize loss and assure proper performance when used, but many of the chemicals are also poisonous.

A chemical storage facility should be (1) located away from areas frequented by people and animals; (2) constructed of fire-resistant materials and have a concrete floor; (3) be maintained cool, dry, and well-ventilated; (4) posted as a pesticide storage area when used for pesticide storage; and (5) kept locked, with keys provided to a foreman.

Pesticides and growth regulators should be stored in separate cabinets and appropriately labeled. Chemicals should be kept in their original containers at all times. Containers should be kept tightly closed to prevent volitilization of liquid formulations or the adsorption of moisture by certain fertilizers or wettable powders. If a leak or break is discovered in a container, the contents should be transferred to an identical container. A current inventory should be kept of all pesticides and growth regulators in the storage. Also, containers should be marked with the date of purchase, and identifying materials such as 2,4–D that require special handling can be color-coded. Consult the label for special storage conditions that may be required for a particular pesticide and for information on the proper disposal of empty containers.

SUMMARY

Storage facilities are used by nurserymen to maintain postharvest quality of plants, for winter protection of cold-sensitive species, for the temporary storage of propagation material, to facilitate processing and marketing of nursery products, for the conditioning of plants, and for the storage of seeds, equipment, and supplies. A multiplicity of structures are used to modify the environment and gain control of temperature, humidity, air quality, and various biological organisms. By proper storage management, it is possible to maintain plant quality for extended periods of time following harvest, thus permitting extension of the market season and the radius of the market area. Proper use of storage facilities also ensures against the loss of tender plants due to desiccation or freezing injury and protects supplies and equipment from spoilage, deterioration, and theft.

REFERENCES

ALDHOUS, J. R. 1964. Cold storage of forest nursery plants. J. For. 37:47–63.

ANONYMOUS. 1938. Does freezing injure planting stock? J. For. 36:1244–1245.

———. 1967. Is palletized storage feasible with general nursery stock? Am. Nurseryman 126(2)11.

BAILEY, V. K. 1969. Bare root storage of deciduous stock. Am. Nurseryman 130(5):15.

BRADLEY, K. 1959. Refrigerated storages. Am. Nurseryman 110(5):104.

CHADWICK, L. C., and HOUSTON. 1948. A preliminary report on the prestorage defoliation of some trees and shrubs. Proc. Am. Hort. Soc. 51: 659–667.

COOK, H. A. 1959. Plastic foam structure for low-cost storage. Am. Nurseryman 109(12).

CUNNINGHAM, J. L., and G. L. STABY. 1975. Ethylene and defoliation of ornamental lime plants in transit. HortScience 10(2):174.

CURTIS, O. F., JR., and D. R. RODNEY. 1952. Ethylene injury to nursery trees in cold storage. Proc. Am. Soc. Hort. Sci. 60:104–108.

DAVIDSON, H., and R. MECKLENBURG. 1974. Overwintering of evergreens in plastic structures. HortScience 9(5):479–480.

DEFFENBACHER, F. W., and E. WRIGHT. 1954. Refrigerated storage of conifer seedlings in the Pacific Northwest. J. For. 52:936–938.

DILLEY, D. R. 1972. Hypobaric storage—a new concept for preservation of perishables. Annu. Rep. Mich. State Hort. Soc. 102:82–89.

DUFRESNE, P. 1970. General information on cold storage of nursery plants in jacket-cooled stores. Proc. Int. Plant Propag. Soc. 20:352.

FLEMER, W., III. 1970. Cold storage in the nursery. Am. Nurseryman 131(9):7.

FLINT, H. L., and J. J. MC GUIRE. 1962. Response of rooted cuttings of several woody ornamental species to overwinter storage. Proc. Am. Soc. Hort. Sci. 80:625.

GOUIN, F. R. 1973. Winter protection of container plants. Proc. Int. Plant Propag. Soc. 23:255.

HALL, C. W. 1965. Problems of humidity and moisture in agriculture. Humidity Moisture 2:87–94.

HARTMAN, H. T., and C. J. HANSEN. 1957. Effect of season of collecting, indolebutynic acid and pre-planting storage treatment on rooting of Marianna plum, peach and quince hardwood cuttings. Proc. Am. Hort. Soc. 71:57–66.

HAVIS, J. R. 1964. Root hardiness of woody ornamentals. HortScience 11(4): 385–386.

KRAHN and DARBY. 1971. The "Filacell" system for refrigerated vegetable storage. Proc. Can. Soc. Hort. Sci. 10:24 (summary).

LARSEN, F. E. 1967. Five years results with pre-storage chemical defoliation of deciduous nursery stock. Proc. Int. Plant Propag. Soc. 17:157.

——. 1969. Pre-storage promotion of leaf abscission of deciduous nursery stock with bromodine. J. Am. Soc. Hort. Sci. 95:231.

——. 1969. Promotion of leaf abscission of deciduous tree fruit nursery stock with abscisic acid. HortScience 4(3):216–218.

——. 1971. Pre-storage promotion of leaf abscission of deciduous tree fruit nursery stock with bromodine-ethephon mixtures. HortScience 6(2):135–137.

——. 1973. Stimulation of leaf abscission of tree fruit nursery stock with ethephon-surfactant mixtures. J. Am. Soc. Hort. Sci. 98(1):34–36.

——. 1975. Chemical nursery stock defoliant needer. Am. Nurseryman 142(7): 12.

LENTZ, C. P., and E. A. ROOKE. 1957. Use of the jacketed room system for cool storage. Food Tech. 11(5):257-279.

____, L. VAN DEN BERGE, E. G. JORGENSEN, and R. SAWLER. 1971. The design and operation of a jacketed vegetable storage. Can. Inst. Food Tech. J. 4(1):19-23.

LUMIS, G. P., and E. W. FRANKLIN. 1973. Winter studies show effective use. Am. Nurseryman 137(9):40-43.

LUTZ, J. M., and R. E. HARDENBURG. 1968. Commercial storage of fruits, vegetables and florist and nursery stocks. USDA Agricultural Handbook 66.

MC GUIRE, H. L., FLINT, and E. P. CHRISTOPHER. 1962. Cold storage of Christmas trees. Univ. R.I. Agric. Exp. Sta. Bull. 362.

MILLER, E. J., J. A. NEILSON, and S. L. BANDEMER. 1937. Wax emulsion for spraying nursery stock and other plant materials. Mich. Agric. Exp. Sta. Spec. Bull. 282.

NEILSON, J. A. 1930. Recent information on paraffining nursery stock. Natl. Nurseryman 38(47):5-12.

NYLAND, R. D. 1974. Fall lifting for overwinter cold storage of conifers. Appl. For. Res. Inst. State Univ. N.Y. Coll. Environ. Sci. For. Res. Rep. 22.

PETHERAM, H. D., and H. G. PORTERFIELD. 1941. Cold storage of deciduous planting stock. J. For. 39:336-338.

PRIDHAM, A. M. S. 1952. Preliminary report on defoliation of nursery stock by chemical means. Proc. Am. Soc. Hort. Sci. 59:475-478.

PRYOR, R. L., and R. N. STEWART. 1963. Storage of unrooted softwoody azalea cuttings. Proc. Am. Soc. Hort. Sci. 82:483.

SCHNIEDER, E. F. 1965. Survival of rooted cuttings of three woody plant species after low temperature storage. Proc. Am. Soc. Hort. Sci. 87:557.

SNYDER, W. E., and C. E. HESS. 1956. Low temperature storage of rooted cuttings of nursery crops. Proc. Am. Soc. Hort. Sci. 67:545-548.

TICKNOR, R. L. 1968. Defoliating roses with chemicals. Pacific Coast Nurseryman 17(11):21-22.

TOY, S. J., and J. P. MAHLSTEDE. 1960. Prolonging dormancy of nursery stock by increasing the concentration of carbon dioxide in the storage atmosphere. Proc. Am. Soc. Hort. Sci. 74:774-784.

____, J. P. MAHLSTEDE, and F. G. SMITH. 1961. Some effects of coating the canes of dormant rose plants with melted paraffin wax. Proc. Am. Soc. Hort. Sci. 77:583.

UOTA, M., J. M. HARVEY, and R. W. LATEER. 1959. Commercial packaging and storing of bare root rose bushes. USDA Marketing Res. Rep. 308.

VANDERBROOK, C. 1956. The storage of rooted cuttings. Am. Nurseryman 103(9):10.

WELLER, H. A. 1958. Propagation—dollars and sense. Proc. Int. Plant Propag. Soc. 8:54–58.

WORTHINGTON, T., and D. H. SCOTT. 1957. Strawberry plant storage using polyethylene liners. Am. Nurseryman 105(9):13.

ZELENKA, J. 1967. Overwintering evergreens under poly in northern climates. Proc. Int. Plant Propag. Soc. 17:351.

SUGGESTED READING

DE HERTOGH, A., W. CARLSON, L. AUNG, and A. F. G. SLOATWEG. Bulb forcers handbook. Netherlands Flower Bulb Inst., Inc., New York.

GAFFNEY, J. J. 1978. Humidity: basic principles and measurement techniques. HortScience 13(5):551–555.

GRIERSON, W., and W. F. WARDOWSKI. 1975. Humidity in horticulture. HortScience 10(4):356–360.

HOCKING, D., and R. D. NYLAND. 1971. Cold storage of coniferous seedlings, a review. App. For. Res. Inst., N.Y. State Univ. Coll. For. Syracuse Univ. AFRI Res. Rep. 6.

MAHLSTEDE, J. P., and W. E. FLETCHER. 1960. Storage of nursery stock. American Association of Nurserymen, 230 Southern Building, Washington, D.C. 20005.

SMITH, E. M., ed. 1977. Proceedings of the Woody Ornamentals Winter Storage Symposium. Coop. Ext. Serv., Ohio State Univ.

Chapter 14

Shipping of Nursery Stock

The shipping of nursery stock is the operation in the nursery-to-market chain that is most vulnerable to loss of plant quality; control of the plant material usually passes from the seller to the buyer via a third party, the carrier (Fig. 14-1). Considerable forethought, planning, cooperation, and coordination by all three parties are needed to prevent losses. Each of the parties has a vested interest in the operation and should take the necessary positive actions to ensure that the products ordered are delivered in the best possible condition, in the right quantities, grades, varieties, and at the right time.

PLANT MATERIAL

Nursery stock is a perishable product. Because it is living material, it has moisture and temperature requirements that must be provided for during shipping. The variety of plant material shipped by nur-

Figure 14-1 Staging area for loading and shipping of nursery stock. (Courtesy Monrovia Nursery Co.)

series ranges from dormant seedlings to large shade trees in full leaf weighing many tons. This necessitates considerable variations in the methods of packaging and means of transportation. Most small plants are dug bare-root during the dormant season and are shipped in packages or in large nursery boxes; the roots must be kept damp and the plants maintained in a dormant condition. Damp, aged, shingletow, or similar material spread about the roots during packaging provide the needed moisture. Temperatures of 35-40°F to maintain dormancy during shipping are obtained by using a carrier equipped with refrigeration. If delivery can be effected in 5 days or less, the temperature can range between 30 and 70°F without serious injury to the plants. However, either a long delay enroute or exposure to a temperature below freezing or above 80°F could result in injury to the plants.

Large plants are typically dug B&B with plain, treated, or plastic burlap about the soil ball. Some nurserymen support B&B stock within wire baskets. In some parts of the country, the root ball is contained within a wooden box. In the past, most large trees were transplanted during the dormant season, but with the advent of mechanical tree diggers, they can now be moved in full leaf. The plants should be taken from the field immediately after digging and placed in a cool, humid area and the root balls and foliage watered to minimize water stress.

Plants in full leaf must be shipped at a temperature above freezing but as low as practical to reduce transpiration. Shade trees in full leaf, nondormant evergreens, and container plants transported in open trucks should be protected with a strong, Saran tarpaulin during shipping. The Saran Tarpaulin (90% shade) provides a barrier to the sun's rays and excessive wind damage but allows heat to escape. Spraying deciduous plants in full leaf with antitranspirants is a beneficial practice when the RH of the ambient atmosphere is above 85%. The film remains effective for several weeks. However, at low RH the antitranspirant film cracks and peels from the surface of the leaf within 2-3 days following treatment; its long-term effectiveness is minimal. When transporting large trees on open carriers, the trees and tarpaulins must be tied down securely to avoid wind whip and possible physical damage when the vehicle passes through a tunnel or under a low bridge. Some of the positive actions that can be taken to help ensure the viability of plant material during shipping are summarized in Table 14-1.

Desiccation during shipment can be minimized by watering the plants prior to digging and utilizing rapid methods of transport. When delays in transport happen, the plants are subject to drying out. When possible, keep the plants in a cool, humid area; ventilate if in a closed van, and water balled or containerized stock. Plants that arrive in a wilted condition should be placed in shade and watered immediately. If the critical wilting point has not been reached, the plants can be saved. Balled and burlapped plants should be misted or watered with the aid of a root feeder. Dormant bare-root plants will benefit either by being immersed into a tank of cool water or by being buried in a moist medium (sawdust, wood chips, soil) for several days to allow the buds to absorb water.

Freezing damage can be avoided by selecting rapid methods of transportation and avoiding shipment when low temperatures are predicted for the proposed route or by using carriers with heated trucks. The greatest cause of cold temperature injury to nursery stock during shipping is delays with railroad cars during winter months. Plant material that arrives with frost on the foliage may not be injured, provided that the low, critical temperature for the species was not reached (Table 13-1). Frosted shipments should be placed in a cool area (35-40° F) and allowed to thaw gradually prior to handling.

Table 14-1 Suggested moisture control, temperature, and other actions to ensure successful shipping of plant material

Class of plant material	Moisture control	Temperature (°F)	Notes
Dormant			
Bare root (roses, shrubs, fruit trees, shade trees, and small fruit trees)	Damp, aged shingletow about roots or poly liner within container	35-40	Shipped in nursery boxes
Packaged (roses, shrubs, fruit trees, and small fruit)	Damp medium in package about roots	35-40	Individually packaged; shipped in nursery boxes
Perennials (flowering, strawberry plants)	Poly liner within container	28-35	Shipped in nursery boxes
Balled and burlapped			
Shade trees			
Dormant		30-50	Tipped and tied
In leaf	Water[a] prior to digging; store in cool area with high humidity	40-60	Tipped and tied
Evergreens			
Dormant		30-50	Stacked on balls; tarp if in open truck
Nondormant	Moisten soil[a] prior to shipping	40-60	Stacked on balls; tarp if in open truck
Containerized			
Small sizes (1-5 gal)	Watered and drained[a] prior to shipping	40-60	Decked or stacked 3-5 high on cans
Large sizes (barrels)	Watered and drained[a] prior to shipping	40-60	Tipped and tied Saran tarp if in open truck

[a]Water adds considerable shipping weight, 8.34 lb/gal. Root ball should be damp, never dry, and seldom wet to field or container capacity.

BUYER'S RESPONSIBILITIES

The buyer of nursery stock initiates the transaction by completing a purchase order which lists varieties, size, quantity, and price per unit. It is also the buyer's responsibility to specify shipping instructions, including shipping dates, means of transportation, and any special handling procedures. Orders should be placed as early as possible, and a confirmation of the order obtained from the seller to assure a contractual obligation. Dates of delivery should be stated so that plant material will arrive on time. Avoid the use of "will advise" for time of shipment. The seller will hold such orders in the inactive shipping file until advised to ship by the buyer. It is better to supply the seller with a delivery schedule that allows the grower some flexibility in his or her digging and shipping program, but assures timely delivery of quality stock. When time of delivery is important to meet a deadline in a planting program or material is being advertised in a garden center merchandising program, this information must be communicated to the seller so that he or she can take the necessary steps to assure timely delivery. A lead time of 2 weeks is usually the minimum required to process a large order.

In addition to the shipping date, the buyer should clearly indicate where to ship the plants, particularly if the plant material is to be shipped to a place other than to his or her place of business. This is especially true for plant material being shipped to a landscape construction site. In some cases the hour of delivery may be important. Landscape contractors may want to specify the hour of delivery to assure that workers and equipment will be available to unload large B&B trees.

If a specific means of transportation is desired, this information should be provided to the seller, or the buyer must arrange for the necessary transportation. When shipping instructions are not provided, it is left to the best judgment of the shipper who acts as an agent for the buyer, since most purchases are FOB the seller's nursery. If the buyer sends a truck to pick up the plant material, he or she should have some concept of the size and weight of the load (see Appendix H) and supply a vehicle that will accommodate it. It is also his or her responsibility to provide the necessary tarps, ropes, and materials to protect the plants and to secure the load.

The buyer should become acquainted with the seller. A visit to the nursery will help to determine the quality of the plant material and to become acquainted with the total production and shipping operation. Details of the purchase agreement should be discussed and agreed upon. Many large wholesale production nurseries have a minimum total order in dollars that will be accepted, and in some cases a minimum quantity within a size class (e.g., 10 BR shrubs, 5 B&B trees, 20 1-gal containers, or 5 5-gal containers). Handling procedures should be discussed and agreed upon to assure a maximum degree of quality control. The buyer should make the necessary financial arrrangements with the seller and provide a number of credit references if he or she is a new customer.

Unloading and servicing of the plant material upon delivery is the buyer's responsibility. He or she should have an appropriate area available to receive, store, and protect the plants. In most situations the plants will need water, and if bare root, the material will have to be heeled-in to protect the root system from desiccation or exposure to freezing temperatures. One-year-old wood chips make an excellent mulch for this purpose.

Special equipment is needed for unloading large B&B trees. The practice of rolling B&B plants off the truck-bed can break the balls and result in premature death of the plants. A forklift, a tractor equipped with a front-end loader, or a small crane is much more effective and less damaging to the plant material.

The plant material should be inspected and counted immediately upon arrival and any discrepancies from the order as booked should be brought to the attention of both the seller and the carrier. The buyer has the right to open damaged cartons and examine the contents prior to signing the delivery receipt. A detailed description of damage, if any, should be noted on the delivery receipt, dated, and endorsed by consignee and carrier. This information should be sent to the seller within a 10-day period of receipt of the order. Failure to do so is tacit acceptance of the order as delivered. Plants that arrive in a frozen, dried, or pest-infested condition should be called to the attention of the state plant inspector to obtain a professional judgment on the quality of the nursery stock.

SELLER'S RESPONSIBILITIES

The seller has the responsibility of digging, assembling, packing, and shipping the order. All stock shipped shall be of the size, grade, quantity, and quality specified in the order and should conform to the latest edition of *American Standards for Nursery Stock*. The seller's responsibility begins upon receipt of the order.

One of the first decisions that the seller must make is to accept or reject the order. First, is the plant material available for sale, and second, does he wish to make a contractual obligation with the buyer? If the customer is new to the nursery, he or she should check credit references and discuss financial arrangements. The stock records should be checked for inventory count by variety and size to either confirm the order or to communicate the necessary adjustments to book the order. Upon acceptance, the appropriate quantities are deducted from inventory for sale. The invoice (Fig. 14-2) is typed and copies sent to appropriate individuals for action, with a copy to the buyer, which confirms the order. In small to medium-

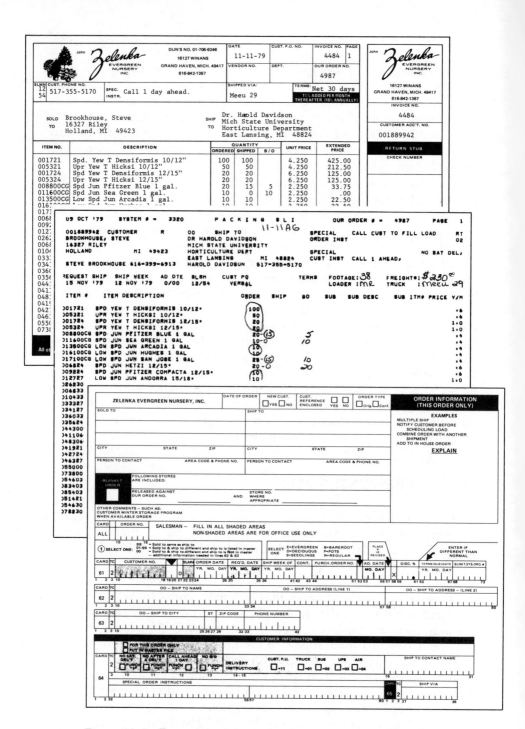

Figure 14-2 Examples of forms used to process an order by a large, wholesale production nursery. (Courtesy Zelenka Nurseries.)

sized nurseries, most of this paperwork is accomplished by a staff of trained clerks employing standard forms and following standard operating procedures. Larger firms accomplish much of the paperwork for booking, invoicing, and inventory control by the use of computers (Fig. 12-6).

The process of assembling, packing, and shipping of the order requires considerable coordination within the nursery and with the carrier. Nurseries that operate on a seasonal basis with a peak shipping season in the spring generally designate a key employee as shipping clerk, whereas nurseries that are shipping 10–12 months of the year employ or contract for a traffic coordinator.

The traffic coordinator or shipping clerk is responsible for arranging the most dependable, rapid, and economical means of transportation. He also coordinates assembling and packing of the order. Upon receipt of the order in the shipping department, it should be keyed to a shipping date. Orders that must arrive at the buyer's site on a specific day or hour of the day should be noted on the shipping schedule to assure timely delivery.

The traffic coordinator can select from a number of means of transportation, each with advantages and disadvantages. Air freight is fast but expensive and is generally utilized for lightweight shipments needed in a hurry. Bus freight and United Parcel Service (UPS) are used for small, lightweight shipments (less than 50 lb/package) that can be delivered within a 2- to 5-day period. Both of these require that the shipper bring the material to the terminal and the buyer pick it up at a terminal, although UPS will deliver. Railroad boxcar, a common method of shipping nursery stock in the past, is now used only on a limited basis. The railroad boxcar takes from 6 to 10 days for direct shipment from coast to coast, but at times delays of 3 weeks or more are encountered. The charge is based on 100-lb units/ mile, with a minimum shipping charge that is often two or three times the 100-lb rate. Although most wholesale nurseries that ship via railroad boxcar are equipped with a railroad loading dock, few buyers have railroad siding and docking facilities, necessitating double handling at the receiving end.

Motor freight is the most common means of shipping nursery stock. Direct motor freight can pick up plant material at the production site and deliver directly to the seller, avoiding multiple handling and delays often experienced when material moves by common carrier and passes through various terminals enroute.

When it is necessary to ship less than a truckload (LTL), the traffic coordinator can arrange a pooled or split load if two or more orders are to be delivered in the same geographic area of the country.

Pooled loads require more coordination to assemble and are more costly, since a stopover charge is added to each order. But pooled loads are less expensive and are generally delivered faster than LTL shipments. Motor freight is charged on a mileage basis per trailer. Thus, it is advantageous to obtain a full load or to split-load rather than employ LTL shipments.

Bare-root plants are normally packaged in the storage area and delivered to the loading dock. Containers for shipping nursery stock should be sturdy; preferably only those that can withstand a 250-lb test should be used. This is to prevent breakage during shipping and crushing of containers that are on the lower layer. Overwatering plant material prior to boxing for shipment in fiberboard-type containers soaks and weakens the container, contributing to breakage and damage to plant material.

Containerized and B&B material are picked up at the growing or storage sites and delivered to the loading dock. Many forms of mechanical equipment are utilized in packaging and loading. Automatic bundling, tying and strapping machines (Fig. 14-3) aid in packaging bare-root orders. Forklift trucks lift and transport heavy loads about the nursery and into the carrier (Fig. 14-4). Some nurseries employ self-tracking lowboy trailers or electric carts to transport container material. Where possible, pallets of various types and endless belt units are employed to expedite the movement of plant material in the loading process.

Plant material loaded into railroad cars or motor freight trailers must be carefully stacked to avoid damage to the plants, and shifting of the load during transport. At the same time, maximum advantage of the total space available can be taken. Small B&B plants and those in metal containers are generally stacked three to four tiers high, whereas plants in nonmetal containers are generally shelved to avoid breakage of the containers. B&B trees in wire baskets require that the trunks be protected with some form of padding to avoid injury during loading and transport. Split loads shipped in closed vans can be divided with a barrier to aid in unloading and to minimize loss of plant material destined for the next stop enroute.

Accurate records must be maintained. A careful count of plants and packages must be made at the time of loading to assure that the buyer receives what was ordered and that the seller bills the customer for the material shipped. The seller is under obligation to conform to the most current issue of *American Standards for Nursery Stock*. All stock must be correctly labeled; in some states plants must be tagged with their botanical name. Following loading, the seller must provide the carrier with a copy of the invoice and other appropriate informa-

Figure 14-3 Automatic nursery stock tying machine. (Courtesy Saxmayer Corporation.)

tion. In split loads, it is advisable to place the invoices in separate envelopes and to mark them with information that the driver will need to expedite delivery. This information generally includes buyer's name, place of delivery with any special directions, time of delivery if applicable, and telephone numbers of people to contact in

Figure 14-4 Forklift aids in loading nursery stock. (Courtesy C. E. Lewis.)

the event of a delay. At the time of departure, the shipping clerk should notify the buyer, either by telex or by telephone, of the expected time of arrival and the name of the carrier.

In addition to shipping records, it is desirable that the party who arranges for the shipping maintain an up-to-date file on each carrier hired to haul plant material. The file should contain copies of the carrier's certificate of insurance and permits to operate a motor vehicle in the various states enroute. The certificate of insurance is needed to assure fiscal responsibility in the event of an accident, and up-to-date permits assure transit within the various states.

It is desirable for the seller to obtain cargo insurance when arranging shipments by exempted carriers not booked through a trucking broker. The seller holds title to the plant material until it is delivered either to the buyer or to a common carrier. Nurserymen who hire trucking firms are advised to contract their trucking needs through a reliable trucking broker who will arrange the necessary details and carry the appropriate cargo insurance.

Most traffic controllers maintain an order board, updated twice daily, so that sales and administrative staff can quickly respond to inquiries relative to shipping of orders.

CARRIER'S RESPONSIBILITIES

The carrier is responsible for transporting the plant material from the seller to the buyer. In most situations the carrier (railroad, motor carrier, bus, UPS, or U.S. mail) is a third party, but in some situations the buyer may send a truck to pick up the plant materials or the seller may deliver in one of his or her own trucks. Nevertheless, it is necessary for the carrier to comply with local, state, and federal laws pertaining to the operation and maintenance of motor carriers. The Interstate Commerce Commission (ICC) is the agency of the federal government that regulates motor carrier transportation interstate and across international boundaries. The ICC regulates motor transport by various economic regulations, which apply only to commercial carriers who do hauling for hire; nurserymen who do their own trucking, under a farm license, are exempt from the economic regulations. However, truck safety regulations, administered by the U.S. Department of Transportation (DOT) apply to all owners of trucks operating in interstate commerce. These regulations are contained in *Federal Motor Carrier Safety Regulations* published by the DOT, available from the Superintendent of Documents in Washington, D.C.. Topics contained in the regulations are qualification of drivers, driving of motor vehicles, parts and accessories necessary for safe operation, notification, reporting and recording of accidents, hours of service of drivers, inspection and maintenance, and driving and parking rules. Every employee who does interstate trucking should be provided with a copy of the regulation, be required to read and understand the regulations, keep an updated driver's log, and turn it in for inspection on a regular basis.

Although nurserymen are exempt from the economic regulations of the ICC, they are subject to the federal highway use tax. This tax is imposed on all motor vehicles or vehicle-trailer combinations having a taxable gross weight of more than 26,000 lb. The Internal Revenue Service (IRS) publishes a schedule showing taxable gross weight for various motor vehicles and vehicle-trailer combinations. The tax must be reported and paid to the District Director of the IRS.

In addition to the federal regulations, many states and local communities have laws or regulations pertaining to the operation of motor vehicles. Nurserymen who transport nursery stock into other states should be acquainted with the applicable laws and regulations. Most of these regulations relate to traffic, weight limitations, truck size, safety equipment, and taxes. They are partially summarized in the *Reciprocity Guide for Private Truckers,* available for a fee from the U.S. Trucking Association. The carrier applies for and maintains an up-to-date file of all necessary permits, which should be checked periodically by the shipper.

Interstate truckers are subject to the economic regulations of the ICC under the Federal Motor Carrier Act. They must obtain a license from the commission, which also regulates rates, territories, routes, insurance coverage, and so on. However, Congress has exempted agricultural and horticultural commodities from the act, thus allowing truckers who haul plant material for nurserymen greater flexibility in service and rates. The exemption holds only if exempted commodities are carried in the truck or trailer combination at any one time. If a trucking firm transports a mixed load of exempt and nonexempt material, it is subject to the economic regulations. Table 14-2 lists some of the exempted horticultural commodities. As a result of this special exemption, many for-hire truckers devote a major portion of their effort to servicing nurseries and other agricultural industries.

Since drivers are primarily responsible for the operation of their vehicles and loads, they should supervise loading and tie-down to

Table 14-2 Partial list of horticultural commodities exempted from coverage under the Federal Motor Carrier Act

---

Bark
Bulbs
Christmas trees
Containers, crates, boxes
  (used to move exempted commodities or being returned for reuse)
Flowers, cut or growing
Grass seed
Greenery
Humus
Leaves
Manure, natural or dried
Nursery stock
Peat moss, dried, shredded, baled
Plants: flower and vegetable
Roots, asparagus, mint, rhubarb, etc.
Seeds
Trees
Wreaths
  (natural with small amounts of foundations or decorative material)

---

assure proper weight distribution and securing of loads (Fig. 14–5). To avoid economic penalties for overweight, a weight estimate of the load should be made at the time of loading (Appendix H). Most truckers can estimate the weight of the load by the pull on the engine as they leave the loading dock. To obtain an accurate weight, the trucker can have the load weighed at a local business (grain elevator, foundry, etc.) that is equipped with the necessary scales.

Figure 14–5 Shade trees loaded and tied for shipping. (Courtesy Studebaker Nurseries, Inc.)

REGULATED CARRIERS

Some nursery stock, primarily boxed and packaged material, is shipped via regulated motor carriers. They charge rates regulated by the ICC and can transport only within the geographic area specified in their certificate of operating authority. Long-distance shipments can pass through a number of terminals and be transported by a number of carriers enroute to the consignee, which can result in delays and possible injury to the plant material. To avoid delays, buyers can request "through routing" from the carrier that will make the final delivery. This information should then be communicated to the seller, who will make the necessary arrangements. If the buyer cannot obtain through routing, he or she should request the shipper to select the best routing available. However, many shippers select "open routing," which passes the responsibility to the carrier to route the shipment; this often results in delays.

Regulated carriers must issue a bill of lading for each shipment received for transport. The bill of lading provides a description of the product (contents, number, weight, size, etc.). The product should be described in wording that conforms to the motor carrier's classification requirements. To do otherwise can result in higher rates. For example, a shipment of bare-root shrubs boxed and marked "dormant nursery stocks" or "perishable nursery stocks" would cost more to ship than the same shipment boxed and marked "shrubs, other than balled in earth, tops tied and roots wrapped." The latter wording conforms to the motor carrier's classification. Also, some carriers refuse to handle perishable shipments. To avoid this possibility, nurserymen should avoid the use of "Perishable" but mark the bill of lading "Do Not Delay! Early delivery requested." When possible, labels on containers should be in large, easy-to-read print and placed on the front and back of the container rather than being typed and placed on top of the container. Only the name and destination of the buyer need to be on the outside of the container. The bill of lading contains all other necessary information.

Upon delivery the regulated carrier must present a freight bill covering the shipment, listing rates assessed; total charges to be collected; special charges (with details); and the route, including name of carriers that participated in the shipment and terminals through which the shipment moved. This information is needed in the event a claim or lawsuit should be filed against a carrier for damages to the plants suffered while in transit.

If it should become necessary to file a claim for damages or overcharges against a carrier, nurserymen should engage a traffic service agency. The traffic service agency will also audit freight bills for overcharges and provide assistance in tracing and expediting shipments that are lost or delayed in transit.

Freight Charges

Freight charges are based on a rate per mile for truck and trailer of a given size. Many nurseries, especially those that produce container-grown plants, provide a schedule of shipping charges. These charges are established for zones of delivery, at various distances from the production site. The charges are stated either as truckload or LTL-zone rates (Table 14-3).

Pooled deliveries are also booked on a rate per mile plus a stopover charge for each partial loading. If all customers are in the same geographic area, the charge per customer can be proportioned either by weight or space. However, where there is considerable difference

Table 14-3 Example of shipping charges from container production nursery
to 10 delivery zones[a]

A. Truckload Rates [maximum load: 6500 1-gal containers or equivalent (1 5-gal = 2 3-gal
= 4 1-gal)]

Zone	Price
1	$ 200
2	250
3	300
.	.
.	.
.	.
10	1500

B. Less-Than-Truckload Rates

Zone	Price		
	1 gal	5 gal	3 gal
1	$0.05	$0.25	Double 1-gal rate
2	0.10	0.50	
3	0.14	0.60	
.	.	.	
.	.	.	
.	.	.	
10	0.25	1.40	

[a]Each distal zone increases by a radius of approximately 100 miles.

in mileage between stops, a more equitable basis for proportioning
charges is the adjusted LTL charge. This charge can be obtained by
first calculating a LTL reduction factor, which is applied against the
LTL charge for each customer. The LTL reduction factor is obtained
by dividing the total freight charges for a pooled load by the total
charges for LTL delivery to each customer. The factor is then used to
adjust the LTL charge to each customer. For example, LTL charges
to three customers are $400, $600, $800, whereas the total pooled
cost is $1400. The LTL reduction factor is 0.78 and the adjusted

charges are $310, $470, and $620. With the aid of a simple desk calculator, these calculations can be made rapidly and accurately.

The traffic coordinator or shipping clerk can estimate cost of shipments with the aid of official state highway maps, a Rand McNally road atlas, or a mileage guide for major cities available from the Household Goods Carrier's Bureau.

Many individual truckers give allowances to nurserymen who load or unload LTL shipments aggregating 10,000 lb or more in one calendar day. Firms that load or unload LTL shipments totaling 10,000 lb or more should negotiate with truckers for the "Loading/Unloading Allowances." Although the allowance may be only a few cents per 100 lb, in the course of a year the amount can be sizable, particularly to heavy-volume shippers or receivers.

Shippers should consider executing a "no-recourse clause" on bills of lading on collect shipments. Failure to do so leaves the shipper liable to pay any uncollected freight charges that the carrier is unable to collect from consignee. Executing the no-recourse clause could save the shipper from having to pay uncollected charges if the consignee should happen to go bankrupt.

A package express service, known as XpressPAX, is available through the Greyhound Bus Company. For a nominal fee the bus company provides an appropriate-sized shipping container, packing materials, and assistance in packing shipments. It can frequently provide same-day service to points up to 300 miles.

SUMMARY

Shipping of nursery stock is an operation of considerable importance to nurserymen. Individual nurserymen and nurserymen's organizations have spent and will continue to spend considerable time and energy trying to assure delivery of quality plants to the customer. At the first meeting of the American Association of Nurserymen in 1876, transportation of nursery stock was a topic that received major attention. Delays in shipment and high transportation rates were the primary complaints of the day. However, with positive action on the part of all parties—shipper, carrier, and buyer—directed toward maintaining plant quality during the postharvest preplanting period, it is possible to deliver the product to the ultimate customer in a condition that is a credit to the grower and to the activities of the carrier. "Green survival—it depends on you," the motto of the AAN, is most appropriate when applied to the operation of shipping of nursery stock.

REFERENCES

AMERICAN ASSOCIATION OF NURSERYMEN. 1963. Transportation Summary, AAN Newsletter 580:1-19.

HALL, G. C., and C. E. WHITCOMB. 1976. Antitranspirants: an investment or an unnecessary expense? Am. Nurseryman 144(2):14.

OSSIAN, W. 1973. Shipping nursery stock today. Am. Nurseryman 138(1):20; 138(2):14.

U.S. DEPARTMENT OF TRANSPORTATION. 1975. Federal Motor Carrier Safety Regulations. Title 49: Transportation, p. 123.

SUGGESTED READING

Guide to Maximizing Recovery of Loss and Damage Claims. 1978. AAN Transportation Consultants–Bohman Industrial Traffic Consultants, 335 East Broadway, Gardner, Mass. 01440.

Chapter 15

Wholesale Marketing of Nursery Crops

The wholesale marketing of nursery crops can be discussed from a number of viewpoints, depending on how one views the marketing process. The retail garden center manager, the mass merchandiser, landscape architect-designer, landscape contractor, wholesale salesman, production nurseryman, and so on, are all involved in wholesale marketing, and each has very personal requirements and interests in the process. Each of these individuals will define the marketing of nursery crops differently. Each will also positively or negatively evaluate the current nursery crop marketing process in relation to how well it satisfies his or her own needs. Marketing, as defined by Kohls, is "the performance of all business activities involved in the flow of goods (in this case nursery crops) and services from the point of initial agricultural production until they are in the hands of the ultimate consumer." Owing to a lack of space in this text, only the wholesale marketing of nursery crops to retailers such as garden centers, landscapers, and mail-order nurserymen will be considered.

The flow of nursery crops from the producer to the retailer is quite complex, in part because of the vast variety of nursery crops, the rapid expansion of the nursery industry, and the long distances that nursery crops are shipped from producer to consumer. A study of the nursery industry in Michigan revealed that approximately 75% of the nursery stock sold at the retail level was produced out of the state. Nursery crops were shipped into Michigan from a majority of the states in the continental United States. At the same time, many wholesale production nurseries in Michigan sell 75% or more of their crops out of the state. A similar marketing pattern would be expected in most of the major nursery market areas in the United States except California, where imports are limited by local competition and stiff import regulations, and Florida, where many of the plants grown are not hardy in other areas.

SPECIALIZATION IN PRODUCTION NURSERIES

There are a variety of reasons for the long-distance shipments of nursery stock in the United States. A specific nursery crop may be more economically produced in one section of the country because of a more optimal climate and soil, lower land and labor costs, greater availability of technically trained employees, lower-energy requirements, longer growing season, and possibly more progressive nursery management. Many production nurseries also specialize in the type of consumer they serve as well as in the nursery crops they produce, and therefore serve a broader geographic area. The same species and cultivar of shade tree, for example, will be grown, pruned, harvested, packaged, and labeled quite differently, depending upon whether the tree will be merchandised through a garden center in early spring as a packaged plant, or through a landscape contractor as a balled and burlapped plant in late summer. The production nursery manager frequently makes irreversible cultural, harvesting, and packaging decisions which commit the nursery crop to a specific type of marketing channel and consumer. The same variety of plant produced in a similar manner will be needed by different retail markets in different stages of growth, different quantities, delivery schedules, labeling, prepricing tags, types of cultural care information, and reorder potentials. State laws in some states dictate part of this.

Most production nurseries, to obtain the benefits of specialization, have directed their nursery crop production to serving a relatively narrow segment of the market. In this way the management of a nursery can more efficiently provide the nursery crop and the necessary services needed by a specific type of retail marketing firm. Developing a successful, profitable wholesale marketing program for a nursery crop begins with an understanding of the needs and nature of the customer. Too often a marketing program begins with a specific product that must be sold. A marketing program should not be a crisis-solving activity. It is an essential part of the nursery management process and must be considered early in the planning and organization of a production nursery.

TYPE OF NURSERY CROPS NEEDED BY LANDSCAPERS

A landscape nurseryman has specific plant needs and will usually want larger plants than will retail garden centers. The nursery stock will usually be B&B, boxed, or container-grown, with very limited quantities purchased as bare-root plants. This in part reflects the reduced maintenance and extended transplanting and sales season, as well as improved transplantability of B&B, boxed, or container-grown plants compared to bare-root plants. If the landscaper is buying plants for a landscape project, specific plants and sizes may be called for by the architect, which in some cases may be produced by a limited number of nurseries.

Timing Deliveries for Landscapers

During the past 15–20 years, the landscape planting season has gradually expanded into the summer and winter seasons as a result of cultural and technical innovations. Landscape planting can now be carried out most of the year, except for certain types of tender landscape plants. However, the ability of workers and equipment to function properly under existing weather conditions will reduce efficiency during the winter season. A landscaper therefore has a more constant need for plants throughout the year than do garden centers, which have pronounced spring and fall seasons.

The landscaper may want to schedule the delivery of plants to a landscape site on a specific day or in some cases at a specific hour of the day to improve efficiency and eliminate the damage to plants resulting from reloading and excessive handling.

Landscapers may frequently purchase rather large quantities of the more commonly used nursery stock which they plan to hold in their own lath, shade area, or temporarily plant in their own fields until needed in a future landscape project. This provides a convenient, inexpensive, immediately available source of landscape plants. Some will produce larger trees and specimen plants which are difficult to find in production nurseries. Other landscapers will purchase only those plants needed on a current landscape project.

Price Quotations for Bidding

Some landscape projects are bid months or even years before the landscape project begins. The production nursery may need to guarantee a price, 1, 2, or even 3 years before delivery in order for the landscaper to submit a bid. Wholesale nursery catalog prices are usually valid for only part of the year; therefore, special price quotations are needed from the wholesale nursery. Large production nurseries supplying quotations will usually want to know the name of the project the landscaper is bidding, particularly if the landscape project is large enough to approach exhausting the regional supply of one size or variety of landscape plant. A number of landscape contractors obtaining prices and guaranteed delivery for the same project will create the illusion of a shortage, which drives prices up and prevents other landscapers from preparing a competitive bid. A production nursery can supply price quotations and guarantee delivery to many landscapers if they are bidding the same landscape project. This keeps the prices down for the landscapers and increases the chances of the production nursery supplying the plants for the project being bid. Production nurseries also may want the opportunity to supply all the plant needs for the project, providing a more efficient shipment to the site and volume discounts on plant material.

Services Provided by the Nursery Broker

In the larger market areas, an independent broker buys in large quantities and may maintain nursery stock on a sales lot in order to wholesale it to retailers. The nursery broker may also provide the service of finding and procuring unusual specimen plants needed by the landscape contractor. Nursery stock brokers may not handle or store landscape plants, but in effect serve as sales representatives for a number of production nurseries. This type of broker may be asked by the landscaper to obtain prices for all plant needs, saving considerable time and expense for the landscaper. The broker may arrange for the digging and delivery schedules if needed. Because of the volume handled by a broker and knowledge of the availability of nursery stock, the broker may be able to arrange efficient, combined order shipments with a reliable trucker, realizing substantial savings in the cost of plants and transportation.

TYPE OF NURSERY CROPS NEEDED
BY GARDEN CENTERS

In contrast to landscapers, retail garden center managers are usually not interested in a broad selection of rare or unusual landscape plants and have short, high-volume spring and fall sales periods. A large northern chain of retail garden centers, Frank's Nursery Sales, Inc., reported 11.3% of their sales in the first quarter of 1975, 39.1% in the second, 20% in the third, and 29.4% in the fourth quarter of the year. The fourth-quarter sales (October, November, and December) are primarily Christmas-related items. The dominance of the second quarter (April, May, and June) spring plant sales in retail garden centers is a serious challenge for garden center managers. Well over half of the plant sales in most garden centers will occur during the second quarter of the year. Garden centers in mild climates will have more uniform sales throughout the year as a result of a longer growing season.

A garden center's merchandising program often begins in winter with the sale of indoor plants, bird seed, pet supplies, and crafts. Spring sales begin with the display of grass, vegetable, and flower seeds, dormant packaged bare-root perennials, deciduous plants such as roses, fruit trees, flowering shrubs, and fertilizers. In the northern United States, this sale begins with the first comfortable spring days. Dormant plant sales will be followed by B&B or containerized plants and bedding plants. Peak sale opportunity for landscape plants such as flowering shrubs and trees may be only the week or two that the plant is in bloom in the community. The garden center manager will usually develop an advertising program which is fixed weeks or even months in advance of the sales period. This program will be timed to promote those types of plants that attract the interest of the consumer. Advertising programs might also feature sale-priced items called *loss leaders,* specifically chosen to increase traffic in the store.

Timing Deliveries for Garden Centers

The timing of nursery stock deliveries for retail garden centers is one of the most important challenges for the production nursery specializing in serving garden centers. Many garden center managers will buy only from those production nurseries that demonstrate the ability to deliver their products consistently when requested. Consumers in the northern United States are interested in purchasing nursery stock the first few warm days in spring, particularly if they occur on a weekend. This does not allow sufficient good weather for a northern nursery to harvest plants from the field, package, and deliver nursery stock to the garden center in time for early spring sales. Southern nurseries have a distinct advantage in providing early, deliveries for northern garden centers. Many northern nurseries utilize a variety of different storage facilities to hold nursery stock harvested and packaged during the preceding fall and winter (see Chapter 13). This allows the northern production nursery to ship fall harvested nursery stock in early spring before the local climate would permit field harvesting.

The sale of nursery stock in garden centers is highly dependent upon the weekend weather. A rainy cold weekend will almost stop sales, whereas a warm sunny weekend will stimulate demand substantially. A production nursery specializing in providing nursery stock for garden centers must be able to respond to a good-weather weekend by accelerating deliveries. The production nursery must also be able to deliver nursery stock according to the retailer's scheduled advertising program. A garden center loses not only the potential sale but customer confidence when an advertised plant is not available as a result of limited supplies. The short duration of garden center sales requires that every available display space to be filled with plants, and that a maximum effort be made to restock as soon after sales as possible.

TYPE OF NURSERY CROPS NEEDED
FOR MAIL-ORDER NURSERIES

The mail-order nursery uses a sales catalog as well as other forms of advertising to sell nursery stock that will be delivered for the most part via parcel post or a parcel service. Mail-order catalogs are usually mailed in mid- to late winter, but early fall catalogs specializing in fall planted bulbs are also common. This industry is particularly sensitive to parcel post rates and makes every effort to reduce the bulk and weight of its nursery products and catalogs. Most mail-order items are either bare-root dormant plants or are grown in small, lightweight containers. Nursery stock is usually dug in the fall, processed during the winter, packaged, and shipped in early spring. Lightweight dormant plants are usually moistened and wrapped in moisture-proof material, frequently sealed in polyethylene bags, and packed in cardboard containers. The mail-order catalog has been the single most important public source of information and sales motivation for the entire nursery industry, including garden center sales and landscape plantings.

Timing Deliveries for Mail-Order Nurseries

The scheduled shipment of mail-order nursery stock is usually based on the estimated time of optimal planting weather for the particular area to which it is being shipped. The entire marketing area (frequently a major segment of the continental United States) will be divided into zones having the same planting dates. A mail-order nursery frequently limits shipping season to only a few months to allow the consumer to plant nursery stock at the best time of year for plant survival.

WHOLESALE NURSERY
SALES ORGANIZATIONS

A variety of different types of nursery sales organizations and agreements with nursery salespersons can be found in the industry. Some production nurseries will hire their own staff who work on a salary and/or commission to sell the nursery's products. The nursery's market area might be divided into districts so that each is the exclusive area for one salesperson. The sales actually booked by the salesperson as well as orders made directly by customers that were originally contacted by the salesperson are his or her accounts and contribute to sales commissions. The sales staff frequently spends a great deal of time personally visiting each customer in the district, providing marketing and management information. It usually takes a number of years of travel before the salesperson can develop the maximum sales potential in the district.

Some nurseries have a separate sales division which markets the nursery's products and, as mentioned earlier, may market plants and related items not produced by the parent nursery. This provides a more complete line of products and services and makes for a more efficient sales organization. Nursery brokers sometimes called representatives or "reps" operate their own independent sales organizations, selling on commission products from a number of production nurseries. These individuals will only book orders. The shipments will originate from the production nursery. A rep will, in most cases, be able to provide a complete line of nursery crops and related products as well as arrange for special shipment, delivery, and other services. The rep receives a commission on all orders personally booked and all orders direct to the production nursery from customers the broker originally contacted. A rep can sell a more complete line than most salespersons representing a single nursery (and the rep usually will write larger orders in a smaller territory than will most salespersons). Both brokers and salespersons will frequently provide assistance in developing advertising programs, display patterns, delivery timing, loss-leader sales, and so on, for retail garden center managers. They may provide data on the previous years' orders, delivery dates, and reorders to assist the buyer in developing this year's purchasing decisions. They are also excellent sources of nursery industry information as a result of their travel and experience with the industry.

Selling nursery stock to discount or department stores with garden center sections usually involves dealing with a head buyer in the home office and the manager of each store. Frequently, the time, quantity, and nature of the initial shipment is established by the buyer in the home office, and subsequent reorders originate with the store manager. The nursery sales force may have to contact each of the individual store managers as well as the head buyer. Many discount or department stores and some garden center managers want large color tags with the botanical and common names and a picture to help identify and sell the plant, and some will want the nursery stock prepriced.

Buyers may also directly contact production nurseries in order to gain more information on the price, quality, and availability of nursery crops. Many buyers for mail-order, garden center, and landscape firms will periodically visit production nurseries searching for new sources of plants as well as new types of plants. Buyer trips to production nurseries are one of the best ways to evaluate the quality and availability of common as well as unusual types of landscape plants, and are encouraged and sometimes sponsored by production nurseries. Many landscape contractors will make extensive searches for unusual, high-quality plant material to add variety and interest to their landscape designs.

STANDARD UNITS OF NURSERY STOCK

Wholesale nursery stock is usually priced in no more than four or five of the following units: 1, 10, 25, 30, 50, 100, 250, 500, and 1000. The unit price may reflect the savings resulting from not having to break bundles or pallets in storage and the savings involved in processing a few large orders as compared to many small orders. The pricing by unit discounts may also be as much the result of traditional practice as it is a reflection of current actual costs. Some nurseries give a discount on total sale rather than numbers of plants. Some wholesale catalogs may indicate that different plants in unit quantities may be combined as one order to receive an even better unit price. In some cases no unit price under 10 or 25 is listed or accepted, or an additional charge may be made for units of less than 10 or 25 of one item. Prices for orders substantially in excess of the 1000 rate are usually negotiated. A wholesale buyer such as a landscape designer or contractor may want to personally select the plants in the production field in order to obtain a specific shape or form. Some nurseries will indicate that this is possible only with an additional 20% charge for the special service.

SHIPPING AGREEMENTS

All wholesale prices are listed in the catalog as FOB (free on board) the production nursery. The buyer bears the shipping cost. In some cases the production nursery will operate its own trucks and is fully responsible for any damage during shipment. In most cases nurseries arrange shipment for the buyer, but the sale is still under the standard FOB terms (see Chapter 14). Additional boxing, packaging, or bailing beyond that normal for harvesting the crop is usually done by the production nursery for an additional charge, but without additional profit.

WARRANTY

In many cases a wholesale catalog contains the statement that no warranty is expressed or implied as to the description, productivity, quality, viability, or any other matter of the nursery stock sold, and that the nursery will not be responsible for the result secured upon transplanting. However, most nurseries warrant their plants to be true to name and in a healthy condition when shipped. The survival of nursery stock, as well as the subsequent growth and production of flowers, fruit, and so on, is to a large degree the result of the care the plant receives during storage and after transplanting. It is not reasonable for the production nursery to be responsible for the performance of the plant. Wholesale catalogs may also indicate that the production nursery accepts no responsibility for the warranty the buyer may give to his customers, including any governmental department or agency.

NURSERY CROP MARKETING CHANNELS

Nursery marketing channels, as mentioned earlier, reflect the nature and location of the consumer, the optimal production environment, and to some degree the existence of management expertise and availability of labor. The marketing channels for nursery stock sold by retailers in the northeastern United States were documentd by E. Jarvesoo in 1969. It is very probable that some of the plant materials in this survey were purchased from a specific area but not grown there. Materials are often purchased from the other production nurseries and wholesaled again in order to provide a more complete line of nursery stock. As shown in Fig. 15-1, over $\frac{1}{2}$ (51%) of the shade trees sold in the northeast were shipped in, Tennessee (34%), Oregon (8%), and Ohio (6%) being the largest suppliers. Approximately $\frac{1}{3}$ (35%) of the deciduous ornamental trees (flowering trees) were shipped into the northeast, with the majority coming from Oregon (18%), Ohio (7%), and Tennessee (4%). It is interesting to note the change in rank of Oregon and Tennessee when comparing shade trees and flowering trees.

In contrast, evergreen trees, narrowleaved evergreen shrubs, and broadleaved evergreen shrubs were predominantly purchased in the northeast. This could be expected because the northeastern states are a major production area of evergreen trees and narrowleaved and broadleaved evergreen shrubs for the states east of the Mississippi River. Approximately $\frac{1}{5}$ (19%) of the deciduous shrubs and $\frac{1}{2}$ (40%) of the roses retailed in the northeast were shipped in (Figs. 15-2 and 15-3).

Surveys in other major market areas would be expected to yield similar relationships reflecting the production advantages available in various areas of the continent. As a general rule, production areas will supply nursery crops to market areas having a more severe winter climate and a later spring. This is not always a north-south relationship, but might reflect the climatic protection provided by the lake effect, such as the Great Lakes or maritime climates along the coasts. The warmer-to-colder climate shipment of nursery crops reflects the advantages offered by longer growing season, reduced winter injury, and overwintering costs as well as the ability to spring-harvest field-grown nursery stock and deliver it to a retail outlet for the first

Figure 15-1 Sources of supply and main destinations of deciduous shade trees, northeast, 1963.

Figure 15-2 Sources of supply and main destinations of deciduous shrubs, northeast, 1963.

Scale of miles

0   200   400   600   800   1000

Figure 15-3 Sources of supply and main destinations of roses, northeast, 1963.

Scale of miles

0   200   400   600   800   1000

spring sales. In some cases the development of spring growth and flowers can be delayed in common cold storage in order to time flowering for maximum sales in northern retail market areas.

Selling Southern Grown Nursery Stock in Northern Markets

There appear to be limits to how much milder or warmer the production climate may be in relation to the consumer's climate. Most of the northeastern retail outlets surveyed by Jarvesoo did not report the purchase of woody nursery crops (with the exception of roses) in 1963 from zones 8, 9 and 10 (Figs. 15-1, 15-2, 15-3). It would seem apparent that many outdoor nursery crops moving from warmer to cooler climatic zones (Fig. 6-5) are rarely shipped to a climatic zone more than 20°F colder (mean annual minimum temperature). Exceptions to this relationship include roses and some juniper and arborvitae species. A number of reasons for the limitation in movement of nursery crops to colder climates can be proposed. The distances involved may make freight costs prohibitive. However, as shown in Figs. 15-1, 15-2, and 15-3, substantial quantities of nursery crops are shipped from the west to the east coast of the United States. Plants grown more than two climatic zones warmer may be in full growth during early spring shipment and be vulnerable to frost damage. The cost of delaying growth and flowering by cold storage to avoid frost damage may be prohibitive. Many nursery crops adapted to northern climates have specific cold-exposure requirements for breaking dormancy and specific day-length requirements for vegetative growth, flowering, and the development of low-temperature hardiness. These requirements of plants adapted to northern climates may preclude their efficient growth in production climates more than two climatic zones warmer.

A number of nursery crops, such as *Cornus florida* and *Cercis canadensis,* can be found growing in native stands over a range of four climatic zones. However, these native stands have developed into ecotypes that are adapted to a specific habitat and are not necessarily capable of surviving over the entire range for the species. This has been found true with almost every species of native woody plant that has been studied. If a specific plant variety is genetically adapted to the climate of a northern market, the fact that it has been grown for a number of years in a much milder climate will not alter that genetic potential. It will be able to develop its full genetic potential for low-temperature hardiness when grown for one growing season in the northern climate to which it is genetically adapted.

Many nursery crops are reproduced vegetatively as "improved" varieties and few data are available concerning their climatic limitations. If information is lacking concerning the climatic limitations of a new variety, it might be advisable to purchase these nursery crops from production nurseries in a similar climatic zone. The flow of nursery crops from the site of production to the ultimate consumer is quite complex and is changing with the development of new technology, new nursery crops, and the changing costs of transportation versus production.

Obtaining Marketing Information

The degree of specialization in marketing channels results in a considerable challenge for both the buyer and seller of nursery crops. The American Association of Nurserymen publishes an annual booklet *Sources of Plants and Related Supplies,* (see Appendix A), which lists production nursery sources for more than 1600 varieties of commercial nursery crops and related supplies. A similar service, available in *Nursery Report,* is provided by the Landscape Materials Information Service, Callicoon, New York. The botanical name of each variety of nursery crop is followed by a listing of production nurseries offering it for sale, with size and quantity of the nursery crop. This booklet provides a broad base of current information for the wholesale buyer of nursery crops and is financed by membership dues of those firms listed as well as those firms obtaining the published listings.

Many state nursery trade associations provide listings of the production nurseries in that state producing various categories of crops, such as shade trees, deciduous shrubs, fruit trees, indoor foliage plants, ground covers, and so on. Additional information for the buyer is available in both the classified and unclassified advertising in nursery trade journals and trade association publications such as the *American Nurseryman, Nursery Business, Home and Garden Supply, Southern Florist and Nurserymen, Pacific Coast Nurserymen, The Voice of MAN,* and others (Appendix C). In many cases the production nursery's advertisement in a trade journal is very brief, providing only the name, address, telephone number, and the type of crops produced. The wholesale buyer may obtain the production nursery's current catalog by contacting the nursery. The wholesale nursery catalogs provided by production nurseries are the most detailed and accurate source of information concerning the availability of nursery crops.

Marketing at Nursery Association Meetings

Trade association meetings provide an additional opportunity for buyers to contact production nursery salespersons and to become aware of the availability of various types of nursery crops. These contacts may be informal discussions between buyers and salesperson or may be the result of an exhibit in a formal trade show. Most state, regional, and national nursery trade association meetings are partially financed by fees charged for exhibit space in the trade show rooms and are a major attraction for the meeting. A broad range of plants as well as pesticides, fertilizers, specialized landscape construction equipment, supplies, tools, and production nursery equipment are on display at most nursery trade shows. The trade fair is certainly one of the most effective opportunities for production nurserymen and wholesale buyers to meet. The actual sales booked at the trade exhibit are commonly less important than the subsequent sales made as a result of the contacts made during the trade exhibit.

Booking Wholesale Nurseries Crop Orders

There has been a gradual change in the purchasing practices for nursery crops. A number of years ago most orders were booked 3–5 months before spring delivery, and the traditional state and regional annual trade meetings, held during the winter season, provided an ideal time for ordering plants. Orders for nursery crops, particularly from garden centers, are currently placed well before the winter season. Some of the newer regional trade exhibit meetings are scheduled in summer or early fall, allowing orders to be booked 6–9 months before spring delivery. The dates for state and regional meetings are usually consistent from year to year to eliminate conflict between meetings.

A number of regional trade shows have become major sales events for the industry: the Western Association of Nurserymen, Trade Show and Meeting, Kansas City, Missouri; the Garden Living Industries of the Eastern United States, Kiamesha Lake, New York; Mid-America Trade Show, Rosemont, Illinois; Mid-Atlantic Nurserymen's Trade Show, Cockeysville, Maryland; Southern Nurserymen's Association Trade Show, Atlanta, Georgia; TAN-MissLark Regional Convention, Nursery and Garden Supply Show, Houston, Texas; and Pacific Horticulture Trade Show, San Diego, California; and others. In some cases the regional trade shows have an educational program in addition to the trade exhibit.

Almost every state having a substantial market for nursery crops has a state nurserymen's association meeting with a trade fair. The state meetings, in many cases, have strong educational programs in conjunction with the Cooperative Extension Service and their land grant university. These meetings also deal with the issues and challenges facing the nursery industry, including relations with the state legislature and various regulatory agencies.

Pricing Nursery Stock

The pricing of nursery stock is primarily based on supply and demand. Pricing of nursery stock is also influenced by production costs, plant quality, and the service and reliability of that service provided at delivery. The changes in prices for nursery stock are not at a uniform rate for all types of plants. The reported mean cost of the same plant material for 1972 and 1974 in an NLA bidding exercise illustrates this point:

Plant material	*1972–1974 change in price*
2–2½-in. shade trees	+61%
2–2½-in. flowering trees	+70%
18–24-in. spreading evergreens	+11%
2–¼-in. potted ground covers	+14%

Two methods are commonly used to establish the current price. A production nurseryman may use the current wholesale catalog from another large nursery serving the same marketing area. The nurseryman will set his or her price using the nursery catalog as a guide. The other method is based on an evaluation of the future supply-and-demand relationship for that particular nursery crop. Obviously, the cost of production will provide the lower limits of wholesale prices, particularly if that crop is going to continue to be produced. The sales organization, commission salespersons, and brokers are a valuable source of information concerning the supply and demand anticipated for specific nursery crops and marketing channels.

Projecting Future Sales

Changes in the supply and demand for a specific plant will reflect adverse growing conditions in a particular production area, changes in consumer demand, and the national economy. The garden center industry tends to expand, at a somewhat greater rate, increasing demand for garden-center-type plants during periods of general economic recession. Apparently, when consumer earnings decrease, the consumer spends more time and effort on "do it yourself" gardening and landscape projects. The demand for plants used in landscape construction, on the other hand, is influenced by public building programs, such as highway landscaping, low-income housing, educational facilities, medical complexes, shopping centers, and so on, as well as major industrial complexes. Changes in the volume of landscape construction are commonly found 2–3 years or more after changes in the volume of building construction. Landscaping is usually accomplished 2–3 years or more after the beginning of general construction on the project. The relative demand for plants used in landscape construction can be estimated by noting changes in construction starts and allowing sufficient time for the delay between construction starts and landscape planting. Unfortunately, the 3- to 6-year or longer crop cycle from propagation to harvest is too long in most cases to take full advantage of reliable economic predictions and changes in the construction industry.

The future demand for nursery stock can be enhanced by a number of other procedures. The development of a patented landscape plant allows the production nursery to control production and therefore the supply of that plant to the consumer. The number of patented landscape plants has dramatically increased in the past 10–15 years, for a variety of reasons. Advertising patented plants to both wholesale and retail consumers is more obviously rewarding to the nursery owning the patent because it develops demand only for those specific nursery crops. The ability to create demand through advertising and to control supply has stimulated the investment in breeding and selection programs for patented landscape plants.

The demand for the entire spectrum of nursery crops could be stimulated by the growth of a coordinated national advertising program such as the nursery industries National Marketing Council (NMC). NMC provides a common nationwide advertising theme and materials which can be used by a local retail nursery. Wholesale growers financially support NMC, which distributes themes, advertising artwork, as well as materials for radio, direct mail, television, transit advertising, and in-the-store merchandising aids equally to landscape firms and retail garden centers.

A well-coordinated cooperative advertising program of sufficient size could have a major impact on the nationwide demand for nursery crops and the growth of the entire nursery industry.

Developing a Marketing Program

The development of a wholesale marketing program for a production nursery begins with an analysis of the needs of the customers: garden center buyers, landscape contractors, city foresters, and other nurserymen. These needs reflect, in part, the needs of the ultimate customers. The market analysis is followed by a production study of species to be produced, cultural requirements, production methods, rotations, costs, and so on. These data are then evaluated against an estimate of potential income from future sales and against product competition to determine an estimate of probability for success of the program.

A successful marketing program for nursery products requires the input of as much factual production and marketing data that are available, matched with the best estimates of future demands, price structure, and potential product competition. Management must integrate all of this information and continually modify production and sales programs to remain economically sound in a constantly changing market environment.

SUMMARY

Wholesale marketing of nursery crops is rapidly changing as a result of many factors, especially changes in market demands, production technology, and modes of transportation. In recent years, the marketing phase has quite possibly changed more than any other aspect of nursery management. The nursery industry of the United States continues to expand, creating many new opportunities for profitable marketing. But, because of its relatively small size as compared with other industries, it is difficult for nursery managers to obtain good market information. Currently, the best information is obtained through various trade associations, trade journals, and from attendance at trade shows and meetings. Hopefully, the Nursery Marketing Council, established in 1977, will serve as the major source of market information for the industry.

The growers' ability to anticipate market demands is a limiting factor in the growth of the nursery industry and poses one of the most significant marketing challenges for the nursery industry of the future.

REFERENCES

BENDER, F., and V. BENSEN. 1968. Marketing channels of floricultural products and ornamentals in Maryland. Agric. Exp. Sta. Univ. Md., College Park, Md. Misc. Publ. 642.

FRANK'S NURSERY SALES, INC. 1975. Ann. Rep. 6399 E. Nevada, Detroit, Mich. 48234.

JARVESOO, E. 1969. Procurement and sales practices of retail outlets for ornamental nursery products. N.J. Agric. Exp. Sta. Rutgers Univ. Bull. 824.

THE NURSERY INDUSTRY AND FLORICULTURE, PROJECT '80 RURAL MICHIGAN NOW AND IN 1980. 1966. Agric. Exp. Sta. Coop. Ext. Serv. Mich. State Univ. Res. Rep. 43.

"PARTNERS FOR PROFIT." Nursery Industry Cooperative Advertising Program (NICAP) A.A.N., 230 Southern Building, Washington, D.C. 20005.

PLANT HARDINESS ZONE MAP. USDA Agric. Res. Serv. Misc. Publ. 814. Superintendent of Documents, Government Printing Office, Washington, D.C.

TWENTY-NINTH NURSERY REPORT. 1967. Landscape Materials Information Service. Calicoon, N.Y.

SOURCES OF PLANTS AND RELATED SUPPLIES. 1973–74 ed. An Allied Landscape Industry Service, American Association of Nurserymen, 230 Southern Building, Washington, D.C. 20005.

Chapter 16

Estimating and Bidding of Landscape Projects

A landscape estimate or bid is a proposal in which a landscape nurseryman or landscape contractor translates the landscape architect's or landscape designer's plans into reality for a specific price. A landscape architect is, in many states, a licensed professional who provides the landscape design, may supervise the letting of bids to landscape contractors, and supervises the construction project but does not do the construction. A landscape designer is not licensed, but provides the landscape design and may do the entire construction project. For the purposes of this discussion we will refer to both types of individuals by the term "landscape designer." The landscape planting must survive, mature, and satisfy the expectations of the owner and the designer. This goal requires considerable cooperation and communication among the owner, the landscape designer, and the contractor.

ESTIMATING LANDSCAPE PROJECTS

The majority of residential landscape projects are designed, estimated, sold, and developed by the same individual or firm. Competing landscape firms do not have the opportunity to submit a bid proposing to develop the same landscape design for the customer. Estimating differs from bidding primarily in that an estimate does not face competition by other nurserymen for the same design. Competition is primarily between differing designs rather than between differing prices.

A landscaper may submit an estimate either agreeing to install the planned landscape for a fixed price or submit a budget that approximates the cost of the planned landscape. The budget will be reviewed periodically with the owner as the project progresses, indicating the actual costs as the landscape is developed. An estimate is an approximation of the anticipated costs of the project, but it can be very precise. Usually, however, estimates are not as detailed or precise as a competitive bid and allow greater flexibility to accommodate unforeseen conditions or to modify the landscape design during construction. Problems encountered by the estimator or bidder, such as interpretation of specifications, owner concerns, substitutions, bonding, contracts, guarantees, and design modification, are eliminated or can be more readily solved by the landscape designer-contractor when they are a single firm rather than two firms. However, considerable experience, information, and skill in a variety of unrelated areas, including landscape design, sales ability, business management, plant availability, personnel management, plant culture, and construction techniques are needed by the landscape designer-contractor. Many landscape construction firms begin with the owner serving as designer, estimator, salesperson, and contractor, but as the firm expands the responsibilities are divided, allowing for more specialization by employees and owner. Even the landscape designer and the contractor being members of the same firm (sometimes called a turnkey operation, because the project is locked into one firm) does not eliminate the possibility of misunderstanding, nor does it preclude the necessity for constant communication and sensitivity to the roles of the other members of the team.

Landscape firms wishing to expand their volume of business or variety of work frequently contact landscape designers and even owners of future landscape sites before the landscape plans are developed. The purpose of this contact is to develop the necessary communication and trust that must exist in order to successfully complete a landscape project.

COMPETITIVE LANDSCAPE BIDDING

Competitive landscape bidding will be discussed in detail since it requires the most precision and detailed preparation. The general principles of bidding apply in landscape estimating but are usually less rigorous. Most landscape projects financed by public funds and many largescale private projects are designed by a professional landscape architect who prepares detailed plans, with complete specifications and procedures. These projects are then released for competitive bidding to qualified landscape contractors.

Landscape Specifications

The development of detailed landscape construction specifications is essential when the lowest bid is to be accepted. Suggestions for writing landscape construction specifications and examples may be obtained from the *Handbook of Landscape Architectural Construction, The Landscape Architect Reference Manual,* and *Off the Board, Into the Ground.* The formal landscape plan and written specifications serve as legal documents describing the work to be done. Plans and specifications must be carefully prepared by the architect and completely understood by the contractor preparing a bid. When writing landscape specifications, the designer must have the cooperation of landscape contractors, who should be involved in updating and improving the specifications. Professional associations of landscape architects and landscape contractors periodically meet at the national and regional level to jointly develop and revise specifications that reflect new construction techniques and current standards. Regular meetings of designers and contractors at the local level are essential to maintain communication and to ensure that full advantage is made of new technology.

The Invitation to Bid

The initial step in the bidding process is the invitation to bid. This might be an informal message in the case of small private work or a published invitation to bid public projects. The form of the invitation to bid public work is determined by law and must be followed rigidly in order for a bid to be considered. There are a number of sources where contractors may obtain information concerning construction projects that are open for bidding. Public advertising in newspapers, trade magazines, and journals and posted public notices are required for most public landscape contracts. Reporting services such as the *Dodge Reports,* published by the F. W. Dodge Company, list new projects and may include a list of bidders, award of contracts, or cancellation of projects previously announced. The Associated General Contractors, local building association, and landscape contractor groups also provide announcements of construction projects. The F. W. Dodge Company also provides a service called SCAN, which is microfilmed copies of the contract specifications. These may be kept to serve as a record of the specifications that the landscape firm bid upon. The contractor may have to make a deposit for the specifications and plans necessary for bidding if the scale of the project warrants the charge.

Many projects are not open to bid by all landscape contractors. The designer may personally select contractors he feels are qualified to complete this type of landscape project. The designer and owner may also refuse the low bid and select a higher bid from a landscape contractor who they feel will do better work. However, this is rarely done when the designer has asked a selected group of contractors to bid the project. Considerable sales ability may be involved in bidding landscape projects. Landscape construction projects may be given to a landscape contractor based on the firm's reputation and the quality of its work, with only an estimate of the cost of the project. But in most cases the owner of the site must know what the proposed landscape project will cost. The cost of the proposed project will be estimated by both the landscape designer and by landscape contractors submitting competitive formal bids on large projects. In some cases (more commonly involving designer-contractors), the owner may request and receive a budget or estimate of the cost. The final cost of the project should vary only slightly from this budget. There may be considerable negotiation among owner, designer, and contractor in order to modify specifications and reduce the cost of the project so that it will meet the owner's budget.

Bid Bonds

A bid bond must accompany a bid when it is submitted. This is to assure that if the contract is awarded, the bidder will sign the contract. The bid bond is an indication that the landscape contractor is submitting a serious bid and that he or she will accept the contract if it is offered. It is purchased by each bidder from a bonding agency, possibly through an insurance agent. The bonding agency will usually require financial data from the landscape firm, including previous volume of work and current commitments. If the landscape contractor refuses the contract, he or she forfeits the bond, which is commonly 10–20% of the bid, and the bonding agency will pay the owner the face value of the bond or pay the difference between the original bid and the next-higher bid. Once the bid is accepted and contract is signed, the cost of the project is fixed. If the acceptance of the lowest bid is not possible owing to lack of funds or other reasons, no bids are accepted and the entire project may be modified and released for another bidding.

The Decision to Bid

The ultimate objective of a bidder is to obtain the project for his or her firm and produce a profit. The estimator or bidder must arrive at a figure that is low enough to qualify and be accepted, but high enough to make a profit. Without a profit there would be no future for the landscape firm. The decision to bid should be based on a management review of the particular project with a complete up-to-date set of plans and specifications. There is a constant temptation for a contractor to bid every landscape job that becomes available. The decision to bid should be based on an evaluation of a variety of factors. Management should outline the nature, size, and location of landscape projects and the quantity of construction work that the firm can most competitively perform while maintaining the reputation and public image it has and hopes to enhance. The legal requirements or terms of the contract should be fully understood before bidding, and in many cases may require the services of a lawyer to evaluate. The legal aspects of landscape construction as they exist in California have been well documented in *Landscape Management* by J. M. Griffin. Statutes will vary in other states, but the basic principles will usually be quite similar.

Landscape Contracts

Two basic types of contracts are commonly used in landscape projects. The first is a single contract between the owner and a prime contractor who is responsible for the entire construction project. He will subcontract portions of the project, such as the landscape, to other specialized contractors. The prime contractor is responsible for the supervision, direction, and payment of all subcontractors. In this system a landscape contractor may contact the prime contractor and prepare a bid for the landscape project. The prime contractor will incorporate this bid adding on a markup for his or her costs of supervision and direction as a part of the entire bid. The relationship between the landscape contractor and the prime contractor is most important. The landscaper is usually the last contractor on the project and must finish before the prime contractor can receive final payment from the owner. The second type of contract is a system of separate contracts between each contractor and the owner. The owner selects each contractor and then either the designer or the owner will assume responsibility for the supervision and development of the entire project.

There are a variety of financial agreements between the owner and contractor which may be incorporated into either of two general types of contracts. In the first general type of contract the owner agrees to pay a lump sum at the completion and acceptance of the project. Any changes in the initial specifications of the project are negotiated individually. A second type involves a unit price agreement with a payment for each unit of work accomplished. The total cost of the project will vary with the amount of each item used in the project: top soil, number of trees, square yards of sod needed to complete the project, and so on.

Landscape construction contracts with either owner or prime contractors may have a number of provisions, such as time of starting and completion, the percentage and schedule for payments as the project progresses, and the specifics of the acceptance and final payment of the job. Complex contracts may require the evaluation by a lawyer experienced in contract law.

Performance Bonds

A number of types of bonds may also be required by both owner and prime contractor in addition to the bid bond discussed earlier. A performance bond ensures that the contractor will do the work according to the specifications and complete the project as agreed in the contract. This bond is usually for the amount of the bid.

Bonds are purchased by the contractor from security companies, which thoroughly investigate the landscape firm for its technical and financial status as well as credit record, equipment, and experience. The cost of the bond will, of course, depend on its cash value, but will also depend on the type of construction and the nature of the bond the security company will establish. The security company will establish the maximum bonding capacity it will provide for each landscape contracting firm requesting bid and performance bonds.

On-Site Visit

After deciding to submit a bid, the bidder should visit the landscape site, particularly on large landscape projects or those in unfamiliar geographic areas. A checklist of things to consider during the on-site visit is an important aid in bidding. Table 16–1 is a suggested list of factors to consider while on the site. Each firm should develop its own individual checklist. This list should be periodically updated as experience with new equipment, problems on the site and, experience with other contractors dictates new concerns. Consideration during this visit should be given to all items that will affect the cost of doing the job and the potential survival of plant materials. Soil characteristics (type, pH, slope, surface and subsurface drainage, and obstruc-

Table 16–1   On-site visit check before bid preparation

   I. *Ecologically Related Items*
       Location and condition of topsoil, stockpile of topsoil
       Subsoil type
          Soil pH
          Soil drainage
          Rocks and debris
       Location and condition of trees to be saved or moved
       Location of elevation markers
       Local sources of fill and topsoil
       Potential microclimatic conditions
       Appropriate plant selection for site
       Time of year job must be done

  II. *People-Related Items*
       Potential vandalism
       Availability of labor and housing
       Local landscape licenses and fees
       Labor union relationships
       Parking and traffic congestion problems

 III. *Utility-Related Items*
       Availability of storage facilities
       Location of construction boundaries
       Availability of dump and charges for dumping
       Source of water
       Accessibility of site by road
       Potential weight limits on access roads
       Identification and location of underground/overhead utilities[a]

  IV. *Other Problems*
       Knowledge and experience of supervisor
       Contractor cooperativeness and past record of payment
       Availability of subcontractors and special equipment

---

[a]Prior to construction or planting, landscape contractors should call "Miss Dig." The telephone number is in most phone books.

tions) play an important part in landscape development and should be considered in detail. If topsoil is to be stockpiled, what is it like? Is it uniform and free of debris, and is there room on the site for the stockpile? Subsoil material may be on the surface by the time landscaping begins, and the nature of it may become most important. A check should be made of property and construction site boundaries, underground utilities, and obstructions that might present problems during construction. Utility companies will often aid in locating their facilities. The availability of water and its cost, the accessibility to the planting site, buried debris from construction, areas for material and equipment storage, and potential for vandalism all affect the cost of completing the job and should be considered. At some seasons of the year public road restrictions or road construction may limit movement of heavy vehicles. On large jobs at distant sites, a check should be made of the availability of housing if labor crews are to be housed in the area. The contractor should check on the availability and cost of labor and the various labor unions which will be involved in the contract. On some large landscape construction sites requiring a variety of local union laborers, contact with local union representatives may be a most important on-site contact. The on-site visit is an information-gathering exercise and an attempt to anticipate potential problems and to resolve them before the construction phase. The contractor may wish to have the architect meet him or her at the construction site or arrange a personal contact to discuss problems uncovered during the on-site visit.

MATERIAL-QUANTITY SURVEY
AND DETERMINATION OF COSTS

The actual bidding process begins with the preparation of the material-quantity survey and to a substantial degree is derived from the survey. The material-quantity survey (a complete list of all types of materials needed) should be the most precise portion of the entire bidding procedure. The landscape designer has specified the plant materials, quantities, and procedures to be followed on the site. The bidder is obligated to check the architect's plant material list and calculations with the actual landscape plans. The actual plans are the final definitive source of information. Any conflicting data or questions resulting from the specifications and plans should be checked with the designer as soon as possible to permit changes if necessary. The bidder's material quantity survey should cover every aspect and area of the landscape project. The nomographs (Appendices F and G), as well as the *Landscape Data Manual* and *Landscape Designer and Estimators' Guide,* (Appendix A) provide the necessary conversion factors for volume, weight, grade changes, rates, and area calculations necessary in preparing a precise material-quantity survey. A standard checklist of materials needed in landscape construction, based on past experience, should be kept up to date and used to check for errors and omissions in the material quantity survey. It is important that the data be double-checked, because an error at this point is compounded many times in the final bid. The bidder may consider subcontracting part of the project on large sites or unusual projects, and a separate material-quantity survey should be prepared for subcontracted portions of the landscape construction project.

Material Costs

After the material-quantity survey is completed, costs can be applied and the material priced. Plant material as well as other material costs should be based on firm bids or prices in writing from suppliers. This is particularly true with large quantities, unusual materials, or during periods of rapid general economic inflation. Some landscape projects may be bid many months, or even years, before actual landscape construction begins, making firm pricing at the planting date most important. In some cases it might be advisable to make a partial payment for scarce plants as soon as the bid has been awarded in order to assure availability. It is not enough to know the price that certain species are listed at in a nursery catalog. The plants may be unavailable or the prices may have increased since the time of listing.

When considerable competition for the bid is anticipated, a more competitive bid may be obtained by an extensive search for low priced plant material that meets specifications. When contacting a production nurseryman about prices on plant material for a specific landscape job, give the production nursery the opportunity to bid the entire plant list. The nurseryman may be able to provide overall economies as the result of full-truck freight rates and moving a larger quantity of plants, including some he may have in oversupply. All material costs should include freight to the landscape contractors yard or landscape site. It is almost impossible to compare the cost of materials from different parts of the country without knowing the freight cost involved.

The 1974 National Landscape Association (NLA) bidding exercise reported a variation in the cost of plant materials from 10- to more than 20-fold (Table 16–2). While this range in price is difficult

Table 16-2 Example of variability in plant material costs as reported in
1974 National Landscape Association bidding exercise

	Costs	
	Mean	Range
2½-in.-caliper shade trees	$40.50	$12.00–90.00
2½-in.-caliper flowering trees	30.20	6.00–66.00
Pine	21.25	2.25–60.00
Spreading evergreen	7.60	1.15–15.00
Ground cover	0.30	0.10– 0.75

to accept, it does illustrate that variation and savings might be
obtained by a thorough search for prices. Another NLA bidding exercise showed that landscape contractors doing considerable competitive bidding (50% or more) paid from 8 to 28% less for all plant
material than those doing noncompetitive bidding or estimating. It
might be advisable for a landscape contractor to turn the plant
material survey lists over to a nursery agent representing a number
of nursery suppliers. The agent's widespread knowledge of plant
availability and sources, his or her ability to combine shipments and
save freight, and the savings in time to the contractor provide a substantial service for the landscaper. Some nursery agents specialize in
providing plant material for landscape projects and are able to
schedule the digging, shipment, and delivery to the landscape site on
the date scheduled for planting. This saves handling costs and possible reduction in quality that might accompany the storage of plants
by the landscape firm and reshipment to the landscape site.

Landscape nurserymen that produce some plant materials often
have a competitive bidding advantage. According to the NLA bidding
exercise 3, landscape nurserymen producing their own 2½- to 3-in.-
caliper trees charged 7–20% less for them than did landscape contractors purchasing the same plant material from other nurseries
(Table 16-3). The price charged by the landscape nursery firm for

Table 16-3 Example of plant material cost variation between those purchased by landscape contractor and those grown by landscape
nurseryman

Plant material	Caliper (in.)	Purchased cost	Grown cost
Ginkgo biloba	2½–3	$93.00	$78.00
Liquidambar styraciflua	2½–3	89.00	71.00
Ulmus parvifolia	2½–3	86.00	80.00

plants it produces should cover the actual cost of growing the plants, including overhead expenses, and return a profit for the firm. Large trees were the only type of plant materials reported to cost less if grown by the landscape contractor. Growing large trees can result in considerable savings in freight charges to the landscape contractor-nurseryman. Producing certain types of specimen plants or the collection of plants from natural stands may be advantageous to some landscape firms in that it provides a supply of unique plants unavailable elsewhere and may provide work for employees during slow periods of the year. Other types of plants (ground covers, deciduous shrubs, evergreens, and small trees) were reported to be less expensive if purchased rather than grown by the contractor. The same bidding exercise indicated that certain plant materials cost less if purchased within 200 miles, while others cost less if purchased more than 200 miles away (Table 16-4). These reported costs included freight, storage, and handling, and therefore probably reflect differences in the range of optimum growing conditions for different landscape plants.

Some plants may grow best within very limited geographic areas, whereas others may grow well almost anywhere. These results should not be interpreted to indicate that all firms should buy certain plants

Table 16-4 Example of variation in cost of plants shipped less than 200 miles compared to plants shipped more than 200 miles

Plant materials	Caliper	Mean cost	
		200 miles or less	More than 200 miles
Local source costs less			
Magnolia soulangeana	3–4 ft	$11.40	$ 12.40
Ginkgo biloba	2½–3 ft	89.40	101.15
Liquidambar styraciflua	2½–3 in.	78.50	99.50
Ulmus parvifolia	2½–3 in.	75.00	95.25
Euonymus fortunei 'Coloratus'	2½ pt.	0.30	0.35
Distant sources costs less			
Thuja occidentalis	3½–4 ft	$ 9.75	$ 5.50
Cornus florida	6–8 ft	19.00	16.90
Juniperus virginiana 'Ketelleer'	4–5 ft	17.30	7.50
Viburnum opulus	3–4 ft	8.20	5.25

at a distance of 200 miles. They do illustrate the advantage of a thorough search for a variety of sources of plant material. The landscape bidder should carefully consider the range of sources of plant material available to him or her. Plant quality never improves with the distance shipped. Before making the decision to grow or buy plant materials, a thorough examination must be made to identify the direct and indirect costs of each course of action, then choosing that which produces the greatest profit. The decision to grow certain types should be periodically reexamined to determine if it continues to be a profitable decision.

Direct Costs

Direct costs (sometimes called planting costs) are those expenses that are directly related to specific plant materials or operations, for example, the cost of labor and the cost of equipment used by the landscape contractor in planting a tree. The estimate of labor and equipment costs are usually based on the quantity and nature of the materials to be installed or other site modifications indicated on the landscape plan. Labor requirements are often difficult to estimate because of the variables of weather and site that influence the efficiency of labor and equipment. When bidding larger, more complex jobs, the foreman or site supervisors may provide valuable suggestions for cost-saving construction methods. It is rare that a landscape installation can be performed in only one way, using a standard crew and equipment. The selection of a construction method of procedure should be made after considering the limitations imposed by the site, other contractors working on the site, weather, completion date, and costs of the alternative methods.

Markup Factors

Many firms use a simple markup factor to estimate the total selling price of landscape plants. This system is more commonly used by firms doing complete landscape projects, including the designing, selling, and construction. The wholesale price of a plant (or retail sales lot price) is multiplied by a markup factor to obtain the price of the plant installed in the landscape. The markup factor provides for labor, equipment, and overhead costs as well as anticipated profit. Commonly used factors are two to five times the wholesale price.

The appropriate markup factor is usually derived from the landscape firm's previous years' financial statement. If, for example, last year's total gross landscape sales were $150,000, and $50,000 of that was the cost of plants installed, the markup factor of three could be used this year. [If a plant costs $25 (wholesale price), the selling price (installed price) would be $75.]

A somewhat more complex system uses a different markup factor for trees, shrubs, evergreens, and ground covers, reflecting average difference in planting costs. One of the problems inherent in estimating costs with a markup factor is that the labor and equipment needed to install landscape plants are not consistently related to the wholesale price of the plant. Plants of the same size, requiring similar time and effort to install, may vary two to three times in wholesale price. The wholesale cost of plants is not necessarily related to the cost of landscape planting, particularly when the landscape firm is hundreds of miles from the producing nursery. A wholesale nursery catalog lists *Acer saccharinum* cv. Pyramidal, 3- to $3\frac{1}{2}$-in. caliper at $68.50 and *Crateagus viridis* cv. Winter King 3- to $3\frac{1}{2}$-in. caliper at $115.80. The use of the markup factor for estimating costs would set the cost of one tree almost twice that of the other. Since they are approximately the same size, planting costs should be similar.

Equating direct expenses (labor and equipment costs) to the material costs can result in considerable error in a bid, particularly on larger landscape construction sites. The labor and equipment utilized in planting a slow-growing expensive plant is the same as the labor and equipment utilized in planting the same-size inexpensive rapidly growing plant. Ratios will overestimate direct expenses for expensive plants and underestimate for inexpensive plants. Ratios will work satisfactorily if landscape projects are not competitively bid and have similar plant types and costs.

Productivity Data Method

A more precise method for estimating direct expenses is based on productivity data expressed as labor- or machine-hours required to perform a given activity, such as planting a certain size tree or seeding on 1000 ft^2 of lawn. The most reliable source for this information is the firm's past landscape construction projects. Average labor productivity data from other firms may be useful in evaluating alternative methods but are of limited value in bidding. Valuable data for bidding can be obtained by using a combination work-order daily time card for each crew such as that shown in Fig. 16–1. Each day the crew foreman fills in materials installed and activities performed by his or her crew corresponding to the hours for each

DAILY TIME SHEET

Foreman __J. Smith__ Date __4/19/80__ Day __Mon.__ Job name __Mc Pherson residence__

Truck __#7__ Sheet __/__ Of __/__ Address __201 Linden St.__

Comments: __Has nasty dog, be sure it is__ City __Golden Valley, Indiana__
__inside. Pick up planting plan at office__ Phone (__317__) __345-4324__
__before leaving.__

Quan-tity	Operation and materials	Size	Com-pleted	J. Smith	Al Johnson	Casey Brown	Bill Black			Total	Unit
	Load			½	½	½	½			2	
	Travel			1½	1½	1½	1½			6	
2	10' Acer ginnala	28"B&B	✓		1¾	1¾				3½	
18	18" Forsythia 'Lynwood'	1 gal	✓	1¾			1¾			3½	
30	18" Lingustrum 'Regal'	"	✓	2	2	2				6	
3	3' Virbrunum clentatum	2 gal	✓				¾			¾	
4.5	yd³ gravel, mulch	—	✓	¾	¾	¾	2			4¼	
	Non-productive			0	0	0	0			0	
	Travel			1½	1½	1½	1½			6	
	Unload			0	0	0	0			0	
			Total	8	8	8	8			32	

(Column headers across top: 1 2 3 4 5 6 — Job completed [x])

Figure 16-1 Example of daily time sheet used to account for time and materials associated with landscape construction. Foreman completes the sheet at the close of each day. Unit is computed by office staff. (Courtesy Theodore Brickman Co.)

worker and piece of equipment. Every labor-hour of payroll turned in must have an activity indicated (travel time, nonproductive time, etc.) for this system to work. As these data accumulate, the estimator can develop averages as well as high and low productivity data for all the activities within the firm. As new methods, materials, or equipment are developed, the time data will change. It is important for the foreman and crew to understand that time checks are necessary to develop up-to-date data for future bidding. The initial reaction of the crew may be that the boss is developing a system to see if they are working as fast as possible. If in fact the time data are used as evidence to obtain more productivity, some foremen will juggle time data so that their crews look good. This destroys the accuracy of the data for bidding purposes and creates an undesirable environment for effective communication and motivation. The time data also allow the bidder to accurately check the bid and potential profitability as the project progresses. Productivity data would be expressed in labor-hours, equipment hours, and, for some types of equipment, miles of operation. This allows for the use of productivity data even though the wage rates and fringe benefits for labor change and the cost of equipment rental or ownership change.

Systems for Compiling Landscape Productivity Data. There are two basic systems for compiling planting time productivity data. The first is based on the size of the plant shoot system (Table 16–5), and the second (Table 16–6) on the size of the root system (diameter of the soil ball, container, or box). The plant root system uses fewer size categories than the plant shoot system, and under most circumstances plants having the same size root system (ball, container, or box) require a similar planting time. The size of the root system determines the size of the planting hole, amount of backfill, and efforts required to move and position the plant. The lower number of plant categories required by using the plant root system would save time and improve the accuracy in estimating planting costs. Table 16–7 suggests categories for collecting time data on other types of landscape operations.

Table 16–5 Plant-shoot categories for estimating planting time

Evergreens	*Shrubs*	*Shade trees*	*Ground covers*
18–24 in.	18–24 in.	Height	Rooted cuttings, bare root
2–2½ ft	2–3 ft	6–8 ft	2½-in. pots
2½–3 ft	3–4 ft	8–10 ft	3-in. pots
3–3½ ft	4–5 ft	Caliper	4-in. pots
3½–4 ft	5–6 ft	1½–2-in.	
4–5 ft		2–2½-in.	
5–6 ft		3–4-in.	

SOURCE: Originally prepared for National Landscape Nurserymen's Association by Harold Hunziker, Hunziker's Inc., Landscape Nurserymen, Niles, Mich.

Labor and Equipment Costs. After the total hours of labor required for a project have been estimated, they are multiplied by labor-cost rates to estimate labor cost. Labor cost is a large factor in landscape construction work, and the rates must accurately reflect the total cost of labor. Labor costs should include the base wage rate, cost of fringe benefits, nonproductive time (if not part of your productivity data), paid holidays, pension or retirement contributions, vacations and various types of essential hospitalization, and accident and unemployment insurance payments. The landscape employer

Table 16-6 Suggested plant-root-system categories for estimating planting time

Ball diameters (in.)		Hedges (in.)
12 or less	49–54	12 or less
13–18	55–60	13–18
19–24	61–66	25–30
25–30	67–72	
31–36	73–78	
37–42	79–84	
43–48	85–90	

SOURCE: Information supplied by Theodore Brickman Co., Long Grove, Ill.

Table 16-7 Suggested labor productivity categories for selected landscape operations

Linear feet (ft)	Square feet (ft²)	Cubic feet (ft³)
Edging	Grading	Spreading
Straight	Hand	Gravel
Curved	Machine	Mulch
	Laying	Soil
	Brick	
	Cobblestone paving	
	Precast concrete	
	Plastic	
	Sod	
	Walls and steps	
	Sandstone	
	Limestone	
	Railroad tie	
	Seeding	
	Hand	
	Machine	

SOURCE: Information supplied by Theodore Brickman Co., Long Grove, Ill.

must usually charge two or three times the base average pay rate to cover total labor costs (Table 16-8). The hourly rate charged for equipment should reflect depreciation, licenses, cost of storage, repair, insurance, and fuel. The annual cost of owning or leasing and operating a piece of equipment for 1 year should be recovered in the charges for the total hours of operation for that piece of equipment in one year. Obtaining the cost of owning equipment also has the ad-

Table 16–8 Landscape labor costs for an employee working 40 hours per week with 2 weeks' vacation and six paid holidays

Total hours	40/week × 52 weeks	2080 hours
Less:		
Vacation (2 weeks)		80 hours
Holidays (6 days)		48 hours
Coffee-break period (2–10 min/day)		72 hours
Nonproductive (30 min/day)		122 hours
		322 hours
Hours of productive work		1748 hours

Direct labor costs (DLC):

$$\frac{2080 \text{ paid hours} \times 5.00^{a}}{1748 \text{ productive hours}} = \qquad \$5.95$$

Indirect labor costs (per hour):

F.I.C.A. tax	0.17	
Unemployment tax	0.18	
Health, workmens' compensation		
insurance	0.28	
		0.63

Overhead labor costs (per hour):

Office (est. 15% of DLC)	0.89	
On-the-job supervision		
(est. 20% of DLC)	1.19	
		2.08
Total labor cost per hour:		$8.66

[a]Dollar values for example only, values will vary with hourly rate.

SOURCE: Modified from Lawrence Backman, Am. Nurserymen Vol. 118, no. 11, p. 9 (1963).

vantage of allowing the estimator to determine if it would be less expensive to rent or lease equipment rather than own it.

Critical Path

One of the time factors necessary to bid large landscape projects is the total time required for completion. The *critical path method* (CPM), devised for the building construction industry, is useful in estimating the minimum time required to complete complex landscape construction projects. The critical path is a list of operations in the most efficient order of occurrence; for example, installation of an irrigation system and large shade trees should be completed before finish, grading, and seeding. To make up a simple CPM flowchart, the various activities (jobs requiring time) required to complete the job should be listed on separate small pieces of paper. The activities should be arranged in sequence, such that the activity to the left must be completed before the following activity. Those activities that must be done at the same time are placed above each other and those activities independent of any other activities may be distributed below other activities in the flowchart in such a manner as to provide a uniform work rate for the entire project. The sequence of activities can then be diagrammed on a single sheet of paper as a CPM flowchart, with arrows indicating the sequence of activities (Fig. 16-2). Each activity is assigned a duration of time for completion. The times indicated under each activity are not the total hours of labor required but the time from starting to finishing that particular activity. The use of more equipment and workers for a particular activity may shorten the time required to complete that activity and make the entire project more efficient by reducing the total time required for completion.

Computing the CPM total time in days will provide the total duration for the project and provide a preliminary organization for the job. When the firm obtains the contract, the CPM flowchart will provide an opportunity to check the project as it progresses against estimates. The CPM flowchart can be a very useful management tool in bidding, planning, and carrying out a large landscape project.

Overhead Costs

Overhead expenses are those costs essential to the operation of the business which cannot be assigned or are too time-consuming to assign to a particular product or specific work activity. A typical list of expenses is shown in Table 16-9. It is tempting for a manager to include many unidentified costs in overhead and to ignore them. It requires less record-keeping time to assign all equipment maintenance expenses to overhead. A more precise bid can be prepared if the hourly operating cost of a piece of major equipment includes its own depreciation, storage, fuel, and oil as well as maintenance charges. Management should determine if detailed costs should be assigned to labor, equipment, selling expenses, and nursery production or if these costs should be assigned to a general overhead. The decision may be based on the relative size of the cost under consideration and the bookkeeping expense involved in assigning the cost either to

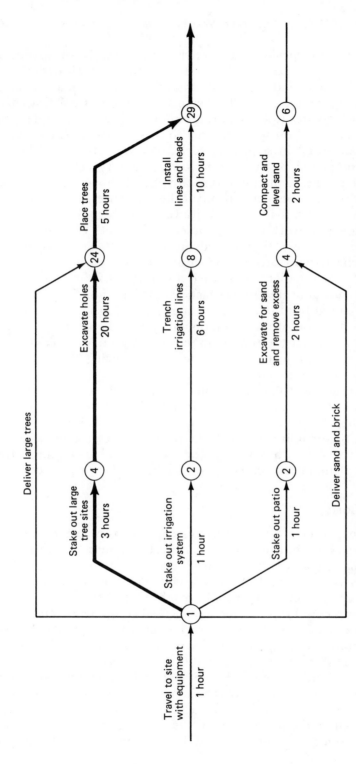

Figure 16–2 Critical path method diagram; the critical path is illustrated by the heavy line.

Table 16-9 Overhead reported by landscape firms[a]

Overhead item	Gross sales (thousands of dollars)			
	100	*100–225*	*225–500*	*500+*
Owner salaries	10.82	9.51	7.29	4.51
Office salaries	6.17	4.32	4.35	2.76
Depreciation	5.10	3.31	2.89	1.25
Insurance	4.45	3.33	3.77	2.18
Rent or mortgage	4.56	2.10	2.19	7.50
Taxes: payroll	2.17	2.64	2.56	2.29
Travel and entertainment	3.17	0.98	0.82	0.70
Taxes: income	1.90	1.26	1.04	0.65
Operating licenses and taxes	1.12	0.50	0.53	0.66
Interest on bank notes	1.06	1.00	0.51	1.77
Advertising	1.39	0.10	1.79	0.66
Maintenance	0.90	0.93	2.45	2.29
Office supplies	0.84	0.47	0.75	0.36
Telephone	0.81	0.65	1.27	0.42
Utilities	0.61	0.71	0.72	0.49
Taxes: property	0.54	0.86	1.41	0.32
Interest on notes	0.55	1.52	0.88	0.34
Professional services	0.55	0.45	0.81	0.63
Contributions	0.55	0.23	0.09	0.23
Dues and subscriptions	0.37	0.30	0.27	0.46

[a]All data are expressed as a percentage of gross landscape sales obtained from NLA.

overhead or to a specific product or work activity. As a general practice, costs of a substantial size should be assigned to a specific product or activity as direct expenses. This allows for more precise bidding and for more precise comparisons of alternative business procedures.

Overhead also includes management salaries. The management salary is distinct from a business profit and is assigned to overhead as operating expense. Owners frequently have difficulty determining a fair salary to assign themselves, as distinct from profit on their investment in the business. The assignment of owners' salary should be based on what salary would be necessary to hire someone to manage the firm or what the owner could earn managing or working for some other landscape contractor. Owner-managers will actually earn the sum total of salary plus profit, but for management purposes the owner's salary must be assigned fairly.

The overhead cost that is to be assigned to a given landscape bid is obtained from an accurate accounting of the last year's overhead costs. If total overhead last year was $30,000, and total landscape construction earnings last year were $100,000, the overhead percentage for last year was 30%, based on total earnings. If $100,000 of landscape construction is anticipated again this year, the overhead add-on percentage based on material and direct expenses is obtained by dividing last year's overhead by estimated material and direct expense costs.

$$\frac{\text{overhead}}{\text{material and direct expenses}} \times 100 = \frac{\$30,000}{\$70,000} = 42.8\%$$

If $200,000 of landscape construction is anticipated and if overhead will be the same as last year ($30,000 per year), then the overhead add-on percentage is lower:

$$\frac{\$30,000}{\$170,000} \times 100 = 17.6\%$$

As the volume of landscape construction increases, over a short period of time, many overhead costs will usually not increase as much, resulting in a more competitive bid. Conversely, if the anticipated volume decreases, and only $50,000 of landscape construction is anticipated this year and overhead remains at $30,000, then the overhead add-on percentage must increase:

$$\frac{\$30,000}{\$20,000} \times 100 = 150\%$$

During periods of reduced landscape construction volume, the overhead add-on percentage must increase to ensure that overhead expenses will be met. An increasing overhead add-on percentage places the bidder in a less competitive position, unless overhead expenses can be reduced dramatically.

Contingencies

Contingency funds are sometimes included in an estimate to provide for cost items that are overlooked or could not be foreseen at the time of bidding. Some firms allow 5–10% for contingencies such as bad weather, delay in delivery of material, strikes, and so on. The contingency fund may reflect a lack of confidence or experience the firm has with the type of construction in a particular project. Contingencies can become a crutch for poor estimating practice. Contingencies should be items that cannot be foreseen rather than cost items that are difficult or time-consuming to estimate.

Warrants

The warranty (or guarantee) cost will vary with the length and terms of the warrant required in the bid specifications. They may vary from 1 to 2 months, one growing season, or 1–3 years. The warranty on a small landscape project may be bid as a percentage add-on based on previous experience. The estimated warranty cost on larger projects will change depending on a variety of factors, such as the length and nature of the warranty in the bid specifications, the nature and adaptability of the plant material to the site, the level of maintenance, whether the contractor or owner maintains the landscape, potential vandalism, environmental pollution, and unusual microclimates. Charges for the warranty may vary from 1 to 15% of the total cost of the project; 5% is an average charge.

Profit

There are probably as many different ways for figuring profit in landscape construction as there are systems for estimating other portions of the bid. Profit should be clearly understood to be a financial factor added to the total cost of the project and distinct from all costs related to the landscape project, such as office overhead, managerial salaries, and advertising. A business manager should expect to make a fair profit on his or her investment, and a profit is essential to ensure a healthy future for the firm. Profit may be calculated as a percentage add-on to the total cost of materials, direct expenses, and overhead. Some nurserymen figure profit only on materials or on materials and labor. The anticipated profit percentage used in preparing a bid may change depending on the contractor's evaluation of competition, the firm's need for work, the risk and difficulty inherent to the job, and the necessity to compensate for losses encountered on previous projects.

When the owner desires a cost-plus agreement the contractor is paid for the construction costs and may be paid either a profit fee calculated as a percentage of the construction costs, or a fee fixed prior to signing the contract. A third agreement involves a profit agreed to in the contract and a guaranteed maximum cost. This type of agreement may also contain provisions to allow the contractor to share in any savings that result in a cost reduction below the guaranteed maximum cost.

IMPROVING YOUR ABILITIES TO BID

The bidding process begins with very precise construction plans and specifications and ends with very speculative estimates of contingencies and warrants. The final bid that is submitted reflects the bidder's need and desire for the job as well as an estimate of competitors' bids. Good bidders, like good poker players, know their competitors. Estimators should attend bid openings, recording their own bids and those of all competitors. A backlog of competitors' bidding patterns is invaluable. It might prove pointless to submit a bid against certain competitors, thus saving the expense of bid preparation.

Never destroy calculations used in estimating unless they are proven incorrect. Estimating work sheets should clearly show the original values to allow comparison with actual costs of the project and corrections made for future bidding. For very large projects, two or more estimators in the same firm should prepare independent bids for comparison before submitting a jointly approved bid. Small portable electronic calculators are a valuable tool for more precise bidding. A calculator, however, will only deliver accurate estimates if correct information is fed into it.

It would be beneficial to visit those landscape projects which were bid but lost in order to evaluate the specific materials and techniques utilized by the successful bidder. This will provide valuable information about your competitor and the landscape architect supervising the job. If the completed project reflects a different type or quality of materials and techniques than you understood from the specifications, it might be well to discuss the difference with the architect supervising the project, to improve your understanding of the architect's expectations for future projects.

SUMMARY

The goal in competitive bidding is to submit a bid which is low enough to obtain the project but high enough to make a profit. Estimating and bidding of landscape projects often begin with very precise, definitive information—landscape plans and specifications—but often end with relatively imprecise estimates of contingencies, weather conditions, and competitors. Experienced bidders reduce to a minimum the amount of imprecise estimates that goes into a bid. They develop definitive labor and material cost information relative to the various operations commonly associated with landscape projects and follow carefully and apply all the steps in bid preparation: the decision to bid, on-site visit, material-quantity survey, materials costs, direct costs, overhead, contingencies, warrants, and profit. Successful bidders are also aware of and adjust their bids to the personnel problems related to the project including: owners, architects, laborers, labor unions, and competitors. Successful bidders of landscape projects are, generally, highly competitive people who enjoy a challenge and are capable of mastering the resources available.

REFERENCES

CLOUGH, R. H. 1972. Construction project management. Wiley–Interscience, New York.

FOSTER, R. H. 1960. Contracting. John Wiley & Sons, Inc., New York, p. 382.

GRIFFIN, J. M. Landscape management. California Landscape Contractors Associations, Inc., Redwood City, Calif., p. 287.

JENSEN, F. E., and P. J. KINSCHLING. 1976. Better management for profitable bidding. Am. Nurseryman 143(2):709, 6669.

MECKLENBURG, R. A. 1976. Competitive landscape bidding; a summary of NLA bidding exercises. National Landscape Association, 230 Southern Building, Washington, D.C. 20005.

SUGGESTED READING

CARPENTER, J. D., ed. Handbook of architectural construction. Prepared by members of the American Society of Landscape Architects and the Associated Landscape Contractors of America, 1750 Old Meadow Road, McLean, Va. 22101.

CARPENTER, P. L., R. D. WALKER, and F. O. LANPHEAR. 1975. Plants in the landscape. W. H. Freeman and Company, Publishers, San Francisco.

DODGE, F. W. Reports. McGraw-Hill Information Systems, New York. Issued daily from 18 centers.

GRIFFIN, J. M. 1972. Landscape data manual. Building News, Inc., Los Angeles, Calif.

THE LANDSCAPE ARCHITECTS REFERENCE MANUAL. 1977. Basic Information Service Inc., Orange, Calif.

LANDSCAPE DESIGNER AND ESTIMATOR'S GUIDE. National Landscape Association, 230 Southern Building, Washington, D.C. 20005.

ROBINETTE, G. O. 1908. Off the board/into the ground. Kendall/Hunt Publishing Company, Dubuque, Iowa, p. 307

SCAN MICROFILM SERVICE. F. W. Dodge Corporation. McGraw-Hill Information Systems, New York.

Appendix A

Partial List of Books and Bulletins Pertaining to Areas of Nursery Management Not Covered in this Book

PLANT PROPAGATION

NURSERY STOCK MANUAL. 1975. J. G. D. Lamb, J. C. Kelly, and P. Bowbrick. Grower Books, London.

PLANT PROPAGATION PRINCIPLES AND PRACTICES. 1975. H. T. Hartmann and D. E. Kester, Prentice-Hall, Inc., Englewood Cliffs, N.J.

PROCEEDINGS OF THE INTERNATIONAL PLANT PROPAGATORS' SOCIETY. 2295 Hillsdale Way, Box 3131, Boulder, Colo. 80303.

SEEDS OF WOODY PLANTS IN THE UNITED STATES. 1974. USDA Agricultural Handbook 450. Superintendent of Documents, Washington, D.C.

PEST CONTROL

SCIENTIFIC GUIDE TO PEST CONTROL OPERATIONS. 1978. P. Villard. Harvest Publishing Co., New York.

TREE FRUIT AND ORNAMENTAL PESTICIDE GUIDE. Thompson Publications, Box 9335, Fresno, Calif. 93791.

DISEASES:

DISEASES AND PESTS OF ORNAMENTAL PLANTS. 1978. P. P. Pirone. John Wiley & Sons, Inc., New York.

DISEASES OF FOREST AND SHADE TREES OF THE U.S. 1971. USDA Agricultural Handbook 386, Superintendent of Documents, Washington, D.C.

DISEASES OF SHADE TREES. 1978. T. A. Tattar. Academic Press, Inc., New York.

FOREST NURSERY DISEASES IN THE UNITED STATES. USDA Agricultural Handbook 470. Superintendent of Documents, Washington, D.C.

INSECTS:

A GUIDE TO INSECT INJURY OF CONIFERS IN THE LAKE STATES. 1976. L. F. Wilson. USDA Agricultural Handbook 501.

INSECTS AS PESTS. 1973. H. S. Zinn and G. S. Fichter. Doubleday & Company, Inc., New York.

INSECTS OF EASTERN PINES. A. H. Rose and O. H. Lindquist. 1973. Canadian Forestry Service Publ. 1313. Information Canada Center, 221 Yonge St., Toronto, Ontario, Canada M5B1N4.

INSECTS THAT FEED ON TREES AND SHRUBS, an illustrated practical guide. 1976. W. T. Johnson and H. H. Lyon. Cornell Univ. Press, Ithaca, N.Y.

WEEDS:

DIAGNOSIS AND PREVENTION OF HERBICIDE INJURY. 1976. Bulletin Office, Michigan State Univ., East Lansing, Mich. 48824.

HERBICIDE HANDBOOK. 1974. Weed Science Society of America, 309 West Clark St., Champaigne, Ill. 61820 ($5.00).

NEBRASKA WEEDS. 1975. Nebraska Department of Agriculture, Lincoln, Neb. 68509 ($8.50).

WEED SCIENCE, PRINCIPLES AND PRACTICES. G. C. Klingman and F. Ashton. John Wiley & Sons, Inc., New York.

GARDEN CENTER MANAGEMENT

OPERATING A GARDEN CENTER, 5th ed. 1957. J. J. Pinney. American Nurseryman Publishing Co., Chicago.

PROFITABLE GARDEN CENTER MANAGEMENT. 1978. L. Berninger. Reston Publishing Company, Reston, Va.

OTHER PUBLICATIONS

LANDSCAPE DESIGNER AND ESTIMATORS' GUIDE. American Association of Nurserymen, 230 Southern Building, Washington, D.C. 20005.

SOURCES OF PLANTS AND RELATED SUPPLIES. American Association of Nurserymen, 230 Southern Building, Washington, D.C. 20005.

A TECHNICAL GLOSSARY OF HORTICULTURE AND LANDSCAPE TERMINOLOGY. 1971. Horticultural Research Institute, 230 Southern Building, Washington, D.C. 20005.

Appendix B

Addresses of Nursery-Related Organizations*

All-America Rose Selections
P.O. Box 218
Shenandoah, IA 51601

American Association of Nurserymen
230 Southern Building
15th and H St. NW
Washington, D.C. 20005

American Association of Nurserymen's
Group Insurance Trust
230 Southern Building
15th and H St. NW
Washington, D.C. 20005

Associated Landscape Contractors
of America
1750 Old Meadow Rd.
McLean, VA 22101

Garden Centers of America
230 Southern Building
15th and H St. NW
Washington, D.C. 20005

The International Plant Propagator's
Society
2295 Hillsdale Way, Box 3131
Boulder, CO 80303

*Addresses subject to change.

International Society of Arboriculture
3 Lincoln Square, Box 71
Urbana, IL 61801

Landscape Materials Information
Service
Callicoon, NY 12723

Mail-Order Association of
Nurserymen, Inc.
210 Cartwright Blvd.
Massapegua Pk., NY 11762

National Arborist Association
3537 Stratford Rd.
Wantagh, NY 11793

National Association of Plant Patent
Owners
230 Southern Building
15th and H St. NW
Washington, D.C. 20005

National Landscape Association
230 Southern Building
15th and H St. NW
Washington, D.C. 20005

Nurserymen's Protective Association
c/o McGill & Son
Fairview, OR 97024

Southern Nurserymen's Association
3813 Hillsboro Rd.
Nashville, TN 37215

Wholesale Nursery Growers
of America
230 Southern Building
15th and H St. NW
Washington, D.C. 20005

Appendix

Trade Journals Related to the Nursery Industry

American Nurseryman
310 South Michigan Ave.
Chicago, IL 60604

Arborist News
P.O. Box 426
Wooster, OH 44691

Florist & Nursery Exchange
434 S. Wabash Ave.
Chicago, IL 60605

Garden Industry of America
Box 1092
Minneapolis, MN 55440

Grounds Maintenance
1014 Wyandotte St.
Kansas City, MO 64105

Home & Garden Supply Merchandisers
2501 Wayzata Blvd.
P.O. Box 67
Minneapolis, MN 55440

Landscape Architecture
Schuster Bldg.
1500 Bardstown Rd.
Louisville, KY 40205

Landscape Design & Construction
2048 Cotner Ave.
Los Angeles, CA 90025

Landscape Industry
850 Elm Grove Rd.
Elm Grove, WI 53122

Lawn/Garden/Outdoor Living
1014 Wyandotte St.
Kansas City, MO 64105

Midwest Landscaping
1706 W. Chase Street
Chicago, IL 60626

Modern Garden Center
208 James St.
Barrington, IL 60010

Northwest Garden Supplier
311 Henry Bldg.
Portland, OR 97204

Nursery Business
850 Elm Grove Road
Elm Grove, WI 53122

*Addresses subject to change.

Nursery Product News
9800 Detroit Ave.
Cleveland, OH 44102

Pacific Coast Nurserymen & Garden
   Center Dealer
832 S. Baldwin Ave.
Arcadia, CA 91007

Southern Florist & Nurserymen
P.O. Box 1868
Fort Worth, TX 76101

Turf-Grass Times
218 19th Ave.
N. Jacksonville Beach, FL 32050

Weeds Trees and Turf
9800 Detroit Ave.
Cleveland, OH 44102

Western Landscaping News
1623 S. La Cienega Blvd.
Los Angeles, CA 90035

Appendix D

Approximate Metric Conversions

Unit		*To metric*				*From metric*		
Length	inches	×	2.5	=	centimeters	×	0.4	=	inches
	feet	×	30.5	=	centimeters	×	0.033	=	feet
	yards	×	0.9	=	meters	×	3.3	=	feet
	miles	×	1.6	=	kilometers	×	0.62	=	miles
Area	inches^2	×	6.5	=	centimeters^2	×	0.16	=	inches^2
	feet^2	×	0.09	=	meters^2	×	11.1	=	feet
	yards^2	×	0.8	=	meters^2	×	1.1	=	yards^2
	miles^2	×	2.8	=	kilometers^2	×	0.36	=	miles^2
	acres	×	0.4	=	hectares	×	2.5	=	acres
Mass	ounces	×	28.0	=	grams	×	0.035	=	ounces
	pounds	×	0.45	=	kilograms	×	2.2	=	pounds
	tons (2000 lb)	×	0.9	=	tonnes (1000 kg)	×	1.1	=	tons
Volume	teaspoons	×	5	=	milliliters	×	0.2	=	teaspoons
	tablespoons	×	15	=	milliliters	×	0.007	=	tablespoons
	fluid ounces	×	30	=	milliliters	×	0.03	=	fluid ounces
	cups	×	0.25	=	liters	×	4.17	=	cups
	pints	×	0.47	=	liters	×	2.1	=	pints
	quarts	×	0.95	=	liters	×	1.06	=	quarts
	gallons	×	3.8	=	liters	×	0.26	=	gallons
	feet^3	×	0.3	=	meters^3	×	35.0	=	feet^3
	yards^3	×	0.76	=	meters^3	×	1.3	=	yards^3
Temperature	(Fahrenheit $-32°$)	×	0.56	=	Celsius	×	$1.8 + 32°$	=	Fahrenheit

Appendix

Rate Per 1000 Ft² Nomograph

Area

acres   sq. ft

Quantity
of
material

Rate
Per 1,000 (sq. ft)

Rate Per Acre Nomograph

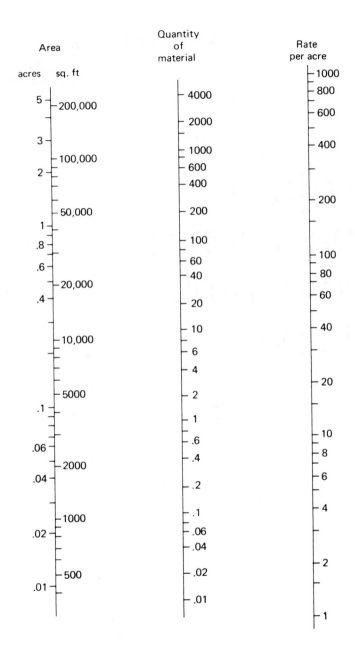

Area

acres   sq. ft

Quantity
of
material

Rate
per acre

Appendix G

Fertilizer Proportioner Nomograph, 100 ppm*

*To obtain other ppm concentrations, multiply by appropriate factor. For example, to obtain 200 ppm, multiply ounces per gallon by 2.0; to obtain 50 ppm, multiply by 0.5.

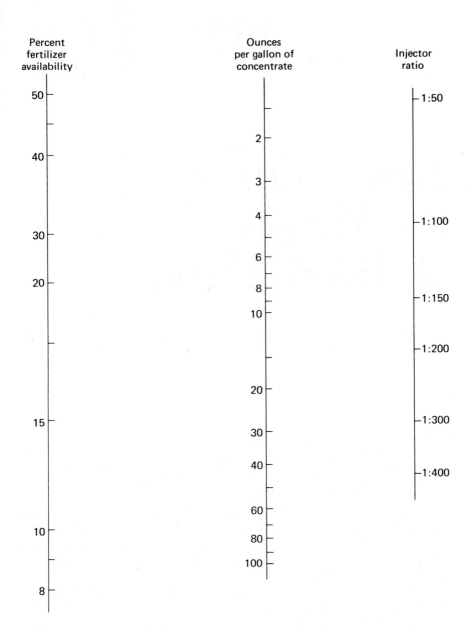

Percent
fertilizer
availability

50
40
30
20

15

10

8

Ounces
per gallon of
concentrate

2
3
4
6
8
10

20
30
40

60
80
100

Injector
ratio

1:50

1:100

1:150

1:200

1:300

1:400

Appendix H

Determining the Weight of B&B Plants

Nurserymen, landscape contractors, and arborists have need, periodically, to determine the weight of B&B trees. They need to estimate weight in order to determine what type of equipment will be necessary to move the plant or plants, estimate cost, and plan transportation routes in accordance with weight restrictions on some roads during the spring-thaw season in certain parts of the country. The weight of B&B plants is dependent upon a number of factors, including the size and species of the plants, the size and shape of the ball, and the soil type, including its moisture content.

The *weight of small plants,* whether they are B&B or in containers, can be readily determined by weighing plants in selected sizes and determining the total weight by multiplying the number of plants within a size class by the average weight of the class. When a group of selected small plants was subjected to a volume/weight analysis, the results indicated that the weight of B&B plants was directly related to the volume of soil, which was related to the type of root system; shallow-rooted plants weighed less than relatively deep-rooted plants. There was also a correlation between ball size and digging time (Table H–1).

Determining the weight of larger plants is a little more challenging, since the weight must be estimated without the use of scales. This can be done by either calculating the weight of the soil ball plus the weight of the tree or by abstracting the estimated weight from a weight table or graph. Various formulas have been suggested for calculating the weight of the soil ball, including:

(1) $W = \frac{2}{3} (D^2 \times d) \times 110$ (dimensions in feet)

(2) $W = \frac{2}{3} (D^2 \times d) \times 0.075$ (dimensions in inches)

(3) $W = \pi \dfrac{d}{3}(r_1^2 + r_1 r_2 + r_2^2) \times 110$ (dimensions in feet)

where D = diameter of top of the ball
d = depth of the ball
r_1 = radius of the top of the ball
r_2 = radius of the base of the ball
π = 3.1417

For each formula, certain assumptions are made. In (1) and (2), it is assumed that the volume of the soil approximates two-thirds that of a cube-like block, whereas in (3) it is assumed that the weight of

Table H–1 Volume/weight/digging time relationship of selected B&B evergreen shrubs

	Average weight of B&B plants (lb)	Average ball volume ft³	Proportionate weight of soil (%)	Average time to B&B (min)
Japanese holly 18–24-in. crown deep rooted	52.8	0.63	90.6	10.1
Pfitzer juniper 18–24-in. crown deep-rooted	50.3	0.63	95.9	8.7
Evergreen azalea 18-in. crown shallow-rooted	22.1	0.45	90.1	5.2

SOURCE: After R. W. Pease.

an "average" cubic foot of soil is 110 lb, whereas formula (2) assumes that it is 0.075 lb/in.^{3} (129.6 lb/ft^3).

The weight of a tree can be determined by estimating the volume of the tree and multiplying by the average weight of a cubic foot of wood. The volume can be estimated by measuring the diameter (caliper) of the tree, determining the square-foot area (Appendix I), and this value multiplied by the effective height of the main stem or primary branches. (A subjective assessment must be made as to the effective height.)

The weight of a cubic foot of wood varies considerably from species to species. Wood in the red oak group averages 64 lb/ft^3, whereas northern white cedar is a relatively light wood weighing 28 lb/ft^3. However, on an average the wood of most trees used for landscape purposes weighs approximately 55 lb/ft^3. Thus, a tree 10 in. in diameter, 1 ft above ground level, and 60 ft tall would have an estimated weight of 1800 lb (0.545 ft^2 × 60 ft × 55 lb/ft^3). These calculations are based on the assumption that the total volume of the tree approximates the volume of a cylinder whose caliper and height can be measured.

If these assumptions are valid and since the *American Standards for Nursery Stock* recommends certain minimum depths for balls within a specific size class, it is possible to calculate the approximate weights for balls within these classes and to plot these data onto semilog paper (Appendix J), from which the weight can be read directly without further calculations. A second curve can be drawn depicting the combined weight of the tree and soil ball.

REFERENCES

AMERICAN STANDARDS FOR NURSERY STOCK. American Association of Nurserymen, Washington, D.C.

PEASE, R. W. The balled and burlapped pack for ornamental shrubs and trees. W. Va. Univ. Agric. Exp. Sta. Bull. 432, October 1959.

PIRONE, P. P. Tree maintenance, 5th ed. John Wiley & Sons, N.Y.

TREE PRESERVATION BULL. 1, U.S. National Park Service.

WOOD HANDBOOK. Forest Products Lab., June 1940. Superintendent of Documents, Washington, D.C.

Appendix I

Area of Circles in Square Feet

Diameter in inches and half-inches

$A = \pi r^2 = 1/4\pi d^2 = 0.7854d^2$		
Diameter	*0.0*	*0.5*
1	0.006	0.012
2	0.022	0.034
3	0.049	0.067
4	0.087	0.111
5	0.136	0.165
6	0.196	0.230
7	0.267	0.307
8	0.349	0.394
9	0.442	0.492
10	0.545	0.601
11	0.660	0.721
12	0.785	0.852
13	0.922	0.994
14	1.069	1.147
15	1.227	1.310
16	1.396	1.485
17	1.576	1.670
18	1.767	1.867
19	1.969	2.074
20	2.181	2.292
21	2.405	2.521
22	2.640	2.761
23	2.885	3.012
24	3.142	3.275

Approximate Weight of B&B Plants

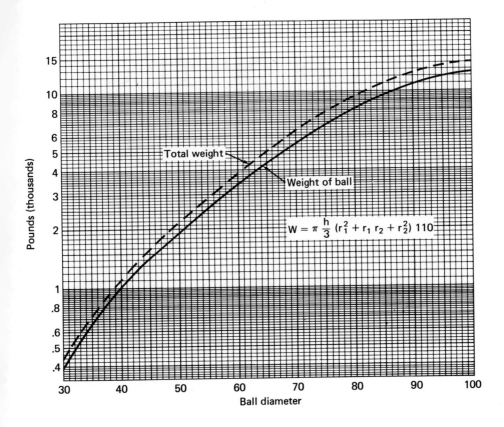

Pounds (thousands)

Ball diameter

Total weight

Weight of ball

$$W = \pi \frac{h}{3} (r_1^2 + r_1 r_2 + r_2^2) \, 110$$

Appendix K

Values for Selected Rates of i

Future value $(1+i)^n$ and present value $1/(1+i)^n$

Year	6% FV	6% PV	8% FV	8% PV	10% FV	10% PV	12% FV	12% PV	15% FV	15% PV	20% FV	20% PV	24% FV	24% PV
0	1.0000	1.0000	1.0000	1.0000	1.0000	1.0000	1.0000	1.0000	1.0000	1.0000	1.0000	1.0000	1.0000	1.0000
1	1.0600	0.9434	1.0800	0.9259	1.1000	0.9091	1.1200	0.8929	1.1500	0.8696	1.2000	0.8333	1.2400	0.8065
2	1.1236	0.8900	1.1664	0.8573	1.2100	0.8264	1.2544	0.7972	1.3225	0.7561	1.4400	0.6944	1.5376	0.6504
3	1.1910	0.8396	1.2597	0.7938	1.3310	0.7513	1.4049	0.7179	1.5209	0.6575	1.7280	0.5787	1.9066	0.5245
4	1.2625	0.7921	1.3605	0.7350	1.4641	0.6830	1.5735	0.6355	1.7490	0.5718	2.0736	0.4823	2.3642	0.4430
5	1.3382	0.7473	1.4693	0.6806	1.6105	0.6209	1.7623	0.5674	2.0114	0.4972	2.4883	0.4019	2.9316	0.3411
6	1.4185	0.7050	1.5869	0.6312	1.7716	0.5645	1.9738	0.5066	2.3131	0.4323	2.9860	0.3349	3.6352	0.2751
7	1.5036	0.6651	1.7138	0.5835	1.9487	0.5132	2.2107	0.4523	2.6600	0.3759	3.5832	0.2791	4.5077	0.2218
8	1.5938	0.6274	1.8509	0.5403	2.1436	0.4665	2.4760	0.4039	3.0590	0.3269	4.2998	0.2326	5.5895	0.1789
9	1.6894	0.5919	1.9990	0.5002	2.3579	0.4241	2.7731	0.3606	3.5179	0.2843	5.1598	0.1938	6.9310	0.1442
10	1.7908	0.5584	2.1589	0.4632	2.5937	0.3855	3.1058	0.3220	4.0456	0.2472	6.1917	0.1615	8.5944	0.1164

Appendix L

Relationship Between T, RH, VP, and VPD

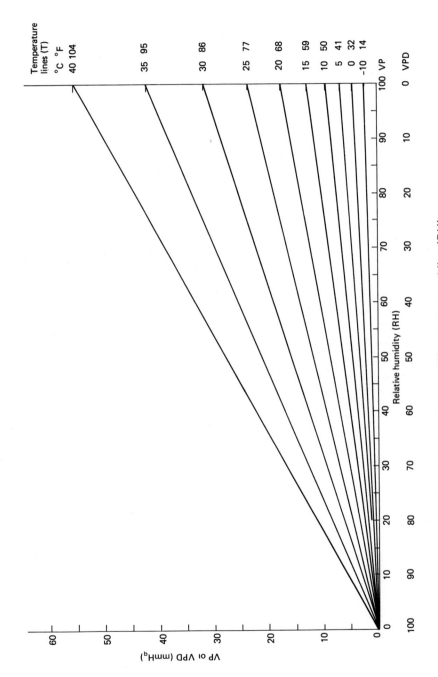

Relationship between temperature (T), relative humidity (RH), vapor pressure (VP), and vapor pressure deficit (VPD). To obtain VP at selected T, read RH scale from left to right. To obtain VPD at selected T, read RH scale from right to left.

Index